'Development and learning are the cornerstones of Human Resource according to Monica Lee in this important re-appraisal. Conceptualising the self as person, whole, rich and multiplex puts warm flesh around the arid bones of "agency" and accords with the experienced realities of those who work in HRD'.

—*David Weir, Professor Emeritus, Northumbria University, UK*

'Monica Lee weaves a fundamental understanding of what it is to be an individual in society, acting and reacting to the problems and possibilities that social—and especially organisational—life creates. This challenging manifesto offers thoughtful scholarship and perceptive craftsmanship in social investigation within the strong architecture of a sensitive and highly reflective autobiography'.

—*Oliver M. Westall, Emeritus Orator, Lancaster University, UK*

'This book is a real page turner, it does not read like a standard "management book" and it combines current knowledge, timeless wisdom with striking narrative style—it does not just make a "contribution to knowledge"—it is a truly inspiring invitation to pursuing a living path to knowledge that matters through reflexive engagement with organizing, management, ideas and life itself'.

—*Monika Kostera, Jagiellonian University, Poland*

'When she calls for interdisciplinary, multilevel, dynamic approach informing managerial education—we should hear a call for a civic, open, value-driven education of responsible citizens capable of creating and negotiating organizational scaffoldings for evolving social agencies'.

—*Slawek Magala, Erasmus University-Rotterdam, the Netherlands*

'Monica's model of holistic agency provides the foundation for the book's structure which draws—amongst others—on Greek philosophy, evolutionary psychology and the science of climate change to inform her understanding of HRD. This breadth of influence reminds us that we live in a world of fluid boundaries; if we are concerned with encouraging learning and development in organisations then we do well to remember that the boundaries we create are necessarily ethnocentric and a response to our socially constructed epistemologies and views of the world. I recommend this book to scholars and practitioners who are interested in, and open to, challenging views on the very idea of Human Resource Development as an area of practice, as a subject of study and as a response to local and global development challenges'.

—*Carole Elliott, Roehampton University, UK*

'For HRD practitioners the world over, this book challenges us to reinvent who we are and to magnify our impact on society. It would be impossible to read this book and not come away seeing our work in a totally different light'.

—*Darren Short, Sr. Director Learning & Development, GoDaddy, US*

'Despite the breadth and range, the content is unfailingly relevant and applied directly to building the case for and explicating Monica's account of the nature of HRD. You will, in the pages of this book, gain understanding of and insight into complex concepts such as self, other, agency and structure, but more importantly how they fit and connect with each other to provide understanding of HRD. As a reader, you will benefit from the grace and wisdom of a true polymath'.

—*Jim Stewart, Coventry University, UK*

'In this book, Monica Lee confronts the legacy of the past. In hindsight, this book may come to be considered as one of the first contributions toward a critical HRD approach that, in the author's words, "seeks to understand more by looking through the cracks in the rhetoric of the mainstream portrayal of HRD"'.

—*Adrian Carr, University of Western Sydney, Australia*

'Breath-taking, outstanding, illuminating and immense, *On The Nature of HRD* is an incommensurable feat which puts HRD at the centre of Humanity, its main questions and its principal endeavours. A phenomenal achievement done by only one individual. The big advantage is cohesion, strength and humanism—*On The Nature of HRD* looks more like a map, the map of Mankind's struggles done by a very skilful, extremely informed, superintelligent and amusingly witty cartographer'.

—*Eduardo Tomé, Universidade Europeia, Portugal*

'Lee "writes like life"; her work is not a neat package with a singular answer. Instead it is messy, filled with emotion, steeped in reflective insight; it confronts us to question. She has changed the way I, and countless of my students, have come to understand what HRD can be . . . can become'.

—*Jamie L. Callahan, Drexel University, US*

'Dr. Lee has been known throughout her career as a trailblazer, challenging traditional thinking. You may not agree with everything that she writes, but this is a must-read book for everyone serious about how we research and practice HRD and management'.

—*Gary N. McLean, Professor Emeritus,*
University of Minnesota, US

'This well-written book models the deep reflection and criticality we should all engage in as we "become" better HRD scholars and practitioners. Dr. Lee set out to offer an auto-ethnography that would help us to grapple with the deep and nuanced complexity of HRD—and in successfully doing so, she offers us a gift that can help us all to question, interrogate, and stretch for possibility in our individual and collective futures'.

—*Wendy Ruona, University of Georgia, US*

'I find this book to be a transformative read. It has brought the "human" right front and centre into discussion of the essence of HRD. This book will inform our thinking and research endeavours for many years to come'.

—*Thomas Garavan, Edinburgh Napier Business School, Scotland*

'Monica Lee takes us on a ride of discovery by way of autoethnographic reflection, identity work, consciousness, agency, actor-networks, and power/ knowledge. The result is a profound rethinking of HRD as a humane process of development'.

—*Albert J. Mills, Saint Mary's University, Canada*

'Exploring the nature of HRD through autoethnography provides a unique perspective of our multidisciplinary field and triggers critical reflections on the meaning and future of our field and on us and our relationships as human beings and professionals in our increasingly complex, global environments'.

—*Maria Cseh, George Washington University, US*

On the Nature of Human Resource Development

The nature of human resource development (HRD) has been, and remains, a contested topic—the debate was sparked in part by Monica M. Lee's seminal 2001 paper, which refused to define the discipline of HRD, but has been accentuated by increasing globalisation, political unrest, inequality, and the erosion of boundaries. Should HRD now be seen as more than 'training', or a subfunction of large Western bureaucracy? This book represents a very wide view of HRD: that it is at the core of our 'selves' and our relationships, and that we continually co-create ourselves, our organisations, and our societies. These ideas are hung upon a model of holistic agency, and supported from sources as diverse as evolutionary psychology, science fiction, the challenges of transitional economies, and the structural uncertainties of contemporary society. Examining the tensions between self and other, agency and structure, the book draws inspiration from an almost-autoethnographic approach. This yields a text that is personal, entertaining, and easier to read than many academic tomes—yet considers the depth and development of the human condition, and locates HRD within that.

Monica M. Lee is a Chartered Psychologist, a Fellow of CIPD and RSA, and Associate Fellow of the British Psychological Society.

Routledge Studies in Human Resource Development
Edited by Monica M. Lee, Lancaster University, UK

HRD theory is changing rapidly. Recent advances in theory and practice, how we conceive of organisations and of the world of knowledge, have led to the need to reinterpret the field. This series aims to reflect and foster the development of HRD as an emergent discipline.

Encompassing a range of different international, organisational, methodological and theoretical perspectives, the series promotes theoretical controversy and reflective practice.

For a full list of titles in this series, please visit www.routledge.com

On the Nature of Human Resource Development

Holistic Agency and an Almost-Autoethnographical Exploration of Becoming

Monica M. Lee

Routledge
Taylor & Francis Group

LONDON AND NEW YORK

First published 2016
by Routledge

2 Park Square, Milton Park, Abingdon, Oxfordshire OX14 4RN
52 Vanderbilt Avenue, New York, NY 10017

Routledge is an imprint of the Taylor & Francis Group, an informa business

First issued in paperback 2018

Library of Congress Cataloging-in-Publication Data
Names: Lee, Monica M., author.
Title: On the nature of human resource development : holistic agency and an almost-autoethnographical exploration of becoming / by Monica M. Lee.
Description: New York : Routledge, 2016. | Series: Routledge studies in human resource development ; 25 | Includes bibliographical references and index.
Identifiers: LCCN 2015045007 | ISBN 9781138781092 (hardback : alk. paper) | ISBN 9781315770260 (ebook)
Subjects: LCSH: Career development—Philosophy. | Personnel management—Philosophy. | Organizational sociology. | Industrial sociology.
Classification: LCC HF5381 .L346 2016 | DDC 658.3/12401—dc23
LC record available at http://lccn.loc.gov/2015045007

ISBN: 978-1-138-78109-2 (hbk)
ISBN: 978-1-138-61800-8 (pbk)

Typeset in Sabon
by Apex CoVantage, LLC

To Chas,
For over 45 years of love and support,
I Love You.

Contents

SECTION 3
Aspects of Other

SECTION 4
Aspects of Agency

SECTION 5
Aspects of Structure

Figures

Foreword

It is with great pleasure that I write this foreword. I have had the privilege of knowing Monica Lee since the late 1980s and worked directly with her during that time in the years when I was chair of the University Forum for Human Resource Development and Monica was the Forum's executive secretary. Prior to that, I worked with Monica and Professor Jean Woodall on an ESRC-funded project, which led to three books being published in what many term 'Monica's' Studies in HRD series, of which this book is the latest instalment. As part of these collaborations I have enjoyed many discussions and debates with Monica on the meaning of HRD and have been an avid follower and reader of her work. What has been evident in all of my experience of Monica is her eclectic views of HRD and her deep thought on the possibilities and potentialities of HRD, rather than its boundaries and limits, characterised best perhaps by her 'refusal to define HRD' (see Lee, 2012). This book is the latest evidence of those views.

What is well known by those who have worked with her and is clearly evident in this book is that Monica Lee has learned a lot in her life. If we can make such distinctions here, this learning has been achieved through living her life, which includes experiences not 'given' to many such as major brain trauma; through engaging in and researching HRD practice; and through studying academic accounts and explanations of human experience drawn from most disciplines of both the natural and social sciences. This book shares the results of that learning in the form of her 'holistic agency' model of the nature of HRD. The model is the result of analyses of issues ranging from macro-concepts such as climate change and globalisation to micro-interactions of individuals in learning groups or management teams. The unifying focus of these analyses is a detailed and forensic examination of the human condition. Chapters in the book range across research from brain science, philosophy, evolutionary biology, and evolutionary psychology, as well as the perhaps more expected fields associated with the study of organisations and management. Despite that breadth and range, the content is unfailingly relevant and applied directly to building the case for and explicating Monica's account of the nature of HRD. Personally, I find little or nothing to argue with in the content and find myself informed, educated, and persuaded by the arguments presented in the book.

I am truly grateful that Monica has decided to share her learning. Her work as represented by this book is in my view of inestimable value to those who study and practise HRD—and many beyond. You will, in the pages of this book, gain understanding of and insight into complex concepts such as self, other, agency, and structure, but more importantly, how they fit and connect with each other to provide understanding of HRD. More importantly still, though, the book provides inspiring insights into life and the human condition. As a reader, you will benefit from the grace and wisdom of a true polymath. I sincerely hope that when you come to the end you experience the same sense of gratitude and satisfaction that I experienced, and the same sense of time well spent in reading the learning of the author.

Professor Jim Stewart
Professor of Human Resource Development
Coventry University

Acknowledgements

I recount several of my personal experiences in this book. As the people I have come into contact with have affected me, so have they changed me and my understanding of my world.

The bad experiences have made me think and have left their mark on me. I hope I am stronger now for having come to terms with these—and so I thank the people involved.

I much prefer the good experiences, however, and I have had many of them. The friendship, support, and challenge of colleagues, and the love and support from friends and family have been wonderful. Thank you.

I first presented the core of the ideas expressed in this book in 1991. In so far as all my work has sprung from this way of thinking, it has developed into an account of my view of the world. The coherence of this book is largely due to Carole Elliott, Oliver Westall, and Jamie Callahan, who read an early draft, and each, in their own way, pointed out that just because something is in my head it does not mean that it is available to the reader! They also gave me some excellent encouragement, so I would like to thank them deeply for their support and feedback, and point out that the faults that remain with this book are mine and not theirs.

I must also mention the great role played by my close family: Chas, Graham, Parissa, Michael, Miriam, and Heidi. You might not know it, but, over the years, you have contributed much to this book – just by being and becoming who you are. Thank you.

May your journeys be interesting, challenging, enjoyable, and fulfilling.

About the Author

Monica M. Lee is a Chartered Psychologist, a Fellow of CIPD and RSA, and Associate Fellow of the British Psychological Society. She was Executive Secretary to the UFHRD, Founding Editor in Chief of *Human Resource Development International* (1998 to 2002), and editor of the Routledge monograph series Studies in HRD. She came to academe from the business world, where she was Managing Director of a development consultancy. She has worked extensively in Central Europe, The Commonwealth of Independent States, and the US, coordinating and collaborating in research and teaching initiatives. Recent books include *Human Resource Development as We Know It* and *HRD in a Complex World*. She also has a smallholding and is actively involved in the farming and broadband communities. She is intrigued by the dynamics around individuals and organisations, and most of her work is about trying to make sense of these.

1 Introduction

This book is about the nature of HRD. I disagree with the view that HRD is a subset of HRM, the poor sister of the real world of management. In this book I argue that HRD is much, much more than that. Those people involved in the initial breakdown of the field of 'management' into its subsets, and those who have just followed in their footsteps without considering the implications of such categorisation, have not come to grips with the importance of the influence of development in forming our very existence. I posit that 'HRD' is shorthand for what is at the core of our being and our becoming. HRD is thus at the centre of our understanding of our lives, our relationships with others, and the emergence of our futures.

I appreciate the boldness of these claims, and in this book I seek to support my ideas with evidence from a wide variety of sources, from evolutionary psychology, Greek philosophy, and arguments about climate change, to name but a few. Because this book is about people and relationships, and the way in which individuals and societies work together, I also make use of evidence from people and situations that I have encountered and engaged with. Elements of this book could therefore be seen as autobiographical, but the stories are not told with this intent. My aim is to use parts of my experience almost like case studies in order to add strength to my line of thought.

When teaching quantitative methods, one of my favorite examples showing the problems of correlation versus causation is associated with childbirth. There is a common belief that the older the woman the more likely the child is to have birth defects and later problems, and indeed there is a correlation between the mother's age and genetic defects. However, as I point out to my classes, this is not a causal relationship. The majority of older women have older men as partners, and an examination of the data shows that it is the age of the man, not of the woman, that is of importance here. The biological explanation for this is that the woman's eggs are all formed at birth whereas the man's sperm is continually created anew through cell division. As the man ages there is an increasing (though still small) chance of mutations developing (LePage 2014).

I have used this example many times because, as well as demonstrating the dangers of correlation, it also demonstrates the reach of a patriarchal society that assumes such problems are attributable to women. Much fun can be had with this when encouraging debate with students. I was surprised, however, when one person came to me several years later, and explained how this point had radically altered her life. She had been in her late thirties when we met and did not wish to risk bringing into the world children with genetic problems associated with elderly primagravida. However her partner was much younger than her and following my lecture they explored what I had said and decided to risk a family. They now have very healthy children.

I had seen this from an academic point of view: as an interesting example to rouse thought and discussion. I associated it with norms and assumptions. After she came to me to thank me, however, it was also about the immediately personal side of family life and of someone I knew and liked well. The critical dispassionate academic balanced against the individual and personal. This book is also about those two aspects of our existence, the quantitative and qualitative going hand in hand. I draw upon our vast human experience of scientific knowledge whilst also pulling in my own individual experience and understanding, as do we all when we try to make sense of the world. I reject the idea that the world can be seen and understood entirely through either the scientific lens or the personal lens.

We live in a world of structure; we structure our conception of our world. The very way in which we perceive and make sense of things has structure created through our biological perceptual processes. As individuals we create our own, unique, understandings and conceptual structures, forged through genetics and experience. As societies we develop shared structures, and shared understandings. Collectively we have created a world of structure, have refined and defined, have honed our knowledge to create edifices of science and learning. Our understanding of cause and effect, and the manipulation and building of relationships between abstract concepts, have enabled us to go beyond our evidence-based existence to speculate, experiment, and create new understandings and structures.

We need the surety of such scaffolding, we need glossaries and definitions, we need rationalistic thinking and scientific breakthroughs, mathematics, statistics, and the hard sciences. We all need to understand them because in understanding them we can also understand their frailties and appreciate when they might not be of much use. We need to be able to understand when to step away from those structures lest they become prisons. We also need to appreciate quite how fragile they might be.

I have a background in experimental psychology and I specialised in test theory and cognition at a time when computers were large and housed separately in hot noisy rooms and PCs didn't exist; a time when statistical calculations were all done by hand, including multivariate analyses. Nowadays, we plug some numbers into the computer and out pops the answer. We risk losing the deeper understanding of how the test works and what it really means. The mere existence of statistical results gives the analysis the appearance of being important and correct. However, my knowledge of quantitative methods makes me wary of the way in which they can be used to provide authority.

The application of lots of multisyllable words and statistical analyses gives the appearance of accuracy and truth. Talking in the third person whilst using obscure language provides authority (Lee 2010). What it can hide is sloppy thinking, erroneous use of statistics, and personal bias. As with the example above, false correlations slip into our cultural understanding and are rarely challenged. If we delve into the data that we are presented with, we can find personal and cultural biases intruding. My preference is, therefore, to balance the presentation of data with an open acknowledgement of the personal side of its impact. In this way people can make up their own minds about the import of what I am saying and the biases I might be exposing. Of course this does rely upon me being as open as I can—to myself as well as to others.

The account I present in this book is not about traditional 'HRD' or 'HRM'; it is not about practice, or theory, or professionalism, or ethics, or any such area of study—though it does touch upon all of these things. This book is much messier. It is about us and our relationships: how we change and change others—and how others change us; how we interpret and structure and manage our lives—and how we don't. This book balances the personal and the wider picture, across both the content and the delivery. For want of a better word or description my approach is best described as autoethnographic in that I use my own experiences as a basis upon which to build a bigger picture (though see Chapter 5 for a discussion of this).

Although my experiences are unique to me, they are just a springboard that I use in my attempt to pull together an integrative model of holistic agency that I developed in the early 1990s and have been playing with ever since. I tried to publish my model at that time, and got good reviews, but also rejections—the reason being, quite rightly, that I should either publish it as a series of papers, or in a book, as it was too large to publish in a journal. It was at this time that I developed the Studies in HRD series with Routledge, with my book intended to be the first in the series. I then had a cerebral haemorrhage and the book remained a nice idea, and the series flourished without it! Since then, my areas of enquiry over the years have been widespread. Because of the width of my model I never really settled to focus on one research area; instead, driven by the 7,000 or so words needed for an academic publication, I looked at one or another small corner of the whole so that each paper I wrote only reflected part of my interest. Also, because of the scope of my interest I have published in a wide range of outlets, some quite obscure. In this book, long in development, I bring together my ideas in a way that presents a more coherent whole. Each chapter is based around a paper I have written, and, for those who are interested in the history of such things, I have given details of the antecedents of each chapter in Chapter 20 at the end of this book.

SECTION 1. SETTING THE SCENE

The book comprises five sections. The first section sets the scene, looking at what we might mean by HRD, what the roots of HRD might be, how we might seek to understand HRD, and what methodological choices we have in furthering our interpretation. The first two chapters in this section focus upon what HRD might be, whilst the last three focus upon methodologies. I start by asking 'what is HRD?' in Chapter 2. I suggest that there are two main ways of looking at the world—the scientistic, being world of structure, and the phenomenological, becoming world of agency. I argue that HRD cannot and should not be defined, yet we need to be able to focus on what we are looking at, so how can we know it? If we cannot define it, can we describe it in other terms? To some extent, the rest of this book fans out from this one paper to give the wider rationale.

Chapter 3 presents two key archetypal structures that dominate the way in which we perceive the world—namely, self and other, and agency and structure. These archetypal structures are derived from evolutionary psychology. They underlie my model of holistic agency and I take the organisation of this book from them. These archetypal structures provide a conceptual basis for my description or understanding of the way in which we interact with others and make sense of our existence in the world—in other words, they explicate the roots of HRD. In this chapter I also start the process of dissecting the apparent surety of our existence, or at least our understanding of it. I describe the development of humanity through the lens of complexity and co-creation, and present the notion of holistic agency as a core concept of the book. The following four sections of the book link directly to the polar ends of the archetypal structures, so there is one section each on self, other, agency, and structure. The idea of holistic agency that I developed in this chapter permeates the book and is addressed more directly towards the end of the book.

Chapter 4 looks at the representational nature of our thoughts, our language, and our depictions. This is an important theme throughout the book—how we know what reality 'is' and how we construe our own reality. When we question our understanding of reality in this way we are also questioning the distinction between epistemology and ontology. In a world of transience and interpretation how can we know anything for sure? It follows that in making sense of the world, autoethnography is a powerful methodological choice for HRD, and, to a large extent, that is the approach adopted here.

Chapter 5 exposes the nature of the book in more detail, through an exploration of methodological choice. Our methodological choice depends upon the way in which we want to find meaning and the sort of meaning that we focus upon. I suggest that the nature of HRD lends itself to mixed methods in which quantitative statistical information is interpreted alongside a more qualitative and personal understanding.

The final chapter in this section (Chapter 6) is the only one that is not written by me, although I am the focus of it. One of the problems of using self as a springboard or basis of wider understanding is that it is easy to fall into the trap of self-referential narcissism, and so I was reluctant to include the interview here. One of the referees of this book, however, reminded me that knowledge of the author and their biases is an important aspect of understanding and judging the value of what the writer is attempting to say. I therefore include the interview in the hope that you, the reader, will examine it with a critical edge so that it informs your analysis of my arguments.

In this first section of the book, therefore, I present a typology of typologies built upon two archetypal constructs. These are derived from evolutionary psychology and are a fundamental part of how the human condition has developed. In order to understand and work with the implications of these notions we need to adopt (or at least borrow) the language and perspective of complexity theory. Through this process I have tried to come closer to what I would see is the nature of HRD. That nature is about process and I describe it as the glue between the representations. For the want of a better term I call it holistic agency. This section is, therefore, largely conceptual in nature. However, in order to make sense of our search for meaning we need to balance a scientific focus on facts with an understanding of the personal and individual. In a similar manner, I shall argue that holistic agency is about construing both the wider picture and action within it. In order to develop a balanced picture, we need to step aside from the conceptual on occasion, and consider the individual and the world of action. That is the reason why much of the research in this book is presented as from an autoethnographical stance, and it is also the rationale for the following four sections of the book.

The Rest of the Book

The next four sections are devoted to the four polar ends of the two archetypal constructs that are identified in the first section. As discussed in Chapter 3, as our ancestors developed the pattern of bearing live young that needed parental care for survival they also developed the pattern of behaviours and emotions that bonded parent and child in a dependent relationship. Thus their first great archetypal system has to do with attachment, affiliation, caregiving, care receiving, and altruism. As the child grew, was replaced by other children, and eventually became a parent themselves, so 'self'—and as a necessary and integral part of that process, 'not-self', or the 'other'—emerged. Therefore, that the first fundamental dynamic played out in each person's life is that of self and other. This pervades the whole of our existence and is the core of self-development literature.

The nature of an archetype is that it does not really exist; it is not achievable. Instead, it is a conceptual embodiment, a pure vision of what is being alluded to. As will be seen in the text, none of the chapters are, or can be, exclusively about one or other of the polar ends. Each can only be known by what it is not, and so in looking from one archetypal pole to another, each contains elements of the other. Therefore, although the following sections are separated, I trust that if you read through you will find many links from one section to another, and question why on earth I clustered them as I have. I can only say that this was a rather awkward exercise and was done for the sake of clarity. I hope, also, that I have offered a hint of conceptual coherence. This can perhaps be better described visually, through a thought experiment to which you will unfortunately need to imagine colour, as this book does not stretch to colour illustrations.

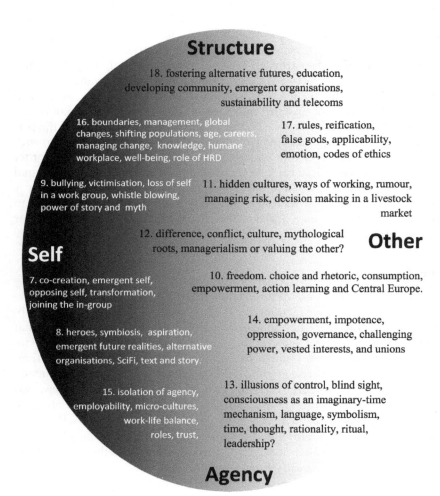

Figure 1.1   Representation of Sections 2 to 5

Imagine a dot of pure red colour that gradually dissipates as it spreads out. That could not represent an archetype, as the colour red does exist and is achievable; however, it is that sense of dissipation from an intense core that I am trying to describe here. As an aside, it is interesting to note that even the correct wavelength for red light is hard to define. It is given as a range (~ 700–635 nm) and has no one singular point. Imagine a colour red dissipating across the ball, which on one side is deep red, and on the other is uncoloured. So, here we could call the notion of 'self' deep red. Imagine the other side is deep green, the direct opposite of red, which we could call 'other'. If we move across that coloured ball we move from a sense of self to a sense of other, with a muddy sort of brown colour in the middle where they are balanced. Thus one end of the self-other archetypal structure could be said to contain nothing of the other end. The same could apply to the structure-agency archetypal construct. The chapters in each of the following four sections of this book focus upon one pole, but as they are about real-life experience they would be located somewhere within the imaginary colour wheel in Figure 1.1. Bear in mind that this location is achieved by thinking of where they are less applicable, rather than where they should 'be'. I have no desire to place them too firmly in one spot, thereby offering an oversimplified representation of a messy world.

SECTION 2. EXPLORING *SELF*

This section focuses on the first of these poles, namely self. Although this can only be understood by what it is not (other), the chapters in this section are chosen as they focus more on self than on other. I start by questioning what is meant by 'self', and explore the notion of the emergent self, in which self is clarified through what one is not, and notions of self emerge from interaction with the other. This is done through negotiating entrance into a new group and trying to find out what that group stands for and what might be entailed by acceptance into the group. The way in which self is challenged and changed by other is discussed.

Chapter 8 questions the direction of the emergent self. I pose different possible futures as presented in science fiction writings and ask what the implications might be for the way in which we develop, work, and live. Two main futures are developed: the lean mean heroic machine, which is contrasted with the co-created storytelling environment. These two themes echo through the book in different guises. The process of looking to the future is not meant to imply that we are the sole agents that create our future. Instead, as we co-create our understandings of self and other so we work towards co-creating the world in which we wish to live. As with the discussion in earlier chapters it is a matter of becoming rather than being, but I suggest that some thought about what we might be becoming, about our direction of travel, is merited.

The third chapter in this section (Chapter 9) is set in a supposedly enlightened environment, within which some staff are bullied to the edge of endurance. This illustrates the self submerged by others, and honed through the sandpaper of interaction with others. As before, the self is not seen in isolation, but through interaction. In this case the interaction is toxic leading to illness and loss of *self*. Such bullying is quite common, but is surprising here because of the self-described supportive environment in which it occurred.

SECTION 3. EXPLORING *OTHER*

The chapters in the previous section focused on self, asking what is meant by *self*? What of the future self? And what of the effects on self of a hostile environment? The chapters in this, the third section of the book, focus on the opposite end of the archetypal structure, the pole of 'other': which is, indubitably, also about self. Each chapter is in some way about the rules that individuals negotiate when coming together to form a group. The chapters here focus on freedom of choice, decision-making, and conflict, all of which come into play as we interact with others.

In Chapter 10 the scene is set in Central Europe shortly after the Velvet Revolution of the late 1980s and early 1990s, in which the rhetoric of the free-market economy was dominated by notions of freedom and choice. A large programme based upon action learning is described, the value base of action learning also being about freedom and choice. However, despite the rhetoric of the programme and the intentions of all involved, I question how much freedom and choice was actually available. As in the previous chapter and throughout this book the freedom of agency rubs against the strictures of structure.

The second chapter in this section (Chapter 11) follows the notion of decision-making, this time located in the boardroom and focused upon negotiating the group appetite for financial risk. This chapter also exposes the idea of a hidden culture associated with farming and the countryside that has cooperative values more akin to the storytelling future described in Chapter 5, than to the heroic cut and thrust that one would expect to find in most boardrooms. As an aside, I appreciate that culture is a very problematic concept, but I use it here as a form of shorthand; it is discussed in more detail in the chapters themselves.

Chapter 12 finishes this section by exploring differences in the approach to conflict and suggests that the nature of the conflict differs according to the extent to which the participants interpret the conflict as an attack on their core values. For those who see their idea of their self to be under attack the conflict is personal, bitter, and hard-fought. When notions of self are not implicated in this way the conflict is seen as a matter of negotiation. The chapter documents times when managerialism has uncritically attacked notions of self and turned negotiation into bitter conflict.

SECTION 4. EXPLORING *AGENCY*

The previous two sections explored self and other—the first great archetypal construct that dominates the way in which we perceive the world. The last two sections of the book explore the polar ends of the second archetypal construct: namely, agency and structure. As discussed previously, both sections contain elements of the other—how can one have agency without structure and vice versa. The difference in focus between the two sections is that in the first there is greater concentration upon the effect that the agent has upon the structure, whereas the latter focuses more on the effect the structures have upon the agent.

The first chapter of this section, Chapter 13, looks at consciousness and questions the extent to which we are conscious agents in our lives. Following a description of my experiences of blind-sight after my cerebral haemorrhage, I adopt a more theoretical approach to establish the idea of consciousness as an imaginary-time processor: an evolutionary side effect. Previous chapters have talked about how we live in a world of representation, not reality; this chapter takes those ideas further and shows how we live also in a world of memory. Everything we see and hear is memory. We do not function in the immediate, even though we feel we might. We talk of ourselves as if we were the agents of our destiny; we seek control of our environment and others, believe ourselves to be superior because of our consciousness, attribute luck to our good traits; but is 'I' the conscious me, or is it my brain that that is really running the show? Who, or what, is the agent here? I suggest that, in the same way that our brain makes many of our decisions prior to our awareness of them, so too the leaders of organisations have, in practice, a retrospective leadership role.

The idea of the agent as someone in charge and driving the team forwards is further questioned in the second chapter (Chapter 14) with a look at what is meant by power and empowerment. This is set in a small primary school and is told as the story of the individual fighting against several bureaucratic structures and the power that is wielded by them. The question of who had the power, and the nature of that power, remains. This extends the notion of power to include aspects of the individual's interpretation of the situation and of themselves—what might be termed agency.

In Chapter 15 I suggest that managers have become agents moving through micro-cultures. The rhetoric is about being an accessible team player, yet the flatter structure forces greater isolation upon the manager. This is explored through a model of different ways of working that is discussed with change agents who present a picture of the agent carefully picking their way through cultural boundaries as they attempt to achieve their goals. The rhetoric of the structure is contrasted with the reality of the isolation of agency. The notion of the agents patrolling the boundaries of the micro-cultures they come into contact with is discussed in terms of holistic agency.

SECTION 5: EXPLORING *STRUCTURE*

This final section explores further the idea of structure. The first chapter in this section (Chapter 16) presents a wide-ranging conceptual review that outlines a world that is physically and mentally structured by us—as we create structure we establish boundaries that form our existence. Initially one might question why global happenings should have an impact upon the local practice of HRD, but this is part of my thesis. We create the structures of society and nations, of organisations and groupings, of free-market and controlled economies. I present a global picture of shifting boundaries and change, and follow global changes through to examine the implications they have for populations, organisations, and you and me. My exploration leads to the view of the agent, me/I/we, within a web of interpretations and changes.

Chapter 17 is about the rules that people develop as they establish structures, so that they can work together. Many of the rules and ways of working are subconscious; they reify our cultural and social expectations. I use the idea of codes of ethical conduct to suggest that these rules, although well-intended, are often chimeric. Despite the structures we build, our ethics boil down to on-the-spot decision-making, a case of enforced agency that is largely independent of wider societal rules.

Chapter 18 is the last chapter in this section, and it questions the sort of future society we might be colluding with. I use the example of a community telecoms company to explore alternative and emerging forms of organising, one that avoids a focus on the short term and the worst excesses of capitalism. As management educators, and HR professionals (and thus agents of change), are we empowering others, helping them to be agents of their own lives—or are we fitting them into holes designed by others? What role do we want to play in our becoming?

CONCLUSIONS

Chapter 19 concludes the book with a brief overview of the main threads of my argument in laying out the idea and a model of holistic agency. Although, to some extent, this is a conceptual exercise, I am also asserting that in exploring the nature of HRD we need to adopt a wide, holistic, view of the world; seeing it, structuring it, and creating it, as interacting elements, processes, and peoples. As part of that world we are agents (by our existence and our nature) and also pawns, and thus we influence the balance, acting within different arenas and across barriers; fostering emergent co-creation within the principle of becoming. As agents within this holistic world we will never 'become' what we aspire to, as we are always becoming—but we might sidestep becoming along a path we want to avoid.

The final chapter, Chapter 20, is a short exploration of the background to the work this book is based on. Throughout this book I have made much use of my own experience of being and becoming to illustrate my line of thought. My experience is the vehicle, but it is the picture that I am trying to transport. I take the risk that the intrusion of my experiences, unique to me, and thus only partially relevant to you, the reader, can weaken or distort this picture. However, don't all convincing pictures have their roots in the empirical? What use is a theory if our own experience gives lie to it? In our journey of becoming, as we try and make sense of our world, we pull together threads from many sources and avoid dissonance in our understandings. I hope that you find this book presents a picture that balances theory and the empirical across the wide spread of holistic agency. I hope I have built a convincing picture of a wider, more complex world than the one we sometimes feel reduced to. The world we live in is the world of becoming, a world that we co-author.

REFERENCES

Lee MM (2010) 'Finding a Voice', in Hatcher T & Rococco T (Eds) *The Handbook of Scholarly Writing and Publishing*: 102–114. San Francisco, CA: Jossey-Bass.
LePage M (2014) 'Testicular Timebomb', *New Scientist* 22 February: 46–49.

Section 1

Being, Becoming, and Almost-Autoethnography

This first section is designed to establish the foundations for the two core elements of the book—notions of becoming and autoethnography. In this section I present life, and thus what we do and think and say, as part of a process of becoming. We never quite get there—partly because 'there' is an unreachable place. This does not necessarily mean that we are striving to become something else, but rather, that regardless of whether or not we are happy in the place that we are, we are in a state of flux—things always change.

The first chapter in this section (Chapter 2) argues that to define HRD is to deny it nature of becoming. I contrast two main ways of looking at the world—the scientistic, being world of structure, and the phenomenological, becoming world of agency. Despite the dynamic nature of our existence, and despite the fact that we are always in the process of becoming, much of our interaction is ruled by the need to specify, to characterise, to define. This is particularly true of our scientific endeavours, through which we build a world of stability that is held together through the framework of knowledge. We need to understand the facts, the causes, and the correlations of our world. We need that scientific framework to understand our 'being' in the world. But—hanging on to that framework and spilling through and around its interstices as individuals, collectives, societies, we are all in the process of becoming. The divorce between the rationalistic scientistic approach and the humanistic approach permeate this book.

However, how can we make sense of the world if we don't define? In Chapter 3 I look at the evolutionary roots of HRD in order to see if we can describe, or understand, it in other terms. I present the rationale for two key archetypal structures that are derived from evolutionary psychology and dominate the way in which we perceive the world: namely, self and other, and agency and structure. The latter two reinforce the debate in the previous chapter. I explore how these dominate our thinking and our understanding of the world and how our style of learning and being is passed on to others. Because of the universal nature of the structures they can be seen to underlie many of the models we have of management, organisation, and development. I take the organisation of this book from them. They provide a conceptual basis for the understanding of the way in which we interact with others and make sense of our existence in the world, represented as a typology of typologies, a meta-typology upon which I build my model of holistic agency. In order to understand and work with the implications of these notions we need to adopt (or at least borrow) the language and perspective of complexity theory. I introduce the idea of holistic agency here, but it permeates the book and is, in essence, how I conceptualise HRD.

Chapter 4 looks at the representational nature of our thoughts, our language, and our depictions. This is an important theme throughout the book—how we know what reality 'is' and how we construe our own reality. When we question our understanding of reality in this way we are also questioning the distinction between epistemology and ontology. In a world of transience and interpretation how can we know anything for sure?

Chapter 5 exposes in more detail the nature of the book through an exploration of methodological choice. Our methodological choice depends upon the way in which we want to find meaning and the sort of meaning that we focus upon. I suggest that the nature of HRD lends itself to mixed methods in which quantitative statistical information is interpreted alongside a more qualitative and personal understanding.

The final chapter in this section (Chapter 6) is based on an interview with me, conducted by Darren Short. One of the problems of using self as a springboard, as I do in this book, is that it is easy to fall into the trap of self-referential narcissism. I was therefore reluctant to include the interview here; however, a referee reminded me that knowledge of the author and their biases is an important aspect of understanding and judging the value of what the writer is attempting to say. I therefore include the interview in the hope that it enables you, the reader, to examine it with a critical edge, and so inform your analysis of my arguments.

The first section of this book, therefore, is largely conceptual in nature. However, holistic agency is about construing both the wider picture and action within it. Similarly, in order to make sense of our search for meaning we need to balance a scientific focus on facts with an understanding of the personal and individual. Ethnographical methods are a powerful choice for HRD, and that is the reason why much of the research in this book is from an autoethnographical stance.

The next four sections, and indeed the rest of the book, are devoted to the four polar ends of the two archetypal constructs. The nature of an archetype is that it does not really exist; it is not achievable. Instead, it is a conceptual embodiment, a pure vision of what is being alluded to. As is discussed in the introduction, none of the chapters are, or can be, exclusively about one or other of the polar ends. Each can only be known by what it is not, and so in looking from one archetypal pole to another, each contains elements of the other. Therefore, although the following sections are separated, I trust that if you read through you will find many links from one section to another.

2 Defining HRD?

This chapter suggests that whilst it might be necessary to define HRD for political reasons, there is a strong case that HRD should not be defined on philosophical, theoretical, and practical grounds. I set the case for considering HRD (and life in general) as a continuous developing process and suggest that to proffer definitions of HRD is to misrepresent it as a thing of *being* rather than a process of *becoming*. I also suggest that in defining the field we additionally run the risk of disengaging from the moral and personal dimensions of HRD.

I decided to start the book from this line of thought, as it provides a gentle, and classically based, introduction to notions of *becoming*. To some extent much of what I want to talk about in this book is normal life and living, but from a lens that includes a sense of continual progress or change. As I argue in Chapter 5, this is at odds with our developmental practice of knowing things, conceptually labelling them and setting them in place, as in an embodied manner: an important part of the way in which we conceptualise is to try and build boundaries around the concept.

In almost any educational situation it is common practice to first define the area or subject that is to be studied. It is generally considered to be good practice if the syllabus and content that are to be taught are derived from such definition, if the students are actively encouraged to study and revise in the light of this structure, and if the assessment and evaluation of students, staff, and course reflect and reinforce the coherence of the whole. This notion of *good practice* holds some moral force: a *good* teacher, trainer, or HRD professional is someone who lays out the subject clearly and coherently. To fail to do so, in the predominant Western model of education, is to be a *bad* educator. I suggest that this approach does particular disservice to the development of those who wish to become HRD professionals, as the notion and practice of HRD is dynamic, ambiguous, and ill-determined. I firmly believe that philosophy and theory need to be rooted in practice (see Chia & Holt 2008 for a discussion of this), and thus I draw upon the experience of the life cycle of a master's programme that I designed and directed, in order to illustrate my arguments.

SETTING THE SCENE: AN MSC IN HRD (BY RESEARCH)

In the early 1990s I designed an MSc in HRD (by Research) at Lancaster University, UK, having previously spent twenty years working for others and myself in the field. This was dual qualification, offering both professional and academic qualifications for international cohorts of senior HRD professionals. Most of what had been written about HRD at that time did not really reflect my own professional experiences, and it felt hypocritical to be regurgitating the literature in the knowledge that it presented an idealised chimera. I therefore designed the course to reflect the way in which I understood my role as an HRD professional, and as an educator of others. It seemed to me that in my professional life, whilst I carried a central core of understanding from each experience that came my way, I, and my understanding, shifted and changed according to that experience—and each experience influenced, and was influenced by, future experiences. I could never say 'this is the organisation', 'this is my role', and 'this is what I am doing', as I could never manage to complete or finalise any of these states.

Similarly, as an educator, I could not identify with any firm body of knowledge and say 'this is what is needed'. I could see that people needed knowledge, but that most of what they needed would be situation specific: The knowledge needed by an Angolan participant would be very different to that needed by someone working in Hong Kong; working multinationally required different knowledge and skills than working with small and medium-sized enterprises; working in the voluntary sector appeared fundamentally different to working with the corporate sector, and so on. I could see that people would need to shift and change to emerge into new roles and selves. There did seem to me to be some meta-level areas of activity in what I did, and it was these that I tried to capture as workshop topics. The design, therefore, avoided specification, or at least, the specification beyond basic structure and process, as can be seen in Figure 2.1. In brief, the programme consisted of eight four day workshops, over one and a half years, and was assessed through three guided work-based research projects, an international placement, a learning log, an open-book examination, and a dissertation.

The programme was not completely content-free, as participants derived implicit delineations of the area to be studied from the brochure and the interviews. Each workshop had a different focus, and it could be argued that there was an overriding definition in practice, but there was no set content or syllabus, and no area that had to be known to satisfy assessment criteria. The process of each workshop followed the Kolb model, but shifted daily between a focus on the academic (theory), followed by (reflection) on the professional self within group, and then a return to the focus upon the individual (planning), before the return to work (experience). Specialists were invited during the first two days of each workshop and were asked to present different views to the group about the workshop topic, with specific instructions to be controversial and to follow their pet theories. For

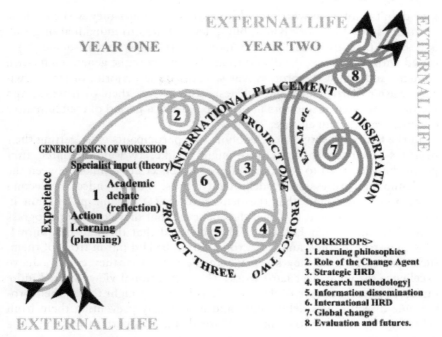

EXTERNAL LIFE

YEAR ONE   YEAR TWO

GENERIC DESIGN OF WORKSHOP
Specialist input (theory)
Academic
1 debate
(reflection)
Action
Learning
(planning)

Experience

INTERNATIONAL PLACEMENT

PROJECT ONE

EXAM etc

DISSERTATION

PROJECT THREE   PROJECT TWO

2   **6**   **3**   **7**   **8**

5   **4**

WORKSHOPS>
1. Learning philosophies
2. Role of the Change Agent
3. Strategic HRD
4. Research methodology]
5. Information dissemination
6. International HRD
7. Global change
8. Evaluation and futures.

EXTERNAL LIFE

Figure 2.1 Outline of the MSc HRD (by Research)

each half day the group lived in the world of that specialist and, given the diversity of each group, there was lots of discussion and hard questioning. I would refuse to clarify, and insist that each person had to come to their own decisions on the differing views presented. I was very determined in ensuring that the third day shifted to one of *no* content. It was called 'academic debate' as it was set aside for the group to work with the ideas from the previous two days and with their own processes, contextualising theory with practice. This was, initially, hard for the participants, and proved to be particularly hard for those academic co-tutors with no counselling experience. The majority of participants came from pressured lives in the world of business where they felt they had to be continually *doing* something. The reflective nature of the day was hard for them and quite often they got stuck. Occasionally I would jump in with some exercise or idea to shift them, but despite the real pain sometimes associated with the processes of self-within-group, evaluations showed that each group eventually came to value this creation of a reflective space.

Whilst the whole programme was based on principles of action learning, (Lee 1996) the fourth day made this more explicit. The group split into subgroups of about six people each, and these were run as a facilitative action learning set. Each person would have about an hour (even if they said they didn't want it) in which to address whatever issues they wished. These normally started as work issues, but quickly shifted to individual or group issues, and then, over the next year, moved increasingly towards issues associated with completing the dissertation. This programme generated its own content, and whilst the process was structured the majority of the knowledge wasn't. Participants had full responsibility for their own work, and the tutors acted as facilitators in order to enforce a period of contemplative openness rather than closure.

In the first workshop of each cohort, the participants were getting their bearings—feeling what the course might be like. Two months later, after people had returned to work and started to reflect upon links between the academic and professional sides of their lives, they attended the second workshop. It was here that the defining of HRD became paramount in most people's minds. It was as if they believed that they could not progress until they knew what HRD 'is'. They believed that through this knowledge their future study and work roles would be laid out in front of them, such that so long as they knew where the path was, they could achieve excellence through sheer hard work. These traditional views shifted quite rapidly, but for a couple of days it was as if they thought that I, their programme director, was deliberately and maliciously preventing them from achieving, by refusing to define HRD for them. This pattern was the same for each cohort.

This programme generated significant income and proved to be extremely successful with the students, many of whom keep in touch and say that it has fundamentally changed their lives. About 85% obtained promotion or changed jobs during or directly after the programme. All participants had to have at least five years' professional experience, and even though about a quarter came with little academic experience, the majority of students achieved exceptionally good academic results, with about a fifth subsequently registering for their PhD. On all the normal criteria it was considered to be an extremely successful programme, yet, despite this, the programme was short-lived and recruitment was terminated after only four cohorts. One reason for this is that it adopted a philosophy and practice fundamentally different to that of normal academe.

THE PHILOSOPHICAL CASE FOR REFUSING TO DEFINE HRD

I am referring here to the academic world view—the archetype or myth of academe—the 'norm' (which is, of course, never really lived just because it is so 'normal'). I discuss the nature of the archetype in Chapter 3 of this book, and try to convey its all-pervading influence. When we think of an academic person, or academe in general, we tend to envision ivory towers, theoretical debate, careful experimentation, scientific method, and so on. These views even permeate applied areas of study such as management and HRD. As Boyacigiller & Adler (1991) point out, the bulk of early management research was done on (and in) white US bureaucratic organisations, and our current understandings of management theory and practice are derived from this culturally specific and non-representational sample. The very nature of this compounded the bias. Early research was assumed to apply to all management, and it was assumed that management was a singular global concept without national or situation-specific boundaries, that there were right and wrong ways of managing, and that it was possible to derive a single global set of tenets for best practice. These views are still around and actively promoted, despite ample evidence of their fallacy—see Chapter 16 for a more detailed discussion of management.

More generally, academe is normally associated with 'scientism'—a belief in the supremacy of reductive rationalistic scientific thinking. This approach pervades academic theorising and shapes and influences all forms of knowledge considered acceptable by the academic community, and this becomes self-fulfilling. Those who do not conform to the control mechanisms of format, style, and scientific method are told that they are not sufficiently 'scholarly'. This is, however, just one way of looking at the world. It has an ancient and strong lineage, but there are other forms of world view.

Western modes of thought build upon two great and competing pre-Socratic world views. These derive from that of Heraclitus, a native of Ephesus in Ancient Greece, who emphasised the primacy of a changeable and emergent world, and that of Parmenides, his successor, who insisted upon the permanent and unchangeable nature of reality. Parmenides's view is reflected in the continued dominance of the belief that science constitutes the most valuable part of human endeavour. This leads to an atomistic conception of reality in which clear-cut, definite things are deemed to occupy clear-cut, definite places in space and time. Thus causality becomes the conceptual tool used for linking these isolates, and the state of rest is considered normal while movement is considered as a straightforward transition from one stable state to another. 'This *being* ontology is what provides the metaphysical basis for the organisation of modern thought and the perpetration of a system of classificatory taxonomies, hierarchies and categories which, in turn, serve as the institutionalised vocabulary for representing our experiences of reality. A *representationalist* epistemology thus ensues in which formal knowledge is deemed to be that which is produced by the rigorous application of the system of classifications on our phenomenal experiences in order to arrive at an accurate description of reality' (Chia 1997: 74). A *being* ontology is conceptualised with one 'true' reality, the units of which are tied together in a causal system. The truth is out there, we just have to find it!

In contrast the Heraclitean viewpoint offers a *becoming* ontology in which ' . . . how an entity becomes constitutes what the actual entity is; so the two descriptions of an actual entity are not independent. Its being is constituted by its becoming. This is the principle of process . . . the flux of things is one ultimate generalisation around which we must weave our philosophical system' (Whitehead 1929: 28 & 240). Cooper (1976) suggests that within such a *process* epistemology the individuals involved feel themselves to be significant nodes in a dynamic network and are neither merely passive receivers nor dominant agents imposing their preconceived scheme of things on to that which they apprehend. All are the parts of the whole, and the parts, and the whole, change and develop together. From this point of view, there is both one and many realities, in which I myself come into being both through interacting with and being constituted within them, and the knowing of these realities is never final nor finished.

Integral to living within a process epistemology is the personal quality of what might be called 'hanging loose', or 'negative capability', as described by the early nineteenth-century English poet John Keats: 'And at once it struck me, what quality went to form a man of Achievement . . . meaning Negative Capability, that is when a man is capable of being in uncertainties, mysteries, doubts, without any irritable reaching after facts and reason' (Keats, Letter to George and Tom Keats, 21st December, 1817). This quality is one of resisting conceptual closure, and thereby creating the necessary 'space' for the formulation of personal insights, and the development of foresight and intuition, is a quality that is vital for counselling and other helping professions, and one that *should* be within the remit of all HRD professionals. All my experience in HRD and life (not that I can easily separate them) points me to belief in a world of becoming, one of process epistemology and negative capability. It could be that I am out of step with the 'real world', but I suggest that the Parmenidean house of cards that we construct around us to provide clarity, certainty, and delineation, will tumble in the wind of close examination. This house of cards stands on the strength of unique definitions by which every concept has its own rightful and static place in the order of things. In contrast, from the Heraclitean perspective, the meaning and boundary of concepts is negotiable. In the following section I shall briefly report on previous work I have done with the notion of development, and illustrate that despite being central to our ideas of HRD, even that concept is debatable.

THE THEORETICAL CASE FOR REFUSING TO DEFINE HRD

Most would agree that, to be meaningful, the definition of something needs to encapsulate the properties or qualities of that which is being defined, such that it can be recognised uniquely from the definition and thereby distinguished from those that are not being defined. This causes problems, even with something as conceptually solid as a cat. We all know that a cat is reasonably small, furry, that it meows, purrs, has four legs and tail, and so on. But, what if it is missing some or all of these attributes? Is it no longer a cat if it is mute, or has lost a limb, or all of its fur? When does a cat stop being identified as a cat? We have an idealised concept of a cat, but is the cat in front of us the same as that ideal or canonical cat? (See Chapter 4 for a further discussion of this.)

This sort of description of what a definition might be, is, in itself, one of *being* rather than *becoming*. We could, however, say that a definition of something need not be fixed or permanent, but instead, it could take the form of a working definition. If enough people use a word in a particular way, and know what is meant by it, more or less, then there is tacit agreement about the meaning of that word and its qualities, such that it could be deemed to be *becoming* defined. We might, therefore, get a rough feeling for a word by looking at the way in which it is used. I attempted to develop a working definition of the word 'development' by examining promotional literature aimed at HRD professionals (Lee 1997a). I found four different ways in which the word 'development' was used. In the first approach, *development as maturation* was used as if to refer to a predetermined stage-like and inevitable progression of people and organisations. Development was seen as an inevitable unfolding, and thus the developmental force is the process itself, which, in turn, defines the end point. The system, be it an individual, a group, or an organisation, was seen as being a coherent entity with clearly defined boundaries existing within a predictable external environment. The organisation was discussed as if it were a single living element, whose structures, existence, and change were capable of being completely understood through sufficient expert analysis. Concepts such as empowerment and change-agency were irrelevant in an approach that was essentially founded upon deterministic principles, with no place for unpredictable events or freedom of individual choice.

In the second, *development as shaping,* people were seen as tools who could be shaped to fit the organisation. Here, development is still seen to have known end points, but these are defined by someone or something external to the process of development. The organisation was stratified and senior management defined the end point for junior management—the wishes of the corporate hierarchy created the developmental force. This approach assumed that there was something lacking, some weakness or gap, that could be added to or filled by the use of the appropriate tools or blueprint, and that such intervention was necessary. Individuals, including their aspirations and their values, as well as their skills, were malleable units that can be moulded to suit the wider system. Empowerment and individual agency could be part of the developmental agenda, but not in their own right. They were an acceptable developmental end point only if ratified by senior management: empowerment became a tool to enhance performance and decision-making.

Development as voyage was seen as a lifelong journey upon uncharted internal paths in which individuals construed their own frames of reference and placed their view of self within this, such that the person constructed their own version of reality in which their identity was part of that construct. This was described as an active process in which the individual was continually reanalysing their role in the emergence of the processes of which they were part. In so doing they were also confronting their own ideas, unsurfaced assumptions, biases, and fears whilst maintaining a core of ethicality and strong self-concept (Adler 1974). Development involved a transformative shift in approach that enabled critical observation and evaluation of the experience, such that the learner was able to distance themselves from it rather than replay it. Experiencing became a way of restoring meaning to life (Vasilyuk 1984). The external world (including organisation and management) might mirror or catalyse development, but it was the individual who was the sole owner and clear driving force behind the process. Empowerment was to be within the individual's own terms, and had little regard for organisational objectives.

Development as emergent was seen to arise out of the messy ways by which societal aspiration became transformed into societal reality: 'the individual's unique perceptions of themselves within a social reality which is continuously socially (re)constructed' (Checkland 1994), in which 'individuals dynamically alter their actions with respect to the ongoing and anticipated actions of their partners' (Fogel 1993: 34), and in which they negotiate a form of communication and meaning specific and new to the group and relatively inaccessible or undescribable to those who were not part of the process (see Chapter 17). Selfhood was described as a dynamic function of the wider social system, be it a family grouping, a small or medium-sized enterprise, a large bureaucracy, or a nation, or parts of each, and as that system transformed so did all the participants. Emergent development of the group-as-organisation was seen to be no different from the development of any social system, and was not consistently driven by any single subsystem, be it senior management or the shop floor. Discussion about planned top-down or bottom-up change was irrelevant, as the words themselves imply some sort of structure to the change. This approach is, of course, in direct conflict with traditional ideas that organisational change is driven by senior management; however, Romanelli & Tushman (1994) offer empirical support for rapid, discontinuous transformation in organisations being driven by major environmental changes (and see Chapter 16 for further discussion of this).

It would be very simple to place these in a nice two-by-two matrix, as in Figure 2.2. The two-by-two matrix is pervasive and well understood in management, but it is a tool of being, rather than becoming. The lines are solid and impermeable, the categories fixed. Instead, the Venn diagram in Figure 2.3 helps us imagine these different views of development as areas of concentration, in which it is as if the most concentrated 'essence' of that which we are examining is in the centre of the area, and, as it diffuses outward, it mingles with the essences of the other areas.

Despite finding alternative ways of representing these findings, which might help address the problem of how to represent the sorts of working

		IDENTITY	
		UNITARY	CO-REGULATED
END POINT	KNOWN	MATURATION: Development through inevitable stages	SHAPING: Development through planned steps
	UNKNOWN	VOYAGE: Development through internal discovery	EMERGENT: Development through interaction with other

Figure 2.2 A Two-by-Two Matrix of Development

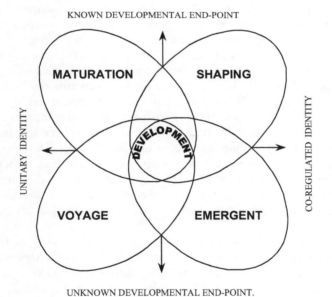

Figure 2.3 Four Forms of Development, After Lee 1997a

definitions associated with becoming, we cannot avoid the fact that there appear to be four fundamentally different working definitions of development. Each of these carries with it a particular view of organisation, and of the nature and role of HRD, and is used under different circumstances. When talking of our own development we normally address it as if it is a voyage. When senior managers talk of organisational development they normally talk of it as if it were shaping. When social theorists talk of development they normally adopt a maturational or emergent perspective, depending upon their theoretical bent. Development is clearly not a unitary concept.

THE PROFESSIONAL CASE FOR REFUSING TO DEFINE HRD

The many ways in which the word development can be used indicates the many different roles that the professional developer might adopt. For example, the role of the developer in the maturational system has the sureness of the (relatively) uninvolved expert consultant who charts the inevitable unfolding of the stages. The developer within a shaped system is the process expert who can not only clearly help senior management identify an enhanced future, but can also apply the tools necessary to ensure that such a future is achieved. Such developers purport to sell a better, and otherwise unobtainable, view of the future to individuals, groups, and organisations plus the blueprint to get there. Those that are being developed are encouraged or moulded to meet the end criteria, regardless of whether such criteria are enhanced skills, positive attitudes, or the achievement of corporate objectives. The role of the developer from the perception of voyage is one of helping others to help themselves (Rogers 1951). In this case the developer brings expert skills that help the individual recognise their self-imposed bounds and widen their horizons, but does so without calling upon the power of expertise that describes a particular path and end point as best for the individual concerned. In emergent systems there is little role for a developer as the developer holds no unique or special status. Developers are as similar and as different as each other member is, and although they perhaps have fewer vested interests in political machinations (and thus might be able to view circumstances more objectively), they are as directly involved in the life of the organisation as any of the individuals they are supporting in co-development.

Let us step back for a bit, and take a Parmenidean view of the world, and examine what is meant by the definition of HRD. In this world view we have the two-by-two matrix, and four different definitions of the word development, only one of which can be what we really mean, while the other three need to be renamed. When we talk about *human resource* development however, the situation becomes clearer. A *human resource* is a commodity—something to be shaped and used at the will and needs of the more powerful. The role of the HRD professional is clear, and, by implication, so is the nature of organisation and management. Senior management set the objectives within a clearly defined organisational structure, in which HRD is a subset of the larger HRM function.

If we accept the common meaning of the words then there is no alternative to HRD as an activity and profession in which development is about shaping individuals to fit the needs of the organisation, as defined by senior management. Integrity, ethics, and individual needs are not important within this conceptualisation, and need only be considered if the circumstances call for hypocritical lip service to them. A Parmenidean definition of HRD, therefore, might be along the lines of 'the shaping of the employees to fit the needs of the employer'. This approach is described as performance improvement by Weinberger (1998) in her examination of theories of HRD, derived mainly from US literature. It is less prevalent in other countries (Geppert & Merkens 1999; Grieves & Redman 1999), and most human resource professionals (including those in the US) do not describe their own work in this way (Claus 1998; Sambrook 2000). They, and the professional bodies, are increasingly paying attention to the ethical aspects of the profession. Some might still see HRD in this way, but for many, the profession has slowly moved on to incorporate notions of integrity and ethics, and also to reflect, at least in part, the notion that people are central to the organisation, and thus the strategic role that their development can play.

There is, however, a strong drive to define HRD, particularly within the professional and qualification-awarding bodies in the field of practice. They need to do so for political reasons—in order to patrol their boundaries, maintain their standards, and bolster their power base. The professional bodies have, in general, abandoned (at least in part) theoretically derived definitions of HRD and instead have adopted a practice-based view, in which they attempt to promote what they see as 'best practice' through the establishment of their professional standards. These standards do not necessarily reflect what is happening in practice, but instead mirror what the professional bodies would *like* to see happening. As illustrated in Chapter 10, standardisation across disparate systems of HRD is likely to have been achieved through cultural imposition, with the accepted standards or definition in practice belonging to those cultures with the loudest voices. Even if the rhetoric is of the dominant culture, the practice often remains that of the hidden, or underlying culture (see Chapter 11). Clearly, professional and qualification-awarding bodies do provide definitions of HRD, and these definitions are generally suitable to meet their political needs, but this localised and self-serving activity is fundamentally different to that of trying to understand or encapsulate the field of knowledge and activity that is HRD. Perhaps the only way to address the need to encapsulate what is meant by HRD is to draw permeable outlines around this complex of activities that we all know and, for want of any other term, choose to call HRD.

THE PRACTICAL REASON FOR REFUSING TO DEFINE HRD

The idea of a generally acceptable definition of HRD achieved via the processes of standardisation becomes particularly unrealistic when we look at the degree of variation in practice across the globe. As McLean & McLean (2001) demonstrate, it is simply not feasible to seek global standardisation or definition based upon current practice. They conclude that definitions of HRD are influenced by a country's value system, and the point of the life cycle of the field of HRD in that country, and that the perception and practice of HRD differ according to the status of the organisation, whether it be local or multinational. We can proffer, with some accuracy and completeness, localised definitions in practice or working definitions. However, descriptions of current practice become increasingly meaningless as the variation in practice increases. Furthermore, as soon as these definitions are encased in course brochures, syllabi, professional standards, organisational literature, or other such statements of fact, they stop becoming and *are*. Thus the very act of defining the area runs the risk of strangling growth in the profession by stipulating so closely what the practice of HRD is, or should be. In consequence it is unable to become anything else, and so we reach the heart of the argument.

HRD theorists and professionals are increasingly talking and acting as if the process that we call HRD is dynamic and emergent. Organisational theory, and HRD theory, are starting to explore areas of complexity, and the notion of process itself. In order to accommodate the variation they found in definitions of HRD, McLean and McLean offer a global processual definition, namely: 'Human Resource Development is any process or activity that, either initially or over the long-term, has the potential to develop adult's work-based knowledge, expertise, productivity, and satisfaction, whether for personal or group/team gain, or for the benefit of an organisation, community, nation, or, ultimately, the whole of humanity' (322). Even such a global definition, however, does not meet everybody's requirements—Why is it limited to adults? What of all the child workers in the world? The authors did not include them in the definition as they considered the fact of child labour to be one of the negative aspects of HRD practice. Thus the definition is really a statement of how the authors would like the field to become, and not how it *is* (see Chapter 16).

HERACLITUS AND MORAL RESPONSIBILITY

The views of Heraclitus and Parmenides could be seen merely as two philosophical stances, with little to do with the bottom line of teaching people about making money through managing people in organisations. However this is a limited view of the field, the theory, the practice, and the role of HRD, as it focuses upon one particular culturally specific and dominant way of working and end product. From the Parmenidean perspective, no other viewpoint captures the essence of existence, yet from the Heraclitean perspective the Parmenidean view could be one among many—all of which together comprise existence. Therefore, despite the dominant focus, in the West at least, on scientistic definition and measurable outcomes, a broader view of the field shows that the practice or the 'doing' of whatever we mean by HRD is also a process of becoming. There are parallels here between this and the emergent system of development I describe above. This system reflects the messy ways by which societal aspiration becomes transformed into societal reality. Society develops with no clear end point and with its emergent activities as the drive behind change, rather than the edicts of the hierarchy (Lee 1997b). From this perspective, HRD could be seen as that which is in the processual bindings of the system, which links the needs and aspirations of the shifting elements of the system, between and across different levels of aggregation, as they are in the process of becoming. Yet while these words are sufficiently general to describe the process of socialisation, per se, they are not a definition of HRD.

To summarise this point, acknowledgement of the Heraclitean cosmology as a descriptor of the metaphysical basis of existence carries with it a moral responsibility that is not entailed by the Parmenidean cosmology. The act of definition, for the followers of Parmenides, is that of clarifying what exists. This might be complicated or problematic, but its moral valency is no different to that of emphasising or copying the lines of a line drawing. It is just describing what already is. In contrast, the act of definition within the Heraclitean cosmology is equivalent to the act of creation. To define is to intervene in the process of becoming, it is to assert a right way, and what should occur. It is to make moral judgements about what is good and bad, and to state these is to attest not only to their legitimacy, but also to the superior power or higher status of the attester. To define is to take the moral high ground and to assert one's power, and, by doing so, it is to deny the right of others to impose their own view on the becoming of HRD.

The world in which we move is political—all our actions and inactions can be seen as statements of power, but in the Heraclitean cosmos we are responsible for the exercise of that power in a way that does not occur in the Parmenidean cosmos. My attempts to maintain a space of negative capability and lack of definition within the master's programme in HRD that I described earlier, was more than an educative ploy. It was an attempt to ensure that each person developed their own, emergent view of HRD, rather than adopting the one propounded by the teacher, which they would end up wearing like an old ill-fitting raincoat. In this way, HRD was different for each person and emerged out of their experiences: 'It is not enough to insist upon the necessity of experience, nor even of activity in experience. Everything depends upon the quality of experience which is had . . . every experience lives in further experiences' (Dewey 1938: 27).

I was lucky to be able to run my master's programme as I did for four cohorts. Many higher education institutions would not have countenanced it nor accepted its notion of self-generating content. Having ensured that its systems of verification and quality management were sufficient, the university was happy for it to continue indefinitely. However, its fate was sealed by a replay of the philosophical debate that took place two and a half thousand years ago in Ancient Greece. My Heraclitean vision for HRD lost out to a fear of difference and a desire to control the uncontrollable. Whilst acknowledging how very hard it is at times to live in a Heraclitean world, I wish to redress the balance and propose that, certainly as far as HRD is concerned, there is no alternative. I will not define HRD because it is indefinable, and to attempt to define it is only to serve the political or social needs of the minute—to give the appearance of being in control. Instead I suggest we seek to establish, in a moral and inclusive way, what we would like HRD to *become,* in the knowledge that it will never *be,* but that we might thus influence its *becoming.*

Before moving on to the next chapter I would like to highlight the importance of the two paradigms discussed here. The Parmenidean paradigm (of a being ontology and representationalist epistemology within a structured world) and the Heraclitean paradigm (of a becoming ontology and process epistemology) are picked up in the next chapter. They can be seen within the second underlying archetypal process that I present there: that of structure and agency.

The refusal to understand HRD through its 'definition' forces us to examine HRD through its 'nature'—hence the title of this book. It presents a different way of looking at the world, one that is alien to many people raised in the Western traditions of scientism. The presenting focus of this book is HRD, but the arguments I use are applicable to a much wider arena. For example, Capra & Luisi (2014) have put forward a comprehensive account of a systems view of life from a physical and biological perspective: an account of how the world operates as a holistic, networked system in which every part depends on every other. The words used to describe this might be different, but the underlying approach resonates with that of Heraclitus, and it is this approach in which individuals and societal groups are part of a wider interlocking and interactive system that is the foundation for this book.

REFERENCES

Adler PS (1974) *Beyond Cultural Identity: Reflections on Cultural and Multicultural Man. Topics in Culture Learning: 2.* Honolulu: East-West Culture Learning Institute.

Boyacigiller N & Adler NJ (1991) 'The parochial dinosaur: Organisational science in a global context', *Academy of Management Review* 16(2)262–290.

Capra F & Luisi PL (2014) *The Systems View of Life a Unifying Vision.* Cambridge: Cambridge University Press.

Checkland P (1994) 'Conventional wisdom and conventional ignorance', *Organisation* 1(1)29–34.

Chia R (1997) 'Process Philosophy and Management Learning: Cultivating "Foresight", in Management', in Burgoyne J & Reynolds M (Eds) *Management Learning:* 71–88. London: Sage.

Chia R & Holt R (2008) 'The nature of knowledge in Business Schools', *Academy of Management Learning & Education* 7(4)471–486.

Claus L (1998) 'The role of international human resource in leading a company from a domestic to a global corporate culture', *Human Resource Development International* 1(3)309–326.

Cooper R (1976) 'The open field', *Human Relations* 29(11)999–1017.

Dewey J (1938) *Experience and Education*. Reprint 2007. New York: Simon and Schuster.

Fogel A (1993) *Developing through Relationships*. Hemel Hempstead: Harvester Wheatsheaf.

Geppert M & Merkens H (1999) 'Learning from one's own experience: Continuation and organisational change in two East German firms', *Human Resource Development International* 2(3)25–40.

Grieves J & Redman T (1999) 'Living in the shadow of OD: HRD and the search for identity', *Human Resource Development International* 2(2)81–103.

Keats J (1817) 'Letter to George and Tom Keats, 21 December Hampstead'. (http://www.poetryfoundation.org/learning/essay/237836?page=2) Accessed 16/2/2013.

Lee MM (1996) 'Action Learning as a Cross-Cultural Tool', in Stewart J & McGoldrick J (Eds) *Human Resource Development*: 240–260. London: Pitman.

Lee MM (1997a) 'The Developmental Approach: A Critical Reconsideration', in Burgoyne J & Reynolds M (Eds) *Management Learning*: 199–214. London: Sage.

Lee MM (1997b) 'Strategic Human Resource Development', in Torraco R (Ed) *Academy of Human Resource Development Conference Proceedings*: 92–99. Baton Rouge, LA: Academy of HRD.

McLean GN & McLean LD (2001) 'If we can't define HRD in one country, how can we define it in an international context?', *Human Resource Development International* 4(3)313–326.

Rogers CR (1951) *Client Centred Therapy*. Boston: Houghton Mifflin.

Romanelli E & Tushman ML (1994) 'Organisational transformation as punctuated equilibrium: An empirical test', *Academy of Management Journal* 37: 1141–1166.

Sambrook S (2000) 'Talking of HRD', *Human Resource Development International* 3(2)159–178.

Vasilyuk F (1984) *The Psychology of Experiencing*. Trans 1991. Hemel Hempstead: Harvester Wheatsheaf.

Weinberger L (1998) 'Commonly held theories of Human Resource Development', *Human Resource Development International* 1(1)75–94.

Whitehead AN (1929) *Process and Reality*. New York: Free Press.

3 Evolutionary Roots and Holistic Agency

In the last chapter I described paradigms of a becoming ontology (agency) and a being ontology (structure) in terms of Greek philosophy, but in this chapter I address these differently and look for entirely different sources for my discussion of these concepts. I present the rationale for two key archetypal constructs that dominate the way in which we perceive the world: namely, self and other, and agency and structure. Many of our current approaches to understanding HRD, management, and our lives and relationships can be seen through the lens of these archetypal constructs. They permeate how we and other social animals construe relationships, and are core to our being.

Because of the width of this view I synthesise notions from several different fields and employ the language of complexity. In so doing I accommodate the disparity that exists between different branches of the social sciences through the provision of a holistic overview that accords with the idea of a coherent scientific body of knowledge. I use a Jungian typology to reinforce the parameters of the four archetypes by which organisation and individuals have been interpreted, and locate this within findings from evolutionary psychology, thereby building a meta-typology of the human condition. I conclude by suggesting that this can best be understood through the notions of relationship and dialectics, and by examining some of the implications this approach holds for the field.

BASIC TENETS

A Mismatch Within the Social Sciences

As the various branches of social science have developed, the way in which they build accounts to explain the world and our existence within it have moved away from each other and from the natural sciences; thus, for example, psychology and sociology present different world views. In discussing this Barklow et al. (1992) note that the natural sciences have retained a common root in their development, such that any move forward needs to fit with both its 'home' discipline, and also be concurrent with all others in order to be accepted. This has not happened in a consistent way within the social sciences. In adopting a post-scientific perspective postmodernism has challenged many of the contradictory yet self-sustaining frameworks that have developed. Yet in creating a world that is devoid of structure other than our own unique and individual structuring of it, postmodernism is actively engaged in preventing constructive (or 'with structure') dialogue between the various disciplines of the social sciences (though see Cilliers 1998). Calas & Smircich (1999) suggest that one legacy of postmodernism is that the boundaries between the disciplines are softening. Notions of complexity can act as bridges between the disciplines (Boisot & McKelvey 2010; Lee 2003; Youngman & Hadzikadic 2014) and provide the ideal vehicle by which a meta-view of human existence can be established and within which apparently contradictory world views can be accommodated.

In bringing together notions from diverse fields of social science in order to make my argument, I am not doing full justice to any of them. This diversity presents a challenge both to the ability to create a coherent account, and also to the foundations of such an account. Each subset of my argument has its own literature and language. A word used in one account may be used in a subtly different way in another, such that the implications and meanings of the word become distorted in a hybrid account such as this. These words, however, are signifiers of deeper meanings, and it is those deeper meanings that I seek to access here.

Archetypes, not Paradigms

It is for this reason that I talk here about archetypes rather than paradigms. A paradigm is a shared set of views with the explicitly defined propositions that contribute to understanding and are transparent to others who are not view holders (Kuhn 1970). They are definable, and formalised through language that 'enables a set of explicit statements to be made about the beliefs and propositions (and their corollaries) that enable everything that must be expressed to be expressed in a self-consistent way' (Yolles 1999). Paradigms are incommensurable, and grow and die, to be replaced by new paradigms. In other words, paradigms are conceived of as 'things', and are given existence in their own right. The paradigms discussed in the previous chapter were presented as separate entities, entirely different opposite ways of working. When describing the same sort of concepts as archetypes, I am using similar words but mean something different.

I want to make it clear from the start that in talking about archetypes I am not talking about things that can be defined or formalised. An archetype can be conceptualised through what it is not, but it has no existence in its own right, and its conceptualisation could be called into question if there existed an entity or system that uniquely demonstrated all the qualia associated with it. Similarly, as is implicit in the typologies that I introduce later on, archetypes can be seen as commensurate, in that entities and systems contain within them the potential for demonstrating the qualia of all quadrants of the typology—but in differing strengths or preferences. These might change over time, but the underlying archetypal structure does not.

A similar distinction can be made between typology and taxonomy (Smith 2002). In a typology the dimensions are based on the notion of an ideal type and represent concepts rather than empirical cases (Weber 1949). They are descriptive rather than explanatory or predictive, and can be subject to the problem of reification (Bailey 1994). Taxonomies differ from typologies in that they classify items on the basis of empirically observable and measurable characteristics. They are associated more with the biological than the social sciences (Sokal & Sneath 1964), and are used in classification schemes and classificatory methods such as cluster analysis. Although the two are conceptually distinct, they can be hybridised in practice; for example, Hotho (2014) derived taxonomy of business systems from international typologies.

Complexity

In so far as paradigms are coherent and incommensurate ways of thinking about and portraying the world, then the ideas presented here are rooted in the relatively new paradigm of complexity. Central to complexity theory is the idea that a complex system is more than 'just' a complicated system (Price 2004). A complicated system or a problem might be very complicated indeed, but with time and effort all its parts, and its whole, can be measured and understood. In contrast, a complex system might be quite simple, yet its parameters cannot be measured or quantified (in the normal sense) and the whole is more than the sum of the parts. However much we atomise the different parts we can never get to the essence of the whole. In this there is similarity between postmodernism and complexity theory; however, unlike postmodernism, complexity theory suggests that whilst aspects of complex systems cannot be measured in the normal sense, we can infer relationships between the constituent parts and subsystems, and we can deduce global underlying principles. It follows from this that we cannot define what we 'know' in any unique sense because all that we know about something is rooted in its relationship to other things—we know it by what it is *not,* its antithesis, as much (or more) than by what it *is*. Despite losing most of its identifiable parts, we still think of the poor cat in the previous chapter as a cat, because, for example, we 'know' that it is not a dog, or a fish—and so on.

There is no requirement that a complex system be uniform in nature. It may have subsystems that appear in structure and function to be significantly different to each other and from the whole, yet each is in relationship to the others and to the 'environment' of the whole, and the whole is in relation to the wider environment. This relationship might be one that is in a state of 'far from equilibrium', yet the system maintains dynamic coherence and adheres to its global underlying principles. As Ball (2014) reports, there is a good argument that all living things 'live at the edge of chaos', and that if we are to better understand our world the search should be for overarching principles, not picking at details.

Rationality and Emotion

Orthodox management theory assumes conscious rational intent by which the individual manager applies systematic processes in order to improve management and output in a rational manner, yet, throughout this book, I query almost every one of these descriptors, and emphasise the importance of 'unorder' in management practices (after Snowden & Stanbridge 2004). Emotions have a pervasive impact on organisational behaviour. They do not just influence people's own actions but also influence others who perceive the expressions (van Kleef 2014). There is an increasing recognition of the need for emotion management for the smooth functioning of wider organisational and societal systems (Frost 2003; McMurray & Ward 2014). However, I am emphasising here much more than the idea that emotion can intrude upon our daily working lives. Emotion underpins everything we do and perceive, our choices or lack of them, our judgements and our being. Most of the time we are not aware of the biases and nuances that form (and inform) us, but they are there, in the background, all the same.

Put another way, however we choose to represent the world to ourselves, however rationally we might wish to account for our engagement in the world, there exist processes that underlie all of humanity, and the principles of complexity theory might provide a language by which we can get closer to an appreciation of them (Tsoukas & Hatch 2001). Further, the diversity apparent between individuals and nations is indicative of self-generating and self-managing subsystems that might be complex in their own right, but which are still parts of the whole, as each derives its identity or being from its opposite (as perceived from the whole), and 'development' in any of these subsystems is synonymous with interaction with the whole.

Gene-Culture Co-Evolution

An example of how the social sciences pay little heed to advances in the physical sciences can be found in the way the literature and practice about changing organisational culture, or difference in cultures, still essentially adheres to the principles of the nature/nurture debate (Pilcher 2013), whereas research in areas such as cultural neuroscience and epigenetics have opened up the field of gene-culture co-evolution. Holmes (2013) described gene-culture co-evolution as similar to a process of self-domestication. The idea of culture affecting genes is well established. The switch to farming 10,000 years ago triggered evolution of extra genes for enzymes used in starch digestion, and other genetic changes that allowed some human groups to digest milk and sugars as adults. Similarly, Talhelm et al. (2014)

studied agricultural communities within China and found that those with a history of farming rice (which required a lot of people working together) were more interdependent and holistic-thinking, whereas those with a history of farming wheat remained more independent. Evolution is also about phenotype change.

We accept that as children grow they develop and are *nurtured* by their culture, and that is distinguished from their essential *nature* that they were born with—their genetic inheritance. However, recent work has shown that bacteria shape our immune system, our body weight, and our mood (Money 2014) and help guide growth of the brain, and our cultural habits influence the quantity and diversity of our gut flora, so influencing our health and culture (De Vreize 2014). Microbial communities differ substantially between homes, and are identifiable by family, and after a house move the microbial community in the new house rapidly converges on the microbial community of the occupants' former house, suggesting rapid colonisation by the family's microbiota (Lax et al. 2014). We take our microbiological environment with us, and it can have a profound effect upon us and may explain, in part, population disparities in mental health across ethnic groups within and across nations (Chiao & Blizinsky 2013).

One of the key mechanisms for this is identified as epigenetics—the vast array of molecular mechanisms that affect the activity of genes (Bird 2013). Epigenetic 'switches' can persist through cell division, and sexual reproduction, such that an environmental event in one generation can affect the phenotype in subsequent generations, providing transgenerational epigenetic inheritance (Daxinger & Whitelaw 2010). For example, undernourishment during pregnancy increases the chances that the next two generations will develop obesity and diabetes, with no effect on the third generation (Thompson 2014). So, environmental stresses in our lives will affect our own genome (Mitchella et al. 2014) and might affect our grandchildren's health. Our epigenome is a snapshot of the major events of our life in which no two individuals have the same pattern—even clones are different—but it can be altered by such simple things as diet, meditation, or counselling (Yehuda et al. 2013).

As we socialise we share microbiota—and the line between nature and nurture becomes blurred. The individual's epigenome can affect their preferences, moods, and emotions. Conversely, culture, and the society they are part of, can affect the epigenome of the individual—and of their offspring. Lots of sharing and influencing without being aware of it!

Memes

Whilst talking about genes, it is worth considering the concept of memes. I explore consciousness in Chapter 13, describing it, not as the pinnacle of achievement, but as a side effect of the evolution of a real-time imaginary processor, through which has developed our ability to work with symbols—symbolism, ritual, myth, language, and so on. I hold that it is this rich *symbolic* cultural life that distinguishes us from other animal societies (and cultures)—not specifically consciousness or language. It is hard to account for the development of symbolic culture solely through genetic evolution. Dawkins (1976) coined the term 'meme' as a 'unit of cultural transmission', leaping like a virus, from brain to brain, through imitation. Memes are said to evolve, like genes and viruses, through natural selection, competing for the scarce resource of our attention. Successful memes grow rapidly (something that has gone viral on the internet, for example). They can be benign (a catchy song perhaps) or malignant (such as scapegoating—see Chapter 9), but in either case they parasitize us and drive us. The influence of memes has become much more obvious since 1976, where ideas and fads can be seen to spread like wildfire across the globe, influencing our lifestyles and choice of mate—cultural evolution interacting and co-evolving with genetic evolution.

Although the idea of memes is relatively new, we have been influenced by symbols and 'units of cultural transmission' since the dawn of humanity. The meme of the meme is itself evolving, no longer entirely through natural selection: many internet memes are now specifically engineered to go viral— the new form of advertising (Rabinowitz 2013). The internet provides the ability to codify and analyse the development of memes, and similarly, network theory offers a quantifiable way of looking at how ideas and 'culture' spread and evolve. The idea of the meme emphasises that information has a life separate from the people and machines that are vehicles for it—and that we might well not be aware of its transmission; it lodges with us and changes us without our realisation.

Subconscious Co-Regulation

Another area of influence that is often hidden to us is that of co-regulation. One of my favourite exercises to demonstrate the effect of different forms of verbal communication uses dominoes. This exercise involves three consecutive sub-exercises in which different pairs (A and B) from the group sit back to back with a matched set of six dominoes on a table in front of each. In each case, A's task is to exactly replicate the array of dominoes that the educator has constructed in front of B. The remainder of the group observes the use of language, metaphors, feelings, and degree of success in the task. In the first task A is only allowed to say 'yes' or 'no', and B therefore has to give instructions (thus modelling the communication of a directive manager). In the second, B is only allowed to say 'yes' or 'no', whilst A has to ask questions (modelling need-to-know communication patterns). The third round allows full communication (modelling open management style). The order of the sub-exercises can be varied; however, the exercise appears to be most effective when presented in the above order.

As might be expected, people find one-way communication problematic, particularly in the forming and posing of accurate questions or directions.

Debriefing can bring out a lot of interesting communication-related learning, but that is not why I mention it here. This exercise also almost invariably demonstrates the rapidly evolving use of common metaphors and language forms, and the communication problems generated if these do *not* develop. For example, regardless of order of sub-exercise or success of task, if the first pair developed a successful common metaphor (such as tombstones on edge and upright) to describe domino orientation, the following pairs continued with that metaphor. If the first pair was unsuccessful in finding commonalty (i.e., if one talked of points of the compass, whilst the other focused upon their visual array), the following pair continued to search for a common metaphorical language.

The metaphors and interpretations that evolve in this exercise provide a nice example of the development of a group micro-culture, which Fogel (1993) terms 'co-regulation'. He defines this as a process through which 'individuals dynamically alter their actions with respect to the ongoing and anticipated actions of their partners' (pp 34), and in which 'the most salient aspect . . . is the emergence of something novel' (pp 31). This is not, however, to imply that these processes are conscious, or easily accessible to conscious control. This exercise skims the surface of what appears to be an underlying and subconscious drive to co-regulate with those around us—to form shared metaphorical interpretations. This process is similar to that described by Hardy et al. (2005), who suggest that effective collaboration emerges out of a two-stage process through which conversations produce discursive resources that create a collective identity.

I want to emphasise here the importance of the subconscious processes involved in co-creation and co-regulation and the drive to work in this way. As in this example, most people are not aware that they are building and using a new language as they work together, yet if it does not develop collaboration falters. These ideas are core to the following discussion, and I will return to this small example later in the chapter.

UNDERLYING PROCESSES

In this section I shall explore what these processes might be through illustration. I do this to emphasise their metaphorical or representational nature. The words employed are used to represent concepts that are themselves socially constructed representations—in other words, whilst there might be some commonality of language between the various constructions discussed here, it must be remembered that the meanings behind the words are dynamic, situated, and ephemeral. One word may mean different things in different contexts and different things to different people (see, for example, Chapter 10). I am therefore trying to explore the parameters of the concepts or meanings behind the words, whilst acknowledging that these concepts are also socially constructed and essentially undefinable.

An Evolutionary Basis

Research into evolutionary psychology and psychiatry (Barklow et al. 1992; Bradshaw 1997) suggests that human (and primate) affectional development progresses through the maturation of specific affectional systems, and that 'all major psychiatric syndromes may thus be conceived as inappropriate expressions of evolved propensities concerned with adaptive behaviour in the domains of group membership, . . . group exclusion, . . . and mating' (Stevens & Price 1996: 29). They argue that there exist two 'great archetypal systems'. The first formative experience faced by our protohuman ancestors would be that associated with parenting and family. As our ancestors developed the pattern of bearing live young that needed parental care for survival they also developed the pattern of behaviours and emotions that bonded parent and child in a dependent relationship. Thus their first great archetypal system has to do with attachment, affiliation, caregiving, care receiving, and altruism. As the child grew, was replaced by other children, and eventually became a parent themselves, so 'self'—and as a necessary and integral part of that process, 'not-self', or the 'other'—emerged. Therefore, the first fundamental dynamic that plays out in each person's life is that of self and other. This pervades the whole of our existence and is the core of self-development literature.

The second formative experience was that of collectivity. For ninety-nine percent of its existence, humanity has lived in 'extended organic kinship groups' of about forty to fifty individuals, comprising six to ten adult males, twelve to twenty childbearing females, and about twenty juveniles and infants (Fox 1989). As predators, they were sufficiently effective not to need to develop large aggregations, flocking behaviour, and high sensitivity to others in the group in order to survive, but they were sufficiently weak that they could only exceptionally survive as solitary individuals. We are therefore left with an awareness of society and its necessary structures and hierarchy, and also of individual agency. This equates to Steven and Price's second great archetypal system, that concerned with rank, status, discipline, law and order, territory, and possessions.

Stevens & Price posit that the search for achievement of archetypal goals occurs throughout the whole of the life cycle, though the presenting face of the goals we seek changes as our circumstances change with age. Our ability at social cognition also changes with age (Vetter et al. 2013). This is the ability to understand intentions, beliefs, and emotions, and is one of the core abilities of interpersonal functioning. It is essential in everyday life as it allows us to predict other people's behaviour and to adjust our behaviour adequately. As we mature we change, and what we want, and our understandings of the world, of others around us, and of our relationships also change—but throughout we are balancing the dual aspects of our collective psyche. These can be seen mirrored in the tensions between self and other, the structured law and the anarchic body (Hopfl 1995), sociology and psychology, or between Giddeon's (1976) structure and agency.

In other words, we can identify two fundamental processes derived from our evolutionary history that continue to affect our humanity and our enactment of our existence. I want to make a clear distinction between the discussion here about the existence of fundamental or underlying processes and our day-to-day appreciation of them. Our daily lives and ways of seeing them are framed by our sense-making of our past and by our anticipation of the future—we each live in our own self-constructed worlds. The surface diversity of our own worlds does not, however, detract from the existence of underlying processes. Our existence is interpreted differently across the spread of our civilisations, but that is a matter of the ways in which we choose to make sense of our existence. These two fundamental processes present the basis for a typology, and are mapped as the vertical and horizontal axes in Figure 3.1.

A Jungian Perspective

Parallels to these notions can be seen in the work of Jung. I am taking some ideas from his enormous contribution to this area, and I am using them in a loose sense to facilitate synthesis with ideas from other fields.

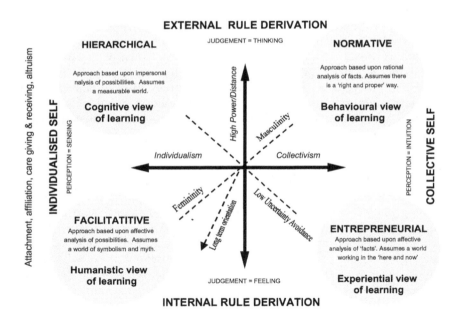

Figure 3.1   Mapping of Typologies

It is beyond the confines of this chapter to delve more fully into his work, but these ideas are not used in a manner that would contradict other aspects of his work. Briefly, Jung suggested that there are four archetypal aspects of psychological orientation that fit together as a whole typology and that can be seen to be associated with the ways in which we perceive our world.

> The quaternity is an archetype of almost universal occurrence. It forms the logical basis for any whole judgement. . . . There are always four elements, four primal qualities, four colours, four castes, four ways of spiritual development etc. So too, there are four aspects of psychological orientation . . . in order to orientate ourselves, we must have a function which ascertains that something is there (sensation); a second function which establishes what it is (thinking); a third function which states whether it suits us or not, whether we wish to accept it or no (feeling), and a fourth function which indicates where it came from and where it is going (intuition). The ideal completeness is a circle or sphere, but its natural minimal division is a quaternity. (Jung 1961: 167)

In other words, whilst everyone seeks to make sense of the world around them, they focus on different aspects of their existence in order to create their account of it. In support of his typology he suggested that there exist two processes (perception and judgement) that are independent of each other, and both are bipolar.

Perception is the process by which individuals make sense (consciously or otherwise) of their surroundings, and is thus mediated by previous understandings, expectation and anticipations, memory and unconscious influences; from the 'promissory notes' of metaphor, myth and rhetoric to primal drives (see Soyland 1994). When gathering information people *prefer* to focus either on the 'here-and-now' information from their senses, *or* on the 'what-if' information they 'intuit' from the possibilities and patterns they see developing. Judgement is the process of deciding which of the many alternative perceptival interpretations available at any one instant to adopt as 'reality'. Judgement is influenced by previous understandings and is more likely to be based upon post-hoc rationalisation than the traditionally accepted view of 'scientifically' weighing up the alternatives and rationally choosing the best option in advance of the final decision. When deciding about the information they have gathered, people *prefer* to make decisions based on objective thinking, by analysing and weighing the alternatives from a wide perspective, *or* to make decisions based on their feelings for each particular situation in an individualised manner.

Typologies

There is strong evidence of individual variation in preferred perceptual and judgemental styles (Reason 1981). Such variation forms the basic premise of the Myers-Briggs Type Indicator (MBTI), a management assessment and development tool for individuals and organisations that is used worldwide and is one of the few such personality tests that have a large body of data to contextualise and help analyse the test results (Briggs Myers & McCaulley 1985). Other researchers have used Jungian dimensions as a basis upon which to build an analysis of their area; for example, Tufts-Richardson (1996) links Jungian typology to individual spirituality by mapping four types of spiritual path, whilst McWhinney (1992) maps four paths of change, or choice, for organisations and society. The Jungian archetypal quartiles are mapped against Stevens and Price's fundamental processes in Figure 3.1.

Hofstede's (1991) typology was developed without reference to Jung. He described national culture by its position along five dimensions: individualism vs. collectivism, low vs. high power distance, masculinity vs. femininity, low vs. high uncertainty avoidance, and short- vs. long-term orientation. Although Hofstede makes it clear that many organisations illustrate a mix of these basic trends, his initial work can be criticised for an overly broad categorisation and delineation of national culture. For example, Poland is classed, alongside Sweden and Germany, as almost centrally balanced between long- and short-term orientation. Yet within his own analysis he found that Poland (as a nation) was a compromise of relatively extreme and disparate tendencies towards either long- or short-term orientation, whilst both Sweden and Germany showed less polarisation. Much of my experience and view on life has to do with the permeability of boundaries, and, indeed, I suggest in Chapter 16 that national boundaries are becoming increasingly eroded, so the idea of creating a model which says that if, for example, you are a Brit then you must have these fixed qualities, is anathema to me. However, for many, the denial of national difference is the politically correct stance; jokes based on nationality would not work if we were not closet classifiers.

Classification and Discrimination

We only know our own characteristics by comparing them with others, finding what we are not. Children as young as 21 hours can infer stability of traits from one example (Gelman & Diesendruck 1999) and by 10 years of age they are as willing as adults to use personality traits to predict behavioural consistency of individuals over time (Kalish 2002). To search out and focus on difference and otherness is part of how we make sense of the world—for example, young children initially categorise others by gender, but by four years old, also by race (Shutts et al. 2013). I see examples of racism quite frequently. Most of the sheep on the farms around my home are white, but I have a flock of Hebridean sheep—they are all jet black at birth, shading to grey in old age. On occasion a mother loses her lamb and so I foster another (usually white) on to her. The process takes several days of seclusion and by the time they go back into the flock it has come to smell like her (melding of smell is a major part of mothering on lambs) and so she accepts and cares for her new small white lamb. Despite the familiar 'flock' smell, the other sheep are not normally so accepting of the colour difference—they will headbutt the lamb if it goes near them, and some will chase it away. Normally that behaviour fades and the lamb becomes accepted, but occasionally one or two sheep will continue to harass it for weeks. The other lambs couldn't care less and play with it as normal. Sheep can be racist too.

TALKING OF ARCHETYPES

We naturally search out difference, whether it is colour, flock smell, or nationality, and those differences do exist, but, as I suggest throughout this book, perhaps the problem is not that something is bounded as such, but where we draw the conceptual boundaries and how permeable we imagine them to be. Hofstede's dimensions can be criticised, but they were derived from a wide spread of data and are illuminative if viewed as relativistic indicators of preference—as archetypal parameters rather than 'reality'.

Also included in Figure 3.1 (in the circles) are associated approaches to learning and organisation. The approaches to learning are picked up again in Figure 3.3 and addressed later in this chapter. The approaches to organisation are derived from Lee (1997a) and are discussed more fully there. Briefly, the 'Hierarchical' quarter is characterised by a system of high leader control in a rationalised environment, in which independent thought, action, and the ability to cope with ambiguity is minimised. The archetypal 'Hierarchical' person is sensitive to the requirements of those in power and to the analytic nature of 'acceptable' contributions. Questioning is allowed, so long as it occurs within the recognised hierarchical structure and conforms to the 'scientific' investigative format.

The 'Normative' archetype is characterised by a particularly strong focus upon the creation and maintenance of behavioural norms supporting a leader-defined vision of the future. Rules of the predominant culture are imposed, under the assumption that without such imposition individuals would have little 'self-control'. Appropriate behaviour is seen to evidence belief in the leader's vision. Ultimate power is awarded to those who can convert others to their view of existence, and thus questioning of these norms is anarchic or heretical behaviour; however, the coercive environment encourages such rebellion.

The archetypal 'entrepreneur' views externally imposed values and codes of behaviour as non-mandatory, and preserves the freedom to question and choose. He or she responds rapidly in a changing environment and is able to be anticipatorily proactive. However, as 'individualists', archetypal entrepreneurs, whilst able to lead others, have difficulty working as equals with others, or as subordinates, potentially falling into a damaging pattern of impotence and rivalry (Stacey 1993).

The facilitative archetype is characterised by cooperative social responsibility within a flexible power structure. This requires the ability to understand the machinations of the external world, whilst maintaining integrity and lack of 'game-playing'. Lack of unidirectional leadership challenges the group decision-making processes, such that the organisation's political system might result in power vacuum and drift.

The conjunction of individual and national foci in the mapping of typologies in Figure 3.1 is intended to highlight the nature of this mapping, by which a 'preference' is interpreted through the extent to which its opposite is realised; in which exploration of the unit under investigation is independent of the 'size' of the unit, and is, instead, linked to the unit's relationship to its wider context. In other words, the 'categories' presented in Figure 3.1 are archetypal and are applicable to any size of grouping (to individuals, organisations, and nations). Similarly, I wish to emphasise that it is not the intention to label the dimensions in a fixed and unique manner, but we do need to understand their qualia better if they are fundamental to our way of describing and enacting self and society.

I discussed four main views of 'management' (Lee 1997a and see Chapter 16 for a more critical discussion): the classical, scientific, processual, and phenomenological. Managers, within the classical view, must be able to create appropriate rules and procedures for others to follow; they must be good judges of people and able to take independent action as and when required. Good managers are assumed to be 'born' rather than 'made'—and so management development is a matter of selecting the 'right' people with leadership potential. The *scientific* view assumes that human behaviour is rational, and that people are motivated by economic criteria (Taylor 1947). Within this view 'correct' decisions can be identified and implemented appropriately through scientific analysis, and thus good management techniques can be acquired by anyone with the right training, and 'training departments' systematically identify and fill the '*training gap*'. Both of these approaches assume a structured and known world based upon rational principles and in which rationality leads to success.

The other two approaches to management assume a world in which agency (rather than structure) is the predominant force. The *processual* view of management assumes that economic advantage will come to those who are best able to spot opportunities, to learn rapidly, and to create appropriate commitment amongst colleagues. Human resource development is seen to help managers develop leadership and interpersonal skills, creativity, self-reliance, and the ability to work in different cultures. Although the individual is the main stakeholder in his or her own development, the direction of the organisation (and thus of an individual's development) remains at the behest of senior management, who, through initiatives such as business process re-engineering (BPR), aspire to mould the organisation and the people within it. *Phenomenological* management differs from processual management by the way in which the activities drive the functions, strategies, and even leadership of the organisation. For many, management is about 'purpose' and 'doing' whilst phenomenology is about the 'study' of 'being'. All individuals are seen to collude with their situation and, through that collusion, are 'together' responsible for the running and development of the organisation (despite some being 'senior management' and others being from the shop floor). 'Management' is about being part of a system whose activities change as a function of the system and of its relationship to its environment.

These four approaches link quite closely to the four ways in which the word 'development' is used in the literature. These were delineated through an entirely different line of research and are described in Chapter 2. An analysis of the literature showed that one meaning of development was to indicate a form of *maturation*—the (inevitable or natural) progression through series of stages of life cycle. When used to indicate *shaping* it similarly implied a known end point to which the individual or organisation was steered by the application of various tools, within a known, quantifiable, and manageable environment. In contrast, the other two uses of the word 'development' that were identified did not have a known end point. Development as a *voyage* was evident in literature about personal development—in which the self was the agent and the object, and development as *emergent,* was evident in social science literature particularly, in which the lines between the individual and the organisation became blurred and the focus was upon co-development and co-regulation.

Figure 3.2 shows a representation of these four forms of development, presented as a typology (in which the lines of the figure indicate the strength of spheres of influence, and not delineations or divisive categories) and maps on to these the four views of management discussed earlier.

This latter point is important and worth emphasising. I am NOT here discussing 'real' differences and saying that there exist four ways of 'doing' management or development—or that management or development are 'things' that can be done, or can be done to. In contrast, I am saying that there appear to be differences in the way that people talk about, or enact, whatever it is that constitutes 'development' or 'management' in their eyes, and that there appears to be some consistency within the realisation of those differences. I have also linked these to different approaches to learning, as I shall build upon these in the next section.

Socialisation and Development

In this section I suggest that these different approaches to the human condition are maintained by socialisation, but more than that, as each approach can be associated with a different view of learning and development so that

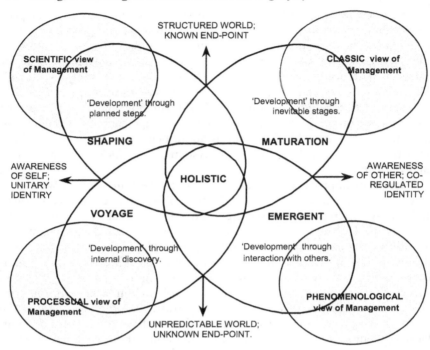

Figure 3.2   Four Types of Development Within Styles of Management, After Lee 1997b

approach is reconstituted and reinforced in its own likeness. Socialisation can be seen as a mechanism by which the tensions and their resolution between self and other, and between structure and agency, are promulgated and emphasised through succeeding generations.

I base my argument on the view that social development is a process of creative interaction in which 'individuals dynamically alter their actions with respect to the ongoing and anticipated actions of their partners' (Fogel 1993: 34). Relationships exist within mutually constructed conventions or frames of reference (Moreland & Levine 1989), and a dynamic view of culture is facilitated (Hatch 1993). Mattingly et al. (2014) suggest that individuals are motivated to grow and improve the self by increasing their capabilities, identities, and resources through a process of self-expansion, which is often achieved through close relationships (Aron et al. 2013). The example given earlier illustrates this process.

Society exists in so far as people agree to its existence—and could be a family unit or a nation. In some way (whether by being born into and thus socialised within it—as in a family or nation, through meeting like-minded people and thus forming friendship groups, or formally through induction into an organisation) individuals come to identify (and be identified

by others) as part of a community. In so doing they help create and collude with underlying values and norms. This process starts at birth and is
a basal acculturation mechanism in which the underlying processes are the
same whether the focus is upon family and friendship groupings, temporary
'micro-cultures', small or large organisations, or national culture (Burns
1977). There is empirical evidence of correlation between the form of parenting and the child's life stance (Bee 1985), and between career and family
history (Cromie et al. 1992). Similarly, there is evidence that choice of curricula, methodological approach, and course design are partially governed
by the value base of the providers, and thus perpetuate that value base (Boyacigiller & Adler 1991). Thus the approach to learning adopted by each
society has a fundamental effect upon the continuation of the parameters of
that particular society (Lee 1996).

In Figure 3.3 different forms of learning were mapped against the archetypal parameters of self and other, and of structure and agency. In practical terms, the 'cognitive' environment carries with it group norms about
received wisdom and the value of qualifications. Power is vested in those
who have achieved qualifications and those who can give them. Cogent
argument carries more importance than does applicability or individual

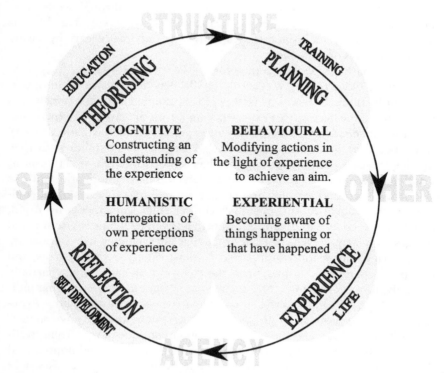

Figure 3.3 Movement Through Typologies (After Lee 1996)

difference. The 'problem' student or heretic (Harshbarger 1973) would be someone who lacked sufficient intelligence to master the required concepts. The 'behavioural' environment focuses upon activity, functionalism, and the importance of the end result. Norms are about identifying competence, and filling the 'training gap' to achieve appropriate levels of competence. The heretic is someone unable to demonstrate the required competence. The 'humanistic' environment focuses upon difference and equality. Received wisdom (in so far as it epitomises a particular view of reality) is inappropriate, as are identifiable and assessable 'competencies' (in so far as they epitomise a 'right' way of doing things). The problem participant is unwilling to explore and share their affective and attitudinal aspects. In the 'experiential' environment the focus is on actionable outcomes—the end justifies the means. The heretic is someone who questions the route, or prefers inactivity. The confidence to act is a prerequisite for learning (Blackler 1993).

I am not suggesting that in real life, learning only occurs within one approach. Instead, it is much more likely that in any situation one learns more holistically (Lee 1996). Honey & Mumford (1989) suggest that 'experience' plays a part in any learning, regardless of whether or not it is acknowledged or focused upon within the educational process. One of the best-known models of experiential learning is that of Kolb (1984), who suggests that the process of learning is cyclical, revolving through experience, reflection, theorising, and planning. In Figure 3.3 this is represented by the large (arrowed) circle. From this perspective, we only really learn by engaging in all aspects of the activity.

Transformative experiences, therefore, appear to be those that force us to (re-)examine our world view (Pascale 1990). Any 'experience' is an opportunity for learning; however, as Dewey (1938) pointed out, 'It is not enough to insist upon the necessity of experience, nor even of activity in experience. Everything depends upon the quality of experience which is had . . . every experience lives in further experiences'. Vasilyuk (1984) takes it further, building the case that all learning that has a transformative effect upon us is derived from a clash between our understanding of the world and our experience, such that learning and change are painful processes of redefinition, and Romanelli & Tushman (1994) offer empirical support for rapid, discontinuous change in organisations being driven by major environmental changes. Similarly, Stevens & Price argue that our changing lives necessitate renegotiating our position with respect to the great archetypal systems, and that 'psychopathology results when the environment fails, either partially or totally, to meet one (or more) archetypal need(s) in the developing individual' (1966: 34). In the terms of complexity theory, transformative experiences occur at bifurcation points, when the system and the environment impact in such a way that the system can either continue in its current, well-travelled pattern, or shift to some way of being that is new and unpredicted (though not necessarily unpredictable). Indeed, the current analysis would suggest that the system is likely to shift to incorporate qualia of a different world view.

Archetypes and Dialectics

I have argued that there exist two main bipolar underlying processes by which the human condition is structured, and that these give rise to four main archetypes. The processes of socialisation, or learning, emphasise particular aspects of our world view, such that the various systems or subsystems, be they individuals, organisations, or nations, have a preference for, or leaning towards, the qualia of one archetype over the others. However, although I have talked of the qualia of the archetypes, I have deliberately failed to define them other than by example. Archetypes, by their nature, are indefinable in the scientist sense, and also, as discussed above, the qualia are unmeasurable other than dialectically (Pascale 1990) by reference to their 'opposite'. Furthermore, that 'opposite' might be different under different occasions or interpretations. For example, as I describe in Chapter 10, in one situation the word 'conflict' was interpreted by some people to be 'contested negotiation' whilst others saw it as 'a fight to the death', and acted accordingly with misunderstanding on both sides. We could extrapolate that for these people the opposite to their views of conflict would be the similar but subtly different qualities of 'easy negotiation' and 'peaceful life'. We live within our own world view yet in order to understand or even describe it we need to compare it with that of others in a dialectic manner. In other words—to know what we are, we also have to know what we are not. We can't categorise the human condition in a positivistic mutually exclusive sense, but we can use the arguments above to develop a dialectically based meta-typology.

I discuss notions of representation in the next chapter, but it is worth digressing slightly here, before the representation of my meta-typology, to emphasise the way in which I intend such a diagram to be interpreted. Deleuze & Guattari (2013: 164) suggest that the diagram 'does not function to represent . . . but rather constructs a real that is yet to come, a new type of reality' making hidden aspects of the world visible and articulable (Hetherington 2011). In this sense they can be seen as an abstract map of power (Rodowick 2001); of interlocking modes of control and forms of resistance (Foucault 1998). Diagrams are not therefore closed systems but evolving and dynamic networks of relations (Butler et al. 2014). From this point of view 'there is no diagram that does not also include, besides the points which it connects up, certain relatively free or unbound points, points of creativity, change and resistance' (Deleuze 1988: 44).

A Wheel of Typologies

Figure 3.4 shows a typology of typologies, or a meta-typology, of the human condition, constructed by plotting the axes of the great archetypal systems against typologies of individual, organisational, and governmental approach and those of individual influence, education, and metaphor (as a form of organisational glue, after Morgan 1986). In other words, it is

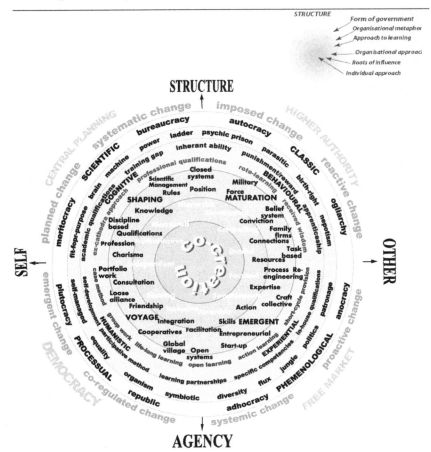

Figure 3.4   A Typology of Typologies (Note the Words Are Indicative, Not Definitional)

intended as a typology that underlies those discussed previously and others in the literature.

This is not intended as a categorisation. Each spoke of the wheel supports the others with no clear distinction between neighbouring typologies, and each is validated dialectically by the qualia of the spoke opposite it. Thus an archetypal individual and organisational approach is represented as if it were located in a radial segment of the wheel (the width of which would depend upon the diversity of the element in question), and the probability of identifying an approach typified by other segments or individual parts of the wheel would be negatively correlated with distance from the primal segment. If this meta-typology is imagined in three dimensions, with the centre forming the tip of a cone, the third dimension represents a continuum moving from micro variables at the apex towards macro variables at the base. In other words, the tip of the cone might represent degrees of aggregation, and the base, large aggregates of elements, yet each has influence upon the other.

When visualised as a cone, however, the meta-typology represents three dimensions, each of which possesses a pole that focuses upon 'individuality', though the import of this is different in each case. This generates multiple layers of meaning that are sacrificed if a one-dimensional form of analysis is adopted. Each segment and type is interpretable in the light of its archetypal opposites within these multiple layers, and thus analysis of the meta-typology is richer if a dialectic perspective is adopted.

An example of the influence the individual can have upon a large organisation can be seen in Connolly (2004), who recounts how the raising of an eyebrow by a senior manager in a meeting delayed an organisational change initiative by several years. Similarly, work exploring gene-culture co-evolution indicates the potential for rapid genetically linked cultural change linked to choice of mate (Laland 1993). This example also indicates the permeable nature of the boundary between individual and society. Individuals might be actively choosing a mate—though factors of background and parenting are likely to mediate in such choice (Duck 1986)—but they are unlikely to be doing so in order to influence societal form. These examples emphasise both the unpredictable influence of individual factors (see Gleick 1987, and chaos theory) and the speed with which such 'inactive' change might occur.

Organisations comprise multifaceted membership and are likely to contain dissidents who might be expected to voice an approach at the polar opposite to that held by the organisation (heresy) or to work outside the accepted bounds of the segment (deviance). Inconsistency of approach might also be found across the levels and/or functions of the organisation (Demirag & Tylecote 1992), and within the individual (leading to analysis within psycho-dynamic frameworks) (Parsons 1951). It can be speculated that level of conflict will be positively correlated with degree of inconsistency both between individual approaches and within aspects of an approach.

Co-Creation

This is a model of types, based on archetypes. This model is not intended to show that individual 'x' is at a particular point in the model, or organisation 'y' can be specifically classified by another point. The import of the model is in the dynamic relationships indicated between the points, not the points themselves. The notion of preferences is critical to interpreting my approach, as is the notion of becoming.

The three-dimensional interpretation of the wheel presents a holistic and interactive overview of the meta-typology that is, in essence, static. Given the notion that individuals and organisations, despite their 'presenting approach', will possess hidden qualia of their opposites and that it is the conflict between these, which are, themselves, part of the environment, or with other aspects of the environment, that generates creative tension and transformation, then it is necessary to introduce a fourth dimension to the meta-typology—that of transformation over time, or dynamism.

As discussed in Chapter 2, from Heraclitus onwards (circa 500 BC) it has been suggested that humanity is in a state of always 'becoming' despite the appearance of structured categorisation and 'being' fostered by Western scientism (Stacey et al. 2000). In other words, our lives are dynamic, and in a state of constant change. Fixed goals, known end points, and clear delineations are tools that we use to provide a sense of stability, but that sense is merely a mechanism and is false with respect to the wider reality of existence.

Individuals, organisations, or nations are all in this state of flux, a state of becoming. They might show a preference for one way of being, or indeed a preference for several different ways of being, but that does not mean that they can be permanently categorised in that way. Indeed, as discussed earlier, part of the process of becoming is finding balance between different poles of the dialectic. As the child grows so the self/other relationship develops. In order to understand our own culture we need to understand what it is not, by experiencing other cultures. In order to develop, to continue becoming, we need to extend our preferences, try different things, explore different ways of being. For a team to work well together, the members need to balance each other, some strong in one thing, others strong in another. A business in which everyone is the same becomes stagnant. It is for this reason that co-creation is at the centre of the model. The act of finding the balance and developing something new holds individuals, groups, and societies together and is at the core of development.

The meta-typology, presented here with lines and detail, is merely an attempt to indicate underlying structures. Those structures exist, however, not as things but as patterns of relationships: a representation of the relationships between other representations. As noted above, even the terminology used is just a representation.

HOLISTIC AGENCY

I have argued that although the terminology differs, the underlying processes permeate our existence. Links between existing work and the meta-typology could be limited to positive correlation with existing typologies along a single axis. For example, Handy's (1981) typology of organisation culture (Power, Role, Task, Person) shows some similarity to the vertical axis. Debates about field dependence/independence in cognitive style (Hayes & Allison 1994) appear to fit more closely to the horizontal axis, whilst those about the way in which individuals and societies are interconnected and mutually influencing are represented by the third-dimensional axis. Similarly, Rasheed & Prescott's (1992) dimensions of complexity and dynamism in the classification of organisational task environments show some similarity to the two diagonal axes. Thus the meta-typology can be linked to one-dimensional measures, such as equity sensitivity (King & Miles 1994), interpersonal orientation (Swap & Rubin 1983), or Machiavellianism (Robinson & Shaver 1973), and is potentially testable in its prediction of relationships between such measures. I note that nearly every two-by-two matrix I come across seems to accord with the meta-typology in some way or another.

It is, perhaps, not surprising to find that two-by-two matrices, as representations of something, accord with other representations, especially if there do exist underlying processes from which we structure our worlds. However, I do not wish to suggest that any organisation or individual might demonstrate all the qualia of a particular typology—to do so might establish them as an archetype! As a complex system the individual might demonstrate forms of behaviour akin to one segment of the wheel (espousing an approach similar to that of the free-market), whilst the observer notes aspects of behaviour that are located within another segment (working within traditional educational methodology and reinforcing respect for position and rules—theory in practice), whilst voicing a preference for a third segment (one that respects 'human values'). Similar multilevel and contradictory behaviour is illustrated in the case given in Chapter 9.

The exploration of inconsistency might lead to greater understanding of organisations in practice (Schein 1985) and point to areas of knowledge that are, at present, under-explored. For example: The form of the model suggests an expansion of Morgan's (1986) typology of organisational metaphor, it supports Buchanan's (1991) call for alternative accounts of change, and it might provide insight into the problems encountered when applying Western-style bureaucracy to African culture (Hyden 1983), or help contextualise inconsistencies in research findings (Judge & Watanabe 1994).

Different parts of the organisation or society might well adopt different configurations, and configurations might change as 'needed'. The activities of the social system are emergent and feed back into it (Weick 1977), they can influence all other aspects of the system, and the system itself can be far from equilibrium. This approach, therefore, denies the ability to 'plan' or 'control' organisational development—it argues for a resource-based view of the organisation in which the role of 'managing' is fragmentary (i.e., Mintzberg 1979) and offers a valuable critique of the established 'discipline' of strategy. In addition, because this view eschews ideas of (real) control by a hierarchy, as well as questions the ability of the organisation to (really) predict or plan, it is more in tune with work that questions the serial and causal nature of our existence (Lee & Flatau 1996; see also Chapter 13).

Integration of the Social Sciences

So how does this link to my earlier points about the integration of the social sciences? Perhaps the earliest discipline was philosophy, from which grew core disciplines of psychology and sociology with their very different views of the world. This can be seen in relation to the meta-typology. If we look at the core disciplines of sociology and psychology, sociology, with its focus on social forces and core debates around structure and agency, can be seen to be aligned along one axis of the representation, whilst psychology, with its focus upon the individual and their relation to the collective, can be seen to be aligned along the opposite axis. Both are looking at the human condition, but from very different perspectives. They understand it differently and employ different techniques to further their understanding

There is, of course, wide variation within each discipline, and many of the fields of study that have developed from these are more hybrid in their approach. Disciplines such as education, politics, law, and anthropology can also be associated with particular areas of the meta-typology (in relation to content and approach), as can hybrid fields of study such as cultural studies, ethnography, ICT, management (including economics, finance, etc.), and organisational studies.

However, these are just titles that are applied to a particular focus on the world, and, if we are to accept my previous arguments, it is inappropriate to delineate one from the other. Indeed, having gone through a period of diversification and delimitation, the rhetoric is now about interdisciplinary and multidisciplinary investigation. It is worth noting, though, that these terms in themselves imply segregation. Whilst there might be a desire to work together across disciplines, the tenets and language of the various disciplines mitigate against this.

There is a need to adopt a flexible view of language (as has been evident throughout this chapter) in order to encompass the multiple specific meanings that have developed around particular words. Take for example (as in Chapter 13) the words conscious, subconscious, and unconscious, which merit a field of study in their own right and mean very different things to a Jungian and to a sociologist. This refining of language cannot be done through definition, as each field defines it within its own terms—it can only be done by a refusal to define and through joint understanding by exemplar.

HRD As the Relationship Between Representations

The more hybrid fields of study can suffer from the diversity inherent in their approach, but also offer a way forward. We can take HRD as an example, though similar things could be said about other hybrid fields. Regardless of one's 'understanding', or the terminology used, that which might be called the development of human resources is located at the dynamic and co-creative interface between the elements of the system, and between subsystems, such that in interacting, they become more than the sum of the parts. Thus the business of HRD, in so far as it exists as a concept and a practice, is concerned with the relationship between the representations. Research into HRD is, in effect, research into the processes that underlie the human condition. The practice of HRD is about influencing the relationships that comprise the glue of the human condition. From this emerges organisational transformation and social change.

In terms of complexity, as we research the human condition we need to be aware that we are researching the intangible and unmeasurable. We can catch glimpses of what we are looking for and we can try to represent or model it—but we need to avoid the temptation to overly objectify or embody that which we research. The 'individual' and the 'organisation' are not unitary bounded concepts—they are part of a whole and are identifiable by their relationship to the whole. As discussed in Chapter 7, they are also moulded, altered, and formed by each other. It is the interactions that are of importance, rather than descriptions of 'purpose'. Similarly, a change in approach requires a change in the language and meaning that is used. For example, it would be inappropriate to talk of 'organisations' as if they had a body and could be anthropomorphised, or of 'people' as if they were machine cogs within 'the organisation' whose function was to 'operate' if we were to adopt a loosely bounded or relativistic view of these elements of the system. When we intervene in the human condition with some aim in mind, both the *'outcomes'* and their 'value' are subject to interpretation. There is no longer necessarily a clear and obvious route between cause and effect—and one person's preferred 'outcome' might be someone else's feared possibility/cause. We can no longer assume that a particular intervention at a particular time will produce a known end point. We lose the gloss of certainty that permeates a well-defined and causal view of the world, one that many HRD professionals feel is necessary for their work as academics, consultants, trainers, etc. HRD and learning are becoming more central to the needs of the nation (as in Watson 1994) and this shift in provision further increases the complexity and uncertainty of enquiry into the nature (and practice) of HRD.

Holistic Agency

I have suggested that there exist 'great archetypal structures' that underlie the human condition, and that these can be identified by their effect upon it, such that human society and thought clusters into four main archetypal world views termed here, for the sake of convenience and bearing in mind the fragility of language, hierarchical, normative, entrepreneurial, and facilitative. The axes by which these are located are bipolar and termed, again, for convenience, self and other, and structure and agency. This forms a meta-typology or representation of the human condition. I suggest that much of human functioning, including ways of examining the world (research methodologies) and interpreting it (disciplines and fields of study) can be mapped against this meta-typology. These great systems and their products are most fruitfully discussed by embracing the language (and thus concepts) of complexity. This recognises that whilst the entity cannot be pulled apart and understood, in a way that a wind-up watch could be, it can be accessed by examining the relationships between the multiplicity of representations that are located within it. Thus the study of the system is the study of the relationships within it, and that study is that which we might commonly call HRD. It follows from this that the practice of HRD is about *agency* in a pluralistic, relativistic, and interpretative world. This involves the search for the patterning of the whole, for dynamic structures, an understanding of the possibilities and their links—a *holistic* approach. Holistic agency is therefore about individual action (or non-action) within a relativistic yet structured world, and thus is about the 'doing' and 'becoming' of HRD.

Figure 3.4 depicts a key part of my conception of holistic agency. The thinking behind it, the way it links into so many other views and models in the literature, and in particular the way in which it builds upon archetypal structures derived from evolutionary psychology strengthen my view of its applicability. However, the model is no good if it remains a pleasing but ultimately sterile account. This figure is a holistic representation of part of my view of holistic agency, but the agency side is as important as the representation. Throughout the rest of this book, I will keep this model in mind but balance the conceptual accounts with accounts of action.

It is the thinking and doing together that comprise holistic agency.

REFERENCES

Aron A, Lewandowski GW, Mashek D, & Aron EN (2013) 'The Self-Expansion Model of Motivation and Cognition in Close Relationships', in Simpson J & Campbell L (Eds) *The Oxford Handbook of Close Relationships*: 90–115. Oxford: Oxford University Press.

Bailey KD (1994) *Typologies and Taxonomies: An Introduction to Classification Techniques*. Thousand Oaks, CA: Sage.

Ball P (2014) 'The Borders of Order', *New Scientist* 26 April: 45–47.

Barklow JH, Cosmides L, & Tooby J (1992) (Eds) *The Adapted Mind: Evolutionary Psychology and the Generation of Culture*. New York: Oxford University Press.

Bee H (1985) *The Developing Child*. New York: Harper and Row.

Bird A (2013) 'Epigenetics: Instant Expert', *New Scientist* 5 January: i–viii.

Blackler F (1993) 'Knowledge and the theory of organisations: Organisations as activity systems and the reframing of management', *Journal of Management Studies* 30: 863–884.

Boisot M & Mckelvey B (2010) 'Integrating modernist and postmodernist perspectives on organizations: A complexity science bridge', *Academy of Management Review* 35(3)415–433.

Boyacigiller N & Adler NJ (1991) 'The Parochial Dinosaur: Organisational Science in a Global Context', *Academy of Management Review* 16(2)262–290.

Bradshaw JL (1997) *Human Evolution: A Neuropsychological Perspective*. Hove: Psychology Press.

Briggs Myers I & McCaulley MH (1985) *A Guide to the Development and Use of the Myers-Briggs Type Indicator*. Palo Alto: Consulting Psychologists Press.

Buchanan DA (1991) 'Vulnerability and agenda: Context and process in project management', *British Journal of Management* 2: 121–132.

Burns T (1977) *The BBC: Pubic Institution and Private World*. New York: Holmes & Meier Publishers.

Butler N, Jeanes E, & Otto B (2014) 'Diagrammatics of organization', *Ephemera* 14(2)167–175.

Calas MB & Smircich L (1999) 'Past postmodernism? Reflections and tentative directions', *Academy of Management Review* 24(4)649–671.

Chiao JY & Blizinsky KD (2013) 'Population disparities in mental health: Insights from cultural neuroscience', *American Journal of Public Health* 103(1): 122–132.

Cilliers P (1998) *Complexity and Postmodernism*. London: Routledge.

Connolly M (2004) *An Investigation into the Generative Dynamics of Organization*. Ph.D. Thesis. Lancaster, UK: Lancaster University.

Cromie S, Callaghan I, & Jansen M (1992) 'The entrepreneurial tendencies of managers: A research note', *British Journal of Management* 3: 1–5.

Dawkins R (1976) *The Selfish Gene*. Oxford: Oxford University Press.

Daxinger L & Whitelaw E (2010) 'Transgenerational epigenetic inheritance', *Genome Research* 20: 1623–1628.

Deleuze G (1988) *Foucault*. Minneapolis: University of Minnesota Press.

Deleuze G & Guattari F (2013) *A Thousand Plateaus: Capitalism and Schizophrenia*. London and New York: Bloomsbury.

Demirag I & Tylecote A (1992) 'The effects of organisational culture, structure and market expectations on technological innovation: A hypothesis', *British Journal of Management* 3: 7–20.

De Vreize J (2014) 'Mayor of Microbe Metropolis', *New Scientist* 14 May 2014: 42–45.

Dewey J (1938) *Experience and Education*. New York: Collier.

Duck S (1986) *Human Relationships*. London: Sage.

Fogel A (1993) *Developing through Relationships*. Hemel Hempstead: Harvester Wheatsheaf.

Foucault M (1998) *The Will to Knowledge: The History of Sexuality: 1*. London: Penguin.

Fox R (1989) *The Search for Society: Quest for a Biosocial Science and Morality*. London: Rutgers University Press.

Frost P (2003) *Toxic Emotions at Work*. Boston, MA: Harvard Business School Press.

Gelman SA & Diesendruck G (1999) 'What's in a Concept? Context, Variability, and Psychological Essentialism', in Sigel IE (Ed) *Development of Mental Representation*: 87–111. Mahwah, NJ: Erlbaum.

Giddens A (1976) *New Rules of Sociological Method*. London: Hutchinson.

Gleick J (1987) *Chaos*. New York: Viking.

Handy CB (1981) *Understanding Organisations*. Harmondsworth: Penguin.

Hardy C, Lawrence TB, & Grant D (2005) 'Discourse and collaboration: The role of conversations and collective identity', *Academy of Management Review* 30(1)58–77.

Harshbarger D (1973) 'The individual and the social order: Notes on the management of heresy and deviance in complex organisations', *Human Relations* 26(2): 251–269.

Hatch MJ (1993) 'The dynamics of organisational culture', *Academy of Management Review* 18: 657–693.

Hayes J & Allison CW (1994) 'Cognitive style and its relevance for management practice', *British Journal of Management* 5: 53–71.

Hetherington K (2011) 'Foucault, the museum and the diagram', *Sociological Review* 59(3)457–475.

Hofstede G (1991) *Cultures and Organisations, Software of the Mind*. London: McGraw-Hill.

Holmes B (2013) 'Life's purpose', *New Scientist* 12 October: 33–35.

Honey P & Mumford A (1989) *The Manual of Learning Opportunities*. Maidenhead, Berks: Peter Honey.

Hopfl H (1995) 'Organisational rhetoric and the threat of ambivalence', *Studies in Cultures, Organisations and Societies* 1(2): 175–188.

Hotho JP (2014) 'From typology to taxonomy', *Organization Studies* 35(5)671–702.

Hyden G (1983) *No Shortcuts to Progress: African Development Management in Perspective*. Berkeley: University of California Press.

Judge TA & Watanabe S (1994) 'Individual differences in the nature of the relationship between job and life satisfaction', *Journal of Occupational and Organisational Psychology* 76: 101–107.

Jung CG (1961) 'Psychology and Religion: West and East', In *Collected Works II*: 167, cited in Jung CG (1963) *Memories, Dreams and Reflections*. London: Flamingo.

Kalish CW (2002) 'Children's predictions of consistency in people's actions', *Cognition* 84: 237–265.

King WC & Miles EW (1994) 'The measurement of equity sensitivity', *Journal of Occupational and Organisational Psychology* 67: 133–142.

Kolb D (1984) *Experiential Learning*. Eaglewood Cliffs, NJ: Prentice-Hall.

Kuhn ST (1970) *The Structure of Scientific Revolutions*. Chicago: University of Chicago Press.

Laland KN (1993) 'The mathematical modelling of human culture and its implications for psychology and the human sciences', *British Journal of Psychology* 84: 145–169.

Lax S, Smith DP, Hampton-Marcell J, Owen SM, Handley KM, Scott NM, Gibbons SM, Larsen P, Shogan BD, Weiss S, Metcalf JL, Ursell LK, Vázquez-Baeza Y, Van Treuren W, Hasan NA, Gibson MK, Colwell R, Dantas G, Knight R, & Gilbert JA (2014) 'Longitudinal analysis of microbial interaction between humans and the indoor environment', *Science* 345(6200)1048–1052.

Lee MM (1996) 'Action Learning as a Cross-Cultural Tool', in Stewart J & McGoldrick J (Eds) *Human Resource Development*: 240–260. London: Pitman.

Lee MM (1997a) 'Strategic Human Resource Development: A Conceptual Exploration', in Torraco R (Ed) *Academy of Human Resource Development Conference Proceedings*: 92–99. Atlanta: AHRD.

Lee MM (1997b) 'The Developmental Approach: A Critical Reconsideration', in Burgoyne J & Reynolds M (Eds) *Management Learning*: 199–214. London: Sage.

Lee MM (2003) *HRD in a Complex World*. London: Routledge.

Lee MM & Flatau M (1996) 'Seriova Logika v paralelnom svete', in Mitzla M (Ed) *Predpoklady Zavadzania ISO 9000 Na Slovensku*: 11–33. Kosiche: IBIS Publishing.

Mattingly BA, Lewandowski GW Jr, & McIntyre KP (2014) ' "You make me a better/worse person": A two-dimensional model of relationship self-change', *Personal Relationships* 21: 176–190.

McMurray R & Ward J (2014) ' "Why would you want to do that?": Defining emotional dirty work', *Human Relations* 67(9)1123–1143.

McWhinney W (1992) *Paths of Change*. California: Sage.

Mintzberg H (1979) *The Structuring of Organisations*. Englewood Cliffs, NJ: Prentice-Hall.

Mitchella C, Hobcraftb J, McLanahanc SS, Rutherford Siegeld S, Bergd A, Brooks-Gunne J, Garfinkelf I, & Nottermand D (2014) 'Social disadvantage, genetic sensitivity, and children's telomere length', *Proceedings of the National Academy of Sciences* 111(16)5944–5949.

Money N (2014) *The Amoeba in the Room*. Oxford: Oxford University Press.

Moreland RL & Levine JM (1989) 'Newcomers and Oldtimers in Small Groups', in Paulus P (Ed) *Psychology of Group Influence*: 143–186. Hillsdale, NJ: Erlbaum.

Morgan G (1986) *Images of Organisation*. London: Sage.

Parsons T (1951) *The Social System*. London: Routledge & Kegan Paul.

Pascale RT (1990) *Managing on the Edge*. London: Viking, Penguin.

Pilcher H (2013) 'Beyond nature and nurture', *New Scientist* 31 August 2013: 44–47.

Price I (2004) 'Complexity, complicatedness and complexity: A new science behind organizational intervention?', *E:CO* 6(1–2)40–48.

Rabinowitz A (2013) 'Why do things go viral, and should we care?', *Nautilus* 5(4). (http://nautil.us/issue/5/fame/the-meme-as-meme) Accessed 24/8/15.

Rasheed AMA & Prescott J (1992) 'Towards an objective classification scheme for organisational task environments', *British Journal of Management* 3: 197–206.

Reason P (1981) ' "Methodological Approaches to Social Science", by Ian Mitroff and Ralph Kilmann: An Appreciation', in Reason P & Rowan J (Eds) *Human Inquiry: A Source Book of New Paradigm Research*: 43–51. Chichester: John Wiley and Sons.

Robinson JP & Shaver PR (1973) *Measures of Social Psychological Attitudes*. Ann Arbor, MI: Institute for Social Research.

Rodowick DN (2001) *Reading the Figural, or, Philosophy After the New Media*. Durham and London: Duke University Press.

Romanelli E & Tushman ML (1994) 'Organisational transformation as punctuated equilibrium: An empirical test', *Academy of Management Journal* 37: 1141–1166.

Schein EH (1985) *Organisational Culture and Leadership: A Dynamic View*. San Francisco: Jossey Bass.

Shutts K, Pemberton CK, & Spelke ES (2013) 'Children's use of social categories in thinking about people and social relationships', *Journal of Cognition and Development* 14(1)35–62.

Smith KB (2002) 'Typologies, taxonomies, and the benefits of Policy classification', *Policy Studies Journal* 30(3)379–395.

Snowden D & Stanbridge P (2004) 'The landscape of management: Creating the context for understanding social complexity', *E:CO* 6(1–2)140–148.

Sokal RR & Sneath IHA (1964) *Principles of Numerical Taxonomy*. San Francisco: Freeman.

Soyland AJ (1994) *Psychology as Metaphor*. London: Sage.

Stacey R (1993) *Strategic Management and Organisational Dynamics*. London: Pitman.

Stacey R, Griffin D, & Shaw P (2000) *Complexity and Management: Fad or Radical Challenge to Systems Thinking?* London: Routledge.

Stevens A & Price J (1966) *Evolutionary Psychiatry: A New Beginning*. London: Routledge.

Swap WC & Rubin JZ (1983) 'Measure of interpersonal orientation', *Journal of Personality and Social Psychology* 44: 208–219.

Talhelm T, Zhang X, Oishi S, Shimin C, Duan D, Lan X, & Kitayama S (2014) 'Large-scale psychological differences within China explained by Rice versus Wheat agriculture', *Science* 344(6184)603–608.

Taylor FW (1947) *Scientific Management*. London: Harper & Row.

Thompson H (2014) 'Famine puts next two generations at risk of obesity', *New Scientist* 223(2978)01. Science, DOI: 10.1126/science.1255903

Tsoukas H & Hatch M-J (2001) 'Complex thinking, complex practice: The case for a narrative approach to organisational complexity', *Human Relations* 54(8)979–1014.

Tufts-Richardson P (1996) *Four Spiritualities*. Palo-Alto, CA: Davies-Black Publishing.

van Kleef GA (2014) 'Understanding the positive and negative effects of emotional expressions in organizations: EASI does it', *Human Relations* 67: 1145–1164.

Vasilyuk F (1984) *The Psychology of Experiencing*. Hemel Hempstead: Harvester Wheatsheaf.

Vetter NC, Leipold K, Kliegel M, Phillips LH, & Altgassen M (2013) 'Ongoing development of social cognition in adolescence', *Child Neuropsychology* 19(6)615–629.

Watson TJ (1994) In Search of Management: culture, chaos and control in managerial work. London: Routledge.

Weber M (1949) *The Methodology of the Social Sciences*. Glencoe, IL: The Free Press.

Weick K (1977) 'Organisational design: Organisations as self-organising systems', *Organisational Dynamics* Autumn: 31–67.

Yehuda R, Daskalakis NP, Desarnaud F, Makotkine I, Lehrner AL, Koch E, Flory JD, Buxbaum JD, Meaney MJ, & Bierer LM (2013) 'Epigenetic Biomarkers as predictors and correlates of symptom improvement following Psychotherapy in Combat Veterans with PTSD', *Frontiers in Psychiatry* 4: 118.

Yolles MI (1999) *Management Systems: A Viable Approach*. London: Financial Times Pitman.

Youngman PA & Hadzikadic M. (2014) (Eds) *Complexity and the Human Experience: Modelling Complexity in the Humanities and Social Sciences*. Singapore: Pan Stanford Publishing.

4 Fact, Fiction, and Representation

The previous chapter introduced the idea of holistic agency based upon two archetypal structures underlying the way in which we play out our lives; it also emphasised the complexity of our being and becoming, and the way in which so much that we 'know' is not as certain as we like to think. This chapter extends this line of thought through an exploration of representation. This is inspired by the circumstances surrounding the withdrawal from my workspace five years after I finished salaried full-time employment. This account leads to questions around the relationship between space and self—the physicality of reality and what constitutes the fact so created. In so doing it picks up the discussion about representation in the previous chapter. That these questions on the nature of 'fact' are asked via the 'fiction' of the autobiographical is also explored. The issues that are raised in this account reverberate throughout the rest of the book.

I am, at heart, a scientist—I enjoy the simple (if complicated) nature of the quantitative side of things, and much of my early work was in experimental psychology. However, like everyone else, I do have key experiences that have impacted upon me—I have written about these (see for example Chapter 13), and my writing has increasingly come to refer to my direct experience. I found myself experimenting with methodology and exploring the notions of researcher as participant and reflective observer. This approach acknowledges and addresses those aspects of social research in which the presence of the researcher and the act of research influence that which is researched, and colleagues have called what I am doing 'autoethnography'. I refer to it as almost-autoethnography, as I discuss in the following chapter. So whilst I have been practising this approach since the early nineties, I can now justify it to the external world by referring to it by name.

The justification for dwelling on my key experiences, for calling them research, is measured by the extent to which they have relevance to a population wider than one. This is, of course, the same for all research, but the bridge between personal learning and 'of import to others' is both more obvious and more fragile in autoethnography. To be seen as 'good' research it needs to be much more than 'just a story'—though the core is a story, it needs to be a contextualised, understandable, often multi-perspectival, critical, criticised, and evaluated account of self in society that throws light on society as well as self.

Autoethnography could be seen as 'fiction' in so far as it is a representation of a perception of a particular happening in a specific time and place to one person, as recounted through that person's interpretative cognition and processing. So what are facts? I shall tell you a story by which to explore this.

ON THE LOSS OF A ROOM

Following a serious illness, in 1999 I retired from full-time work on medical grounds. On my retirement, I was honoured to be awarded life-membership of the university and I was given a room in the department in exchange for the supervision of PhD students. As the person who was dean at the time wrote:

> I like the idea of compensating you for this work in facilities rather than cash. . . . I hope we can agree that having a room will compensate you for the PhD work you might be doing. . . . Do you want to have a very careful tariff? I would rather not—but would like it on the record that your use of the room etc. was in return for the work you will continue to do for the School. (Email from the person who was dean when this arrangement was made, sent to myself and copied to four key senior staff in the Management School and in the HR department of the university, including my head of department at the time, whom I shall call AS.)

To cut a long story short, I was moved out of my room after five years, but continued to supervise students. I therefore expected some sort of recompense for the work I was doing. The dean had left by this time, so the discussion around this centred upon AS. He refused to acknowledge that any agreement existed—which rather surprised me. I produced the documentation discussing and establishing the agreement—some that AS had been copied into, some that he had contributed to, and others that he had generated. It transpired that AS accepted that the correspondence existed but denied that it could be seen as true or factual. He wrote:

> Neither your metaphysics nor your practice involves the idea that there can be truth, to such an extent you do not seem to be capable of recognising that there can be such as a true account of a series of human events. I think you think that there are only points of view that prevail and those that don't. Since I honestly think you do not recognise facts, that you should claim that it is an important rule to stick to the facts is itself deceitful. (Email from AS to me, copied to other senior staff, including the HR department.)

This is a very odd statement for AS to make about someone like myself, who is rooted in experimental psychology (and thus well versed in scientific method, the power of statistics, and normative approaches). Emotionally I was stunned and felt deeply let down by an institution that I had first joined in 1973 and in which I spent a large part of my adult life. I felt particularly betrayed by the HR department and senior colleagues who colluded with this approach through their inaction. Setting aside all these feelings of betrayed loyalty and emotional baggage, what do these two emails tell us?

The line of logic used by AS raises several thoughts. The first is its tortuous nature; in effect the logic of AS's position is 'I state you don't believe in truth or facts, therefore I can abandon selected facts whilst employing the 'fact' that I believe in facts to call you deceitful, whilst also showing by my abandonment of selected facts and adoption of unsupported statements about the other, my lack of belief in the truth'. Thus the selective view of 'fact as usable commodity' leads directly to the denial of the possibility of a true account of a series of human events. This is a view in which all things are relative and personal. Whilst the email attributes this view to me, it is really AS's own view that he is projecting on me, as is evident in his email.

At the same time, the email assumes that it is, indeed, possible to recognise the existence of facts and that there is such a thing as deceit (as opposed to situated and dynamic different viewpoints): It indicates a sense of truth. Regardless of whether or not AS or I really hold this relativistic view, in writing about deceit as he does, AS is echoing a world of right and wrong, and thus of common truth against which such judgements can be made. His argument therefore makes a clear distinction between a relativistic view in which facts and the truth are personal and dynamic commodities, and an absolute view in which there is a single, knowable truth and undisputable facts.

RELATIVITY AND PHYSICALITY

Cross-cultural and postmodernistic influences across the humanities all point to relativistic aspects of our knowing and understanding, yet even if we were to abandon the idea of absolute truth, societal agreements lend themselves to a weaker version of unitary truth. If this were not the case, we would each live in our own fiction, unchallenged by any confluence of reality that could be called fact. It is hard to see how research could be conducted without some agreement about facts and belief in the value of evidence, or how one could be called a researcher without some sense of seeking a wider truth. As demonstrated by the story, complete relativism leads to a self-referential narcissistic black hole in which bigotry is a way of life.

In common with Western tradition, in academia written documentation tends to take precedence over verbal, when the veracity of facts is considered. Thus for the normal population of the university, the documents would be considered to be factual evidence relevant to the discussion. They might be analysed and judged to be a 'true' account. The physical presence of the documents lends them a strength of reality over and above that of the spoken word. We are therefore moving into a realm where neither the relativistic nor the absolute hold sway—but rather one where there are degrees of reality.

A continuum might be deduced, moving from absolute 'true' physicality through to relativistic mental space. The more solid a thing is the better it is known and its parameters agreed upon. Physicality of the room gives a sense of permanence to the identity. The identity is threatened by the removal of the physical aspects—but the physical aspects are not threatened by the removal of the identity. As with the tree falling in the forest, so we have to assume that the room remains after the occupant has left.

It could be argued that our sense of identity is inevitably and of necessity linked to physical space. We exist in physicality—it influences us, and we, in turn, can influence it. We can enter space that is closed to Other (at least in the physical sense) and call it 'private'—a space where we can be—a space which resonates with Martin's (1992) space. Whether physical or mental, such locations are never completely devoid of the influence of others, but the physical does suggest a greater presence or stability of self than is generally perceived in the literature.

This is, perhaps, more evident when the influence of Other is actively engaged—when the physical space is modified for the audience—whether it be different fashions in posters, or the creation of showrooms—to demonstrate power, social standing, and so on. Such demonstrations are a conscious statement of self to the external world and, in turn, reinfluence our 'self'. They are artefacts in the same way that the many faces we use for our multiple social selves are artefacts. But they take more time to change than does the swapping of a persona. Their physicality necessarily brings a sense of permanence; however, such physicality is only known through representation, and permanence is an illusion.

Memory and Confabulation

The illusion of permanence extends to our view of ourselves, our thoughts and memories. I explore the dynamism of self in Chapter 7, but here I want to focus upon the malleability of memory. There are plenty of studies that show quite how malleable memory is, particularly in relation to witness statement and emotional events (Howe 2013). As we experience things we interpret them and try to make sense of them, and that sense-making is not done in a void. It is based upon our prior experience and our anticipations. If we are walking through a dark wood and see a long wriggly shape do we interpret it as a snake or a broken branch? Four friends might attend the same event but are very likely to walk away with four different accounts of that event. Not only this, but each time we revisit a memory we reinterpret it in relation to our current understandings and it can get changed time by time until it bears little relationship to the original event. At times things we have imagined can become a memory (Loftus & Davis 2006), particularly so in old age. And so, we are continually recreating our understanding of the past.

We are also continually recreating our understanding of the present. Although it feels that we are directly involved in the 'here and now' as we go about our daily business, this is not strictly the case. All that we see, hear, or feel does not come directly from our eyes, ears, or skin and into our awareness. Instead, the senses we are aware of, and those we process as if we are experiencing them with immediacy are, in effect, very recent memories. These memories that we call our 'now' suffer all the interpretation and cognitive baggage that our other memories carry. We experience the world entirely through memory, albeit very short-term, and our perceptions and biases are built into our senses. This includes our sense of time. Our 'now' lasts about two to three seconds, which is the period over which our conscious brain fuses our jumbled subconscious experiences into a 'psychological present' (Wittmann 2011). From these short steps of 'now' we create a sense of order and identity. See Chapter 13 for a more detailed discussion of this.

It is worth mentioning false memories or confabulation here (I am using these words synonymously, though there is a slight difference—see Mendez & Fras, 2011). This is the production of fabricated, distorted, or misinterpreted memories about oneself or the world, without the conscious intention to deceive (Fotopoulou et al. 2007). Confabulation is coherent, internally consistent, and relatively normal (Nalbantian et al. 2010) and individuals who confabulate are generally very confident about their recollections, despite contradictory evidence. Older adults and the very young are particularly susceptible to confabulation (Brainerd et al. 2008), and also those with neurological disturbance such as Alzheimer's.

It is possible that confabulation has a self-serving emotional component, by which people cover up a gap in their memory, or understanding of their actions, by creating a plausible 'cover story' (Metcalf et al. 2007). What is particularly interesting for my account here are the little false stories that are told by 'normal' people. There have been many experiments involving pheromones—a classic is when 'Boar Mate' was sprayed on chairs in a dentist's waiting room and significantly altered where women sat. When asked why they had chosen that seat they made up all sorts of semi-plausible stories—and stuck to them. Similarly, split brain studies (in which stimuli are shown to one side of the brain, unknown to the other) have shown people creating false stories to account for their otherwise apparently strange behaviour. We do things without knowing why, and retrospectively account for it in a plausible cover story—one which we believe ourselves.

In Chapter 13 I look at the relationship between brain and body with respect to consciousness, but for the present I note that the feeling that we each hold, that we are rational beings with a sense of permanence and a history of memories, is a nice, comforting illusion. What we know is based upon what we anticipate, which is itself based upon what we have experienced; and what we have experienced is changed and reviewed according to what we know. This is a dynamic re-creation that is largely hidden from us. We do not 'know' sounds, sights, or smells: What we do know, and take to be the real thing, are our memories of these, our representations of them.

Ontology and Epistemology

This approach holds some implications for the study of ontology and epistemology. Ontology is rooted in the Parmenidean view, as described in the previous chapter, and can be briefly described as the study of being. It deals with questions concerning what entities exist or can be said to exist, and how such entities can be grouped, related within a hierarchy, and subdivided according to similarities and differences. In contrast epistemology can be briefly described as the study of knowledge. It questions what knowledge is and how it can be acquired, and the extent to which knowledge pertinent to any given subject or entity can be acquired. As philosophical areas of study these are coherent and distinct. As concepts that might be applied to people and to our own understanding of the world and to our practice as researchers, they are not unitary and the boundaries between them are contested (Thompson 2011).

Our experience of being, existence, the here and now, is based upon our knowledge. Our knowledge of our being, our existence, and the here and now, is based upon our experience. We cannot talk correctly of our knowledge about something (its epistemology) as distinct from its existence and its fundamental being (its ontology) because we interpret its existence through our knowledge of it and vice versa. Although we can step back as philosophers and talk about ontology and epistemology, and although we can talk of entities having an existence independent of our own, when we conceptualise entities, even those directly involved in front of us that we can see and feel, we are talking of memories of these entities. These are conceptualisations, representations, that we have created within a world of representation.

Language

Language, of course, is also a representation. The words employed are used to represent concepts that are themselves socially constructed representations—in other words, the meanings behind the words are dynamic, situated, and ephemeral. One word may mean different things in different contexts and different things to different people (see Chapter 10). It is worth noting, however, that the conceptual structure that underlies our basic vocabulary is consistent across cultures and is based on universal features of human cognition and language use (Youn et al. 2015). Different words, in our own and other languages, can be used to provide different nuances on a concept—there is no one-to-one relationship. Kroll & Bialystok (2013) show that bilinguists activate information about both languages when using one language alone, as do bilinguists using sign language (Zou et al. 2012). As an aside, bilinguists are also better able to ignore irrelevant information, switch tasks, and resolve conflict.

In some sense, however, whether socially constructed or as part of great archetypal underlying processes as discussed in Chapter 3, we reach some agreement such that we believe we understand the same things as others as described by the words that are used (see Chapter 15 for a discussion of this)—we employ definitions and examples, we build upon agreed theoretical bases. We develop an impersonal 'body of knowledge'—largely static, at least at the core, and abstract—but accepted and agreed. However, it is not just the act of agreement between the parties that lends this abstract representational phenomenon the feeling of 'reality'.

REALITY AND REPRESENTATION

The feeling of reality comes with the degree of its embodiment. Hierarchies of understanding, causality, and correlation within this abstract body of knowledge are interpreted as spatial relationships. We talk of core knowledge, the base for our understanding, the edges of the field, and so on. We give it height and depth, and build three-dimensional models of it. In so doing, we give it the 'reality' of an object. This abstract 'thing' comes to hold life of its own, and we construct our reality through its near-physical lens.

Yet, paradoxically, despite its greater feeling of 'reality', our understanding of physical space is also representational. Much is made of the supposed difference between physical space and metaphorical space, yet the appreciation of physical space is the result of interpretation, in the same way that the understanding of speech is the interpreted result of language (Marr 1982). We perceive and interpret physical space through our senses, and we create internal models of objects (including abstract objects) that have spatial-like qualities, but are clearly not spatial in themselves. For example, whether we are examining different but associated words, or different parts of an object, experiments with reaction times show that both take longer to manipulate if they are 'further' from each other (conceptually or physically) than if they are nearer.

Canonicality and Point of View

Interestingly, as I showed through some of my early experimental work (Lee 1989), although the metaphorical space, sometimes called the workspace, in which we process or represent spatial concepts and the representation of spatial objects has some properties similar to those we associate with

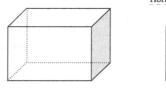

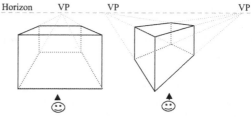

Oblique Projection.
A canonical cube, showing both
front and side faces.

Linear Perspective
In which either the front or the two sides
receding into the distance can be seen, but not
both at the same time. (VP = Vanishing Point)

Figure 4.1   Forms for Projection

three-dimensional objects (such that we imagine and process these representations as if they were 'real'), those representations and the properties of that space take a canonical form. This canonical form is not visually accurate, but does preserve the spatial associations of meanings in the most concept-rich way. In other words, when we say 'table', we generally mean an abstract canonical table rather than a specific 'real' table, so when we 'imagine' a table, we represent it canonically (and unrealistically), and do not build an image of a 'real' table.

What a canonical image lacks is a unique viewpoint. There is nothing to indicate the position of the observer. The mental representation can be mentally rotated and manipulated, but its position in relation to other images and the observer (or imaginer) cannot be specified or deduced without losing canonicality. Canonicality and linear perspective (point of view) entail mutually exclusive systems of projection—see Figure 4.1.

It is paradoxical that despite the visually unrealistic nature of the way in which we represent and think of ourselves as three-dimensional objects surrounded by similar objects in a 3D space, such representation conveys the essence of truth, the here and now, and a sense of reality. Our sense of 'reality' is inherently spatial and inherently canonical. Our particular situated memory of an event or object will contain a point of view as a personal account, but in our perception of it (replaying of it, our conceptualisation of it, our understanding of it), we move from the specific to the canonical form.

The Ubiquity and Commonality of Space

In the same way that we forget that language is representation, so we forget that our understanding of the space around us is also representational—and is imbued with as many layers of meaning as is language. However, to say that all reality is representation is not to say that all representation is individualistic and thus relativistic. The representation of space follows similar rules, regardless of culture or age, thus whilst each of us adopts our own, individual, representation of reality, there are strong and funda-mental similarities between these representations. There are core under-lying perceptual and conceptual processes and archetypal structures that derive from our evolutionary roots and are common to all. We thus have a common representational reality—one which gives precedence to con-crete physical evidence and an element of physicality to our structures of knowledge.

It is therefore unsurprising that this common representational real-ity, based upon our physicality, intrudes upon and is part of our identity. Perhaps this is why such a nebulous concept as our identity is lent spatial aspects—from assumptions about identity made around physical attributes to seeking space in which to find ourselves. What is perhaps more surpris-ing is the way in which the literature and language of research account for physical and mental space as if they were mutually exclusive. At some point, the distinction between physical and metaphorical space collapses in the same way as does the distinction between ontology and epistemology. These are representations of representations, and one cannot be conceived without the shadow of the other.

Canonicality and Fact

It is not surprising, therefore, that I suggest that aspects of canonicality bear similarity to those of fact: that which stands separate from a point of view; that which is agreed upon regardless of one's point of view. It is this canonicality that sets 'fact' apart from 'reality'. This is indubitably so in relation to the representation of space, in which the canonical projection is of the unreal, despite being the one commonly used to represent reality. This also holds in the representation of conceptual architecture. Facts are something apart from the immediate and the 'real', in so far as the real incorporates a privileged perspective—a point of view. Facts are those bits of knowledge, those nodes on the conceptual net, sufficiently distanced from the conceiver's point of view to have gained some life of their own: to stand independent from the observers; to gain some permanence in the conceptual fabric we weave around ourselves.

In so far as facts are distanced from the real, the individual perspec-tive, then they are also unreal—they no longer relate uniquely to the indi-vidual. Instead they resonate with the output of combined viewpoints—to say something is fact or factual is to indicate that there is agreement about the position that this item holds within the conceptual network. In the ter-minology of research, it has validity, reliability, and significance. Of course, to what extent it has each of these is open for discussion, and, as in the example above, just because something is physically 'real' does not mean that it is necessarily accepted as fact.

FACT, FICTION, AND AUTOETHNOGRAPHY

The distinction in the example is no longer one between absolute and rela-tivistic reality but is about the abandonment of fact in favour of the creation of fiction. Earlier I suggested that AS envisaged mutually exclusive concep-tions of reality (relativistic and absolute) that equated to fiction and fact. In this sense, fact is the cornerstone of an absolute universe. I have used notions of representation and space, however, to show that this is a false dichotomy. Instead, as illustrated by canonicality, it all depends on whether or not there is a point of view.

The idea of 'fact' is similar to that of canonicality. Facts have an existence (or at least a representation of an existence) independent of an individual viewpoint. As in the example above, such existence might be reinforced by a physical element (as of the written word), but to be classed as a fact does not necessarily entail physicality—just canonicality. To reject the written agree-ment, as in this case, is to deny the canonicality and, so, the factual status of the agreement. The point of view that is adopted, the fiction that is created, is that with the most power behind it. Facts can be part of a power play in a way that canonicality cannot.

In contrast, I have employed almost-autoethnography (as medium, tool, and exemplar) in an attempt to turn fiction—the story told from the single viewpoint—into fact: to step back and lay the elements on the table in a way that de-individualises that whole. I would question the extent to which this particular piece of work can be seen as an 'account of self in society that throws light on society as well as self'. The society and circumstances that are described here are both rather unusual, but I have not delved far into them. All sorts of fun could be had by building conjectures on the sorts of power play and misinformation that was being spread at senior levels such that those who were copied into these notes conveniently failed to act. A questioning of motives and intentions? Research into the blindness of hierarchy to be pondered on? I have constrained myself to basing my explo-ration upon the 'fact' of the written word, because thereby I am adhering to, and demonstrating, the focus of this assay, in so far as an assay is a subpart or a specimen of the whole.

In other words, I wonder if I am demonstrating the process of turning fiction into fact and turning personal learning into research; by throwing words at it, am I creating an assay of fact rather than an essay on fact?

REFERENCES

Brainerd CJ, Reyna VF, & Ceci SJ (2008) 'Developmental reversals in false memory: A review of data and theory', *Psychological Bulletin* 134(3)343–382.
Fotopoulou A, Conway MA, & Solms M (2007) 'Confabulation: Motivated reality monitoring', *Neuropsychologia* 45(10)2180–2190.

Howe ML (2013) 'Memory lessons from the courtroom: Reflections on being a memory expert on the witness stand', *Memory* 21(5)576–583.

Kroll JF & Bialystok E (2013) 'Understanding the consequences of bilingualism for language processing and cognition', *Journal of Cognitive Psychology* 25(5)497–514.

Lee MM (1989) 'When is an object not an object? The effect of "meaning" in the copying of objects', *British Journal of Psychology* 80: 15–37.

Loftus EF & Davis D (2006) 'Recovered memories', *Annual Review of Clinical Psychology* 2: 469–498.

Marr D (1982) *Vision*. San Francisco: W.H. Freeman.

Martin J (1992) *Cultures in Organizations: Three Perspectives*. Oxford: Oxford University Press.

Mendez MF & Fras IA (2011) 'The false memory syndrome: Experimental studies and comparison to confabulations', *Medical Hypotheses* 76(4)492–496.

Metcalf K, Langdon R, & Coltheart M (2007) 'Models of confabulation: A critical review and a new framework', *Cognitive Neuropsychology* 24(1)23–47.

Nalbantian S, Matthews PM, & McClelland JL (2010) (Eds) *The Memory Process: Neuroscientific and Humanistic Perspectives*. Cambridge, MA: Massachusetts Institute of Technology Press.

Thompson M (2011) 'Ontological shift or ontological Drift? Reality claims, epistemological Frameworks, and theory generation in Organization studies', *Academy of Management Review* 36(4)754–773.

Wittmann M (2011) ' "Moments in Time", Frontiers in Integrative', *Neuroscience* 5(66)1–9.

Youn H, Sutton L, Smith E, Moore C, Wilkins JF, Maddieson I, Croft W, & Bhattacharya T (2015) 'On the universal structure of human lexical semantics', In *Physics Society* arXiv:1504.07843: 1–32, Ithaca, NY: Cornell University Library.

Zou L, Abutalebi J, Zinszer B, Yan X, Shu H, Peng D, & Ding G (2012) 'Second language experience modulates functional brain network for the native language production in bimodal bilinguals', *NeuroImage* 62: 1367–1375.

5 Meaning and Methodological Choice

In previous chapters I have explored what HRD might be and described it as the glue of process between relationships: the interface between individuals, between organisations, and between individuals and organisations. These are not clear concepts; each is influenced by the other and is best understood in the light of the other. I have also put forward the idea that the human condition and the parameters of much of our thinking and being can be seen through a typology of typologies, structured around two key archetypal constructs derived from our evolutionary past. I have presented a picture of a world in flux, and although we try to define and categorise it and present it as a world of being, it remains a world of becoming. Our understanding of the world is derived through interpretation; our senses are based on memory (albeit very short-term) and not immediacy; our perceptions are modified by our understanding of the past and our anticipation of the future; we create stories for ourselves to try and make sense of our own behaviour—and then believe those stories. Yet, within all of this confusion, or perhaps because of it, we still search for clarity and meaning.

This chapter explores the ways in which we choose to derive meaning, and the methodologies we might use to make sense of whatever it is that we might find meaningful. Throughout our lives as we learn and develop we are, in effect, asking questions and seeking answers. We try to make meaning of our lives, even if it is as simple as learning what a cat is, and how a cat is different to a dog—which, actually, is not very simple at all. In so doing we are gathering information and researching. There are of course some differences between this life experience and formal academic research, but the quest for meaning drives us all.

As we go through life building up experience, we are not necessarily aware of the questions we are asking. In academic research, however, the question needs to be explicit. If we don't know the question how can we know whether we have achieved the answer? The 'correct' identification of one's 'research question' and the judgement as to whether or not one has effectively, comprehensively, and skilfully answered that question are central to the way in which our work, as researchers, is measured. This applies to those in the higher echelons of the research community and neophyte research students alike—though the grounds for the judgement might differ. Many a researcher has been told (as was I by my head of department when I first joined academe), 'Review the literature, find the gap, find your question, and then answer it', irrespective of their area of study and personal style. This approach does no favours at all to either party, nor to the field (see Alvesson & Sandberg (2011) for a detailed discussion of formulaic research). As Kilduff (2006) pointed out, good theory comes from engagement with problems in the world, not gaps in the literature.

TWO RESEARCH PARADIGMS

In Chapter 2 I discussed two world views: one that emphasises the permanent and unchangeable nature of reality, with a 'being' ontology and a representationalist epistemology; and another that emphasises the primacy of a changeable and emergent world, with a 'becoming' ontology and a process epistemology. I am using the word 'paradigm' here as outlined in Chapter 3: a world view which guides that of the scientist and provides investigative tools, including theory and its fundamental underpinnings, methods, and standards, for evaluation. (Kuhn 1969; Ritzer 1980). The two research paradigms I discuss here parallel these two world views. My intention in this book is not to pit these against each other as an introduction to methodology, as has so often been done before, because, as I will explain later in the chapter, choice of method is much more complicated than that. I will, however, outline each for the sake of completeness before entering that debate. As an aside, I am using the word 'data' here in its original sense. By this I mean as a plural word, the singular being a 'datum'. So, it is used in the same way that the word 'socks' would be used. Over the last 20 years or so, the American version of using 'data' as a singular word has crept into our vocabulary. I am not adopting that here.

The Scientific Method

Simply put, the scientific approach is to start with theory and then to validate this empirically via carefully controlled enquiry, as was propounded as early as Mill's 'Canon of Induction' in 1872. Experiments are designed by which the truth of null hypotheses can be ascertained—and these are built from, or around, the research question. The research question, therefore, is assumed to be absolutely clearly stated and concisely worded before any experimentation occurs. I have illustrated this in Figure 5.1.

More broadly, scientific method involves the systematic observation of the phenomena being studied and the recording of these observations as evidence, or scientific data, which might include the use of controlled experiments. The researchers then attempt to interconnect the data in a coherent way, free of internal contradictions. The resulting representation is known

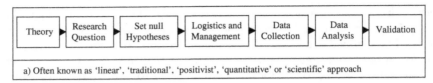

Figure 5.1 Paradigm A: Scientific Approach to Research

as a scientific model. The theoretical model is tested by further observations and additional experiments. If the model is found to be consistent with previous theory and further observations and is able to predict future results, it eventually becomes accepted as a scientific theory. Scientific models often use mathematical language because of the precision and internal consistency inherent in mathematics, but neither mathematical formulations nor quantitative results are essential components of the scientific method. This approach is also referred to as scientism.

Although the scientific process is commonly held to be staged and formulaic, in practice these stages are not neatly separated and do not always occur in the same order. What is essential is the need to match all models and theories firmly against empirical evidence. If a theory does not adequately describe/predict the evidence, it needs to be modified or superseded. However, all natural phenomena are ultimately interconnected, and their essential properties derive from their relationships to other things. Therefore, in order to explain any one of them completely, all the others would also have to understand. This presents an impossible challenge and as Capra & Luisi (2014) point out, crucial to the contemporary understanding of science is the realisation that all scientific models and theories are limited and approximate.

The Phenomenological Approach

The second paradigm is said to start in the empirical world, and then to generate theory, and is discussed in Flick (1998) and illustrated in Figure 5.2. The *Phenomenological* approach focuses on the subjective, unusual, and unexpected aspects of the world around us, as opposed to the normative aspects of the scientific approach. Within this broad description there are a wide range of methodologies (critical incident, ethnography, action research, etc.).

By its nature, research into HRD involves people, with all the variability that entails, and therefore we could assume that there is little role for the scientific approach. This assumption is likely to be wrong, at least in parts. Although strict experimental method is often not used in HR research, the terminology and concepts behind it remain valid for the 'statistical' approach in which people just happen to be the objects that are being measured or

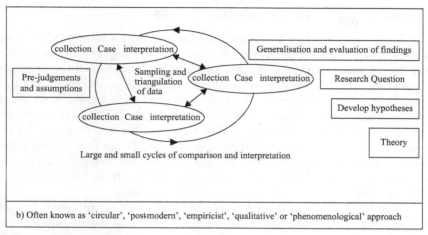

Figure 5.2 boxes and labels:
- collection Case interpretation
- Generalisation and evaluation of findings
- Pre-judgements and assumptions
- Sampling and triangulation of data
- collection Case interpretation
- Research Question
- Develop hypotheses
- collection Case interpretation
- Theory
- Large and small cycles of comparison and interpretation
- b) Often known as 'circular', 'postmodern', 'empiricist', 'qualitative' or 'phenomenological' approach

Figure 5.2 Paradigm B: Phenomenological Approach to Research

sampled. This approach assumes that there is a 'normal' population and that the more data that are gathered the better the description, or the more valid the findings. Hypotheses are established at the beginning (though in this case they are positive hypotheses rather than null hypotheses) and they, and the clearly established and controlled sampling methods, are directly linked to an already established and clearly stated research question. In an excellent polemic, Armstrong & Lilley (2008: 355) lay out the way in which, in the absence of any need to work within and develop an overarching integration of the field, a methodologically pluralistic field 'enables certain favoured texts to circulate within the influence networks of academia, accumulating authority and creating alliances until certain of them achieve quasi-foundational status. . . . Within this socially constructed reality there is a fusion of power and knowledge which places normative limits on the field of enquiry such that the questioning of certain foundational ideas and texts, even on the basis of empirical findings, is taken to symptomize not an active mind or an interesting piece of research but a failure of understanding'.

Although the scientific approach is often characterised by rigour, repeatability, a formulaic mind-set, and quantitative methods, whereas the phenomenological approach is often characterised as messy, lacking rigour or repeatability, directed by fashion, and qualitative methods, it is clear from the above that neither characterisation is accurate. Multiple methods can be used in both approaches, and as illustrated above, qualitative methods can be employed within a scientistic mind-set, and the use of non-parametric statistics can firmly locate quantitative methods within a more phenomenological approach. I do, however, see a fundamental difference between the two approaches, and that relates to the way in which we conceive of the world.

Normative or Unique Viewpoint?

In Chapter 3 I described how we knew that a cat was a cat even if the poor animal had lost most of its identifying features. In Chapter 4 I talked about the use of canonological concepts, and how we conceive of the world in canonological terms. When we think of cats, or dogs, or tables, or other objects, we think of them in an idealised normative form. When we think of things that are particularly close to us, like ourselves, our pets, people we know well, and so on, then we tend to think of (our interpretation of) the qualia that make up those individuals or objects. We see them through our unique viewpoint. So, one of the key distinctions that derives from the way in which we conceptualise the world is whether we are seeking to make or take meaning from a normative or a unique viewpoint.

Normative conceptualisation is central to the scientific approach: finding the norm, deviance from the norm, what is normal for population X, how large does the sample size have to be to establish the norm, and so on. It is what the fashion conscious might do when buying a new pair of shoes, looking around to see what everyone else is wearing and what stands out as different. When we are looking at something from a unique viewpoint we are not concerned with how normal it is, but are focused on its qualia, the aspects that make it unique.

Null and Positive Hypotheses

This leads to a further distinction between the use of the null and a positive hypothesis. The shift from null hypothesis to positive hypothesis is much deeper than might appear on first glance. For example, we could hypothesise that all cats have tails. When we adopt a null hypothesis approach we are saying that the hypothesis we will examine is that some cats don't have tails . . . so, if we find any cats without tails then we know that the original hypothesis is wrong . . . not all cats do have tails. However, if we don't find any no-tailed cats, then we can only say that we don't know . . . that somewhere, undetected by us, there might be cats without tails. This approach offers the absolute certainty that proving the null hypothesis disproves the original.

If we adopt a positive hypothesis, then we say that we have seen lots and lots of cats and they all have tails so all cats must have tails. So—we cannot be absolutely certain that the hypothesis is really true. This is a confirmatory approach to life and is how most of us normally make assumptions about life, but it does lead to the sort of apparent paradox highlighted in *The Hitch-Hiker's Guide to the Galaxy* when Adams (1995) describes the population of the Universe as 'none', saying, 'It is known that there are an infinite number of worlds, simply because there is an infinite amount of space for them to be in. However, not every one of them is inhabited. Therefore there must be a finite number of inhabited worlds. Any finite number divided by infinity is as near to nothing as makes no odds, so the average population of all the planets in the Universe can be said to be zero. From this it follows that the population of the whole Universe is also zero, and that any people you may meet from time to time are merely the products of a deranged imagination.' The questions we ask in this approach are normally about things that we wish to confirm, rather than disprove.

As with the confusion between correlation and causation that I described in the introduction to this book, so the frequent choice of positive hypotheses within the social sciences counts as 'bad science' from the perspective of the scientific approach, whilst giving the chimera of legitimacy to the quasi-phenomenological approach. The sort of questions we ask of the world, the sort of hypotheses we use, depend upon the sort of answers we are hoping to get, and upon our existing theories about whatever it is we are seeking an answer to . . .

One of the problems is that theory is neither well defined or understood, nor is it one-dimensional (Sutton & Staw 1995). A theory could be a guess, conjecture, speculation, supposition, proposition, hypothesis, conception, or model, with those at the formal end of the spectrum more likely to be in print, but, even in print, theory displays high variation in terms of range, focus, interest, complexity, sweep, elegance, level of analysis, presentational character, and implications for next steps in the collective research process (Weick 1995).

THE SEARCH FOR MEANING

Personal Preference

Another problem is that whilst everyone seeks to make sense of the world around them, we do not all focus on the same things. I discussed Jungian theory, and the MBTI in Chapter 3. Mitzroff & Killman (1978) take these ideas and suggest that there are four psychological types which represent basic styles of thinking about and doing science. Their typology of scientists fits well with the meta-typology discussed in the Chapter 3. As can be seen in Figure 5.3, they have clearly and uniquely categorised the different types of scientist. By this I mean that their typology implies that a scientist can be in one group or another, and that if a scientist is in one particular group then the characteristics of that group describe the characteristics of that individual's personality.

This deeply delineated approach is interesting in that it clarifies differences between the way in which researchers think and work, but it does not sit well with the messiness of reality. The same typology can be interpreted through preference, in which different people prefer different ways of making sense of the world, which are associated with different preferences for how research 'should' be structured and conducted. We can also appreciate that these preferences are situated, and are not exclusive personality

	Analytical Scientist	Conceptual Theorist	Conceptual Humanist	Particular Humanist
Properties of the scientist	Disinterested, unbiased, impersonal, precise, expert, specialist, sceptical, exact, methodological	Disinterested, unbiased, impersonal, imaginative, speculative, generalist, holistic	Interested, free to admit and know his biases, highly personal, imaginative, speculative, generalist, holistic	Interested, 'all-too-human', biased, poetic, committed to the postulates of an action-oriented science
Preferred logic	Aristotelian, strict classical logic, non-dialectic, indeterminate	Dialectical logics, indeterminate logics	Dialectical behavioural logics	The 'logic' of the unique and singular
Preferred mode of enquiry	Controlled enquiry as embodied in the classical concept of the experiment	Conceptual enquiry; treatment of innovative concepts from multiple perspectives; invention of new schemas	Conceptual enquiry; treatment of innovative concepts; maximal cooperation between experimenter and subject	The case study; the in-depth, detailed study of a particular individual

Figure 5.3   A Typology of Scientists (Adapted From Mitzroff and Killman 1978, Given in Reason 1981: 8)

differences. What is becoming clear through this discussion is that different sorts of people ask different sorts of questions of the data, of their world, and so get different sorts of answers.

What is also clear is that both the scientific and the phenomenological approaches make a clear distinction between theory and method, yet method can generate and shape theory, just as theory can generate and shape method. 'Theories without methodological implications are likely to be little more than idle speculation with minimal empirical import. And methods without theoretical substance can be sterile, representing technical sophistication in isolation' (Van Maanen et al. 2007: 1147).

Formulaic Research

Although the scientific approach is generally said to spring from theory, whereas the phenomenological approach is held to spring from 'the real world', in fact the empirical context is core to both. If we take it as it is represented in Figures 5.1 and 5.2, above, in the scientific approach much of the formal research has already been done before the empirical work is undertaken, during the designing and planning of the experiments, questionnaires, etc. In the phenomenological approach the development of this core part of the research is a more obvious and central part of the research project, such that under some models (e.g., action research), the 'object' of the research becomes a participant who is given the power to influence (or given co-ownership of) the research question.

These models present an idealised account of the research process—one that Alvesson & Gabriel (2013: 253) criticise heavily as formulaic, saying:

> Quantitative papers usually are entirely uncritical of their methodological premises, based on a naive assumption that responses to questionnaires mirror reality out there or respondents' true beliefs. Qualitative ones tend to give the impression of clear design, rational and linear procedures, separation of theory and data, and a logical step-by-step process from research question to delivery of result. They generally out finesse the actual research process, which usually involves ambiguity, messiness, theory-impregnated data, and leaps of intuition with a post-facto invention of rational methodology. Method sections sometimes resort to grandiose statements about ontology and epistemology, inflating a modest number of interviews into "ethnographies," or routine textual analysis into discourse analysis. Such methodologies whether qualitative or quantitative, are carefully written to avoid any allusions to accidental discoveries or any conclusions that reach beyond the "research questions," themselves carefully formulated to avoid any trouble with unforeseen anomalies or irregularities.

Gap Spotting and Problematisation

Whatever form the research takes, it is built upon a background of thinking and reading, of scouring the secondary data, and of conducting 'thought experiments', all leading to knowledge of the area. The challenge is in how we build on that knowledge. Do we search for the gap as my head of department suggested? Locke & Golden-Biddle (1997) found that that the authors of all the studies they examined either argued that the existing literature was incomplete or misleading and and thus justified the study as able to correct faulty or inadequate existing literature. Locke & Golden-Biddle argue that such gaps are always rhetorically and socially constructed and reflect an arbitrary ordering of work and various rhetorical gymnastics (see also Bluhm et al. 2010).

The problem is that such a formulaic approach takes us away from the empirical heart of research. It reinforces the basic assumptions underlying established theories and reduces the chances of producing really interesting theories, and the institutionalised logic is accepted as more or less unproblematic. The idea of generating the research question through problematisation has been proposed as an alternative to gap spotting (Sandberg & Alvesson 2011). Problematisation involves a dialectical interrogation of the researcher's own familiar position, other theoretical stances, and the literature, in order to identify, articulate, and challenge different types of assumptions, and so formulate research questions that may facilitate the development of more interesting and influential theories. In this way it also contributes to a more reflective form of scholarship.

THE EMPIRICAL CONTEXT

At some stage, all research has to be measured against its empirical context. A formulaic approach might help us get published but it takes us one step further away from the messiness of the empirical. It is by transgressing the formulaic that we are more likely to find our deeper questions answered (Gherardi 1999). Instead of searching for gaps in the literature we should seek to challenge assumptions; to see old things with new eyes; to conduct research aimed at a rich description of organisational realities; to say something meaningful and socially relevant about an important phenomenon that breaks with established, broadly shared taken-for-granted ideas; to allow for serendipity and accident that have long been crucial factors in scientific discovery and technological innovations (Corley & Gioia 2011).

Alvesson & Gabriel (2013) offer the idea of polymorphic research, which involves a diversity and plurality of structures, styles, and approaches, as an alternative to formulaic research. They note that it would not deal directly with the problem of practical relevance, but it would enhance the scope and dissemination of organisational research to wider audiences, and thus foster new uses and applications (Gabriel 2002). Polymorphic research is fostered by adopting a nomadic research trajectory, through which researchers explore alternative texts, methods, and vocabularies; problematise their work and acknowledge uncertainties and doubt; adopt methods based on reflexivity and acknowledge problems in mirroring reality; produce non-standardised texts, and aim for a broader audience. From this perspective empirical material can be seen as a critical dialogue partner rather than a judge of the truth or, as in grounded theory, a signpost to the delivery of theory: the empirical is a source of mystery, which, in itself, offers an interesting source of further thinking, as it encourages problematisation and self-reflexivity (Alvesson & Kärreman 2007).

Mixed Methods

There is an increasing focus on the use of mixed methods: 'To us it seems clear that research is actually more a craft than a slavish adherence to methodological rules. No study conforms exactly to a standard methodology; each one calls for the researcher to bend the methodology to the peculiarities of the setting' Miles & Huberman (1994: 5). Such flexibility can facilitate the sort of problematisation discussed above, by which the research can be approached with few presumptions and an open mind and can draw together widespread data and ideas (Pace 2012). I have already described the empirical world as one of complexity, not easily accessed by a formulaic approach, whether it be quantitative or qualitative, scientific or phenomenological.

As Alvesson et al. (2008) point out, there is a strong belief that the 'collection' and processing of data can prove or disprove various hypotheses and theories. In qualitative research (e.g., grounded theory) it is common to assume that data may guide the researcher to understand specific phenomena and develop theory. However, one of the issues with attempting to access the empirical is the way in which language can construct rather than mirror phenomena, making representation, and thus empirical work privileging 'data', a basically problematic enterprise. The empirical world is not laid out ready for easy access—accessing it as we go about our normal lives is a process of interpretation. Further interpretation, understanding, or research divorces us more from the 'real' world. Yet, the 'real' world stays with us: 'We cannot lift the results of interviewing out of the contexts in which they were gathered and claim them as objective data with no strings attached' (Fontana & Frey 2000: 663).

Reflection and Reflexivity

Reflexivity is an important component in adopting a problematising attitude and a polymorphic methodology as discussed above. It is said to help us engage in theoretically informed interpretations and to support the critical judgement that must be viewed as the cornerstone in research. In fact, the body of literature on reflexivity and reflection is very large, but offers little clarity, and reflexive practice remains a vague concept, with little distinction made in the literature between reflection, reflexivity, reflective enquiry, reflective practice, critical reflection, and critical enquiry (Hamilton et al. 2008).

Alvesson & Sköldberg (2000) suggest that reflection can be seen as the interpretation of interpretation, directed at one theme or one level; in contrast, reflexivity cannot be derived from a single theory or fixed standpoint, but can be seen as multilevel areas of reflection, rejecting 'totalization' or the privileging of a particular dimension. They describe the reflexive process as a repertoire of interpretation, requiring access and willingness to develop several research vocabularies and theoretical perspectives. This links to my discussion above and in the previous chapter about normative or unique viewpoints. From this perspective we could say that in reflection we look at things from a singular viewpoint—in reflexivity we adopt the broader aspect, the canonological, the normative. This presents a quandary;

although I am sure some research can be very reflective, I am not sure that, from this perspective, any work can be truly reflexive. How can we ever really reject the privileging of a particular dimension? Furthermore, the notion of reflexivity is, itself, privileged. Reflexivity is a linguistic construction employed by a subset of researchers informed by particular theoretical influences (Freshwater & Rolfe 2004).

In contrast, Calás & Smircich (1992: 240) talk of reflexivity as the constant assessment of 'the relationship between "knowledge" and "the ways of doing knowledge" ', and Anderson defines analytic reflexivity as a process that 'involves an awareness of reciprocal influence between ethnographers and their settings and informants. It entails self-conscious introspection guided by a desire to better understand both self and others through examining one's actions and perceptions in reference to and dialogue with those of others' (Anderson 2006: 382). It is worth also noting the role that memory plays in the 'self-conscious introspection' of reflexivity (Wall 2008). As discussed in the previous chapter, memory is a fickle thing, and the process of reflection (and reflexivity) is as much one of re-creation as remembering, and is influenced by mood, stress levels, and age (Bender & Raz 2012; Howe & Malone 2011).

There is also a lack of clarity around the role of self in the reflexive process and self-report narratives (de Freitas & Paton 2008). There appears to be little in the literature on complexity of one person holding different views within their own thinking (intra-subjectivity) such as between Winnicott's (1971) 'real' self, which is said to react in a more spontaneous manner, while the 'false' self complies to the expectation of others; or the employment of mental defence mechanisms, such as projection and denial (Conti-O'Hare 2002). Intersubjectivity, when different views are held by different people about the same event, is also a complex factor, particularly for a methodology such as autoethnography, in which the reader plays a crucial part in establishing the value of the research, but for which the words used by the writer do not necessarily engender similar emotions in the reader (Lacan 2005).

Armstrong & Lilley (2008) suggest that the assumption that reflexivity is intrinsically and unequivocally 'good' warrants further investigation, and Srivastava & Hopwood (2009) suggest that for all of the talk of reflexivity there is little of it in evidence. It would appear that reflexivity is a problematic concept. Weick (1999) charts an increasing focus on reflexivity and the 'paradigm wars' in the literature during the 1990s, linking this to a destabilisation of the field of theorising on organisational studies. Similarly, Alvesson et al. (2008) comment that the level of conflict between the formulaic and traditional means of suppressing ambiguity and accomplishing pseudo-rationality (namely data management and technical rules) and the key elements in reflexive research is easily underestimated.

Perhaps it is easier to see reflexivity as an unobtainable goal, something to strive for whilst, because of its very nature, knowing it is unreachable;

something that fosters trustworthiness and points towards truths, rather than stating truths (Erickson 2011). Perhaps it is the principles associated with it, those of interrogating the formulaic, searching for questions and problems, employing a range of methods, and looking to the roots of the assumptions that are made, that we should be attempting to employ. Perhaps we should be focusing more on deep reflection, acknowledging our own presence and viewpoint.

Personal Involvement

Both in the previous chapter and in the next, I hang my colours on the mast and explain how I started my academic life securely based in the quantitative scientific approach and have moved over the years through mixed methods to what might be called autoethnography. Partly this is through selfishness on my part—as I see it, regardless of one's research paradigm, the central core of research is about trying to make sense of the world. The process of finding the 'research question' is the process of structuring that search for meaning, such that it becomes a manageable and achievable task. For most people the best research they do has a deep meaning for themselves; it says something to them about their life. People are often attracted to a particular research area because of questions they are asking of themselves or of their lives. Perhaps they are trying to make sense of a circumstance that they find themselves in, perhaps they are trying to understand or rationalise a particular experience, perhaps they are trying to understand how their story fits within the range of human experience. Such personal involvement with a particular research area, if acknowledged and used, can be a tremendous help in the research process. It is the spark that keeps the researcher going through the late nights when the words have fled the lexicon—it is what keeps the research alive. I have to admit that this sense of personal relevance is certainly what kept me going at times when the words and thoughts would not coalesce.

Also, however, and more seriously, I am most definitely partisan in how I view and present the world. I find any attempt to lay down blanket rules or formulaic approaches to the complexity of human interaction and relationships to be deeply wrong and out of keeping with how I understand the world. They might make life easier, but they divorce us from the complexity of living. I find it anathema to apply the tools of being to the process of becoming. I moved towards a more personal style a long while ago, making use of different methods as seemed appropriate, as best to search out the meaning I was exploring. I have been told that my work is autoethnographic or, in part, theory-enhanced autobiography (Richardson 1999). So, in searching for meaning through this chapter, I am also searching for a better understanding of how I conceptualise my research.

I find that one of the problems with such personal involvement is in trying to understand what it is about myself or my situation that attracts me to a particular area of investigation. I imagine that anyone who has ever supervised research students knows what it is like to be presented with a research proposal, which if it were to be done properly, would be equivalent to at least six PhDs, but which contains within it, somewhere, the one point—the single spark—that encapsulates why that particular topic means something to that individual. The only thing to do is to sit down with the person and question, gradually pulling apart the web until the spark is revealed and the personal focus acknowledged. Obviously research can, and often is, conducted without this personal realisation, but it tends to be a relatively unrewarding hard slog. And so I find myself reflecting on the area and why it is sparking in me. It is almost tautological to say that the more personal the research area the harder it is to stand back from it and objectively make decisions about what is to be researched, how it should be managed, and the interpretation of the findings. Yet some clarity is necessary in order to avoid reflective traps like narcissism, self-indulgence, and a cascading regression of doubt (Gergen 1991). I am one with Adams (1997) as he says, 'There were so many different ways in which you were required to provide absolute proof of your identity these days that life could easily become extremely tiresome just from that factor alone, never mind the deeper existential problems of trying to function as a coherent consciousness in an epistemologically ambiguous physical universe'.

GROUNDED THEORY

Autoethnography shares the roots of ethnography and grounded theory. A key principle of grounded theory is that the researcher begins with a general field of study and allows the theory to emerge from the data with the focus on inductive theory building, not testing: grounded concepts, relationships, and theories are suggested, not proven (Glaser & Strauss 1967). This is achieved by systematically gathering and analysing relevant data using a constant comparative method of analysis (Creswell 2009). Whilst the analytical nature of the approach helped foster the acceptance of qualitative methods in applied social research (Thomas & James 2006), there has been much debate about whether the process has become too formulaic. Charmaz (2000: 524) suggests that 'as grounded theory methods become more articulated . . . guidelines turn into procedures and are reified into immutable rules', and offers an alternative: a constructivist approach in which people create and maintain their own realities by seeking understanding of the world in which they live and by developing subjective meanings of their experiences; researchers interpret a reality, dependent on their own experience and the study of participants' portrayals of their experiences, and do not seek a single, universal and lasting truth. Theory is not divorced from researcher bias and tells a story about people, social processes, and situations that has been composed by the researcher. Nor does it approach some level of generalisable truth, but constitutes a set of concepts and hypotheses that other researchers can transport to similar research problems and to other substantive fields. These assumptions, and the search for a balance between the formulaic and ever-expanding data, are similar to those of ethnography, and the messiness of complexity described earlier. Indeed, Ybema et al. (2009) suggest the use of organisational ethnography through which to study the complex, because of the way in which the ethnographic process forces a trade-off between the width of concern needed for accuracy and the tight focus needed for simplicity.

One of the challenges of ethnography is 'breaking in' to the group that is the focus of the research, whereas self-ethnography involves the study of a group in which the researcher is an established participant, thereby entailing 'breaking out' of taken-for-granted cultural and social structures. This approach has also been referred to as auto-anthropology, autobiographical ethnography or sociology, and personal or self-narrative research and writing, and has been linked to the turn towards blurred genres of writing, a heightened self-reflexivity in ethnographic research, an increased focus on emotion in the social sciences, and the postmodern scepticism regarding generalisation of knowledge claims. The intention is 'to draw attention to one's own cultural context, what goes on around oneself rather than putting oneself and one's experiences in the centre' (Alvesson 2003b: 175). This is similar to 'at-home ethnography', coined by Alvesson (2009). A key problem for at-home ethnographers is, once again, the struggle between closeness and closure, accentuated by the difficulty of researching one's own practice. Closeness provides a rich variety of potential ways of interpreting one's organisation and a great temptation to stay native (Phillips & Jorgensen 2002).

Auto-Ethnography

In contrast to self-ethnography or at-home ethnography, autoethnography researchers put themselves and their experiences at the centre (Ellis & Bochner 2000). Hayano (1979) used the term 'autoethnography' when discussing self-observation in traditional ethnographic research. It is used across a variety of disciplines, and is marked by the adoption of critical enquiry, with the researcher writing about themselves as a researcher-practitioner, with an account that is embedded in theory and research practice (McIlveen 2008); as 'an autobiographical genre of writing and research that displays multiple layers of consciousness, connecting the personal to the cultural' (Ellis & Bochner 2000: 739). Autoethnography involves storytelling, but it 'transcends mere narration of self to engage in cultural analysis and interpretation' and should be 'ethnographic in its methodological orientation, cultural in its interpretive orientation, and autobiographical in its content orientation' (Chang 2008: 43,48); 'as a method autoethnography is both process and product' (Ellis et al. 2011: 1).

As with the debate around the degree of structure applied in the use of grounded theory, so there is a tension between evocative and analytic autoethnography. Evocative autoethnography developed out of a rejection of the traditional realist and analytic ethnographic epistemological assumptions within conventional sociological analysis. Evocative autoethnographers 'bypass the representational problem by invoking an epistemology of emotion, moving the reader to feel the feelings of the other' Denzin (1997: 228). In contrast to the free-form approach of the evocative genre (Ellis 2000), researchers such as Anderson (2006) have argued for a more analytic form of autoethnography that accepts more traditional methods, which keep reliability and validity whilst being informed through autobiographical writing styles, so enabling the self to be represented within a narrative (Broadhurst & Machon 2009). The analytic approach tends towards objective writing and analysis, whereas the evocative tends towards the generation of empathy and resonance within the reader.

Anderson (2006: 374) argues that 'the dominance of evocative autoethnography has obscured recognition of the compatibility of autoethnographic research with more traditional ethnographic practices'. He describes analytic autoethnography as a subgenre in the realist ethnographic tradition, and proposes that a) the researcher is a complete member of the social world under study (CMR); b) they engage in analytic reflexivity; c) their self is made visible within the narrative; d) they engage in dialogue with informants beyond the self; and; e) they demonstrate a commitment to theoretical analysis. 'The definitive feature of analytic autoethnography is this value-added quality of not only truthfully rendering the social world under investigation but also transcending that world through broader generalization' (Anderson 2006: 388). Anderson notes that Adler & Adler (1987) distinguish between two types of Complete Member Researcher (CMR): the opportunistic and convert. The opportunistic are already part of the group before starting the research, whereas the convert join the group for the purpose of research, but in doing so become 'converted'. He likens this to Schutz's (1962) distinction between members' practically oriented, first-order constructs or interpretations and the more abstract, trans-contextual, second-order constructs of social science analysis, pointing out that autoethnographers are expected to be fluent in both first- and second-order constructs. The autoethnographer's understandings, both as a member and as a researcher, emerge not from detached discovery but from engaged dialogue in which they themselves form part of the representational processes in which they are engaging and are part of the story they are telling (Atkinson et al. 2003); to truthfully render the social world under investigation and also to transcend that world through broader generalisation (Snow et al. 2003). The autoethnographic interrogation of self and other may transform the researcher's own beliefs, actions, and sense of self, but as Atkinson et al. (2003: 57) point out, 'We must not lose sight of the ethnographic imperative that we are seeking to understand and make sense of complex social worlds of which we are only part (but a part nevertheless)'.

Whilst Anderson puts the idea of the 'complete member researcher' at the centre of autoethnography study, Chang's (2008: 26) key focus is on self as a relational being that is an 'extension of community rather than that it is an independent, self-sufficient being' (see Chapter 7). This difference is perhaps one of ideology (Creswell 1998), and it emphasises the influence that the researcher can have upon interpretation of the empirical. In essence, autoethnography is about 'using empirical evidence to formulate and refine theoretical understandings of social processes'. Autoethnography offers the methodological advantages of the availability of data and quality of access that provides insider meanings (Atkinson 2006).

Ellis & Bochner (2006) and Denzin (2006) opposed Anderson's proposal on the grounds that it could dilute the current meaning of the term 'auto-ethnography'; it could contain, limit, or silence the researcher's self in the research context; and it could reduce publishing opportunities for those who seek to practise evocative autoethnography. There are also questions about the extent to which analytic autoethnography is usable in practice. Struthers (2012) found that whilst several authors referred to Anderson's five key factors of analytic autoethnography, only DeBerry-Spence (2010) explicitly details their use. Short (2010) incorporates analytic data in his evocative methodology and argues that binary distinctions between different forms of autoethnography may distract from the power of narrative to represent the individual's experiences. I empathise with his point of view. A mix of evocative and analytic brings out the researcher's personal experiences, and can also link these to other participants' perspectives, as well as contextualise and develop the issue through secondary sources and theoretical analysis.

Although my work has been referred to as autoethnographical and some parts of it do fit the patterns described above, the majority of it does not classically follow this model. Whilst the researcher is at the core of auto-ethnography, their role is to bring in data from those around them, and interpret it and present it to the reader in partly digested form. Vryan (2006: 406) suggests that including data from and about others is not a necessary requirement of all analytic autoethnography; and that the necessity, value, and feasibility of such data will vary according to the specifics of a given project and the goals of its creator(s). The work presented in this book is based more upon my analysis of my own experiences, as supported and reflected by the literature and by my understanding of others and the social situations I find myself in, than upon any attempt to give others around me their own voice within my work. In this, I am following more the pattern of the traditional European essay in which thoughts and experiences along with the literature are combined within a narrative.

Boje & Tyler (2009) make a distinction between narrative and story, where a narrative engages a more objective cognitive perception for sense-making and stories engage subjective transcendental consciousness, leading to different outcomes of the same event. This raises interesting resonance with the discussion about normative or unique viewpoints earlier in the chapter. The narrative can be challenged on its representational content (described as content answerability), whereas the story can be challenged on how the reflexivity represented in the story captures the unique lived experience of the person involved in the event—its authenticity (Rolfe et al. 2011) (described as moral answerability). Boje and Tyler note that this distinction is rarely used within autoethnographic accounts. Lack of clear methodological delineation could indicate that the field is under-theorised (Buzard 2003) but it also offers a more 'flexible and fluid' approach (Burnier 2006). In my experience accounts often move back and forth between narrative and story, as moving between looking back on memories in reflection, and analysing critical incidents in a reflexive manner.

Narrative Collage

Kociatkiewicz & Kostera (2012) point out that ethnography can be based on stories gathered in the field and itself take the form of a story, but it remains concerned with social practice and the processes of social construction of reality (Gabriel 2000). By contrast, the narrative approach more closely mirrors traditional forms of human knowledge, the way in which we verbalise our experiences and make sense of the world around us (Czarniawska 2004). Stories are a natural part of organisational everyday life and in order to better understand the processes of organising, we need to know more about the use of symbols and archetypes, organisational legends, and myths (Hatch et al. 2005; Chapter 16). In particular, imagination is important for creative organisational activities, such as entrepreneurship, which is about breaking old patterns in order to test the borders of the possible (Kociatkiewicz & Kostera 2012).

Imagination and collective views of the future can be seen as a powerful kind of reality where innovative and creative thinking can take place, and thus where potential for change originates (Morgan 1993, Chapter 8). Kostera (2006) developed the idea of the narrative collage, by which fictive narratives are collected from a chosen group of social actors concerned with a certain idea or phenomenon. The researcher, having collected the material, edits the stories to form larger wholes, interprets them, and perhaps concludes with a story of his or her own. The design of a narrative collage varies from occasion to occasion, depending on the needs and aims of the project. In this way, narrative collage can reach the social imagination that is unavailable to traditional ethnography. Kostera notes that whilst all involved co-create the collage, the final shape depends on its author/the researcher. Norris (2008: 96) comments that 'although collages are traditionally thought of as products, they can be effectively used in all stages of qualitative research. . . . They are meant to evoke disparate meanings in others and strive to communicate on a metaphoric, rather than a transactional, information-giving level'.

As is evident in several chapters in this book, I do at times explore the imagination, the stories and myths, and the possible futures that we create for ourselves. My work is based within the narrative genre, but I rarely pull in the voices of other participants in order to create the picture. This is partly because I do not really believe that, if I am the mouthpiece and the writer, it is possible to present a voice that is not tainted by my own. It seems to me more honest to acknowledge that all my experiences, all my sources of information, and everything I present here, has gone through the filter of my own interpretation. In order to own that, I need to present it as my own understanding of the events, not as someone else's reality. Perhaps I might better describe my approach as that of a mainly analytical, and at times evocative, autoethnographic narrative with overtones of the classical essay! My intention is to offer a robust and rounded picture, built on empirical observation as well as grounded in the literature, and able to explore the abstract as well as the concrete, thereby offering the reader a better view, and it is, of course, that view or interpretation of the picture, as adopted by the reader, that really matters. Thus the reader of autoethnography plays a crucial part in establishing its value as research. However, if empathic resonance within the reader is seen as an indicator of validity (Ellis & Bochner 2000), then such writing, whether story or narrative, reflective or reflexive, requires an ability to use written words in an evocative manner to enable this resonance (Jaya 2011).

Politics

Without conscious intention I seem to have brought this chapter, in its closing stages, towards Denzin & Lincoln's (2000) fifth choice point applied to discourse analysis: namely, around the form of presentation and the effect of the research. The measure of any research, whether qualitative or quantitative, experimental or autoethnographic, is ultimately about how well it can persuade the research community (and wider community) to the value of the views presented. The methods of persuasion need to be appropriate for the ideas being presented. The more flexible the form of research, the more important the persuasiveness of the writing style. The researcher needs to persuade the sceptical reader, marrying empirical material with insightful interpretation, reflexivity, analysis of the relevant literature, and understanding of the informational needs of the reader. This includes self-critical analysis of the problems, ambiguities, and messiness of working with empirical material, in which dilemmas and uncertainties contribute to the understanding.

Influencing the reader, creating meaning and interpretations that are accepted and can be built upon, hark to debates on the interrelation of power and knowledge (Foucault 1979) and the power relations involved in the construction of meanings. Hall et al. (2008) make a distinction between hard and soft knowledge, and suggest that knowing when to treat knowledge as 'hard' and when to treat it as 'soft' provides a considerable source of rhetorical power. They describe a study of evidence-based medicine, in which Fitzgerald et al. (2002: 1437) found: 'Our data support the view that scientific evidence is not clear, accepted and bounded. There is no one fact, which can be seen as "the evidence". There are simply bodies of evidence, usually competing bodies of evidence'. In this instance ambiguous and soft knowledge must appear to be rendered into reliable, auditable, and checkable, hard knowledge (Power 2004).

It is the act of writing that creates the major illusion of hard knowledge, that the question was clearly established at the 'beginning' of the research, and that all the 'research' was conducted as an inevitable response to that question. Indeed, most research that is written up tells the story as if this is exactly how the research was conducted; nice and clearly linear and logical. To some extent, what the research question does is provide a sense of inevitability about the way in which it must be answered. It is stated in such a way that there can only be one way of addressing it; it provides the feeling of legitimacy and appropriateness to the answer (Thayer-Bacon 2003). It allows the reader to know where the argument is going, and why. Each paragraph addresses a separate or discrete point, and each leads, one from to the other, to what feels by the end of the text, like the 'obvious' conclusion. Most people who have ever done any research know that this is not what really happens, or at least, it is not what happens chronologically. Instead it is the acceptable face of research—the sanitised version in which all the parts, the thinking, the reading, the activity, and the pain are rearranged to make sense to the reader. Thus the research continues to live and develop within the process of writing and rewriting.

The research, the search for meaning, is not isolated from its potential effects. We are political and our research reflects that. In addition, as researchers, we are inevitably engaged in politics—it is only the very lucky few who can conduct research exactly as they wish, with no constraints or compromises. For most of us there is a whole web of factors that influence our research. Some of these might be obvious: the dubious impartiality of 'sponsored' research; restrictions to access or publication of 'sensitive' material; the specific requirements of particular publication outlets; departmental research focus; and promotional possibilities. Less specific factors include resources (Flick 1998) and logistics. For example, I did my PhD just as I was starting a family, so much of my empirical work was conducted carrying youngsters around with me. Thus my choice of organisation to visit was a compromise between the needs of my enquiry and the (sometimes urgently stated) needs of my offspring. Similarly, however much the researcher might think a longitudinal study is needed to address a particular point, if the time frame for the research is short then the emerging research must reflect what is possible—not that which is desirable. Future prospects can also influence the research. A research topic that anticipates and 'solves' an area of organisational concern might lead to a job and team being created for the researcher. A smoothly written dissertation that captures the imagination of the public might (when rewritten) prove the first step on the road to becoming a guru (Lee 1991).

Conclusions

In writing about the research, the search for meaning becomes the search for *giving* meaning. The more persuasive the text, as judged by the reader, the greater the quality of the work. Persuasiveness is not just about inciting emotion but also about linking the ideas and theories in a coherent manner into the empirical world and the existing body of knowledge. However, the very act of mapping changes the geography; the act of watching changes the group dynamics; the act of researching changes the outcome; the act of writing changes the map. The desire for quality remains the same, but it is harder for the author(s) to provide structure, rigor, relevance, clarity of purpose and direction, and so on, when translating the 'real world' into linguistically based symbols, particularly when there is no irrefutable agreement about either the symbols or the underlying structure that they might represent. Perhaps the most important point that I wish to emphasise from this is that research is confusing, just as life is confusing, and that it is OK as a researcher to be confused: the skill is not in ignoring the confusion and pretending that the world is simple, but in taking that confusion and working with it to present it in a form that is simpler, but still true to 'life'. As Alvesson (2003: 190) says, 'The challenge of ethnography, and of most qualitative work, is to be close and avoid closure'.

In the following chapters I present stories of my experiences. Some are written in a different manner to facilitate publication, but all are in some way about what has happened to me, and some are highly emotive for me. I have sought distance from those times, and my intention in this book is to balance the emotive and the analytic, and provide you with the information you need to critically analyse what I am saying. Chapter 6 contains an interview with me written by someone else, and it is included in this book so that you can read it with reference to this chapter. By this I mean that throughout the book I am trying to persuade you to my particular perspective on life, but I don't want to just emotively drag you along. Part of that information is about where I, as the author, am coming from, so that you, as a critical reader, can better judge this book.

REFERENCES

Adams D (1995) *The Hitch-Hiker's Guide to the Galaxy—A Trilogy in Five Parts.* London: Heinemann, Pan.
Adams D (1997) *Mostly Harmless.* London: Heinemann, Pan.
Adler PA & Adler P (1987) *Membership Roles in Field Research.* Newbury Park, CA: Sage.

Alvesson M (2003) 'Methodology for close up studies', *Higher Education* 46: 167–193.

Alvesson M (2009) 'At-home Ethnography: Struggling with Closeness and Closure', in Ybema S, Yanow D, Wels H, & Kamsteeg F (Eds) *Studying the Complexities of Everyday Life:* 156–174. London: Sage.

Alvesson M & Gabriel Y (2013) 'Beyond Formulaic research: In praise of greater diversity in organizational research and publications', *Academy of Management Learning & Education* 12(2)245–263.

Alvesson M & Kärreman D (2007) 'Constructing mystery: Empirical matters in theory development', *Academy of Management Review* 32(4)1265–1281.

Alvesson M & Sköldberg K (2000) *Reflexive Methodology.* London: Sage.

Alvesson M, Hardy C, & Harley B (2008) 'Reflecting on reflexivity', *Journal of Management Studies* 45(3)480–501.

Anderson L (2006). 'Analytic autoethnography', *Journal of Contemporary Ethnography* 35(4)373–395.

Armstrong P & Lilley S (2008) 'Practical criticism and the social sciences of management editorial', *Ephemera* 8(4)353–370.

Atkinson P (2006) 'Rescuing autoethnography', *Journal of Contemporary Ethnography* 35(4)400–404.

Atkinson PA, Coffey A, & Delamont S (2003) *Key Themes in Qualitative Research.* Walnut Creek, CA: AltaMira Press.

Bender AR & Raz N (2012) 'Age-related differences in Episodic Memory', *Neuropsychology* 26(4)442–450.

Bluhm DJ, Harman W, Lee TW & Mitchell TR (2010) 'Qualitative research in management', *Journal of Management Studies* 48(8)1866–1891.

Boje D & Tyler JA (2009) 'Story and narrative noticing: Workaholism autoethnographies', *Journal of Business Ethics* 84: 173–194.

Broadhurst S & Machon J (2009) *Sensualities/Textualities and Technologies.* Eastbourne: Palgrave Macmillan.

Bruner J (2004) 'Life as narrative', *Social Research* 71(3)691–710.

Burnier D (2006) 'Encounters with the self in social science research: A political scientist looks at Autoethnography', *Journal of Contemporary Ethnography* 35(4)410–418.

Buzard J (2003) 'On auto-ethnographic authority', *The Yale Journal of Criticism* 16(1)61–91.

Calás MB & Smircich L (1992) 'Re-writing gender into organizational theorizing: Directions from feminist perspectives', in Reed M & Hughes M (Eds) *Rethinking Organization:* 227–253. London: Sage.

Capra F & Luisi PL (2014) *A Systems View of Life.* Cambridge: Cambridge University Press.

Chang H (2008) *Autoethnography as method,* Walnut Creek, CA: Left Coast Press

Charmaz K (2000) 'Grounded Theory: Objectivist and Constructivist Methods', in Denzin NK & Lincoln YS (Eds) *Handbook of Qualitative Research:* 509–535. Thousand Oaks, CA: Sage.

Conti-O'Hare M. (2002) *The Nurse as Wounded Healer.* Boston: Jones and Bartlett.

Corley KG & Gioia DA (2011) 'Building theory about theory building: What constitutes a theoretical contribution?', *Academy of Management Review* 36(1) 12–32.

Creswell JW (1998) *Qualitative Inquiry and Research Design.* Thousand Oaks, CA: Sage.

Creswell JW (2009) *Research design: Qualitative, quantitative and mixed methods approaches* (3rd ed), Thousand Oaks, CA: Sage Publications.

Czarniawska B (2004) *Narratives in Social Science Research*. London-Thousand Oaks-New Delhi: Sage.

DeBerry-Spence B (2010) 'Making theory and practice in subsistence markets: An analytic autoethnography of MASAZI in Accra, Ghana', *Journal of Business Research* 63(6)608–616.

de Freitas E & Paton J (2008) '(De)facing the self: Postcultural disruptions of the autoethnographic text', *Qualitative Inquiry* 15(3)483–498.

Denzin NK (1997) *Interpretive Ethnography*. Newbury Park, CA: Sage.

Denzin NK (2006) 'Analytic autoethnography, or Deja Vu all over again', *Journal of Contemporary Ethnography* 35(4)419–428.

Denzin NK & Lincoln YS (2000) (Eds) *The Handbook of Qualitative Research*. Newbury Park, CA: Sage.

Ellis C (2000) 'Creating criteria: An ethnographic short story', *Qualitative Inquiry* 6(2)273–277.

Ellis C, Adams TE, & Bochner AP (2010) 'Autoethnography: An Overview', *Forum: Qualitative Social Research,* 12(1)1–18

Ellis C & Bochner AP (2000) 'Autoethnography, personal narrative, reflexivity: Researcher as subject', in Denzin NK & Lincoln YS (Eds) *The Handbook of Qualitative Research:* 733–768. Newbury Park, CA: Sage.

Ellis C & Bochner AP (2006) 'Analyzing analytic autoethnography: An autopsy', *Journal of Contemporary Ethnography* 35: 429–448.

Erickson F (2011) 'A History of Qualitative Inquiry in Social and Educational Research', in Denzin NK & Lincoln YS (Eds) *Handbook of Qualitative Research:* 43–59. Los Angeles: SAGE.

Fitzgerald L, Ferlie E, Wood M, & Hawkins C (2002) 'Interlocking interactions, the diffusion of innovations in health care', *Human Relations* 55(12)1429–1449.

Flick E (1998) *An Introduction to Qualitative Research*. London: Sage.

Fontana A & Frey J (2000) 'The Interview: From Structured Questions to Negotiated Text', in Denzin N & Lincoln Y (Eds) *Handbook of Qualitative Research:* 645–672. Thousand Oaks, CA: Sage.

Foucault M (1979) *Discipline and Punish: The Birth of the Prison*. Harmondsworth: Penguin.

Freshwater D & Rolfe G (2004) *Deconstructing Evidence-Based Practice*. Oxon: Routledge.

Gabriel Y (2000) *Storytelling in Organizations*. Oxford: Oxford University Press.

Gabriel Y (2002) 'Essai: On paragrammatic uses of organizational theory: A provocation'. *Organization Studies* 23:133–151.

Gergen KJ (1991) *The Saturated Self: Dilemmas of Identity in Contemporary Life*. New York: Basic Books.

Gherardi S (1999) 'Learning as problem-driven or learning in the face of mystery?', *Organization Studies* 20: 101–123.

Glaser BG & Strauss AL (1967) *The Discovery of Grounded Theory*. New York: Aldine De Gruyer.

Hall M, Clegg SR, & Sillince J (2008) 'The importance of learning to differentiate between 'Hard' and 'Soft' knowledge', *Communications of the IBIMA* 6: 67–74.

Hamilton ML, Smith L, & Worthington K (2008) 'Fitting the Methodology with the Research: An Exploration of Narrative, Self Study and Autoethnography', *Studying Teacher Education* 4(1)17–28.

Hatch MJ, Kostera M, & Kozminski AK (2005) *The Three Faces of Leadership.* London: Blackwell.

Hayano D (1979) 'Auto-ethnography: Paradigms, problems, and prospects', *Human Organization* 38(1)99–104.

Howe ML & Malone C (2011) 'Mood-congruent true and false memory: Effects of depression', *Memory* 19(2)192–201.

Jaya PS (2011) 'Themes of identity: An auto-ethnographical exploration', *The Qualitative Report* 16(3)745–763.

Kilduff M (2006) 'Editor's comments: Publishing theory', *Academy of Management Review* 31: 252–255.

Kociatkiewicz J & Kostera M (2012) 'The good Manager: An Archetypical Quest for morally sustainable leadership', *Organization Studies* 33(7)861–878.

Kostera M (2006) 'The narrative collage as Research Method', *Storytelling, Self, Society* 2(2)5–27.

Kuhn T (1969) *The Structure of Scientific Revolutions.* Chicago: University of Chicago Press.

Lacan J (2005) *Ecrits: A Selection.* London: Tavistock.

Lee MM (1991) "Playing the Guru: inequality of personal power in relationships", *Management Education and Development* 22(4)302–309.

Locke K & Golden-Biddle K (1997) 'Constructing opportunities for contribution: Structuring intertextual coherence and "problematizing" in organizational studies', *Academy of Management Journal* 40(5)1023–1062.

McIlveen P (2008) 'Autoethnography as a method for reflexive research and practice in vocational psychology', *Australian Journal of Career Development* 17(2)13–20.

Miles MB & Huberman AM (1994) *Qualitative Data Analysis.* Thousand Oaks, CA: Sage Publications.

Mill JS (1872) *A System of Logic, Ratiocinative and Inductive.* London: Longmans, Green.

Mitzroff II & Killman RH (1978) *Methodological Approaches to Social Science.* San Francisco: Jossey Bass.

Morgan G (1993) *Imaginization.* Thousand Oaks: Sage.

Norris J (2008) 'Collage', in Given LM (Ed) *The SAGE Encyclopedia of Qualitative Research Methods:* 94–96. London: Sage.

Pace S (April 2012) 'Writing the self into research: Using grounded theory analytic strategies in autoethnography', in McLoughlin N & Lee Brien D (Eds) *Text— Special Issue, no. 13: Creativity: Cognitive, Social and Cultural Perspectives:* 1–15. Australian Association of Writing Programs.

Phillips L & Jorgensen MW (2002) *Discourse Analysis as Theory and Method.* London: Sage.

Power M (2004) 'Counting, control and calculation: Reflections on measuring and management', *Human Relations* 57(6)765–783.

Reason P (1981) ' "Methodological approaches to social science" by Ian Mitroff and Ralph Kilmann: An appreciation', in Reason P & Rowan J (Eds) *Human Inquiry: A Source Book of New Paradigm Research:* 43–51. Chichester: John Wiley and Sons.

Richardson L (1999) 'Paradigms lost', *Symbolic Interaction* 22(1)79–91.

Ritzer G (1980) *Sociology: A Multiple Paradigm Science.* Boston: Allyn and Bacon.

Rolfe G, Jasper M, & Freshwater D (2011) *Critical Reflection in Practice.* Hampshire: Palgrave, Macmillan.

Sandberg J & Alvesson M (2011) 'Ways of constructing research questions: Gap-spotting or problematization?', *Organization* 18: 23–44.

Schutz A (1962) 'Common-sense and Scientific Interpretation of Human Action', in M. Natanson (ed.) *vol. 1, Collected papers of Alfred Schutz:* 3–47. The Hague, the Netherlands: Martinus Nijhoff.

Short NP (2010) *An Evocative Autoethnography: A Mental Health Professional's Development. (Professional Doctorate of Nursing).* Brighton, UK: University of Brighton.

Snow D, Morrill C, & Anderson L (2003) 'Elaborating analytic ethnography: Linking fieldwork and theory', *Ethnography* 2: 181–200.

Srivastava P & Hopwood N (2009) 'A practical iterative framework for qualitative data analysis', *International Journal of Qualitative Methodology* 8(1)76–84.

Struthers J (2012) *Analytic Autoethnography: A Tool to Inform the Lecturer's Use of Self When Teaching Mental Health Nursing?* Ph.D. Thesis. Lancaster, UK: Lancaster University.

Sutton RS & Staw BM (1995) 'What theory is not', *Administrative Science Quarterly* 40: 375–390.

Thayer-Bacon B (2003) 'Pragmatism and feminism as qualified relativism', *Studies in Philosophy and Education* 22: 417–438.

Thomas G & James D (2006) 'Reinventing grounded theory: Some questions about theory, ground and discovery', *British Educational Research Journal* 32(6)767–795.

Van Maanen J, Sørensen JB, & Mitchell TR (2007) 'The interplay between theory and method', *Academy of Management Review* 32(4)1145–1154.

Vryan KD (2006) 'Expanding autoethnography and enhancing its potential', *Journal of Contemporary Ethnography* 35(4)405–409.

Wall S (2008) 'Easier said than done: Writing an autoethnography', *International Journal of Qualitative Methods* 7(1)38–53.

Weick KE (1995) 'What theory is not, theorizing is', *Administrative Science Quarterly* 40: 385–390.

Weick KE (1999) 'Theory construction as disciplined reflexivity: Tradeoffs in the 90s', *Academy of Management Review* 24(4)797–806.

Winnicott DW (1971) *Playing and Reality.* London: Routledge.

Ybema S, Yanow D, Wels H, & Kamsteeg F (2009) (Eds) *Organizational Ethnography: Studying the Complexities of Everyday Life.* London: Sage Publications.

6   Meet the Author

This chapter stands out from the others in this book because it is based on a paper that is not written by me. This is taken from an interview with me that was conducted and written by Darren C. Short (Avanade Inc.) in 2010. It seems narcissistic to include this in a book written by me, but I hope that you will step past that feeling to see that it is part of the autoethnographic approach described in the previous chapter to understand the author behind the text. Greater knowledge of the author helps the interpretation of what they are saying. Throughout this book I try to emphasise the representative nature of the language we use and the thoughts we present (see Chapter 4). I, as writer, am using all these many words to convey my thoughts, and I hope that you, as reader, understand them in the way that I mean. Your understanding of what I am saying is more likely to match what I mean the more we share a common conceptual raft behind the words. In addition, I hope that you do not just accept what I say, but critique as you read. Part of that critical edge is to consider the personal, social, and cultural biases, often unknown and unacknowledged, that are part of any text. Insight into these can be gained by a wider knowledge of the author. This chapter is therefore included specifically to help you, the reader, critically interpret and perhaps better understand the book.

BETTER KNOW AN HRD SCHOLAR: A CONVERSATION WITH MONICA LEE BY DARREN SHORT

This article is part of a series that aims to better understand the people behind the names we see in journals and conference papers, by examining their careers, motivations, and life histories. What follows is an edited conversation with Monica Lee who, at the time of writing, was a Life Member of Lancaster University, as well as a visiting professor at the Northumbria University. She is a Chartered Psychologist and a Fellow of the Chartered Institute of Personnel and Development (FCIPD). She was a founding member of the University Forum for HRD, the founding editor of the *Human Resource Development International* (HRDI), and is founding editor of the

Routledge series Studies in HRD. Monica is a regular attendee at HRD conferences around the world, and the award for the HRDI article of the year is named after her. She has written many influential articles. The conversations with Monica were conducted by phone on August 12 and 13, 2009. They were recorded, transcribed, and then edited to meet the word count limit for the journal. The editing retained the spirit and voice from the conversations, and the edited version was reviewed by Monica prior to publication.

THE CONVERSATION

DARREN: *I'm conscious that I have become aware of you and your work probably quite late on in your career. So, I'd like to start by asking you to walk me through your career timeline to give me a better understanding of the path you took.*

MONICA: Let me start by taking you back to my childhood. I am dyslexic, but it was never recognised when I was a kid. I was brought up in a family that believed that women should be well behaved ornaments, and so I was sent to convent schools that looked at deportment and things like that. We didn't actually do things like biology, physics, and chemistry. Being dyslexic, it was thought that I was a bit thick, and I was considered naughty because I wouldn't spell properly. But, in 1963, I took the 11+ test, which was a nationwide test largely focused on non-verbal IQ. I got a very high score and came within the top ten in the South of England for that year. Then, teachers and parents put my inability down to being deliberately disruptive and I was regularly punished for not writing or reading properly. The upshot of all of that was I really hated education: I hated school, I hated learning. I hated adults. I quite quickly turned into a truly rebellious and isolated child. But, at the same time, I did well on tests and other things that didn't involve an awful lot of reading and writing, and I was always interested in creating and making things, so I didn't turn too far inwards.

DARREN: *It is interesting for someone so passionate about learning that you started off hating it. What happened to change your thoughts on learning?*

MONICA: Well, I applied to Cambridge to read Education at Homerton College. They had a non-verbal entrance test and I got a really high score. They gave me an unconditional place there, which meant that I didn't have to do my A-levels. So, I was rather an anomaly as I ended up getting into higher education in Cambridge with very poor qualifications and hating education itself, whilst looking to be a teacher because that was something I got into, rather than because I particularly wanted to teach. All the time, I was reacting, rather than saying, 'This is my career; this is what I want to be'. While I was at Cambridge, I came into contact with lots of people who liked to learn and who actually valued education. And by the end of it, I was similar. I really did end up quite enjoying the whole challenge of developing areas of knowledge. Of course, I had enormous gaps to make up, particularly in the sciences and history.

DARREN: *Now, Cambridge is a long way from Lancaster, so what happened to bring you up north to Lancaster?*

MONICA: I met my husband at Cambridge. He came up to Lancaster to do his PhD in pure mathematics, and I came with him. By then, I was thinking I'd be an educational psychologist, so I was one of the first cohort of students to do a psychology degree in the newly established department at Lancaster. Lancaster was unusual in that it required all its undergraduates to have three different areas of expertise. So, I did philosophy, psychology, and maths, because, of course, maths was one of the things I hadn't done much of at school. And, that was really interesting. I did well and on finishing I enrolled to do a psychology PhD, but we were pretty desperate for money. So, instead, I ended up teaching maths at secondary school level, including special needs kids, and I also taught art and pottery. Probably because of my own background and dislike of school generally, I was able to relate quite well to the kids, particularly the problem ones.

DARREN: *This all sounds a long way from HRD, although I can definitely see a link to a passion for learning.*

MONICA: Well, just when I started teaching, the government raised the school leaving age from 15 to 16. I was teaching on the outskirts of Liverpool, and it was kids from farms and from Liverpool, all of whom had thought they were just about to go off and earn lots of money and do adult things. Then they were suddenly told that they were going to have to stay in school for an extra year, so they were very disaffected. This sounds like it's got nothing to do with HRD, but it's actually got a lot to do with it. For example, at one stage there was an enormous fight between these two groups of youths; a couple ended up in the hospital and there was lots of broken furniture. The teachers who were meant to be on playground duty locked themselves in the storeroom. I was just eating my lunch, when someone ran in to say there was a fight. By the time I got there nearly 60 people were involved, but I was just so cross with them that I stood in the middle and ordered them to stop fighting, and they did!

When you think about it, I was only a few years older than them and many of the lads were much bigger than me—they were all very worked up. It was a very silly thing to do and I could have been badly hurt, but I was determined they should stop. What it made me think about later on was the relationship between leadership and power: about just being in the right place at the right time, and the power of conviction or belief that one was doing the right thing.

DARREN: *How long were you teaching?*

MONICA: After five years teaching, I ended up starting a family, and took that opportunity to also do my PhD. My PhD was in experimental psychology. It was quite mathematical really, or at least scientific. However, the assumption from the local community of people I worked with was that as a psychologist I knew all about helping people. At the same time I taught Adult and Further Education, both qualification courses and Adult Returner courses, and became head of psychology at the local FE college. I eventually started a business as a private consultant. So, I sort of sideways got into starting to do more therapeutic and developmental work and became a Chartered Psychologist. Over a period of ten years, I ended up building up quite a strong client base ranging from some very large multinational firms to some very small charities and non-profits. It was all developed by word of mouth and happenstance. I also ended up working at Sunningdale.

DARREN: *Yes, I have heard of Sunningdale and visited the Civil Service College at Sunningdale on many occasions when I was in the British Civil Service.*

MONICA: Well, I was one of their consultants for some while. Through that, I started to move more and more into training and development—from the outside as it were, coming from a background in education and psychology. I became a member of the Institute of Training and Development (ITD), which was the professional body for UK trainers and developers. I just happened to notice an advert for a post at Lancaster University. It was to work on a government-funded initiative (the Management Teacher Development Scheme) to develop staff in management schools across the UK—the aim being to enhance management schools, and thus management within the UK. This is going back to 1988 when management was just starting to be seen as an academic discipline, and as an income generator. I didn't want a full-time job with them, but they wanted a full-time person and made me an offer I couldn't refuse, so I ended up joining Lancaster.

DARREN: *So, the career path has already taken several interesting turns, starting with teaching maths, moving into private consulting, getting more involved in training and development, and then moving into Lancaster University to work on developing people in management schools. Can you talk a little about your role once you joined Lancaster?*

MONICA: When I started, it was absolutely hectic. Within two weeks of joining, we had our first workshop, and I designed the whole three-year rolling programme with Mark Easterby-Smith in those two weeks—it ended up running for six years. I think it had quite a profound effect on some management schools, and some of the people who are currently in the University Forum went through that programme. It was very interesting. At that time management schools focused mainly on economics. The concept of training and staff development was new, and alien, to the academic environment. It was a high-profile job and I was under a lot of scrutiny but the scheme worked well. The management schools were catalysed and internal staff development is now commonplace. I also used some of the ideas from that programme to design and direct wider programmes that were funded by the European Union, working with universities across Central Europe and Russia on separate programmes doing very similar sorts of things. Of course, they were different both in the conception of what was happening and also in the structure of the programmes. It's hard to think back to the circumstances of those times, but the idea of workshops within a university system was just unheard of, particularly week-long workshops where people had really intensive stuff going on. So, it was quite a challenge to the system. The same was true in Central Europe and Russia: that was completely groundbreaking work that brought together senior university and government staff from different institutions and nations at times of great change, and the EU held it as an exemplar project. I was invited to talk to the Swedish Council of Ministers about my work, on behalf of the EU, which was a feather in my cap and very interesting. We were working so hard that there was little time to write. The only real record of it is in my book on Central Europe (Lee et al. 1996, see also Chapter 10). This really gets me to where I started to do much more HRD work. At least, it was then that I started to think of myself as an HRD person.

DARREN: *You have talked a bit about the significance of workshops in your approach to HRD. Did these feed through into your HRD education programmes?*

MONICA: In the early 1990s, I set up the MSc in HRD and the HRD Pathway programme at Lancaster, and these adhered to the notion of workshops. That programme in particular is what I wrote about in my 'Refusal to Define HRD' paper (see Chapter 2 in this book), which was later published in HRDI, because, again, that challenged the norms of university structure. This is going back to the education side of being a teacher, and the belief that you have to be true to yourself and your experiences to be able to come across with any power. It is the idea that you have to be able to design your own learning opportunities, not be spoon-fed with a curriculum—this is what we're doing, this is what HRD is. It's much more about who you are, where you are, how you develop in relation to others. Because you can always go out and find more information if it's information you need, but the development of yourself in relation to others isn't something you can just go out and do. It happens coincidentally. It can't be forced and it can't be easily changed, but you can try and build up situations in which it happens. So, my idea within the MSc was trying to build up such situations, where experienced HRD people and managers could build on their own experiences and thereby create their own curriculum, with obviously a lot of help from the staff. But, the idea was that it was very much student-led.

DARREN: *I know that you have been at Lancaster since 1989, but you have also been a visiting professor at Northumbria since 2002. How did that come about?*

MONICA: Yes, I was proud to be the third professor of HRD in the UK, and the very first female one. It came about with some confusion really. Heather Hopfl at the time was a senior academic in Northumbria, and it was she who brought me in as a visiting professor. Just as that was happening, I had my cerebral haemorrhage, and she also left the university. During the time after she'd left, there was quite a lot of personnel change, and so they found that they had a professor on their hands that they hadn't really expected and didn't really know what to do with. I also was just recovering from having been ill anyway, so, it was quite a slow start. Jim Stewart was a new visiting professor there as well. So, we started by contributing to several staff development days and a couple of workshops. Since then, most of what I've done is to provide support to the staff, initially with a focus on helping them to develop their research profile. It has been quite a laid-back relationship. We've been working together very well. It's a lovely place, a very genuine place.

DARREN: *You mentioned the University Forum for HRD. From my experience, a lot of people within the HRD community in North America have only have a patchy understanding of its history and role. It seems to me that its creation was a critical point in the development of HRD education within the United Kingdom, and more broadly within Europe. Could you tell me a little about how it came about, and your role in its creation?*

MONICA: I have co-authored an article on the creation of the University Forum (Stewart et al. 2009), so let me summarise the background. The University Forum stems from two separate initiatives that occurred in the late 1980s. The first of these was the introduction of national competence-based vocational qualifications in the United Kingdom (NVQs). The second was an initiative by the professional body—the ITD. They already had qualifications at certificate and diploma level and sought to encourage master's-level degree programmes in universities to provide for the continuing professional development of ITD members. Universities providing ITD-related qualification programmes were faced with two challenges: first, to develop new master's-level programmes, and second, to reform existing certificate and diploma programmes so that they would also meet the requirements of the then-new national vocational qualifications. Several universities began a cooperation facilitated by Alan Moon, a retired college principal. The key players also included myself, and people like Jim McGoldrick, John Walton, Bob Hamlin, and Sandra Watson, who were strongly university-based, but also practitioners. These people had come through the ITD, like me, offering courses within the ITD, but at the same time with a university focus too. Out of this cooperation arose a loose network of academics, which became known as the Euston Road Group, named after the location where the group met—at the headquarters of the National Council for Vocational Qualifications (NCVQ). The group agreed and applied some general principles, and the early programmes gained recognition from the ITD.

DARREN: *Was it the Euston Road Group that eventually became the University Forum?*

MONICA: Yes. In the early 1990s, the NCVQ withdrew support from the Group, and so the loose association had to decide whether to continue and, if so, what name to adopt. At the time, there were around 15 academics from around a dozen or so universities actively involved. We decided that there were benefits from continuing and Alan Moon suggested

University Forum for HRD as a name. And so the Forum came into being. The ITD continued to fund Alan's time as the first executive secretary of the Forum. In 1994, the ITD merged with the Institute of Personnel Management, which was strongly focused on personnel or HRM. This created what is now the Chartered Institute of Personnel and Development (CIPD). In 1998, it withdrew funding for Alan's time and thus for the activities of UFHRD. We adopted a new constitution that allowed for subscription fees to be charged. The CIPD is now a valued member of the Forum, and the Forum sees itself rather as a think-tank on HRD issues.

DARREN: *I think that many AHRD members also frequently associate you with the journal Human Resource Development International, and your role as the founding editor. Of course, the HRDI article of the year award is now named after you. Could you tell me about how the journal was started?*

MONICA: Yes, I was thrilled and honoured when the AHRD decided to set up the award in my name—I still am really! I have always been very interested in the relationship between things, how things work, and particularly in the interface between individuals and organisations. I find it very hard to see individuals or organisations as entirely separate entities—they influence each other. That has brought me into conflict with some people at different times because most discipline areas, at least back in the 1990s, were clearly around either individuals or organisations, and I would say, 'No, I'm interested in how they relate'. I remember one staff meeting at Lancaster when I was told, 'Well, you've got to do one or the other. You can't be in the middle'. I replied, 'I want to be in the middle. There's a lot to learn from being in the middle'. With Lancaster being a research university, I had to publish, but was finding it hard because I was looking at that interface. I had to publish in one place or another and, at the time, there weren't any journal or other publication outlets that focused on the emerging interfaces and boundaries in the way that I was trying to do. So, HRDI partly came about because of this.

DARREN: *I remember when HRDI first came out, and the significant contribution it added. The overall philosophy of the journal was different to other HRD journals. So, I wonder whether publishers and other researchers took some convincing to buy into the concept. How difficult or challenging was it to launch HRDI?*

MONICA: This might offend people from AHRD. Initially, in 1996, I was working on contract discussions with Routledge, and we were going ahead great guns. I had the Forum fully behind me too, not necessarily entirely on the principle of what I was trying to do, but because they knew me and were willing to accept me. The Forum made links with AHRD about a year after the first contract was drawn up between Routledge and me, but before the journal was published. I think that the publishers wanted AHRD on board because of the sales it would provide. I welcomed this and agreed to change the contract to include AHRD. However, it seemed that the AHRD leadership of the time didn't understand what I was trying to do, and had no faith in me at all as editor. I think they thought that someone more in tune with the American model of HRD as performance management should be running it. I just got so fed up with the cultural imperialism. It's hard to describe. I'm sure they were doing what they thought was in the best interest of the field. But, as far as I was concerned, they were just trying to impose more of the same formulaic approach. Unless you get those boundaries open, the field just can't develop so easily—it needed to be kept open and fluid and flexible for any development or any challenging to happen. Otherwise, it would merely reinforce the structures that already existed within the field. And the whole idea of HRDI, as far as I was concerned, was to try and challenge all of those boundaries and those interfaces. And that's one of the reasons why I encouraged authors from broader fields, who were well known outside of HRD, but never had anything to say to HRD.

DARREN: *It sounds like you set out to create a journal that reflected your own thinking about HRD.*

MONICA: Yes. My conception of HRD was less to do with training and development, and much more about the relationships between people, about power and authority and leadership, inspiration and creativity; simply much more Jungian, really. You find the same sorts of issues in groups and individuals at work as you do in families, in government, in bigger organisations and small organisations. They just change focus slightly. It is like that with research and practice—under some lights they are very similar or almost the same. Therefore, to me, it makes no sense to restrict focus to a specific subject or to have a research-only journal or a practitioner-only journal.

DARREN: *When you look at it now, how much of your original vision do you still see in it?*

MONICA: I don't know. I think it has changed its focus each time the editor has changed. Jean Woodall came after me as editor, and she provided a more orthodox approach. There are now other journals, such as the one developed by Heather Hopfl, which have taken up the less orthodox positions that HRDI once held and have taken several of the writers that would have otherwise written in HRDI. Peter Kuchinke brought a challenging and thoughtful dimension with him, and I look forward to seeing what will happen under Rob Poel. I think it's finding its feet—it's growing up. At the time when I was doing it, I obviously knew everyone who was involved. Now, there's a new wave of people coming through who I don't have the same contacts with. So, I don't think it's just about the journal. I think it's about friendships and about the relationships as well. If you see things written in a journal by people you know well, you'll automatically read them much more than if you'd see things by people you don't know so well. So, it is maturing and feels less like my baby. But that's probably as much because I'm changing and I've moved away to other things. Not away from it or from the field, but my involvement is in other areas, too. Still, I hope that it retains some of the original vision and maintains some sort of different focus. I established the Routledge monograph series at the same time as HRDI and that is still going strong, and it keeps me involved in fostering a wider focus. The series is better known in Europe than North America, but has some excellent books within it from some authors who are key to HRD. I see it as a way of strengthening the field and I do hope that more AHRD members will contribute to it in the future.

DARREN: *When I look at your published works, it strikes me that you have written on a very wide range of subjects. So, I'm really interested in how you decide where your time goes within HRD. How do you decide which topics to research and write on?*

MONICA: I think this is one of my problems, really. Because of my background as a psychologist, I'm interested in how people relate to others and how that creates societies and influences within societies. And, of course, that's just the whole human condition. It's very much just what I'm thinking about at the time, things that have affected me or things that just attract my interest. Then I'll think about it and write about it. One of my problems is that I haven't had a single obvious focus for my work. So, I think it's very hard for me and for others to say this is what I'm about. This was particularly hard early on in my career as I had no language by which I could adequately describe what I was trying to get across to others. More recently, however, as complexity theory has developed, I have found that the concepts embedded in that match my own quite closely, and so I have come to describe how I see the world in those terms—but though I can now put words to it (Lee 2003), I still remain stuck in the middle without a clearly defined focus!

DARREN: *You must find that there are times when you have to choose to work on just one of the many ideas or concepts that have attracted your interest. So, how do you prioritize the one that gets your time?*

MONICA: Sometimes it's just desperation because I promised to write a paper by such a time, and I've given it a title and a short abstract, and I suddenly realise I have to actually write it. You know, at one stage it was a nice little idea and I thought there might be something to make of it, and then I've committed myself to that. And a year later, I have to flesh it out and think about it properly. Other times, as with 'The Refusal to Define HRD' paper, it's just purely reactions to particular circumstances. I wrote a paper at one stage about consciousness and unconsciousness (see Chapter 13), and that was very much how I think I've worked with the world. I think for most people they see consciousness as a sort of way of directing things and organising things. The decisions that we make have already been made by our subconscious, but we try to convince ourselves we're in control and that we made those decisions in a conscious manner. Perhaps because of my background of being dyslexic, and also through my cerebral haemorrhage when I went back to being dyslexic, I focus much more on concepts than on words, and there is a distinction between what my consciousness is directing me and my unconscious or subconscious, which is really making the decisions. So, I'm more willing to accept that really I'm not in control. I do flit around, and I'm driven by activity rather than necessarily trying to go in a straight line. I just do what comes along and follow paths that intrigue me. If I see something that is trying to control me or other people, I tend to fight against it. And sometimes those fights just can't be won.

DARREN: *You mentioned the dyslexia. You have an amazing track record within academia and practice. To look at the track record, nobody would ever be aware of your dyslexia. I'm interested in how you think it affected you, or how you controlled it.*

MONICA: Well, it still affects me. I often read words wrongly, especially when I am tired. The computer has helped tremendously with spelling. But, I can still be very blasé about using words wrongly because I focus much more on the concepts rather than on the words. I don't have the sort of brain or the sort of attention that focuses on the dictionary definition of the words in the way that a lot of people do. Certainly as a kid, I found it hard to become literate. When I had my haemorrhage in the 1990s, I became fully dyslexic again and could not read anything, and that was just so absolutely frustrating. I couldn't phone anyone because I couldn't read what the numbers were on the phone. I couldn't use the computer as the keyboard just didn't make sense to me. I couldn't even turn the television on. I just got so cross all the time. I must have forgotten it or blocked out the frustration I felt as a child, though I guess that as a kid, you don't know what you should be able to do, and so you don't have the same expectations. But, I had totally forgotten how disabling it is to be illiterate in a literate world.

DARREN: *How did you relearn to read, write, and use computers after the haemorrhage?*

MONICA: I just let my brain do it. I mean this is part of the consciousness bit. I just was willing to accept that eventually my brain would sort itself out. And it has done tremendously well. Certainly for the first three months, every day I would wake up and notice that I could do things that I couldn't do the day before. At first, I couldn't see things because I had multiple vision all the time, and gradually that got sorted. I just went with it. I suddenly got a passion to do jigsaws, and obviously my brain was trying to match patterns better, and suddenly that improved. I was just quite laid-back about it all really, but was determined to keep on going, so I kept on daring myself to do things that I couldn't do before. A lot of it was actually quite scary—trying to walk, for example, when the whole world was spinning round all the time—and it would have been easy to stop and see myself as an invalid. As it is, however, my brain has adapted really well and I am more or less back to normal, which is pretty good for someone who was only given a two percent chance of survival.

DARREN: *I would like to switch topics a little. I am interested in the people who have had an influence on you. When you look back at the different stages of your career, are there particular people who have had more of an influence than others?*

MONICA: I think probably the main turning point for me was right back at the beginning—meeting my husband and other friends at Cambridge and learning that they actually liked and enjoyed education. I found people, particularly my husband, who had a value for education rather than just feeling like they had to do it. Without that, I have no idea where I would have gone because I never had a career plan. As with my writing, I've just done what intrigued me at any one time. I think that I've always chosen things that challenged me. For some reason I have to prove myself a lot. Not to other people, and not for praise. But I do need to prove myself to myself. It's about making things better, making things happen.

DARREN: *You talked then about your husband as being a critical influencer. Have there been others who you feel have had a particular influence on you?*

MONICA: I rate Jim McGoldrick highly, and many others—too many to name. I mean there are a lot of people who I've enjoyed friendships with and talked with and learnt from and developed, yourself included. Everyone I meet impacts upon me in some way or another, but I'm not sure there's anyone who has directly influenced my path as it were. It sounds awful really, and it was the question that I've really been rather dreading you asking because I'm not sure that there's any particular text or anything that has been a key inspiration in that way. Theoretically, I suppose I come from a Jungian, process-oriented, action-oriented position—but that might change. In practice, I have never had a hero (or heroine) or put anyone on that sort of pedestal. I have been influenced more by the things that I've bounced off and the things that helped me think about what I was doing at that particular stage. I think that's partly because I do work at that subconscious, conceptual level, and because there are so many people and so many things that I've come into contact with. I read quite widely. I quite often read science texts, psychology journals, and things like *New Scientist*. Quite often I pull in things from completely different fields that just sort of spark my interest, things like genetics and evolutionary psychology. You would never even think they'd be relevant to HRD, but actually I think they are, and what I have read in disparate fields has inspired my writing. What's going on there influences how I think about things.

DARREN: *I'm conscious in your writing that you've written a lot about the way in which HRD has changed and is continuing to change. So, I'm interested in your perspective on changes in HRD, both looking back in time, and also looking forward. How about we start with looking back?*

MONICA: To some extent the nature of development is going to be the same across times and cultures: People will learn and change and develop. How that is consciously done or how that's enacted or enabled might change depending upon the culture and circumstances, the national structures, and the organisational structures that facilitate that. But, the actual doing of it, the functioning of it, the development of people, happens as part of being a person. So, if we're talking about HRD then we are talking about the conceptualisation of how this is done, then I think there has been quite a change in this conceptualisation. Looking back, training and development or HRD was once seen as making people fit to their jobs within a particular organisation, within a particular organisational structure. Now, over the years, different forms of organisation have arisen as has the acknowledgement that you can have all sorts of different organisational structures. There's been a lot of change in the widening of the concept of what is done in the name of HRD. And that has to go hand in hand with a widening in the understanding of what organisations are about and what management is about too.

DARREN: *Looking ahead, how do you see these changes affecting the role of HRD?*

MONICA: This comes back to the sort of things that I've been writing about more recently, which is about the erosion of boundaries, whether it's national, geographic, organisational, or identity-based boundaries. Not a collapse, but a reduction in the mega-control and to clusters of organisations that work together. Now, I'm sure we'll still get multinationals, but I'm sure that organisations are going to get smaller. People are going to increasingly need to be portfolio workers, and that is going to result in a need for different ways of thinking about HRD. It raises questions like: How do people develop and whose responsibility is it? Is it the individual's? Is it the organisation's? Does the nation want to become more involved in it? Or perhaps different professional organisations? How do they all relate to each other? And also, what sort of ethical and moral dilemmas will result? How will this look in the developing worlds, with people who don't have technology, don't have the resources? I think HRD as a profession is going to increasingly need to be able to help its professionals to address these sorts of questions and issues and to recognise the reason why these sorts of issues exist.

DARREN: *When I look at most HRD education programmes, they generally look very traditional with adult learning, instructional design, evaluation, OD, and so on. There seems to be a big disconnect between what those programmes are seeking to do and the future challenges that you've just described. Given the changes you foresee, what do you see as being the resulting challenge to HRD education?*

MONICA: I think that there are challenges not just for HRD education programmes, but also for the professional qualification routes as well, like that set up by the CIPD. This goes back to the 'no definition' argument. As soon as you define something, as soon as you put boundaries around it, whether it's a qualification programme or an educational academic programme, you say that this is the syllabus, say that this is the way of doing it, and then you set it in stone. You're also saying, 'This is what I think the culture is about, this is what I think organisations are about', and so on. And once you've got that and once you're trying to measure people against standards that have been predetermined, then you have great problems with trying to even recognise that the world is changing, let alone move with that. So, as far as I can see, both the academic institutions and the professional institutions need to take more and more account of the outcomes they are trying to attain, rather than the curricula they want to put in.

DARREN: *The boundaries between traditional HRD, performance improvement, HRM, technology, knowledge management, and OD have essentially blurred to the point where there's no clear distinction. And your descriptions of future challenges appear to blur those boundaries even more. It does appear that HR education is going to need to find a way of addressing that or it potentially becomes obsolete.*

MONICA: Yes, absolutely. I mean, I'm sure qualifications will always be needed, but if there's an increasing divorce between what is taught and what is actually done, people are going to start complaining, if nothing else. If you get a group of students who pay large amounts of money to come on a course and then find it doesn't really prepare them well for what's happening out there, then there will be a financial incentive for programmes to change.

DARREN: *When you look forward to the coming years, where do you see yourself fitting in? Would you see your influence coming more through the way you impact HRD programmes, or maybe through the way you influence others' thinking via your writing?*

MONICA: No, not really. I've tried to influence programmes through external examining and those I've been directly involved in. And, I'm certainly not a lone voice in this. But, I think I'm focusing much more on writing than that now, and I'm not even sure how I will carry on with that. I mean, I'm still writing things that I'm interested in. But, I don't have a plan. I don't have a mission in that way.

DARREN: *We have talked a lot about your passion for HRD, but I want to make sure that we have enough time to find out more about your life outside of HRD. What other interests do you have?*

MONICA: Partly they're outside and partly they're within the wider concept of HRD. On a personal level, I've been always interested in art, pottery, gardening, and sewing. I like creating things, and it's partly an escape. When I get the chance, I will often be sitting making or doing something. We have a smallholding, and we're pretty well self-sustaining in terms of vegetables and animals—we have sheep and hens. The university is at the bottom of the hill, and we're at the top. One day I went down and it was totally awful at work, and I realised that that morning before I'd left for work, I'd helped a ewe give birth and saved the life of her and her lamb. So, that part of my life is very much a stabiliser, and it feels creative even if you're just sitting there watching things grow. It feels much more close to reality, whatever reality is. I just don't like all the organisational politics and game playing. I'm not good with it, and I don't really enjoy it. So, it's nice to be in places where there is no game playing.

DARREN: *You talk about not liking organisational politics, but I know that you have been very active in organisations outside of HRD and have even set them up. The Northwest Gateway Initiative (Lee 2002) is one that comes to mind. To what extent have you found your HRD knowledge and skills useful in those sorts of external engagements?*

MONICA: Each of those initiatives came about because I saw a need within the community and established ways of helping and improving things, in so far as I can. I wouldn't say it was HRD. I think I'd call it more the sort of interest in the human condition, or a way of working with groups and with people. Because, I'm not scared of working with groups, which I think a lot of people are. So, trying to move things forward and trying to influence people, and doing it in that way, yes. I think that has used my skills in a way that brought them together with my interest in helping to maintain a stable community in the area.

DARREN: *All of this community work must have been a heavy time commitment, at the same time as you were continuing to be very active in HRD. How did you find time for everything?*

MONICA: I think I work quite quickly. Again it could be a problem of mine, but also it can be a benefit. I can make decisions quite quickly and easily. I don't try and make decisions early on, I just leave them, and once they need to be made, they're made, whereas I think some people sort of decide and then go against it and so on. When I turn my mind to it, I can just get down and do things. I've always been deeply engaged in life all the time, doing lots of different things. Not necessarily always doing academic work or income-generating work. I mean, one of the things that took up an enormous amount of time was being a school governor and trying to sort out a problem at the school, which I wrote about in the end (see Chapter 14). That took almost a year out of my life for no financial gain.

DARREN: *It is clear that you have had an amazing track record of scholarship and service. How do you sustain that without burning out?*

MONICA: I think I probably have burned out at times. I do need to have projects where I feel that I'm doing some good. And part of my dotting around the place, I think, is keeping my interest up. If I find that I'm getting really fed up with something then it's absolutely hopeless, and I can't keep it up. If I were just stuck doing one thing the whole time, I don't think I could do it. I would just find diversion after diversion, and would have to really force myself into it. I think the nature of the dotting around is what keeps me going.

DARREN: *Monica, unfortunately the time has come to wrap up our conversation. Thank you very much. I found it very interesting to hear about your background, how you got into HRD, how you overcame dyslexia and recovered from your cerebral haemorrhage, how the University Forum was created, and how HRDI came about. As we explored these, you raised several points that I would like to take away and reflect on. I will be giving more thought to the consequences of placing boundaries around HRD, about how we are guided by our subconscious, and about the impact on HRD of future changes to organisations and structures. I was also particularly taken by how you described the way that you choose what you work on as I think that I may have a similar approach but had never been conscious of it before. This is certainly something I want to consider further. Thank you again. This has been a wonderful opportunity to discuss your career, and to better know you as an HRD scholar.*

REFERENCES

Lee MM (2002) 'The Gateway Initiative: A Successful Partnership?', in *Proceedings of Forum on Competitiveness and Cooperation: The Future of Rural Cumbria and Lancashire*: 28–34. North West of England: Centre for NW Regional Studies, Lancaster University.

Lee MM (2003) (Ed) *HRD in a Complex World*. London: Routledge.

Lee MM, Letiche H, Crawshaw R, & Thomas M (1996) (Eds) *Management Education in the New Europe*. London: International Thompson Business Press.

Short D (2010) 'Better know a HRD scholar: A conversation with Monica Lee', *Human Resource Development International* 13(3)361–374.

Stewart J, Lee MM, & Poell R (2009) 'The UFHRD: Its history, purpose and activities', *New Horizons in Adult Education and Human Resource Development* 23(1)29–33.

Section 2

Aspects of Self

In the previous section I presented a typology of typologies built upon two archetypal constructs. These are derived from evolutionary psychology and are a fundamental part of how the human condition is developed. I have argued that the language we use and the concepts that we develop to build our world upon are all representations. We cannot rely upon the notion of fact as something that is pervasive and everlasting, and so we could be seen to be adrift in a world of our own making. However, our understanding of the world is guided by the basic physiological underpinnings of being human, so there are great similarities in how we construe the world. We might look at the world in different ways but our basic understanding of our existence within the world is shared. Our conceptual heritage is canonical. Our thoughts are confirmatory, we build edifices of things that normally happen, and that norm is canonical. In order to build the norm we need to know what is not normal, and so we understand the world through what it is not. One of the key things about archetypes and canonicality is that they are not and can never be real. We do not naturally think of disproving the null hypothesis. When we think in abstract terms of a cat or a table we think of an idealised cat or table, one that could never really exist. That shared canonical structure lends itself to a world where the unrealisable is seen as real. Reality becomes a world of being, a world of structure and certainty.

At the same time we live in a world of individual experience, a world of difference, and a world of different understandings. Whilst we conceptualise canonical cats and tables, we interact with the real things. If I were asked to think of a particular table I would probably refer to my kitchen table: wooden, about waist high, quite long, with four good solid square legs. You might think of something entirely different, though like me, you will probably think of a piece of furniture that can support various items on its top surface. So alongside a collective world view of structure and function we also have a world view of individuality and difference. In order to understand and work with the implications of these notions we need to adopt (or at least borrow) the language and perspective of complexity theory. This allows for a world in which the sum total is more than the constituent parts; in which things can be understood better by what they are not; in which one small action can have a disproportionate effect upon the whole; a world of process, becoming, and emergent properties. In this way I have tried to come closer to what I would see is the nature of HRD: the glue between the representations. For the want of a better term I call it holistic agency: the individual art of becoming whilst walking the boundaries of a holistic view of the world.

The first section of this book, therefore, is largely conceptual in nature. However, holistic agency is about construing both the wider picture and action within it. Similarly, in order to make sense or search out meaning we need to balance a scientific focus on facts with an understanding of the personal and individual. It is for that reason that much of the research in this book is from an autoethnographical stance. The remainder of this book is in four sections that are built around the two great archetypal systems identified in the previous section. As discussed in Chapter 3, the first fundamental dynamic played out in each person's life is that of self and other. This pervades the whole of our existence and is the core of self-development literature.

This section focuses on the first of these poles, namely self. Although this can only be understood by what it is not (other), the chapters in this section are chosen as they focus more on self than on other. I start with Chapter 7 looking at the self that emerges through interaction with the other. I start by questioning what is meant by 'self', and explore the notion of the emergent self, in which self is clarified through what one is not, and notions of self emerge from interaction with the other. This is done through negotiating entrance into a new group and trying to find out what that group stands for and what might be entailed by acceptance into the group. The way in which self is challenged and changed by other is discussed.

Chapter 8 questions the direction of the emergent self. In this I pose different possible futures as presented in science fiction writings and ask what the implications might be for the way in which we develop, work, and live. Two main futures are developed: the lean mean heroic machine is contrasted with the co-created storytelling environment. These two themes echo through the book in different guises. The process of looking to the future is not meant to imply that we are the sole agents that create our future. Instead, as we co-create our understandings of self and other so we work towards co-creating the world in which we wish to live. As with the discussion in earlier chapters it is a matter of becoming rather than being, but I suggest that some thought about what we might be becoming, about our direction of travel, is merited.

The third chapter in this section (Chapter 9) is set in a supposedly enlightened environment, within which some staff are bullied to the edge of endurance. Everything that happened here is thoroughly and completely documented with emails, letters, and internal papers. I have sanitised the account by relocating the happenings to a different country in a different sector, by cutting out several of the more horrendous incidents, and by minimising the characters involved into little more than avatars. As with the varied journey of this account itself, this chapter illustrates the self submerged by others, and honed through the sandpaper of interaction with others. As before, the self is not seen in isolation, but through interaction. In this case the interaction is toxic, leading to illness and loss of self. Such bullying and harassment is quite common, but is surprising here because of the supposedly supportive environment in which it occurred.

7 The Emergent Self

This chapter looks at ideas of developing self through interaction with other, and it is based upon my own experience of trying to become part of an academic grouping that I valued but was new to me. I start by recounting my experiences of negotiating group membership, and then interpret these through introspection and an exploration of supporting literature. The development of one's own reality is presented as a dialectic process of managing the tension between notions of selfhood and individuality, and the subconscious pressure to conform to group reality, such that self, as the 'I', develops in opposition, and feelings of inclusion or exclusion are partially indicative of self-development. This line of enquiry questions the postmodernist view that a lack of a unitary truth or knowledge indicates a lack of underlying process, suggesting instead that collectivity *necessitates* a perceived degree of unity in meaning, theory, and knowledge, and it is this that fosters the affective bonds of inclusion.

EZY: THE ENTITY

My academic friends told me that I must join Ezy—I would love it and it would be good for my research. I joined, wanting to be part of what they were part of—unsure what to expect. I went to my first Ezy conference in anticipation and trepidation, buoyed by knowing that my friends would be there. I met others, all of whom were friendly—big smiles and feelings of inclusion. I took the role of newcomer, wondering what Ezy believes in. I am told it's a nice bunch of people, and it's about extending ideas and openness. 'So is everyone welcome?' I ask. 'Oh yes . . . except for psychologists', says one, and those close share a private laugh. I ask, 'What is wrong with psychologists?' Speaking over each other, the group replied without a hint of irony: 'They label things. They believe in definitive truth. They proscribe a unitary view. They don't allow for divergence or difference'.

I am a psychologist, but I don't believe I do any of these things. I spend the day re-questioning colleagues, aware that in seeking 'Ezy' rather than individual beliefs I am, myself, guilty of imposing the unitary. I am told of belief in postmodernism and deconstruction, chaos and the value of the individual. I see in each the belief that the collective Ezy consensually supports this approach. That evening, nursing a beer, I approach one of the hierarchy. He is relatively friendly, so I start exploring these ideas. When, I wonder, does consensual belief become 'truth', an underlying stratum of unquestioned acceptance? I tell him that despite the rhetoric of difference, Ezy illustrates, to me at least, a uniformity of belief sufficient to be seen as centralised truth. He points to the level of disagreement and discussion that pervades the conference. I point to the implicit rules of engagement that are adopted. He asks me whether I have ever read Derrida, etc. I reply that I am not seeking the official view, I am interested in here and now—his personal construction of the world. He replies with a monologue, scatter-gunning references, one that avoids the personal, has been rehearsed on undergraduates, and is designed to put me in my place; he shows his 'prowess in aggressively competitive conduct' (Knights 2006: 712). Perhaps I should not have approached him at the bar—Bell & King (2010) note that 'contrary to the espoused informality and supportiveness of such occasions, they are highly charged with the exercise of academic power', and others have noted the gendered, machismic nature by which the social networks at conferences are developed (Rowlinson & Hassard 2008). I take it that I must believe (as do the great and good) that there is no truth and there is no knowledge or I must remain alien to Ezy.

I distance myself and ponder the encounters. This is a conference renowned for its commitment to reflexivity. Surely it is worth further exploration. I understand he does not embody Ezy. It was I that labelled him as such based on a snapshot, an ephemeral moment in which he chose to present something in one particular way. However, I cannot know either him or Ezy other than through my feelings—feelings of acceptance or dismissal, value or worthlessness, inclusion or exclusion. I build my knowledge upon a base of affect that links me to others. I knew that for him I was now labelled as 'not-Ezy': that through my questioning of the central and implicit tenets (the deification of references and the unifying belief in lack of unity in meaning, theory, or self) I had gone from deviancy to heresy (Harshbarger 1973): I had been Othered. By asserting views at variance with those of the collective I was instigator of my own rejection—and this sense of rejection was of me as opposed to the initial rationalised rejection of 'all psychologists'.

I want acceptance, but am unwilling to sacrifice my sense of self on the altar of unquestioning belief in order to be seen as a worthy member of the collective. On paper I am a member of Ezy: the collective, and I have equal right to pose my views, if not equal ability to influence. If I follow the rules of engagement I might be able to shift the collective towards just seeing me as deviant, rather than as a heretic outcast.

From one perspective, the remainder of this chapter is an attempt to do just that. From another, it can be seen that I am already operating from within the Ezy beliefs. The case presented above is an emotive and live mechanism adopted to provide me with entrance to the explicit topic under discussion. From a third perspective, I am questioning the way in which we research and create meaning—suggesting that collectivity demands a degree of unity in meaning, theory, and self. I shall argue, through an exploration of development, that self is an emergent phenomenon arising out of the interplay between the individual and the collective, such that feelings of inclusion and exclusion are a natural part of the developmental process.

CO-REGULATION AND INDIVIDUAL FRAMES OF REFERENCE

As discussed in Chapter 3, I support the ideas of social development as a process of co-creation and co-regulation, in which 'individuals dynamically alter their actions with respect to the ongoing and anticipated actions of their partners' (Fogel 1993: 34), and in which they negotiate a form of communication and meaning specific and new to the group (Smith 1992) and relatively inaccessible or undescribable to those who were not part of the process (see Chapter 15). I argue that relationships exist within mutually constructed conventions or frames of reference, which can be mutually dissolved by participants through ratification (Duncan 1991: 345), and thus 'communication, self and culture are just different ways of talking about relationships, different points of view on the same phenomenon' (Fogel 1993: 24), and a dynamic view of culture is facilitated (Hatch 1993). As Bell & King (2010) point out, whilst this culture is undoubtedly heterogeneous and pluralistic, comprising various competing and conflicting perspectives, it has become sufficiently cohesive to be discernible and therefore analysed. This process starts at birth and is a basal acculturation mechanism in which the underlying processes are the same whether the focus is upon family and friendship groupings, temporary micro-cultures, small or large organisations, or national culture.

Notions of Self

I am, of course, presenting a particular view of self here. The majority of autoethnographic accounts present self as a relatively uncontested concept (Burnard 2009). Self as researcher, participant, and author is central to autoethnography, and notions of authenticity rely upon the idea of a true self. Cohen (2009) suggests that existential authenticity loses its meaning in the context of relational selves and should be abandoned along with objective and constructive authenticity.

There is plenty of evidence in support of a stable sense of self (see Chapter 13 for a discussion of the perception of time). Oyserman et al. (2012) point out that people assume that people, themselves included, have a stable essence or core that predicts their behaviour, and Arkes & Kajdasz (2011) argue that who we are matters for what we do, and that what we do reflects who we are. This essential sense of self appears universal, although whether people use adjectives or action verbs to describe their traits, and whether they assume their traits apply within particular situations or across situations, may vary cross-culturally (English & Chen 2011).

Many Western individuals seek an idea of self that reflects unity and purpose (McAdams 1997), some seeking exposure to an array of cultural praxes and ways of life, following the idea of a 'true inner self'. Cohen (2009) found that whilst backpack travellers often cited the search for the inner self as the spur to their lifestyle, several recounted a greater sense of fragmentation through their travels. Similarly Ybema (2010) points out that although identities are often framed as fragmented, fluctuating, and in a state of becoming, the identity literature predominantly builds on narratives of the self that convey the experience of continuity, commonality, and distinctiveness. It can be argued that maintaining a coherent sense of self has become increasingly problematic as notions of choice replace obligation or tradition as a basis in self-definition (Cote & Levine 2002).

This resonates with the different views of development discussed in Chapter 3. On the one hand we have the idea of an inner self and notions of self-actualisation, self-realisation, self-fulfilment, discovering one's self, finding one's self, and self-development, and on the other the relational or cosmopolitan self of late modernity.

Self and Identity-Work

The last 15 years has seen a great increase in research around self and identity; these terms are often used as if they were synonyms, and are commonly explored under identity theory. From our first inklings of self-awareness to our final reflections on the meaning of life, our social interactions define, nurture, and alter our sense of self (Swann et al. 2010). These views retain a core of self with identities as its parts. We talk and act as if our sense of self is stable, but that it is quite natural to have multiple identities, and for these to change. As McDonald (2013: 140) says, 'My personal "coming-out" tale illustrates that identity categories cannot be taken as stable and clearly identifiable. Rather, people's identifications with particular categories of identity can change, and the meanings of these categories are contextually dependent on the personal trajectory of every person who comes to identify with a given category'.

A more sociological approach is to talk of it as 'identity-work'. This is seen as the discourse-based ongoing production of a coherent self, though frequently fragmented, shifting and insecure, with conscious as well as unconscious dynamics (Alvesson 2010). This builds upon Lacanian psychoanalysis, in which everything that is real and unique about a subject is not what is articulated but that which is systematically repressed and excluded, such that identity is about not what is most intimate to a subject but what is missing, or 'extimacy' (Parker 2005: 172). Therefore, although identity work is about constructing the self, this self is an extimacy, a misrepresentation and an illusion (Fink 1995). Language is given a privileged place in notions of identity work, as providing symbolic order formed by social conventions so that articulations of self use signifiers that are not of one's own making and do not represent what is real for that person. Thus individuals unconsciously desire the missing real that always eludes them, so that whatever is consciously articulated as identity or desire is instead an imaginary attempt at obtaining the unobtainable real (Hoedemakers & Keegan 2010). This approach holds that identity is constructed in and through discourse that is generic to all participants, but that each person takes a different and unique position to this discourse (Morrison & Macleod 2013).

These accounts of identity work do, of course, assume that we are language: that our conceptual structures are founded on nothing other than language—a position I contest (see Chapters 3, 4, and 13). However, the importance of a negative ontology for identity work, and the way in which identity is seen to be separate from self, are important for my line of thought. It is perhaps through discussion of identity and identity work, rather than self, that the balance between self and other that I discuss in the previous chapters becomes more apparent. In my focus on self, in this chapter, I am not ignoring the great body of work on identity but seeking to explore the mirage of the stable core.

Personal Norm

I have pointed to different views of what self might be and it would appear that even with a clear, relatively permanent, and singular sense of self there is general acceptance of the dynamic interaction between self and society that influences both. Social norms are seen to help maintain social order (Gintis 2004) and emerge through internalisation in a flexible, dynamic, multistep process through which they are also de-internalised (or compliance-blocked) (Hassin et al. 2009). The idea of a personal norm allows for individual style or preference alongside that which is socially created. It thus accommodates genetically and physiologically related difference in the way people perceive and judge the world and themselves. This norm is not static—the actor becomes the character. It recognises the idea of self as dynamic yet perceptually identifiable, thereby limiting any form of measurement to comparison, either with self or perceptions of others, and denying the possibility of statements of the absolute. It also allows for individual difference in the way in which the learner-as-researcher makes sense of their experience holistically, such that their approach to meaning and their perception of their history and anticipation of the future will influence their current learning. Co-regulation, therefore, recognises that individuals construe their own frames of reference (similar to Piaget's (1972) schemata or Kelly's (1955) constructs), but suggests that these frames need to be dynamic and continually developed in the light of shifting social experiences, without which rigidity of self and relationships will ensue.

The impact of others is therefore an important element in the development of such frames and of the processes through which the world is made sense of. Our notion of self, however, is also influenced through the underlying processes of perception and judgement (Jung 1938). Perception is the process by which individuals make sense (consciously or subconsciously) of their surroundings, and is thus mediated by previous understandings, expectations and anticipations, memory, and unconscious influences (from the 'promissory notes' of metaphor, myth, and rhetoric (Soyland 1994) to primal drives). Judgement is the process of deciding which of the many alternative perceptival interpretations available at any one instant to adopt as reality. Judgement is also, therefore, influenced by previous understandings, etc., and is more likely to be based upon post hoc rationalisation than on the traditionally accepted view of scientifically weighing up the alternatives and rationally choosing the best option in advance of the final decision. Similar processes, termed 'perceived control' and 'self-efficacy', arise in work on reasoned action (Fishbein & Ajzen 1995), in which the two variables are empirically distinguishable (Terry & O'Leary 1995), co-vary to provide a personal norm (Parker et al. 1995), and are also applicable to organisations (Elliott et al. 1995).

Self and other are often entwined in such development. Self-expansion theory suggests that individuals are fundamentally motivated to grow and improve the self by acquiring new identities, enhancing capabilities, developing new perspectives, and gaining resources (Aron et al. 2013). Such expansion is primarily held to be through close relationships in which the identities, resources, and perspectives of the romantic partner become intertwined and cognitively linked to the self (Aron et al. 2004), and, if close, the other's outcomes can be treated as belonging to the self (Mattingly & Lewandowski 2013).

The Development of Social Cognition

Interacting with others and the search for self-expansion could be considered a core part of our nature. We are influenced by our own physiology—I pointed out earlier that our understanding of our self is influenced by our interpretation of our own body language, and we go through defined and definite changes as our self and our understanding of others mature. One of the core abilities of interpersonal functioning is to be able to understand intentions, beliefs, and emotions, and so predict other people's behaviour and adjust behaviour adequately (Vetter et al. 2013). Two key areas of social cognition are the understanding of others' mental states or theory of mind (Perner 1991) and recognition of emotion in others (Adolphs 2003). However, it is worth noting that both develop slowly and do not mature until late adolescence. Young children just a few months old start to distinguish and respond to basic emotions, such as happiness and sadness, and they continue to develop gradually throughout childhood, with a large increase between 5 and 10 years of age (Gao & Maurer 2010). At around 4 years old children start to develop a theory of mind (Wellman et al. 2001) and at around 6 years old this ability becomes more elaborated, with the development of a higher order theory of mind, which is necessary to understand complex mental states like irony (Happé 1994). More complex, so-called belief-based emotions such as embarrassment, guilt, or pride (which are closely connected to mental states, such as intentions or beliefs) are first recognised from about 7 years old (Hadwin & Perner 1991), and a protracted development of higher order theory of mind has been found at about 8 to 10 years, when children begin to understand social faux pas (Rieffe et al. 2005).

There are fewer data available on how these skills develop during adolescence. Magnetic resonance imaging studies show that the brain regions involved in social cognition, including the prefrontal and temporal cortex, undergo the most pronounced and protracted transformation (Gogtay et al. 2004) across adolescence. Adolescents show higher activity in the medial prefrontal cortex (a key brain area for social cognition) than adults (Guyer et al. 2008). It is during this period of major physical, cognitive, and socio-emotional changes that the individual negotiates the self-other divide. Adolescents become more self-conscious (Steinberg & Morris 2001) and develop more complex peer relationships (Lerner & Steinberg 2004). The mature levels of social cognition necessary for complex peer relationships and the possibilities and constraints of social interaction are achieved at about 18 years of age, but until then problematic social behaviour in adolescence is part of the developmental process (Steinberg 2005).

LEARNING AND TRANSFORMATION

This steady maturation of social behaviour, and the drive for self-expansion, go hand in hand with learning that occurs within the whole person—the social being, the perceiver, the judger, the reflector, and the theoriser. It also implies a distinction between cumulative learning (more of the same) and developmental learning (transformative changes). Within the terminology of complexity, learning can be seen as ontologically weak and takes place within the system's existing boundaries, and as such poses no threat to its operational coherence, whilst transformation is ontologically strong, forces a change of boundary, and threatens the system's operational coherence and autonomy. This can be seen in the light of Bartunek & Moch's (1987) description of second- and third-order change, in which second-order change attempts are designed to phrase in particular frameworks in which events are understood (schemata) and phase out others, whereas third-order change attempts aim to help learners develop the capacity to identify and change their own schemata as they see fit. Similar notions of shift can be seen in double-loop/triple-loop learning (Hawkins 1991) and the Rogerian approach, in which a facilitator helps others to help themselves (Rogers 1969). Thus the movement from second- to third-order change involves a transformative shift in approach through some process, either internal or externally facilitated, that enables critical observation and evaluation of the experience, such that the learner is able to distance themselves from it rather than replay it—experiencing becomes a way of restoring meaning to life (Vasilyuk 1984).

Transformation is therefore seen as an active process in which the system (individual or group) is continually reanalysing their role in the creation and development of the processes they are part of, and in doing so is also confronting their own ideas, unsurfaced assumptions, biases, and fears (Argyris 1990). Acting in this manner involves the knowledge and acceptance of a wider repertoire of ways of being and the maintenance of a core of ethicality and strong self-concept (Snell 1993). This is similar to Lane & DiStefano's (1992: 394) commitment in relativism, 'in which a person understands the relativistic nature of the world, but makes a commitment to a set of values, beliefs, and a way of behaving within this expanded world view'. It requires individuals and organisations to create their own models and derive their own views of the dynamics of change, rather than rely on uncritically utilising off-the-shelf accounts of the future (Slaughter 1993).

Transformation is also painful. Schemata are disbanded, the individual's feelings of self-worth are challenged, inconsistencies are exposed, and a contented life stance overturned. It involves stepping outside the known, and cannot therefore be planned for. How can one know what the result of the unknown will be? It is therefore a process forced upon the system by changing circumstance, by which the system's frame of reference is found to be no longer adequate to represent existence (as the system understands it), entailing a need for deconstruction and recomposition. Romanelli & Tushman (1994) offer empirical support for rapid, discontinuous change in organisations being driven by major environmental changes. Similarly, Vasilyuk (1984) suggests that individual transformation is driven by the need for crisis resolution. Transformation, rather than change, therefore is discontinuous and is driven by conflict derived from either internal or external sources

Influence, Control, and Group Membership

Transformative conflict is frequently a result of the processes of influence, control, and manipulation—it occurs in relation to others and is normally a relational process. Control is more about explicit rigidity of frame and the imposition of this on others, denying the existence of their own frames. Manipulation is more about implicit rigidity of frame, such that it is presented to others as dynamic, yet the frame itself is rigid—the flexibility is only within limited and non-frame-threatening parameters. The distinction between the two is similar to Reed's (1992) distinction between control-by-repression and control-by-seduction. Influence is about flexibility of frame, the process through which individual frames most commonly accommodate co-regulation. Theoretically, we all have equal ability (and right?) to influence; however, whether it is gender, race, birth, or some other divider, some individuals are given (by the remainder of the group) differential power to influence the path of group development, thus generating at all times, leaders and followers in the continuing emergence and co-regulation of implicit group norms.

A minimal level of trust, as a key antecedent to cooperative behaviour (Smith et al. 1995), is an important prerequisite of implicit group membership. However, trust is based upon both perceptions of competence and affective bonds (McAllister 1995) and the potential entrant would need to be able to persuade others that their actions are based upon citizenship rather than ingratiation (Eastman 1994), building deeper trust through a process of equitable social exchange (Konovsky & Pugh 1994, see also Chapter 11).

The implicit norms within a group are built through subtle processes of which many group members might not be aware. The groups I talk about here could be family units, groups of friends, work teams, organisations, nations—the size of the group might differ but I contend that the subtle processes of assertion, intimidation, and self-censorship are the same. Studies of organisational culture have traditionally focused on the symbolic and discursive practices through which values, beliefs, and norms are established and communicated (Knights & Thanem 2005). However, culture is thus not just about words, but also about conduct and the 'embodied dispositions it demands and nurtures' (Wacquant 2005: 466). The body is the medium through which socialisation into a culture is achieved (Shilling 2007). As I discuss in Chapter 3, Connolly (2004) documents how the raising of an eyebrow prevented badly needed organisational change for several years.

The different ways in which groups choose to regulate themselves can be seen as the making explicit of such implicit norms of influence and, as I argue in Chapter 3, HRM can be seen as the explicit management of explicit norms within the wider field of HRD. An understanding of who is part of the group and who has the right to influence the boundaries of implicit and explicit group membership therefore gains theoretical and practical importance. For example, accounts of the Japanese philosophy of lifelong employment for organisational members rely upon the raft of casual workers upon which the organisation relies being defined out of existence (Hui et al. 1991). Co-regulation implies that migrant labourers, as contributing towards the organisation, must be seen as participants within it. However, it would be unrealistic to assume that those with peripheral involvement have equal right (to those central to its existence) to influence the future of the organisation. Similarly, Eastman (1994) found that supervisors' behaviour was influenced by their perception of the level of the individual's organisational citizenship behaviour. Supervisors, therefore, can stand as judge and jury on controlling implicit group membership.

Those given the power to influence the acceptable-for-group-membership criteria are likely to be concerned with the preservation of their own framework, and justifiably feel that if someone threatens their frame they will also threaten the collective frame of the group. As the group moves towards cohesion the parameters that support the choice of membership become less changeable (Iles et al. 1990), thus acceptable behaviour becomes rigidified. The potential entrant increasingly becomes seen as an agent of individuation, distinct from the collective will, and a potentially unmanageable and destructive force. Such rigidity leads to difficulty in socialising new members and to the creation of minority groups (Weldon & Weingart 1993).

Othering

Earlier in this chapter I said that I had felt as if I were 'Othered'. I'm referring to the process by which the individual or group is cast into the role of the Other, thereby enhancing sense of group, or self, and reinforcing one's own identity through opposition to the Other. Gabriel (2012) points out that this is a process that goes beyond mere scapegoating and denigration—it denies the Other those defining characteristics of the Same and ultimately any entitlement to human rights. He suggests that the person or group that is Othered is the one in closest physical and symbolic proximity, as it is seen to present a major threat to one's identity and pride. It could be argued that Othering has become core to Western identity and culture (Said 1994) in which many groups are dehumanised on the grounds of race, religion, gender, sexuality, and so on and thus become legitimate targets for bullying (see Chapter 9), exploitation, oppression, and genocide (Blok 2001). Bell & King (2010: 440) point out that 'theoretical sensitivity to power relations does not necessarily prevent participation in practices that are excluding to others or translate into a commitment to transform oppressive, exclusionary practices'.

The Opposing Self

On the one hand I have described Othering and the dehumanising process by which individuals and groups can bolster their sense of self, and on the other I am arguing that transformative processes occur through conflict and that we better know ourselves, and establish our cultures, through opposition. Perhaps one of the lessons of life is to learn how to think of the other without also thinking of them as lesser (Reedy 2008; Chapter 12).

Both the individual and the group would prefer to maintain their existing frames of reference, and expend effort in order to do so. The individual is torn—it is important for the individual's sense of selfhood to maintain life as they know it, yet co-regulated socialisation necessitates elements of reframing. The easier, though non-transformative, route would be for the individual to only seek acceptance from those who are known to be similar—to see life as they do. Similarly, the easy, though non-transformative, route for the group is to only accept implicit membership (regardless of explicit membership-on-paper) from those who are trusted not to unduly influence the group frame. The fact that people can communicate cross-culturally implies that there are fundamental processes common to the different parties—ones that allow a common language of comparison. At a lower level of accretion the conscious or subconscious co-regulation of the creation and maintenance of processual rules of communication can be seen to generate locally bound micro-cultures to which all parties can adhere without, necessarily, sacrificing their root culture, and thus the surfacing of assumptions between members is part of the organisational learning process as well as part of an individual's learning.

The development of selfhood and identity is a statement of individuality in which each individual defines their existence within their own terms. Whilst there exist processes by which individuals collude in the progressive merging of their individual perceptions to create social groupings, the development of one's own reality (cf. Construct Theory) is a process of managing the tension between individuality, and the underlying co-regulatory processes, or subconscious pressure to conform to group reality. Thus the co-regulated reification of implicit group norms leads to alienation, restatements of individuality, and the challenging of the group norms.

At a fundamental level, the self exists in opposition, and thus group development can be inspired, potentially, by the opposing self, thereby providing a descriptive mechanism for dialectical development. Extrapolating from this, there appear to be two different forms of development—that of the individual in opposition, and that of the individual within consensual group development (Fournier & Payne 1994). I suggest that the first leads primarily to individuation, creativity, and innovation, whilst the second leads primarily to the consolidation of group vision and identity. Neither group nor individual development can occur in isolation from the other. In both cases change in isolation might occur, and take the form of further learning; however, development or transformation implies a change of schemata, the adoption of a different world view, and thus requires external input as a catalyst.

Frames of reference, however, are not known in the absolute cognitive sense—much of the knowing occurs through pivotal encounters with the frames of others, encounters that emphasise previously unknown dissimilarity and disjunction. Whether intended or not, encounter with others holds the potential for transformation—potential for challenge to existing frames of reference through tension between self and socialisation, or between group identity and the dissenting individual. The pain and conflict of transformation is therefore closely associated with negotiating group membership and influence, with feelings of inclusion and exclusion.

Ezy and Me

I have resorted to the theories, findings, and constructs of others in an attempt to rationalise my Ezy-related experience and create a debate sufficient to engage others in a process of mutual exploration. I have not been persuaded to accept the truth that there is no truth. I know that we each create our own versions of truth and knowledge, suggesting that the co-regulated processes of social development involve a negotiation of individual frameworks such that truth and knowledge are social constructions and the influencing of the accepted truth and knowledge is a political process. I cannot see anything sufficiently unusual or revelatory about this to merit the assumption that psychologists or other misguided individuals might not accept it. Our formative experiences are based around comparing our versions of truth and knowledge with those of others, and thus it is something we experience from birth. Similarly, something else we experience from birth, and common to all, are the underlying processes associated with the unique emergence of the individual through the developmental tension between the individualistic-self and social-being, balanced through the creation, modification, and rejection of many identities along the way. The notion of societal co-regulation necessitates both underlying processes and unique frames of reference.

My Ezy-related experiences illustrate these points. I joined Ezy (paid my money and became an explicit member) in the hope that I would fit in. My friends represented to me a generic notion of Ezy: the entity, which had a life separate from each of them as members of Ezy, but one that they supported by their presence and influence. I, as an outsider, had no such common framework. I was not yet an implicit member of Ezy—for that to happen there needed to be some co-regulation/co-creation of frameworks.

I set myself the inferential task of framework comparison—I was searching for implicit, dynamic, context-specific, and largely subconscious and undescribable parameters, whose influence I could only judge by my own feelings of rightness and inclusion or otherwise. As I was labelling Ezy as an entity, others were labelling me. The difference was that I was seeking inclusion whilst others were de-individualising me into the generic disliked 'psychologists'. In acknowledging that neither I nor Ezy was a rigidly defined and stable entity I attempted to merit implicit membership by an assertion of selfhood whilst seeking similar assertions from others. Those I knew and valued appeared willing to accept my exploration at face value—exchanging thoughts and opinions such that I felt a sense of commonalty and the synergetic creation of something over and above our existing frames, something personal to us though located in Ezy. The final encounter highlights this. Although I told myself that I was approaching this person as an individual and attempted to act in that way, my underlying motivation was less about friendship and more in line with my noting that he was a representative of Ezy hierarchy—someone who had been given the power to influence the implicit framework of Ezy. Despite my surface attempt at the melding of frameworks the underlying message was clearly one of conflict, and in labelling him (to myself) as an influential subject I gave him the power (which he accepted) to call on the wider interpretation of Ezy as an inflexible edifice in order to emphasise his position inside the temple and thus close the doors in my face. I suspect that, within the terms of the previous section, he did not trust me and saw my behaviour as ingratiating rather than evidence of citizenship.

Gaining Acceptance

The question remains, however—how can one gain feelings of citizenship if, as evidenced here, the implicit criteria are interpretative and emotionally based? There are four main ways in which to approach this. The easiest way would be to adopt an *egocentric* stance, a reassertion of self, and redefinition of Ezy as those-I-already-feel-included-by—in other words, by assuming inclusion and by ignoring and discounting a section of the population that might wish to exclude. Alternatively, one could adopt a *fragmented* approach—deny aspects of self and become a corporate acolyte (Hopfl 1992) spouting the ritualistic dogma despite its clash with experiences and understanding, accepting a schism in one's multi-dialogical framework. Another possible route to acceptance would be *manipulative,* generating apparent acceptance of the dogma, whilst, through an awareness of the dynamic and multi-dialogical nature of Ezy, attempting to seduce each of the parts sufficiently such that the whole comes to accept a modified framework. A fourth approach could be that of co-regulated *transformation*—in which one lets go of the self, trusting that there will be support for one's fragile selfhood through the pain of schematic change, and hoping that others will join the transformation—dynamically shifting the joint perceptions. Having recently played a part in the merger of two firms with different cultures I have witnessed all four approaches at various times, but not as neatly categorised as here!

This chapter represents an attempt to unpick, through empirical and theoretical evidence, some of the complexity inherent in organisational life—a life in which explicit and implicit group membership often fail to coincide. A life in which actors are increasingly being expected to perform across a range of co-regulated micro-cultural boundaries, each of which entails a shifting of selfhood. A life in which individuals and groups are being exhorted to develop, and transform, as if it were a bounded process. A life that often fails to recognise the affective import of these requests, fails to accept the inevitability and importance of emotional response, and thus fails to see the relevance of support mechanisms—preferring instead to rely upon palliatives, denial, and crisis management. If nothing else, this chapter suggests that negative emotions (feelings of exclusion, lack of trust, denial, rejection, and conflict) are an integral aspect of the transformative process, that they are part of the tension between self and other, and thus that they provide a useful arena for individual and group reflection.

REFERENCES

Note: Ezy is a pseudonym for the group from which these data are derived; however, I have had many similar experiences, and thus it also represents a type—a group-into-which-I-seek-inclusion.

Adolphs R (2003) 'Cognitive neuroscience of human social behaviour', *Nature Reviews Neuroscience* 4: 165–178.

Alvesson M (2010) 'Self-doubters, strugglers, storytellers, surfers and others: Images of self-identities in organizational studies', *Human Relations* 63: 193–217.

Argyris C (1990) *Overcoming Organisational Defences*. Boston, MA: Allyn and Bacon.

Arkes HR & Kajdasz J (2011) 'Intuitive theories of behavior', in Fischoff B & Chauvin C (Eds) *Intelligence Analysis: Behavioral and Social Scientific Foundations:* 143–168. Washington, DC: National Academic Press.

Aron A, Lewandowski GW, Mashek D, & Aron EN (2013) 'The Self-Expansion Model of Motivation and Cognition in Close Relationships', in Simpson J & Campbell L (Eds) *The Oxford Handbook of Close Relationships:* 90–115. Oxford: Oxford University Press.

Aron A, McLaughlin-Volpe T, Mashek D, Lewandowski G, Wright SC, & Aron EN (2004) 'Including others in the self', *European Review of Social Psychology* 15: 101–132.

Bartunek JM & Moch MK (1987) 'First-order, second-order, and third-order change and organisation development interventions: A cognitive approach', *Journal of Applied Behavioural Science* 23: 483–500.

Bell E & King D (2010) 'The elephant in the room: Critical management studies conferences as a site of body pedagogics', *Management Learning* 41(4): 429–442.

Blok A (2001) *Honour and Violence*. Cambridge: Polity.

Burnard P (2009) 'A reply to Short and Grants' paper: "Burnard (2007): Autoethnography or a realist account?"', *Journal of Psychiatric and Mental Health Nursing* 16: 670–671.

Cohen SA (2009) *The Search for 'Self' for Lifestyle Travellers*. Ph.D. Thesis. New Zealand: University of Otago.

Connolly M (2004) *An Investigation into the Generative Dynamics of Organization*. Ph.D. Thesis. Lancaster, UK: Lancaster University.

Cote JE & Levine CG (2002) *Identity Formation, Agency, and Culture*. Mahwah, NJ: Lawrence Erlbaum.

Dewey J (1938) (reprint 2007) *Experience and Education*. New York: Simon and Schuster.

Duncan S (1991) 'Convention and conflict in the child's interaction with others', *Developmental Review* 11: 337–367.

Eastman K (1994) 'In the eyes of the beholder: An attributional approach to ingratiation and organisational citizenship behaviour', *Academy of Management Journal* 37: 1379–1391.

Elliott R, Jobber D, & Sharp J (1995) 'Using the theory of reasoned action to understand organisational behaviour: The role of belief salience', *British Journal of Social Psychology* 43: 161–172.

English T & Chen S (2011) 'Self-concept consistency and culture: The differential impact of two forms of consistency', *Personality and Social Psychology Bulletin* 37: 838–849.

Fink B (1995) *The Lacanian Subject*. Princeton, NJ: Princeton University Press.

Fishbein MJ & Ajzen I (1995) *Belief, Attitude, Intention and Behaviour*. Reading, MA: Addison-Wesley.

Fogel A (1993) *Developing through Relationships*. Hemel Hempstead: Harvester Wheatsheaf.

Fournier V & Payne R (1994) 'Change in self construction during the transition from university to employment: A personal construct psychology approach', *Journal of Occupational and Organisational Psychology* 67: 297–314.

Gabriel Y (2012) 'Organizations in a state of darkness: Towards a theory of organizational miasma', *Organization Studies* 33(9)1137–1152.

Gao X & Maurer D (2010) 'A happy story: Developmental changes in children's sensitivity to facial expressions of varying intensities', *Journal of Experimental Child Psychology* 107: 67–86.

Gintis H (2004) 'The genetic side of gene-culture coevolution: internalization of norms and prosocial emotions', *Journal of Economic Behavior and Organization* 53: 57–67.

Gogtay N, Giedd JN, Lusk L, Hayashi KM, Greenstein D, Vaituzis AC, et al. (2004) 'Dynamic mapping of human cortical development during childhood through early adulthood', *Proceedings of the National Academy of Sciences* 101: 8174–8179.

Guyer AE, Monk CS, McClure-Tone EB, Nelson EE, Roberson-Nay R, Adler AD, et al. (2008) 'A developmental examination of amygdala response to facial expressions', *Journal of Cognitive Neuroscience* 20: 1565–1582.

Hadwin J & Perner J (1991) 'Pleased and surprised: Children's cognitive theory of emotion', *British Journal of Developmental Psychology* 9: 215–234.

Happé FGE (1994) 'An advanced test of theory of mind—Understanding of story characters thoughts and feelings by able autistic, mentally-handicapped, and normal children and adults', *Journal of Autism and Developmental Disorders* 24: 129–154.

Harshbarger D (1973) 'The individual and the social order: Notes on the management of heresy and deviance in complex organisations', *Human Relations* 26: 251–269.

Hassin RR, Bargh JA, & Zimmerman S (2009) 'Automatic and flexible: The case of non-conscious goal pursuit', *Social Cognition* 27(1)20–36.

Hatch MJ (1993) 'The dynamics of organisational culture', *Academy of Management Review* 18: 657–693.

Hawkins P (1991) 'The spiritual dimension of the learning organisation', *Management Education and Development* 22: 172–187.

Hoedemakers C & Keegan A (2010) 'Performance pinned down: Studying subjectivity and the language of performance', *Organization Studies* 31(8): 1021–1044.

Hopfl H (1992) 'The making of the corporate acolyte: Some thoughts on charismatic leadership and the reality of organisational commitment', *Journal of Management Studies* 29: 24–33.

Hui CH, Triandis HC, & Yee C (1991) 'Cultural differences in reward allocation: Is collectivism the explanation?', *British Journal of Social Psychology* 30: 145–157.

Iles P, Mabey C, & Robertson I (1990) 'HRM practices and employee commitment: Possibilities, pitfalls and paradoxes', *British Journal of Management* 1: 147–157.

Jung CG (1938) 'Psychology and Religion: West and East', In *Collected Works II*: 167, cited in Jung CG (1961: 416) *Memories, Dreams and Reflections*. London: Flamingo.

Kelly G (1955) *A Theory of Personality: The Psychology of Personal Constructs*. New York: Norton.

Knights D (2006) 'Authority at Work: Reflections and Recollections', *Organization Studies* 27(5):699–720.

Knights D & Thanem T (2005) 'Embodying Emotional Labour', in Morgan D, Brandth B, & Kvande E (Eds) *Gender, Bodies and Work*: 31–43. Aldershot: Ashgate.

Konovsky MA & Pugh SD (1994) 'Citizenship behaviour and social exchange', *Academy of Management Journal* 37: 656–669.

Lane H & DiStefano J (1992) *International Management Behaviour*. Boston: PWS-KENT Publishing Company.

Lerner R & Steinberg L (2004) *Handbook of Adolescent Psychology*. New York, NY: Wiley.

Mattingly BA & Lewandowski Jr GW (2013) 'An expanded self is a more capable self', *Self and Identity* 12(6)621–634.

McAdams DP (1997) 'The Case for Unity in the (post)modern Self: A Modest Proposal', in Ashmore RD & Jussim L (Eds) *Self and Identity: Fundamental Issues*: 46–78. New York: Oxford University Press.

McAllister DJ (1995) 'Affect- and cognition-based trust as foundations for interpersonal cooperation in organisations', *Academy of Management Journal* 38: 24–59.

McDonald J (2013) 'Coming out in the field: A queer reflexive account of shifting researcher identity', *Management Learning* 44(2)127–143.

Morrison T & Macleod C (2013) 'A performative-performance analytical approach: Infusing Butlerian theory into the narrative-discursive method', *Qualitative Inquiry* 19(8)566–577.

Oyserman D, Elmore K, & Smith G (2012) 'Self, self-concept, and identity', in Leary MR & Tangney JP (Eds) *Handbook of Self and Identity*: 69–104. New York: The Guilford Press.

Parker D, Manstead ASR, & Stradling SG (1995) 'Extending the theory of planned behaviour: The role of the personal norm', *British Journal of Social Psychology* 34: 127–138.

Parker I (2005) 'Lacanian discourse analysis in psychology', *Theory & Psychology* 15(2)163–182.

Perner J (1991) *Understanding the Representational Mind*. Cambridge, MA: MIT Press and Bradford Books.

Piaget J (1972) *The Child's Conception of the World*. Totowa, NJ: Littlefield, Adams.

Reed MI (1992) *The Sociology of Organisations*. London: Sage.

Reedy P (2008) 'Mirror, mirror, on the wall: Reflecting on the ethics and effects of a Collective Critical Management Studies Identity Project', *Management Learning* 39(1)57–72.

Rieffe C, Terwogt MM, & Cowan R (2005) 'Children's understanding of mental states as causes of emotions', *Infant and Child Development* 14: 259–272.

Rogers CR (1969) *Freedom to Learn*. Columbus: Charles E. Merrill.

Romanelli E & Tushman ML (1994) 'Organisational transformation as punctuated equilibrium: An empirical test', *Academy of Management Journal* 37: 1141–1166.

Rowlinson M & Hassard J (2008) 'How come the Critters came to be teaching in business schools? Sociology, politics and Punk Rock', *Critical Management Studies Seminar Series,* February, Manchester, England.

Said EW (1994) *Culture and Imperialism.* London: Chatto and Windus.

Shilling C (2007) 'Sociology and the Body: Classical Traditions and New Agendas', in Shilling C (Ed) *Embodying Sociology: Retrospect, Progress and Prospects:* 1–18. Oxford: Blackwell/Sociological Review.

Slaughter R (1993) 'Looking for the real "megatrends"', *Futures* 25(8)351–364.

Smith KG, Carroll SJ, & Ashford SJ (1995) 'Intra- and interorganisational cooperation: Toward a research agenda', *Academy of Management Journal* 38: 7–233.

Smith PB (1992) 'Organisational behaviour and national cultures', *British Journal of Management* 3:39–51.

Snell R (1993) *Developing Skills for Ethical Management.* London: Chapmann Hall.

Soyland AJ (1994) *Psychology as Metaphor.* London: Sage.

Steinberg L (2005) *Adolescence.* New York: McGraw-Hill.

Steinberg L & Morris AS (2001) 'Adolescent development', *Annual Review of Psychology* 52: 83–110.

Swann WB, Rand J, & Bosson JK (2010) 'Self and Identity', in Fiske ST, Gilbert DT, & Lindzey G (Eds) *Handbook of Social Psychology:* 589–628. New York: Wiley.

Terry DJ & O'Leary JE (1995) 'The theory of planned behaviour: The effects of perceived behavioural control and self-efficacy', *British Journal of Social Psychology* 34: 199–220.

Vasilyuk F (1984) *The Psychology of Experiencing: The Resolution of Life's Critical Situations.* Hemel Hempstead: Harvester Wheatsheaf.

Vetter NC, Leipold K, Kliegel M, Phillips LH, & Altgassen M (2013) 'Ongoing development of social cognition in adolescence', *Child Neuropsychology* 19(6)615–629.

Wacquant L (2005) 'Carnal connections: On embodiment, apprenticeship and membership', *Qualitative Sociology* 28(4)445–474.

Weldon E & Weingart LR (1993) 'Group goals and group performance', *British Journal of Social Psychology* 32: 307–334.

Wellman HM, Cross D, & Watson J (2001) 'Meta-analysis of theory-of-mind development: The truth about false belief', *Child Development* 72: 655–684.

Ybema S (2010) 'Talk of change: Temporal contrasts and collective identities', *Organization Studies* 31: 481–503.

8   The Future Self

Please see Chapter 20 for details of the development of this chapter.

THE STORY

I wish to tell you a tale of love and hate, escapism and addiction, and of how an idealistic young girl grew into a woman who feels the need to justify idealism. I shall tell it of myself, but, as you are listening, multiply the one to many—as many have taken the journey. This tale might, at first, appear divorced from the reality of organisations, but it has a bearing on it and we will come to it before the end.

I have, since early childhood, been fascinated by visions of other ways of being. I started on a diet of mythology. Despite being dyslexic I was a keen reader (though a very bad writer) and from the age of seven or eight I would scour the local library to feed my habit. Initially my parents thought nothing of it; if anything they were pleased that I appeared precocious in my tastes. I devoured mythology, moving through the Nordic complexity of heroes and villains, in which the individual's life is led in a blaze of glory, the supporting cast benefits from reflected light, and the hero (and his genetic line) is remembered to eternity, fighting to the cry of death (and eternal reward) before dishonour. I then widened my repertoire to include myths that focused more upon environmental symbiosis—Indian, Native American, and Eskimo myths in which all things have their place and name, a rabbit is as 'valuable' as a man (or woman), and death is an inevitable part of life. These were less acceptable to my parents, as they accorded less with the way in which they viewed life, but were seen as a minor aberration on my part.

As I grew older I appreciated that there are many different ways of representing our past, that the import of these was often mutually exclusive, and that, despite the normality of my existence relative to my acquired mythological heritage, my life within the family was re-accountable within mythological terms—family histories were micro-myths conceived and retold as control mechanisms in order to influence the future. Mythology became timeless. Though rooted in the past, it played an active part in my present and in moulding my future.

By the age of twelve I was hooked on science fiction. My allegiance to myths located in history shifted to myths of the future—to ways of envisaging future 'realities' and the practical, ethical, and philosophical implications these might have for my present and future existence. I became less discreet, and started to withdraw from family life (particularly the chores) in order to read in privacy. My pocket money disappeared at second-hand book stalls and I was truly addicted. My father (being a practical sort of person) saw it as infantile escapism and pressurised me to break the pattern. It did become a form of escapism—there was one tall yew tree that only I was able to climb, and I spent many hours up there, on level with a wild dove's nest, cool in the summer's heat whilst my siblings searched for me; or tossed around in the autumn storms whilst my parents shouted for me—none thought to look upwards. Regardless of the changing circumstances I invariably had a tatty paperback hidden up there with me. I would read and think, and read and think, and escape. As reality became more unpleasant I became increasingly involved in alternatives—my life became one of 'what if?'.

By fourteen I saw my life in terms of control and rebellion, hate and rejection. I was different in many ways—a rebellious female in an intensely patriarchal household; a doubter of organised belief in a strictly religious community; an idealist in a world of practicality—in short, I questioned. I was not alone in the questioning process—my siblings also questioned, but each of us was alone in the form of release we sought, and it took nearly twenty years before we could start to talk about it. Exploring the threads woven by the past, perceptions of these, and the links between these and alternative forms of future, was now central to my way of thinking and my identity. A life in which I was continually denigrated for this approach was intolerable, and I (and my habit) was a focal point for conflict. When things got really dirty and I was disinherited, one of the reasons given for this was my mental instability as evidenced by my liking for science fiction. This monologue, therefore, partially represents an attempt to justify such mental instability.

Futuristic Fiction

To those who are not addicts it is hard to describe the fascination that drives the addiction, or even the wide range of forms that science fiction can take. I do not consider those who read science fiction for the adventures, the daring-do, or the tales of glory to be real addicts. Some forms of science fiction do contain these elements, but readers who search for these can also obtain them elsewhere—they are not essential to the genre. Similarly, science fiction to me is not directly about fictional scientific advances (that may be prophetic, as in H. G. Wells's writing), or voyeuristic—whether sexually (as in John Norman's Gor books) or about difference from the 'norm', as inferred by fascination with little green men from Mars. In fact, the words 'science fiction' are a misnomer, relevant only to a small element of the genre yet applied more widely as a relatively meaningless form of categorisation.

Examples of this futuristic fiction can be seen in what would be more usually termed science fiction and science fantasy, but can also be found in more traditional sources, such as the excellent *Seven Days in New Crete* by Robert Graves (1949). This genre is about creating and exploring the implications of alternative forms of reality, which are, for the sake of convenience, normally set in the future. In reading these works I find that my understanding of my own existence is enhanced—rather as living in a different culture enforces understanding of one's own. It can be argued that all works of art that capture our imagination do so by illuminating elements of our existence—to do this is not the sole prerogative of futuristic fiction. There is, however, something about relaxing the constraints of reality (as defined by our present circumstance) that is both seductive and facilitative. Seductive, in that it fires the imagination whilst being sufficiently divorced from reality to minimise feelings of personal threat, and facilitative, in that the inherent symbolism and mythology addresses a subconscious level of awareness that shifts perceptions in a way that is appreciated upon later reflection. 'Science Fiction writers are limited only by human potential, not human actualities. SF can serve to show women, and men, how large that potential can be' (Sargent 1977: 62).

There is a tremendous volume of available literature, and if I get as far as admitting my addiction and fortuitously finding other addicts, the conversation invariably turns to comparing notes. All too often, however, we then face the disappointment of discovering that we talk different languages—we seek different forms of future reality and read different authors. As future fantasy grows, subdivisions within it are becoming more explicit, each of which adopts a different vision and caters to different tastes. Part of my purpose here is to explore these alternative forms of social engineering.

Posing a particular future under the guise of fiction, is, at one level, nothing more than an abstract exploration. At another level, the initiation and exploration of a particular future, in itself, makes such a future more accessible. I wish to emphasise that I am not concerned here with whether the genre predicts the future, but instead am suggesting that the description of a particular form of future might popularise it sufficiently to make it more realisable. For example, Nicholls (1993a) suggests that 'the US government could never have got away with budgeting such large amounts of the national income on the space programme had the *desire* for space flight, largely catalysed by sf, not been so great'. Similarly, some authors hold, or have held, positions of power from which they could influence the future of society. One example is Paul Linebarger, an army intelligence officer and US governmental advisor, who wrote under the name of Cordwainer Smith. Other authors have used the genre to support political fantasies, deliberately written to influence society (such as H. G. Wells, through George Orwell, and Isaac Asimov, to many of the authors mentioned below).

Future Realities

The majority of writers use mechanisms such as time travel, alternate worlds, the far future, psi powers, and so on, as vehicles for their message, and for some it is the mechanism that fires the imagination and is the focus of the reading and writing. For the purpose of my account, however, I wish to bypass these and explore the view of humanity carried by the vehicle. In doing so I am following McHale's (1987) footsteps when he argues that SF is 'perhaps *the* ontological genre *par excellence*. We can think of science fiction as Postmodernism's non-canonised or 'low art' double, its sister-genre in the same sense that the popular detective thriller is Modernism's sister-genre'. Each author describes their own perceptions and judgements of their existence, yet within this myriad of uniqueness there are two main archetypes into which they can be classified—the heroic and the symbiotic. I do not see these as mutually exclusive or with clear definition, but, as is the nature of archetypes, with fuzzy edges and driven by my perception and judgement of my own 'realities'.

HEROES, VILLAINS, GODS, AND PREDETERMINATION

'For we wrestle not against flesh and blood, but against principalities, against powers, against the rulers of the darkness of this world, against spiritual wickedness in high places' (Ephesians 6: 12, King James Version).

Whilst some assume an antagonism between scientific and religious imaginations, and thus portray science fiction as anti-religious, SF toys with notions central to metaphysics. Values underlying the heroic archetype are 'religious' in nature. This is evidenced by Nicholls (1993b), who suggests that 'god' is the word most commonly used across all SF titles. I see this as a vision focused around power and impotence—in which variants upon super-entities with the ability to create and manipulate whole worlds abound. Man is often seen as a puppet of godlike beings, either in an arbitrary adversarial universe, or else in one whose patterns of meaning are planned by wider powers and in which man's existence is linked to pain and personal striving in the search for cosmic meaning (as in the Neverness series by Zindell). In both cases man is striving against the odds and is (to varying degrees) a tool of fate. The world views tend to be conceptually static, history is cyclical, and the narrative form is almost always the quest for an emblematic object or person. Characters are also emblematic, most commonly working within a dualistic system where good confronts evil, where they are trapped in a pattern that fulfils a predetermined destiny.

Different writers portray the 'godlike' theme in different ways—sometimes questioning the interrelationship between god and man and the responsibilities of both (*Downward to the Earth*, Robert Silverberg, 1971), or questioning the nature of 'godliness' (Dune series, Frank Herbert); exploring the evolution of man into god and the generation of quasi-gods (*Childhood's*

End, Arthur C. Clarke, 1953); or developing the role of the young accidental hero in a world whose 'rules' are driven by gods or godlike powers, but who is normally characterised by flamboyant behaviour and contempt for imperial decadence. Other writers maintain the sense of 'higher' powers, whilst only implicitly invoking 'gods', focusing upon alien beings in race-memory as gods or how a highly civilised society might appear godlike to a more primitive one, with stories (often of colonisation) that are more often about power and responsibility and carry political messages that verge on the metaphysical (the Tales of Alvin Maker trilogy, Orson Scott Card, 1988).

Extreme examples of this can be found in survivalist fiction—described by Clute (1993) as 'male-action story, set in post-holocaust venues where law and order has disappeared, and where there is effectively no restraint upon the behaviour of the hero, who therefore kills before he is killed, demonstrating his fitness to survive through acts of unbridled violence (which very frequently descend into prolonged sessions of rape and sadism)'. It often demonstrates apocalypse pathology—in which life is conducted in anticipation of surviving the holocaust (with the sub-belief that those who might die lack faith and thus deserve to die) and therefore its coming is welcomed. It represents a political agenda in which 'civilian' values are defeated when the 'real' world bares its teeth, and, despite focusing upon the autonomy of the heroic male, also contains elements of predetermination—in that it is the man who is able to realise his true (predetermined) nature that survives.

The emblematic nature of the genre clearly extends to the role of women and of villains.

> Not allowed the variety or complexity of real people, women in sf have been represented most frequently by a very few sexual stereotypes: the Timorous Virgin (good for being rescued, and for having things explained to her), the Amazon Queen (sexually desirable and terrifying at the same time, usually set up to be 'tamed' by the super-masculine hero), the Frustrated Spinster Scientist (an object lesson to girl readers that career success equals feminine failure), the Good Wife (keeps quietly in the background, loving her man and never making trouble) and the Tomboy Kid Sister (who has a semblance of autonomy only until male appreciation of her burgeoning sexuality transforms her into Virgin or Wife). (Tuttle 1993)

It is almost as if women are portrayed as an alien race that is linked to man, yet the alienness is threatening and thus deserves metaphorical subjugation. Even when female heroes are portrayed, they are still cast in a male world—their main interactions are with men, and they are placed within high power-distance scenarios and given a 'masculine' approach to a fight for, or against, power. Take, for example, Robert Heinlein's 1983 *Friday*. A male writer proposing a female hero is unusual, but what sort of hero? Friday is a genetically engineered woman who is assured that she 'can take pride in the fact that *all* of you was most carefully selected to maximise the best traits of H. sapiens'. She has augmented powers, and, as a female sort of James Bond, weaves her way through political plots, fights 'anarchists', kills, suffers torture and rape with casual aplomb, uses sexual manipulation, and, of course, looks fantastic. Upon completion of her tasks, she is given to say: 'I no longer think about my odd and sometimes shameful origin. "It takes a human mother to bear a human baby", Georges told me that long ago. It's true and I have Wendy to prove it. I'm human and *I belong*'.

A woman validates her existence through motherhood! Visions that portray women as 'equals in the fight' tend to be incomplete, and fail to address the wider implications of societal maintenance. Take, for example, cyberpunk, a subgenre (epitomised by Gibson's Neuromancer series) in which women regularly play central, and relatively equal, roles, but in which all but the main characters fail to exist. Cyberpunk is important for my account for another reason. It became popular in the 1980s, and it creates a future in which 'industrial and political blocks may be global rather than national and controlled through information networks; a future in which machine augmentations of the human body are commonplace, as are mind and body changes brought about by drugs and biological engineering' (Nicholls 1993c). The concept of virtual reality is central to cyberpunk, where the world's data networks form a kind of machine environment into which a human can enter by jacking into a cyberspace deck and projecting 'his disembodied consciousness into the consensual hallucination that was the matrix' *(Neuromancer)* and in which the role of the anti-hero becomes heroic. The way in which cyberpunk consciously places itself within virtual realities that are themselves within alternate realities, and its denial of neat aesthetic or moral wrap-up, means that it lends itself to being seen as the SF subgenre closest to postmodernism; see, for example, Jameson (1991), who suggests that cyberpunk is 'the supreme literary expression if not of postmodernism, then of late capitalism itself'.

Postmodernism can be portrayed as a shift in approach, reflecting 'being' as opposed to 'knowing', linked to a qualitative rather than quantitative search for meaning, and a recognition that the world of human experience is multiple and open-ended. My placing of cyberpunk within this archetype is therefore a provocative act. I have done so because I believe that the underlying values within cyberpunk (and postmodernism) remain those heroic endeavours. On the surface cyberpunk is anti-religious; however, at a basal level the machine becomes God and cyberspace his playground, often with godlike entities inhabiting cyberspace. The ethos is clearly one of survival—characters are puppets within a complex environment. However augmented, individuals might, if they learn the rules, commune with God and acquire favoured status. The presenting villain is normally the faceless manipulator, but the real villain is naiveté—the punishment for which is immediate, and often gory, death.

Cyberpunk, with its focus upon young, streetwise, aggressive, alienated individuals and destructive sex, is implicitly phallocentric. Whilst there are some female cyberpunk authors they are few and tend to remain true to the basic tenets of the approach. One of the notable exceptions is Pat Cadigan's 1994 *Fools,* which uses cyberpunk as a vehicle for exploring the implications of 'being' in a world in which one cannot 'know'. The central female character is forced to become both her own god and villain. More generally, female heroes rarely communicate with others—remaining a foil for the masculine characters. 'When women do appear they are usually defined by their relationship to the male characters, as objects to be desired or feared, rescued or destroyed; often, especially in recent, more sexually explicit times, women characters exist only to validate the male protagonist as acceptably masculine—that is, heterosexual' (Tuttle 1993).

The nature of villainy has changed as a reflection of the fears and bigotries of the societies that produced it. For example: the mad scientist and loss of 'humanity' (Stevenson's *Jekyll and Hyde,* 1886), indicating fear and suppression of the darker side of human nature; the idea of alien species and hive mind (*The Midwich Cuckoos,* Wyndham, 1957), in which individuality is subjugated to demands of the mass; the uncontrollable robot, indicating an anti-technology theme; the faceless behind-the-scenes manipulator, exploring a fear of computerised society. An underlying theme central to the whole of this archetype is that of paranoia, the fear of the unknown and the uncontrollable, the fear of loss or breakdown of the integrated self, in which lack of control equals chaos. Something, someone, some predestined future is out there or within us and we are but tools of it—it is bigger, cleverer, and more powerful than us and we need to understand and control it for our physical, emotional, or spiritual well-being, without which we will split asunder. In order to do this we need to become big, clever, and powerful, and in doing so we ensure our longevity and adopt some or all of its characteristics. This is as true for cyberpunk (and reified postmodernism) as for the more obvious examples. Here, the big bad thing is the collective focus upon knowing; the reaction is to propose multiple ways of being, which, however, then become as draconian a way of knowing (albeit different) as that which was being reacted against. Heroes exist to demonstrate the overcoming of temptation from the path of wisdom and the avoidance of ultimate doom—which is seen as temporary and futile existence, death and schism of the self.

EXISTENCE, SYMBIOSIS, AND RELATIONSHIPS

The other main archetype is that which I more usually associate with female authors. I was not searching for a gender split when I first started exploring this story—it crept up upon me unawares. There are few authors that I really appreciate, but each of these clearly questions (rather than plays with) our cultural norms, gender biases, and existence (and the heroic, power-related base they are derived from), and the vast majority of these writers happen to be female. I say they question, because in creating an alternative reality they do so with some attempt at completeness, exploring the implications for maintenance of that society, its procreation and its interrelationships. Whilst some of these visions are based upon the heroic form (as of *Jack the Bodiless* by Julian May, 1991, or *Heroes and Villains* by Angela Carter, 1969) the majority are pastorally based. They are, however, divorced from the subgenre of the pastoral-idyll in that they all, in some way or another, contextualise the 'dark side' as a natural facet of existence—to be embraced rather than feared. Perhaps the epitome of this is in Ursula Le Guin's 1993 *Always Coming Home*. She creates a 'liberal utopian vision, rendered far more complex than the term "utopian" usually allows for by a sense of human suffering' by weaving together stories, poetry, and other aspects of a fictional culture in order to 'force a dialogue with the here and now' (*New York Times Book Review*).

In this sense, the archetype works towards completeness—there is striving, but not of the heroic kind. All is pattern and interrelationships. An example of this can be seen in Storm Constantine's three books of the Wraeththu. The saga is definitely not peaceful, depicting the struggle for recognition of a 'mutant' class (in which masculinity becomes hermaphrodite) that eventually spreads throughout the world, but is one of patterns of relationships between authentic beings, that love and hate, adjust to their circumstance, and develop within an interacting and mutually dependent existence. 'We have the future now, no need to cling to the past. . . . Once it (power) lived in man, but men and women couldn't experience the light and dark of their natures without fear. Perhaps Kamagrian and Wraeththu are the answer. We shall certainly try. Our races as we know ourselves are just the beginning; there is so much more to come, and if we are wise, we shall greet it gladly' (*The Fulfilments of Fate and Desire*, Storm Constantine 1989).

Another (and perhaps less mainstream) example might be Flynn Connolly's 1993 *The Rising of the Moon*—an interesting choice for me because I do not know the gender of the author. This is a tale of rebellion in twenty-first-century Ireland, focusing around the interrelationship between women, women and men, and the patriarchy. It depicts a strife-torn but interrelated and complete society in which the individual chooses and accepts responsibility for their own actions without resorting to the heroic or the villainous. This theme can also be seen in *A Plague of Angels* by Sheri Tepper (1994), in which the heroic myth is directly challenged and reversed. The main characters are both authentic and developed as such, and act as archetypes based upon their own heroic myths within the wider belief of a heroic, star-travelling past. The 'angels' are hunger, war, and sickness:

> 'The last thing they asked me was this: Since man was so intransigent, why was he allowed to go to the stars?' . . . 'Man never went to the stars. . . . His star journey was only a myth. Another in an endless series of man's heroic myths of his own past. Glorious stories to make man the hero, for man always has to be the hero.' . . . 'There is an archetype

we never had in any of our villages . . . The Mysterious Stranger. The one who comes and goes, who sees everything, learns everything. He is needed in this new world.' 'Something within him shuddered and sat up straight, substituting one vision for another. Instead of glory and power, instead of a gleaming shuttle pushed by its tail of fire, this slow creaking wagon behind this flatulent horse. How far to Rigel, or to Betelgeuse? Or did one aspire to a different destination? . . . room perhaps for a Mysterious Stranger. A storyteller.'

A similar use of archetypal characters, that at the same time are real and interconnected, can be clearly seen in Cordwainer Smith's work. Despite predating the majority of other works cited here, and despite the rarity of his work, he is one of the very few male writers whom I would place in this category. His writing epitomises many of the above issues, and he appears to me to explore female sexuality from a 'feminine' point of view (as defined by my own preferences): a point of view in which sex is less about explicit domination and challenge, and more about implicit knowing and being. A 'female' approach to sex is very clear in Megan Lindholm's 1993 *Cloven Hooves,* yet it hardly mentions the 'act'—instead it is a journey of self-development and understanding fostered by relations with others, of which sex is an integral part. The whole book is around sexuality, yet it is hard to find one quote that epitomises it. Sexuality is about self—a state of being. Sex is a fact of life, enjoyable and painful, alongside death and birth.

Both Lindholm and Cordwainer Smith address the dark side of existence in a similar factual and necessary manner. For example, 'The Dead Lady of Clown Town' (1969) uses the 'myth' of Joan of Arc to address deviance, heresy, and death. D'joan, a genetically engineered dog fighting for the rights of the underpeople, adopts passive resistance as an inevitable part of her doglike nature, and eventually gets burnt at the stake—by which time all lives are irrevocably altered. This brief description does very little for the complexity and depth of the existential dilemmas addressed within the short story—the relationship between predetermination and free choice, identity and collectivity, humanity and prejudice, longevity and death, task and enjoyment—and the inevitable role of the accidental hero and the power of the weak. In this, Cordwainer Smith writes of heroism, but from a symbiotic perspective in which the heroic endeavour is the recognition and re-establishment of the dark side—thereby revalidating the light:

I am making a clear connection between maleness and the heroic myth, and femaleness and symbiosis. Before I bring this story to a circle I wish to clarify that I do not see this split as necessarily causal. Women can and do adopt the heroic pattern (keeping up with the Joneses' etc.), and men the symbiotic. I would, however, defend the idea that women tend to tell a story different to that told by men.

If women's work is organised differently from men's, if the day is structured differently, if space is inhabited differently, if styles of verbal communication are different, then it follows that women will have a different sense of beauty and pleasure. Whether this shows up in literature depends on the extent to which women's literary forms are derived from a female culture, rather than determined by literary tradition and critical response (Register 1980).

Furman (1985) suggests that the recurrence of topics, themes, images, and metaphors in the literary works of women is linked to the search for an emancipated self by individuals who react in a collective manner to a common social reality. If the central focus in heroic literature is the preservation of the unified self, then, in contrast, the focus here is upon acceptance of the many sides of the non-unified self. Given that history (and myths) are recounted by the winners and that women are traditionally the non-writers, then we live with a cultural heritage that supports the archetype of the patriarchal hero and the preservation of the unified self.

FUTURE REALITIES AND ORGANISATIONS

In creating alternative futures, futuristic fiction addresses alternative forms of organisation both implicitly and explicitly. Many, such as *The Land Beyond* by Gill Alderman (1992), *Raising the Stones* by Sheri Tepper (1991), or *The Wanderground* by Sally Gearhart (1985), use stories of people who are dissatisfied with their own way of life and thus attempt to establish another as vehicles to explore alternative forms of existence. These can be part of the colonisation subgenre, or as exemplified by the latter, the reaction of an alienated minority to futuristic systems of organisation and governance extrapolated from the present. All futuristic fiction, however, addresses the human condition and displays the author's beliefs about its source, management, and extrapolated future—the more complete representations also explore conditions for and modifiers of that future.

It would be interesting to map the many variations that exist; however, this is not the purpose of my story. Instead, I wish to explore the role that the creation of future realities and past myths plays in our organisational existence. I take a wide view of organisation—in which I suggest that all individuals collude with the systems they are in, and that, at times, they collude with the belief that they should not, or could not, take some responsibility for these systems. I suspect that this attitude can, at least in part, be attributed to implicit belief in predetermination and heroism. We are fed a diet of heroic endeavour. Organisational vision is a future myth, based upon the myths of the past—it is a control mechanism that reinforces the status quo. The system is predetermined—our organisational pattern recreates the aspirations of the founding father (Salama 1995), and our induction and assessment systems support this. We are told that we will climb the corporate ladder if we augment our powers, and learn to understand the system. There is little place for questioning—the deviant might be accepted (if sufficiently close to the higher powers) but the heretic is burnt (Harshbarger 1973). To question the myth is heresy.

We talk of paradigm shift, and the questioning of the rationalist, modernist approach. We talk of the multiplicity of forms of knowing and being, but, as with cyberpunk, we exist within our basal myths—we replace surety of knowledge with rapid communication, flatter structures, power shifts. The search for meaning and expertise becomes the heroic endeavour. The streetwise knowledge worker becomes the hero.

Alternatives?

This has two important elements: the way in which the heroic myth encapsulates (or at least correlates with) predetermination and disempowerment, and the potential impossibility of ever stepping outside our mythological heritage. What alternatives are there? As evidenced above, this is a question central to futuristic fiction and is one that the symbiotic archetype attempts to address. This archetype poses a clear and irrevocable distinction between empowerment and power. Power is the search for betterment over others, the creation of in-groups and out-groups, structures of control and reward, and the inevitability of existence. Empowerment is about equality of value for all things, a realisation and acceptance of the dark side, an appreciation of interconnectedness, freedom of choice, responsibility for that choice, and a belief in the openness of the future. Instead of heroes and villains, good and evil, all is patterns—interconnected patterns of love and hate, life and death. We talk glibly of empowerment, yet, as addressed by futuristic fiction, the effects of this would be profound and far-reaching, and would lead to a society that eschews much of which we hold dear.

The rapid increase in literature addressing the symbiotic archetype indicates that I am just one of many who are looking for alternatives. Authors need to sell books and without a willing audience few would write in this way. Is this just 'fiction', or does fiction influence reality by offering us alternative ideals? The case of B4RN, discussed in Chapter 18, might just be one of many ways forward.

Issues of Choice

I suspect that each individual, group, and nation has their own heroic myth and patterns of power, from the samurai, and the jihad, to respect for seniority. Each has an almost paranoiac fear of their nearest neighbours (often warranted). Heroic mythology and fear seem to be part of the human condition. Similarly, I would not like you to infer that I am attacking all religion and religious belief. I am not. I am trying to explore the pattern and the links—and within that pattern I am suggesting that it is the structures that develop alongside the heroic myth to stabilise it that also trap the individual. You are welcome, therefore, to infer that I see the formalised and widespread organisation of religious belief as frequently based on the valorisation of the heroic and thus a potentially destructive pattern.

With the collapse of the Communist Empire, moves towards sustainable development and strategic alliances, and the increasing focus upon small and medium-sized enterprises, then, perhaps, we are moving towards a time in which the functioning of smaller collections of individuals becomes more pertinent, and in which individuals wish to review the structures they collude with. If the symbiotic archetype is gendered, then perhaps, as the female workforce increases relative to the male, alternative ways of working will become inevitable. If such alternatives are based upon fundamentally different precepts, then our past and future mythology will require redefinition. I cannot see this happening easily.

CHASING THE TAIL

I seem to be plodding along OK, despite my mentally unstable preference for futuristic fiction, to which I am still addicted. I still go and hide, and read, and lose myself in reverie. I welcome the recent influx of (mainly) female authors who force me to question my assumptions whilst presenting me with a view of existence that I can, at least, empathise with.

I have set out to justify my idealism—arguing that my individual idealism is mirrored by all who question the mythology of our existence, that a growing number interpret it as I do. I have suggested that with changing patterns of work, this questioning will increase. That the individually idealistic but collectively disillusioned might together challenge the systems of control and reward. I have presented this as an inevitably growing force—a challenge to the heroic myth that will confront us all and that at least needs to be understood, but, preferably, should be explored and embraced. I have right on my side!

In other words I have established myself as the downtrodden heroine, who, developing some ability with words, attempts the heroic endeavour (late into the night, at cost to body and soul, risking the loss of peaceful family fulfilment) in order to place herself within the parameters of the system by getting another paper published, a step in achieving wider recognition and securing immortality. I am trapped by my own mythology.

This is, perhaps, more noticeable because I have chosen to speak in the first person—to impose my views on others. In reality, is not all establishment of one's own view part of the heroic archetype? I could have pretended objectivity ('60% of the respondents . . .'), or tried the third person ('once upon a time there was a little girl who . . .'). Do we become Sheri Tepper's Mysterious Strangers—storytellers who replace one basal form of myth with another? Are all myths heroic in essence? I am, at least, trying to be obvious and honest in my attempt to influence others. However, taken to the logical conclusion, does not the idea of symbiosis also entail responsibility to ensure that others develop their own views of life? If true to the ideology, should I really not keep quiet? Research might still exist (in theory) if we question but hold back from pontification—but will our jobs remain? Is research therefore irrevocably welded to the heroic archetype? Is the realisation of anything patterning onto the symbiotic archetype a logical impossibility?

There is no end to this story, only questions; however, given my heritage, I cannot leave it at that. As someone close to me (who happens to be a symbiotic sort of male) once said:

'I'm glad I don't have good taste—I can, at least, enjoy life'.
And so ends the story, and so starts the (slightly more) academic bit.

TEXT AND IDENTITY

The shelves are covered with books and articles on management. They contain three main types of literature. The first, the majority, build upon a tradition of knowledge—some of these are deep theoretical tomes, others provide recipes and models of the world of organisations. Each provides, in some way, the surety of an ordered causal reality through which anticipated outcomes can be obtained through planning and control. Identity is a known and measurable thing, and, depending upon the focus of the writer, either organisations or individuals have unitary identities ascribed to them. Where the writer ascribes an identity to the organisation (as if it were a living entity) then the identity of the individuals within it becomes negated or subsumed. In writing about these things, authors validate their argument through rigorous reference to other sources (textual and empirical) interpreted from within the existing body of knowledge.

The second, a sizeable minority, talk of management in a different way. These question and deconstruct the traditional knowledge. They present alternative accounts of reality. Reality, it is suggested, cannot be uniquely defined, is a function of our perceptions, and is best understood by what it appears not to be. Causality is questioned, and planning and control are presented as illusory—chimera created to satisfy our needs for security. Some talk of the role that myths and metaphors play in stabilising and promulgating organisational life. Some talk of emotions and values. Individual and organisational identity is seen as socially constructed and relative. The (artificial) conceptual boundaries between the individual and the organisational are eroded. In writing about these things, authors validate their argument through rigorous reference to other sources (textual and empirical) interpreted from within the existing body of knowledge.

Whilst these two types of literature offer very different world views, and whilst the adoption of one rather than the other appears to necessitate a leap of faith, there are also strong similarities between them. In either case, authors call upon a higher power in order to validate their thoughts. The higher power, the authority, is that of the peer group. On any potential points of issue the peer group is called upon for support—'As Smith and Jones (1999) suggest . . .', or 'following Derrida (1999), . . .'. This is more than a textual artifice. Our existence is surrounded by examples, as in discussions between colleagues in which one person avoids debating the question in hand by employing authoritative reference. As one academic (who shall remain unnamed) acknowledged when challenged, when unsure of her ground she normally refers to 'Bull and Jackson'. These two well respected and frequently quoted (by her) authors happen to be her cleaners whom she has overheard chatting. Much of what they say makes sense, so what is it that makes the charade necessary?

This is similar to playground politics. One child makes a statement that another disagrees with. The first supports it by citing his father: 'It must be true because my dad said so'. The second child replies, 'Your dad's rubbish. My dad is bigger than yours'. The first responds, 'Well, me and my mates all agree, so it must be true', eliciting, 'Oh yes? You and whose army?' At which time it comes to blows. There is one distinction between playground politics and academic debate—at least in the playground the children have the honesty to put themselves behind their own views. They talk of me and you. By the time they reach maturity these children will have learnt that it is safer to hide the 'me' behind an army of references. They will have developed the ability to avoid the personal statement of belief, whilst at the same time manipulating the army of authority in a way that supports their (personal) goal. Some will even have developed so far as to be able to believe that the text they are producing is sufficiently authoritative to contain no personal bias.

It is instructive to make a distinction between the personal spark (the drive) that creates the text, and the voice in which it is written. The text presented in this section has been written in a distant voice. It does not use 'I' in the personal sense, yet clearly, there is someone writing it who has their own view of the world, and their own mix of needs, motivations, and beliefs. The 'I' that wrote this, despite using a non-I form, has had to think of each word and the construction of each sentence. This distantly voiced 'I' has edited, rephrased, sought further meanings, and in working through the communicative effort required, has thought of the other and the impact or influence the emergent text might have upon the other. In thinking of the other, the 'I' has understood better the thoughts that are evolving through the process of writing. Though distant from the surface of the text, the 'I' is central to its creation. In addition, the creation of the text has dynamically influenced aspects of the 'I'. The self-perception of the 'I' changes and develops through the creative process.

The malleable 'I' resides behind all interaction, but, as in the two types of literature described above, it is normally hidden. It is a safer, less exposed position from which to operate. This raises two, linked, questions. What is the nature of the operation, and what is the threat?

Essentially, the creation of text is an attempt to communicate. For some, this might be communication with self; for many, the recipients of the communication might be known or imagined others. Of course, for those who believe in a socially constructed identity, the distinction between self and others is problematic and flexible. Regardless of one's beliefs about the roots of identity, however, the perceived nature of the anticipated recipient of textual communication influences the form and intended function of the text. The text might be intended as self-expression, or, at the other extreme, as a non-attributable contribution to a wider mind-set. In either case, the act of writing involves self and intent. The nature of the operation, therefore, is to in some way influence the selected target group. Texts written in either of the two types proposed at the beginning of this section are normally attributable and designed to further, or to influence, the body of knowledge to which they relate. The selected target group is an anonymous body of knowledge. Adherents to that body patrol its boundaries. There are rules and regulations that must be enforced (the immune system that recognises aberration), and those on the inside are jealous of their maintenance responsibilities (the antibodies that foster integrity of the system).

In other words, despite their different presenting world beliefs, both types of literature (or bodies of knowledge) exist (in operational terms) within the first type—individual identity or expression of self is subsumed within the parameters of the wider anthropomorphised body. Individuals can be identified within this body, but the act of identifying them is an act of disembodying the whole. Text designed to communicate with an individual (albeit someone who, under other circumstances, would be seen as part of the body) will be written in a different form to that designed for the body as a whole. Both are attributable; however, when writing to another person, both the author and recipient communicate as separate entities and identifiable selves. In contrast, when writing to a body of knowledge, the author is pleading entrance (even if masked by citing an existing right of membership). The text is attributable to the author (otherwise how would the body recognise its members?), but the author is a supplicant and must avoid providing cues that might alert the antibodies to a possible breach of the unitary nature of the body.

The understanding of life to which the body coheres (through subsumation of its members within a collective mind-set) would be threatened or challenged by a strong statement of self on the part of another body. A supplicant to the body can minimise this apparent threat by referring to the truth that the body upholds—using textual cues that evidence right of membership as if they were elements of a drug designed to suppress the immune system and minimise the chance of organ rejection. For acceptance, an even more powerful cue than the use of a distant voice is that of extensive reference to signifiers that the body clearly values already. Thus the citing of authorities that are valued by the body, reference to recent thoughts voiced by the body, and use of textual patterns normally employed by the body, all perform the same function, as do recommendations made in sales training. Doorstep sales people are advised to build upon mutual interests, talk about topical issues, and mirror body language and speech patterns in order to gain sufficient acceptance from their client to enable them to clinch the sale.

The threat of exposure of the malleable 'I', therefore, is associated (at least in part) with an embodied view of knowledge. To risk exposure is to risk rejection by one's peers who are acting with the authority of the body behind them. In terms of playground politics, one's peers can legitimately talk of 'me and my army'—so long as they subsume themselves within the authoritative rhetoric. The text presented here has only partially subsumed self. Use of the distant voice and the addressing of recent thoughts voiced by the body (e.g., text, identity, and embodiment) indicate willingness to play, but a lack of complete self-negation—where are the references? I could have provided a raft of supporting names and dates, but I have chosen not to. There are references—but these are not derived from literature central to the academic body of knowledge.

Of the two types of literature presented above, the first is built on scientific principles and is consistent in its assumption and enactment of a unitary body of knowledge. The second is inconsistent in its cry for inconsistency. The boundaries of the second type of literature are patrolled in a highly consistent manner, one which regulates and reifies the 'body' of knowledge. In contrast, if the espoused principles were to be enacted what would they look like?

THE THIRD TYPE OF LITERATURE: THE STORY

There is a third type of literature on the shelves—a type rarely associated with academe (let alone management). We walk into the realm of stories—ideal vehicles for the exploration of identity and emotion, myths and metaphors—but a realm that is dust covered and rarely visited. This presents an account that makes no special claim to external authority, but is, instead, deliberately designed to engage the self of the recipient through the authenticity of the author. It leaves the recipient freedom to make their own sense of the meaning contained within. From this perspective, the story given above is a particularly poor example as there is a clear purpose to it. It is given, in part, to emphasise the different textual forms associated with the same intended message. However, it is also noticeable that the story form allows greater flexibility or layering of intent. Certainly, feedback from those who have read or worked with the story given above indicates that a multiplicity of threads of meaning can be derived from it—the majority of which were unknown to, or go beyond, the author's intention when writing it.

The notion of authenticity, however, is problematic. A truly authentic account might be one of emotional expression of the transient self that is likely to have little to offer recipients, other, perhaps, than an idea of how the author was feeling at that moment. Whilst this might be a valid communicative act, it is unlikely to have a lasting impact upon the way in which others make sense of the world. The urgent debates that pervade the corridors of academe about what is meant by rigor and validity, and about choice of methodology and method, illustrate the complex relationship between personal preference (authenticity?), sense-making (research?), and influential dissemination (authority?). How can any academic account ever be fully authentic? If we are to move beyond the second type of literature, how do we cope with the need for authority?

The story given here does employ authority through the use of references (if not those normally associated with management literature), whilst the first section attempts to play with other authoritative cues. As author, I find it hard to gauge what the effect of such playing has upon you, as you read it. So I shall leave you with some thoughts and questions. I am clear where my initial disquiet about needing to change my textual form has come from— the way I write is an expression of, development of, and reaffirmation of my self. When I write in a form that is intended to be acceptable to the body of knowledge, I effectively have to adopt a different persona, and in doing so my development and reaffirmation are skewed towards making me seen to be acceptable to those that patrol the boundaries of the authoritative mind-set. I am, perhaps, becoming too old and crotchety to do this willingly.

I am also sufficiently self-indulgent to attempt to put this upon the agenda for others. I have justified this by questioning (largely implicitly) whether we need to move beyond postmodernism, and by suggesting that if this is the case, then we need to do so in textual form as well as content—in our acceptance criteria as well as in our methodological approach. I play with the idea of stories as a possible vehicle for this, but what would it do to the body of knowledge if stories were to become an acceptable means by which to seek membership? Would the rules change, or would the body become so disembodied that membership criteria no longer existed?

As a final part to this chapter I want to point out that I have deliberately left the text very much as it was written in the early 1990s. I could have peppered it with updated references but that would have ruined the original intent. It stands on its own questioning what sort of future we might wish to belong to and what the implications of those futures might be. Science fiction has obviously moved on since then and there is a lot in the literature about identity and embodiment, text and voice, heroes and myths, stories and symbiosis. Indeed, I return to these themes again and again. Perhaps, if you do want more detailed and up-to-date academic references, you could read some of the other chapters in this book.

This is a chapter for thought rather than scholarship.

REFERENCES

Alderman G (1992) *The Land Beyond: A Fable*. London: HarperCollins.
Cadigan P (1994) *Fools*. London: HarperCollins.
Card OS *The Tales of Alvin Maker, comprising:* (1988) *Seventh Son;* (1988) *Red Prophet;* (1989) *Prentice Alvin*. London: Legend.

Carter A (1969) *Heroes and Villains*. London: Penguin.

Clarke AC (1953) *Childhood's End*. London: Pan Science Fiction.

Clute J (1993) 'Survivalist Fiction', in Clute J & Nicholls P (Eds) *The Encyclopaedia of Science Fiction*. London: Orbit. http://www.sf-encyclopedia.com/entry/survivalist_fiction accessed 13/1/16

Connolly F (1993) *The Rising of the Moon*. New York: Ballantine.

Constantine S (1988) *The Enchantments of Flesh and Spirit*; (1988) *The Bewitchments of Love and Hate*; (1989) *The Fulfilments of Fate and Desire*. London: Futura.

Ephesians (1958) *The Holy Bible, King James Version*. London: Collins.

Furman N (1985) 'The Politics of Language: Beyond the Gender Principle?', in Greene G & Kahn C (Eds) *Making a Difference: Feminist Literary Criticism*: 59–79. London: Routledge.

Gearhart S (1985) *The Wanderground*. London: The Womans Press.

Gibson W (1984) *Neuromancer*; (1986) *Count Zero*; (1986) *Burning Chrome*; (1988) *Mona Lisa Overdrive*. London: HarperCollins.

Graves R (1949) *Seven Days in New Crete*. London: Quartet.

Le Guin U (1993) *Always Coming Home*. London: HarperCollins.

Harshbarger D (1973) 'The individual and the social order: Notes on the management of heresy and deviance in complex organisations', *Human Relations* 26(2): 251–269.

Heinlein R (1983) *Friday*. NY: Hodder and Stoughton, New English Library.

Jameson F (1991) *Postmodernism, Or, the Cultural Logic of Late Capitalism*. Durham, NC: Duke University Press.

Lindholm M (1993) *Cloven Hooves*. London: HarperCollins.

May J (1991) *Jack the Bodiless*. London: Pan.

McHale B (1987) *Postmodernist Fiction*. Routledge: London.

Nicholls P (1993a) 'Prediction'; (1993b) 'Gods and Demons'; (1993c) 'Cyberpunk', in Clute J & Nicholls P (Eds) *The Encyclopaedia of Science Fiction*. London: Orbit. http://www.sf-encyclopedia.com/entry/ accessed 13/1/16.

Norman J (1966) *Tarnsman of Gor*. New York: DAW.

Orwell G (1949) *1984*. Toronto: S.J. Reginald Saunders & Co.

Register C (1980) 'Review essay: Literary criticism', *Journal of Women in Culture and Society* 6(2)268–282.

Salama A (1995) *Privatization: Implications for Cultural Change*. Aldershot, UK: Avebury.

Sargent P (1977) ' "Dear Frontiers": Letters from women fantasy and science fiction writers', *Frontiers: A Journal of Woman's Studies* 2(3)62–78.

Silverberg R (1971) *Downward to the Earth*. London: Gollancz.

Smith C (1969) 'The Dead Lady of Clown Town', London: Sphere Books.

Stevenson RL (1886) *The Strange Case of Dr. Jekyll and Mr. Hyde*. London: Longmans, Green.

Tepper S (1991) *Raising the Stones*. New York: Bantam Spectra.

Tepper S (1994) *A Plague of Angels*. London: HarperCollins.

Tuttle L (1993) 'Women as Portrayed in Science Fiction', in Clute J & Nicholls P (Eds) *The Encyclopaedia of Science Fiction*: 1343. London: Orbit.

Wyndham J (1957) *The Midwich Cuckoos*. London: Penguin.

Zindell D (1988) *Neverness*; (1993) *The Broken God*. London: Grafton.

9 The Submerged Self

I shall tell you a story, and, as I do so I wonder at what stages reality becomes story and story becomes myth. In part it is a story in the way in which all events of our lives become stories, remembered, revisited, reinterpreted and, over time, reworked to suit our changing sense of self. In this I link myself to Watson's (2000) concept of ethnographic fiction science, in which he demonstrates how ethnographic research accounts can be written in a way that bridges the genres of creative writing and social science. I discuss the development of this story in Chapter 20, where I explain why it is written as if it were in a place far, far away, when really it is about me and my experiences and is all well documented. The events I describe here were briefly alluded to in the previous chapter.

AN INTRODUCTION TO DDT

The story is set in the relatively affluent Western world—let's say a pharmaceutical company in Australia—but is one that can be seen in many places. It is set many years ago and is situated within one department of the company—let's call it the Department of Developing Things (DDT). DDT had quite a few people in it, and many different stories, but I shall concentrate on just a few here. Some of my focus is on the relationship between DDT and the wider company, but most is upon the dynamics within DDT. This story is about favouritism, discrimination, bullying, harassment, and whistleblowing. It illustrates some intriguingly bad management practices, which contrast with the humanistic and developmental values espoused by the characters, DDT, and the company involved.

The characters in this story worked together in different combinations on many different projects, but over the years, and without really knowing how it happened, they developed three main groupings. Though there was some correlation between the groups and seniority, it was not strong. These groupings developed through people's attitudes to each other—not through management structure. I will call the first of these groups the Whites. They were all white, but my reference is to neocolonialism in management (see

Chapter 16) and the idea of whiteness, which is not just a matter of phenotype or skin colour, but is about power and privilege: 'Whiteness . . . is the production and reproduction of dominance rather than subordination, normativity rather than marginality, and privilege rather than disadvantage' (Frankenberg 1993: 236).

The Whites were stratified. At the top were two male senior staff (Bill and Ben). During the period covered by this story, Bill was initially head of DDT, followed by Ben in the later stages. Other Whites were a male junior member of staff (Brad) and one older woman (Bertha) and another woman, Bo, who was considerably junior. Neither yet had their qualifications and Bill, Ben, and Brad often referred to them collectively as 'the Women'.

I shall call the second group the Subalterns. This faction was smaller, subordinate, and withdrawing. They included one senior male (Doug), a mid-rank female (Dora) and male (Dave), and a junior male (Dick) and female (Dot). They were non-hierarchical and flexible in their roles, and banded together in reaction to the Whites. They were subjected to subtle bullying by which their views were often ignored in meetings, and their work was openly treated as a side issue to the 'real' work of DDT—later in this story they became increasingly 'Othered', and so became part of the third group: the Others.

I describe the process of 'Othering' in Chapter 7, by which an individual or a group dehumanises the 'other' and thereby strengthens their own view of self. Unlike the Subalterns, the Others became isolated in reaction to the Whites. They included a woman (Cass) who had recently joined DDT to do a senior job. Bertha had applied for this post and though her application had been supported by the Whites, it was firmly rejected by senior management external to DDT. In addition to Cass there were also two younger female staff (Clara and Chris), and overseas trainees (Cliff and Cora). Their skills, knowledge, and work were appropriated where possible and otherwise rejected, and some behaviour towards them resembled planned and deliberate vindictiveness.

Mobility and Promotability

Some of this interplay can be seen in people's career paths. For example, when a new senior post was advertised Bill and Ben managed the shortlisting process. Dora and Chris, both highly eligible for the appointment, were told that no internal applications would be accepted. Brad, who did not specialise in that area of work, was then found to be on the shortlist, and it transpired that his application had been written with help from Bill and Ben. Several members of DDT complained in writing to Bill and Ben about both the process and the result. Despite that, when the Managing Director (MD) queried such a weak internal appointment he was told unambiguously by Bill and Ben that the appointment had unanimous support from all in DDT.

Bill and Ben were happy to lie to senior management and it was only by bypassing them that promotion for non-Whites was possible. Cass was told in an open meeting that she was unpromotable and would not be supported. She therefore applied for promotion directly to the personnel department, and the promotions panel questioned why she had not been put forward earlier.

Promotability was linked to prestige of work, which was rated by internal measures, and because of the predominance of senior staff in the Whites, their areas of work were rated most highly. Other forms of work were categorised as 'not in areas central to our needs', even if those areas were classed as prestigious by those outside DDT.

The idea of more valued areas of work offered a key route for discrimination, yet such discrimination was not applied evenly and it was clear that what was really valued was the status of the person doing the work not the work itself. For example Brad was given time off and preferential treatment because he was a junior member of a prestigious project that was being led external to DDT. At the same time Cass was leading a directly comparable project within DDT but this was discounted as irrelevant for work allocation and ignored internally. In total Cass achieved a large amount of sales revenue, none of which was acknowledged internally. Interestingly, at one stage DDT had to account for itself to the MD, and at that time it put forward five initiatives in defence of its right to continue to exist—four of these initiatives were Cass's, though her leadership of them was not acknowledged.

Dave was refused any support from Bill and Ben in seeking promotion and eventually walked straight into a much better job elsewhere. Dot and Dora made sideways moves within the company rather than remain in DDT, and Dick and Clara left DDT, describing it as racist and sexist respectively. Ten years later Clara described continuing bad dreams of her time there and the 'poisonous atmosphere' she endured. Twenty years later Chris and Cass met and remembered their experiences with bitterness, still trying to lay the ghosts to rest. This is not unusual. Lillemor et al. (2006) describe the long-term impact of workplace bullying on victimised employees who report being 'marked for life'. Similarly, Mikkelsen & Einarsen (2002: 98) state that 80.5% of employees claim that 'no other event in their life affected them more negatively than the bullying'.

So much talent was wasted, so much discrimination and hurt, but how could it happen?

McTernan et al. (2013) argue that bullying presents a particularly severe form of psychosocial risk as it directly threatens the sense of self. The sub-theme throughout this chapter is about how the individual's understandings of themselves were eroded by the actions of others, and I shall return to this at the end of the chapter, but for now I shall focus on bullying and DDT.

The Cost of Bullying

Workplace bullying is widespread yet under-reported and its extent is likely to be underestimated (Lutgen-Sandvik et al. 2007). Most definitions of bullying suggest that repetition is important; however, bullying can occur with a single act (Cowie et al. 2002). Bullying may also intensify over time, particularly if the initial behaviour is unchallenged (Lutgen-Sandvik 2003). Lee & Brotheridge (2011) compared workplace bullying with bullying elsewhere and found that young children found bullying to be relatively acceptable whereas those aged 15–17 and mothers considered bullying to be less acceptable. Interestingly, 10- to 15-year-old pupils and workplace employees gave more justification of bullying and were more likely to attribute the situation to victim's responsibility.

The literature suggests three main forms of bullying: direct interpersonal bullying, depersonalised bullying, and subtle bullying. Interpersonal bullying entails explicit behaviours and malicious personal intentions and has received far more attention in the literature than depersonalised bullying (Samnani 2013). This refers to the contextual and structural elements of organisational design, which in effect bully the employee. However, the vast majority of bullying is relatively subtle (Lee & Brotheridge 2006). Subtle or covert bullying can include withholding important information, excessive monitoring, persistent criticism, excessively high workloads, social ostracism, gossip, shouting and yelling, personal jokes and insults, and taking credit for an employee's work (Fox & Stallworth 2005). Such behaviour may be difficult to detect, may be misinterpreted, and may be implicit or hidden. For example, repeated acts of incivility can constitute bullying, and a meta-analysis (Jones et al. 2013) shows that this subtle kind of discrimination can be just as harmful to its targets as its more overt manifestations. Indeed, Samnani (2013) argues that subtle bullying is likely to be more harmful than explicit bullying as it is less obvious to the recipient and more difficult to interpret and defend against. Reacting strongly towards the perpetrator is most likely to halt bullying; however, bullying is likely to intensify when the recipient fails to recognise what is happening (Baillien et al. 2009). Bullying is also more prevalent when laissez-faire leadership is present (Skogstad et al. 2007).

The description of DDT given above showed depersonalised bullying through discriminatory structures. These could be maintained because it was the Whites who interfaced directly with the rest of the organisation and prevented almost all interaction with others. Therefore, in promoting a negative or non-positive image of the achievements of these people, the Whites maintained their apparent right to dominancy—so justifying the self-fulfilling aspects of such negativity. They were the senior staff and they would be believed. Each of the Others who succeeded in breaking out of this negative cycle did so by accessing the wider organisation directly.

WORKLOADS

Discriminatory structures could also be seen in the allocation of work, and nicely illustrate the power of fiction over fact. When Cass joined DDT people were allocated workloads through discussion, and there was a certain lack of clarity about what work people actually did. Remember—this story is set many years ago, when data management and spreadsheets were quite new. Cass designed a workload spreadsheet in order to illustrate her claim that she was overloaded. Bill presented the idea to the MD as his own and it was adopted as a cross-company management tool and a standard was stipulated, along with a system of remissions for particular tasks.

Within the department, remission for projects was to be agreed on a pro rata basis with Bill and Ben. Remission rates for revenue generation were a problematic area. Bill and Ben decided that people had to 'buy' themselves out unless the work was of value to DDT, then it would be counted in the individual's workload even if it brought in less revenue. Only those projects conducted by the Whites ever fell into the category of 'value to the group'. For all other projects, any time that was outside the 'paid days' was not recognised, and so the person had to do the work but was given no time allowance in which to do it.

This was exacerbated by the way in which Bill and Ben failed to ratify the workload statements presented by the Others, and so did not properly take into account their existing workload. This failure included the inability to quantify the number of the roles and the nature of the work that such people had, as well as the more nebulous parameter of project revenue. Each year a 'draft' workload would be produced that significantly underestimated the workload of some people and overestimated the load for others. Bill and Ben would then suggest that finalising it would be conducted on an individual basis. They were never easily available when the non-Whites wished to discuss their workloads, and thus 'estimates' went uncorrected. The MD received the draft versions, which showed that each of the Whites worked over their expected load, whilst each of the others failed to meet, or only just met, the targets. The story of individual workloads that was told to the company was thus backed by hard, yet erroneous, figures. In believing the figures the hierarchy failed to question the story, and so a vicious circle developed and continued in this fashion for many years.

Stress and Ill Health

In order to highlight the implications of this, let us look at the effect it had upon Cass. She became increasingly ill and had time off for work-related stress. Work was allocated at a DDT group meeting and there was an allocation meeting planned during her absence. Cass wrote to all members of the meeting, stating her health problems and specifying her workload as measured objectively by the established company criteria (but not as given in the previous year's 'draft' allocation sheet). As measured by the criteria, she was carrying a total workload of 388 working days a year (excluding weekends and holidays). On hearing nothing for some while Cass made an appointment to see Ben to discuss this. He said that he had thrown the details of her workload in the bin. Her case had been discussed at the meeting and he supported Bertha's view that Cass was trying to use emotional blackmail to cover up the fact that she couldn't cope. Cass's health continued to deteriorate and she eventually suffered a cerebral haemorrhage linked to hypertension, but that is a different story (see Chapter 13).

There is a lot in the literature about workplace bullying and detrimental effects on the health of the recipient, including stress and anxiety, insomnia, a lower self-image, and poorer mental health. Anxiety and depression are amongst the most frequently reported conditions (Einarsen & Mikkelsen 2003; Einarsen et al. 2011) and bullying causes more long-term illness and trauma than all other types of work-oriented stress (Brewer & Whiteside 2012). This includes symptoms analogous to the formal diagnosis of post-traumatic stress (Kreiner et al. 2008). Medically related absence rates for victims of bullying are 1.2 times higher than for other employees (Kivi-maki et al. 2000). The relationship between bullying and depression has been consistently verified across a number of occupations and work settings (Hansen et al. 2006) and according to World Health Organization estimates (2001), depression is the leading cause of disability worldwide and will be the second leading contributor to the global disease burden by 2020. Diestel et al. (2013) found that high levels of emotional exhaustion particularly affected high-level work performance (though low-level tasks were not affected), so it is quite likely that Cass's standard of work was being affected by the treatment she received, but this does not detract from the fact that the DDT workload meeting explicitly ignored the figures showing that Cass was being grossly exploited, choosing instead to believe a story that absolved them of usury.

WHISTLEBLOWING

Cass responded by writing to the MD, enclosing details of her full workload and explaining that her only option was to refuse to work on one of the projects allocated to her. The MD agreed that her workload should be reduced immediately. She stopped working on that project, but in retaliation Bill and Ben withdrew all secretarial cover from her. Such retaliation was explicitly related to exposing the underbelly of the cover story.

Goffman (1990: 231) suggests that any social establishment has a front region, which is a place where 'performance is presented', and a back region, where 'performance of a routine is prepared'. Protective performance practices such as loyalty, discipline, and circumspection hinder backstage information from being shared. In a situation 'in which organizational authority is challenged, an event that normally occurs "backstage" in organizations' is suddenly brought front stage, and 'the potential loss of face is greater for all involved' (Near & Jensen 1983: 6). Negative reaction towards whistle-blowing can be seen as a way of controlling the back region information and thereby preventing the cost of a 'loss of public face' for the organisation. From this perspective whistleblowers are troublemakers and retaliation is justified against organisational members who are perceived as 'rocking the boat' (Rothschild & Miethe 1994). According to the spiral of incivility, wrongdoing and subsequent actions may 'escalate into a spiral of conflict' (Andersson & Pearson 1999: 458) as occurred in DDT.

(Bjørkelo 2013) found that whistleblowing is often followed by retalia-tion and bullying that can be performed by both managers and colleagues. Official reprisal can take the form of 'demotion, transfer, reprimand, refer-ral to a psychiatrist, as well as many unofficial reprisals such as social isola-tion, threats, ostracism as well as pressure to resign' (McDonald & Ahern 2002: 22). For example, Cass submitted a paper for publication to a special issue of a journal of which Bo was guest editor, and after receiving posi-tive comments from three reviewers Bo wrote to Cass, formally accepting the paper for publication. Shortly after that Bo entered into a relationship with Bill, and months later, when Cass was expecting to see the paper in print, Bill (not Bo) told Cass that her paper had been rejected. He should not have been party to any of the decision-making processes, and having been formally accepted, Cass should have been notified of any reasons for change, but she was never notified and no reasons were ever given. She then submitted the paper to a more prestigious journal and four months later it was accepted without revision, but the timing of this rejection was impor-tant. Cass was going through a promotions board, and the removal of that publication from her CV at that time affected her chances.

Whistleblowers suffer health problems similar to those described the bul-lying above (Rothschild & Miethe 1999). Both whistleblowers (70%) and non-whistleblower witnesses (64%) reported stress-induced physical prob-lems associated with involvement in a whistleblowing situation (McDon-ald & Ahern 2002).

Without doubt, the withdrawal of all secretarial support increased Cass's workload tremendously, but all the extra work was completely hidden. It was at this stage that she started the process of moving sideways to another department. She had time owing to her and wished to move with her full allowance, but Bill and Ben claimed that she had had that time already. Once again, Cass addressed the hierarchy and produced relevant correspon-dence and so eventually received her full entitlement, and so the cycle of whistleblowing and harassment continued.

Depersonalised bullying through the creation of structures that discrimi-nated against non-Whites was largely led by Bill and Ben and strongly sup-ported by Brad. The majority of the personal attacks were led by Bertha and supported by Bo. Bertha was never challenged by any other White, however illegitimate or vicious the attacks became. Indeed Bertha claimed she spoke the 'truths' that others did not have the courage to say. Some attacks were physical, such as a cup of coffee and saucer thrown across the room at Dick when he disagreed with her in a meeting. Others were verbal—several of the Others, including Cass, were told many times by the White women that they were 'not the right sort' and would never be trusted. Almost every meeting resulted in some sort of bullying, such that at one stage Cass initiated a grievance against DDT, and at another, contacted Personnel Services directly to start proceedings. Both times the bullying stopped for a short while and she withdrew the grievance—whether she should have done so is another question.

More problematic was the treatment of some of Cass's junior staff. Bertha was put in charge of all junior staff, and she regularly 'lost' the paperwork for Cass's, so they and Cass had to redo it many times. In addition, when Cass was ill, Bertha took full responsibility for them and she told Cliff several times that he was not fit to be there—without any evidence. He eventually started to sue over her treatment of him. Cora was abused so many times that on entering the building she would take a long diversion up the stairs, across the top corridor, and back down so she approached Cass's room from the other direction, rather than the few steps that led past the offices in which Bertha and Bo worked.

At one stage Bertha changed the contracts of all Cass's junior staff, thereby invalidating their visas, resulting in Cliff and Cora becoming illegal aliens. This was not a mistake. The authorisation for the changes was in writing from her, and claimed to be on behalf of Bill. It is hard to know whether this claim was true because of the level of rumours and mistruths that circulated in DDT. What is certain is the amount of pain and additional paperwork that these actions caused Cass and her staff, and the complicity of the Whites in this obstructionism and indirect aggression towards people and things that Cass valued.

The Right to Punish

I talk of punishment, as the Whites felt that the others needed to be controlled and, as Bill was fond of saying, 'brought into line'. They acted as if they, and particularly Bertha, saw themselves as only doing what was required to assert the authority of the system. However, although, when dealing with the rest of DDT, the Whites summoned the wider organisation as the authority behind many of their actions, they clearly did not believe in the importance of this wider authority. They misled it, and presented it with half-truths, using it as was convenient for their purposes. Their invocation of a higher authority was opportunistic, manipulative, and without respect for that authority itself. Their 'right to punish' was rooted in the group dynamics.

The espoused culture of DDT was collective. Policy, structure, and decisions were discussed at group meetings, and the role of head of department was rotated. As is clear in the earlier sections of this chapter, such espousal of collectivity was not matched by equality of opportunity or voice, but DDT was more collective than many other departments in the organisation. Bullying can be prevalent in collective cultures as victims are disinclined to seek social support from the members of their in-groups, as this might lead to a disruption of harmony in the in-group (Taylor et al. 2004). Leung et al. (2005) found that avoidance and non-confrontational strategies are generally preferred in collectivistic cultures in disputes of high intensity with in-group members and with superiors; thus, a negative climate is associated with increased perceptions of bullying and decreased perceptions of psychological health. Those witnessing the bullying are more likely to turn away and avoid becoming involved, to the extent that it becomes the elephant in the room: the situation 'whereby a group of people tacitly agree to outwardly ignore something of which they are all personally aware' (Zerubavel 2006: 2). Such a thing is so conspicuous that significant effort is required to avoid noticing it.

More women than men report bullying and workplace aggression (Lee & Brotheridge 2011) and bullying in DDT was partially gender-based. The majority of people that were bullied were female, and the direct personal bullying was largely conducted by women. Hoel et al. (2001) concluded that men who felt threatened by women managers resorted to bullying as a way of excluding them from advancement, and that could be applied to the way in which Cass was treated. However, the gender issues in DDT were more complicated than that. Bertha often described herself as the 'wise woman' and she, and the other Whites, referred to her actions as those of 'intuitive womanhood', and she at times described herself in terms of the Goddess. Few were willing to counter her emotional outbursts and many voiced fear of them, but if they were considered on their own they were no more than that. If Bertha was the Goddess, Bo was a handmaiden—benefiting from favouritism in return for attending to the needs of the White males, reinforcing their roles, doing their dirty work. Taken together, 'the Women' gained the mystic strength of the feminine. Furthermore, the very nature of DDT, focused as it was upon relationships and development, meant that (at least on the surface) the feminine was honoured; intuitive womanhood was privileged.

In contrast, although she was female, the rationality that Cass used to counter systemic emotionally laden inequality was described (initially by Bertha, but later by others) as 'a threat to intuitive ways of being and a betrayal of femininity and sisterhood'. Her workload spreadsheet that was adopted by the MD was seen by the Whites as too quantitative. It also transpired that her letter to DDT setting out her workload was rejected as much because it presented the data in figures and tables (and was thus termed scientistic and masculine), as because of the message it carried. Cass was seen not only to have taken Bertha's job, but also to deny the feminine mystique. However, whilst paying lip service to the power of intuitive womanhood, the White males continued to see themselves as separate to (and threatened by) the women—so much so that Bill at one stage proposed that finances would be eased if all the women in the section were to be put on the same salary regardless of experience or qualifications. This was not a joke. The men were in thrall to the feminine myth, but did not necessarily like it.

Some of the Whites' behaviour, especially in the establishment of the systems, was clearly self-interest—Whites got career advancement, more money and/or more time to do what they wanted. Those who spoke out against injustice became a focus for punishment and most moved job to avoid it. Others described themselves as 'victims' in the more classic sense of not fighting back, and keeping quiet in the hope that the gaze of the predator would move on—they became subsumed and hidden. On the face of it each was serving their own needs; however, to act in this way was alien to the nature and espoused beliefs of all those concerned, and despite some individual gain that might have accrued, the real power that was driving the behaviour was based in story and myth.

POLITICALLY SKILLED—BETTER BULLIES

Despite the popular characterisation of bullies as socially inept misfits, they are highly skilled socially and can use this skill in organisationally dysfunctional ways (Ferris et al. 2007). Politically skilled bullies are better able to choose the most vulnerable targets for their abuse; to identify specific points of vulnerability in their victims; to bully in ways that will be the most psychologically painful for their targets (Treadway et al. 2013). They are better able to mask their behaviour so that it goes undetected by others, and to use their bullying behaviour to build broad coalitions of supporters and pools of resources that will facilitate their own job performance. They are less likely to be viewed as bullying by their superiors and powerful others (Treadway et al. 2007).

The Whites were highly politically skilled and for the majority of the time, they were able to reframe the situation in a way that absolved them from any questions. One tactic was to throw the responsibility on to the person being bullied and overlook the ways in which the imbalance of power limited mutual influence (Stark 2007). Martin & Klein (2013) point out that whilst most relationships involve degrees of mutual influence it can reasonably be argued that a position of neutrality during bullying colludes through inaction with the abuser and allows the organisation to turn its back on its ethical responsibilities (Rhodes et al. 2010). For example, a pervasive rumour circulated by Bill was that two of 'his' women kept on fighting, and that he had to 'control' them (referring to Bertha and Cass). This served several functions. It maintained his appearance of control and authority. It reframed the external viewer's interpretation of events from bullying to a catfight. It fed the underlying currents of sexism within the organisation in a humorous way that enhanced his reputation, whilst demeaning those of the women.

Witnesses

There were many witnesses to this story: internal witnesses to single acts of violence, through multiple acts of gossiping, to structural changes that impacted all in DDT; external witnesses who saw what was going on but did little, including the trade unions who declined to become involved; and the senior management and HR, who had a paper trail of complaints and problems from many different people in DDT as well as high turnover and health-related absence, yet failed to ask any questions. Bullying was evidenced in so many different ways in DDT and throughout the 10 years that this story covers that it was impossible for any member of DDT not to become involved in it in some way.

Brewer & Whiteside (2012) point to increased awareness of the extent to which witnesses of workplace bullying and employees that are not directly involved may also be affected almost as severely as the victims. In addition to the stress, anxiety, and ill health that may occur, witnesses of workplace bullying also report decreased job satisfaction, productivity, commitment, and loyalty to the organisation (Hoel & Cooper 2000). When witnesses overtly challenge the bullying behaviour it is likely to stop; however, if witnesses fear becoming the next target then they are likely to support the perpetrator or become silent spectators (D'Cruz & Noronha 2011).

As reported earlier, the Others were each deeply affected by the treatment they received, yet they felt they received little support (Strandmark & Hallberg 2007). It is possible that those who were not directly involved did not realise the severity of the issue. Hoel & Beale (2006) point out that subtle bullying can be difficult to detect for the recipients and thus it might be even more difficult to detect for witnesses, especially if that bullying is masked by demands for work efficiency (Parzefall & Salin 2010). As a result, witnesses who, through sense-making processes, choose not to believe that an employee is experiencing bullying will be less likely to lend support to them, and instead, rationalise that they are unnecessarily complaining and risking team cohesion, thereby placing the blame on the recipient of the bullying. Workplace bullying has the potential to penetrate across employees, workgroups, and departments in an organisation through the imitation of negative behaviours and the resulting spiralling effects of negative acts (Cortina et al. 2013: 283).

A RATIONALE?

In this story people depersonalised their own colleagues to the extent that it was felt to be legitimate to ignore all factual information about workloads, giving preference to personal bias and reinforced by the stories individuals told to themselves and others. They chose to overlook rational argument and group needs. They chose to ignore emotional pain evidenced by others. A group of civilised, well-educated, and, individually, very nice people colluded (by commission or omission) in an environment rife with harassment and bullying.

One thread through this is power within local struggles (Gramsci 1971; see also Chapter 14). The story told here illustrates the complex relationship between formal power of position in the organisation, which is, itself, compromised by incomplete knowledge as passed up through the power structure, and the more nebulous, though still powerful, aspects of 'power'. It shows the power of facts and figures being overturned by the power of rumour and gossip. It shows managers as fallible emotional creatures, unfettered by the bounds of logic.

Two intertwined forms of story developed. Those for internal consumption developed in a way that justified what would otherwise be seen as inappropriate behaviour. In developing stories to support unjustifiable behaviour the storytellers needed to either believe (or appear to believe) the stories they were telling, or admit that their behaviour was unjustifiable. In this way, it seems to me that the storytellers became victims of their own stories. Having started on a particular path of self and group deception there was no easy alternative other than to continue on, and reinforce, that path.

The stories told to the outside world were slightly different. They were designed to provide a plausible explanation for some of the rumblings that were evident to external watchers. These stories were pervasive and believable, both because they were 'good' stories, in that they amused and entertained, and because of the hierarchical power of the storytellers. These stories gained power because of the power of the teller(s), and the stories were used to reinforce the power of the hierarchy. These stories were more powerful than the facts and in many cases they were designed to mislead, or redirect the organisational gaze away from the factual evidence. These stories were told with particular vehemence, as to question the authenticity of the story was to call into question the appropriateness of the power of the storyteller(s).

In such incidents direct evidence was used to counteract the story that had been circulated, but until that evidence was produced it was the story that was believed, and in each case the story circulated more widely around the company than did the evidence and counteraction. For example, when seeking to leave, Cass was told by several senior staff from different departments that they could not see why she wished to move department, as she would have to carry a full workload in her new place and not be able to cruise as she had up until then.

THE POWER OF STORY AND MYTH

The culture of DDT was known to be difficult before Cass joined, and she was warned that Bertha was very angry with her for being appointed to the job from which Bertha had been rejected, but Cass did not expect to become the focus for the sorts of behaviour described here. Cass described herself as increasingly being forced into the role of outsider, an isolate who did not accept the position given her. She also became an observer and, at times, commentator. She saw herself becoming a truth seeker standing out against injustice and fighting a corrupt system, on behalf of herself and others. Her role became ever more mythical and obdurate. She was the Wild Card, the Joker, and the Fool (Graves 1949)—in not following the myth-based rules (as played out by the Whites), she became the agent of chaos.

She was a threat that could not be incorporated into the feminine/masculine goddess-based power play voiced and enacted by Bertha and Bo. This undercurrent of sexist tension rippled through the whole organisation, but was particularly excised within the Whites as that was where the power play was, and where the male and female roles were most clear. The battle of the sexes and the need for control were played out upon the stage of myth, and it was the mythical nature of the roles that was, at times, openly referred to, and which sucked the players in. She was demonised and became an avatar for 'not us'—the outsider; the unknown. She was seen as the archetypal 'Other'. This avatar was particularly invoked at times when the Whites wished to emphasise their power—as an aid to delineating the group boundaries and a legitimation for the denial of unwelcome views. ·

She also eventually saw herself as a Cassandra. Her links with the wider organisation enabled her to act outside the group—they also helped her better understand some of the wider political issues faced by the group. She several times tried to feed these back to the Whites, but her comments were taken as interventions in the power play, though that was not her intention. They were met aggressively and she found herself further vilified, even though almost everything she foretold came to pass. Indeed, that she was consistently proved right seemed to further acerbate her Othering.

Over time she became isolated, depressed, and stressed. She lost confidence in her ability and in her judgement. She started to fear interactions with others and avoided social situations. She lost her belief in her own ability and in her sense of self. She had to fight not to see herself in the cardboard cut-out terms with which she was portrayed. She dreaded going to work and meeting those who were supposed to be her close colleagues who eroded her 'self'. She had been naïvely confident in her ability to work alongside Bertha and the rest of DDT. She did not know what her 'self' had been, she could not say what her 'self' was now: She could not say exactly how she changed but she did know that she was no longer the social, engaged, and enthusiastic person that she had been when she first started DDT. This was not about changing social identity, changing hats or persona; this was much deeper. Her self became eroded, submerged by the onslaught of Othering. (Cass: 'As I read this, over 30 years on, I still see this as a very dark time; still wake up with nightmares about it. The hurt has faded, but it has fundamentally altered me'.)

Perhaps if there is a moral to this story of power it is about the power of stories, but myths don't need morals—we play to them and incorporate them, and they drive us without our knowing. Other than Bertha, the majority of characters in the story rarely referred to themselves in mythical terms, yet did, at times, refer to their ways of being with labels borrowed from myth. At those times they recast themselves, borrowing 'divine afflatus'. They garnered the courage to be brave, brilliant, and inspired (though not necessarily to be humane)—to stand above the normal. This enhanced focus cascades even to the seeking of the myths underlying this story of pain as well as power—reviewing it in mythological terms creates an understanding and a closure that is not available through discussions of behaviour or power.

A final thought: The nature of the group of people meant that it was particularly susceptible to the feminine mystique and the Goddess-based rules. Yet, as epitomised in Graves (1949), the tool of the Goddess is the Fool and the Agent of Chaos. The Goddess eschews the rule-bound and the customary. Perhaps Cass was not as divorced from the Goddess as she was portrayed.

REFERENCES

Andersson LM & Pearson CM (1999) 'Tit for tat? The spiraling effect of incivility in the workplace', *Academy of Management Review* 24(3)452–471.

Baillien E, Neyens I, Witte HD, & Cuyper ND (2009) 'A qualitative study on the development of workplace bullying: Towards a three way model', *Journal of Community and Applied Social Psychology* 19(1)1–16.

Bjørkelo B (2013) 'Workplace bullying after whistleblowing: Future research and implications', *Journal of Managerial Psychology* 28(3)306–323.

Brewer G & Whiteside E (2012) 'Workplace bullying and stress within the prison service', *Journal of Aggression, Conflict and Peace Research* 4(2)76–85.

Cortina LM, Kabat-Farr D, Leskinen EA, Huerta M, & Magley VJ (2013) 'Selective incivility as modern discrimination in organizations evidence and impact', *Journal of Management* 39(6)1579–1605.

Cortina LM, Magley VJ, Williams JH, & Langhout RD (2001) 'Incivility in the workplace: incidence and impact', *Journal of Occupational Health Psychology* 6(1)64–80.

Cowie H, Naylor P, Rivers I, Smith PK, & Pereira B (2002) 'Measuring workplace bullying', *Aggression and Violent Behavior* 7: 33–51.

D'Cruz P & Noronha E (2011) 'The limits to workplace friendship: Managerialist HRM and bystander behaviour in the context of workplace bullying', *Employee Relations* 33(3)269–288.

Diestel S, Cosmar M, & Schmidt K (2013) 'Burnout and impaired cognitive functioning', *Work & Stress* 27(2)164–180.

Einarsen S & Mikkelsen EG (2003) 'Individual effects of exposure to bullying at work', in Einarsen S, Hoel H, Zapf D, & Cooper CL (Eds) *Bullying and Emotional Abuse in the Workplace:* 127–144. London: Taylor & Francis.

Einarsen S, Hoel H, Zapf D, & Cooper CL (2011) 'The concept of bullying and harassment at work: The European tradition', in Einarsen S, Hoel H, Zapf D, & Cooper CL (Eds) *Bullying and Harassment in the Workplace*: 3–40. Boca Raton, FL: Taylor & Francis.

Ferris GR, Treadway DC, Perrewe PL, Brouer RL, Douglas C, & Lux S (2007) 'Political skill in organizations', *Journal of Management* 33: 290–320.

Fox S & Stallworth LE (2005) 'Racial/ethnic bullying: Exploring links between bullying and racism in the US workplace', *Journal of Vocational Behavior* 66(3)438–456.

Frankenberg R (1993) *White Women, Race Matters: The Social Construction of Whiteness*. Minneapolis: University of Minnesota Press.

Goffman E (1990) *The Presentation of Self in Everyday Life*. London: Penguin Books.

Gramsci A (1971) *Selections from the Prison Notebooks*. London: Lawrence & Wishart.

Graves R (1949) *Seven Days in New Crete*. London: Quartet Books.

Hansen AM, Hogh A, Persson R, Karlson B, Garde AH, & Orbaek P (2006) 'Bullying at work, health outcomes, and physiological stress response', *Journal of Psychosomatic Research* 60: 63–72.

Hoel H & Beale D (2006) 'Workplace bullying, psychological perspectives and industrial relations: Towards a contextualized and interdisciplinary approach', *British Journal of Industrial Relations* 44(2)239–262.

Hoel H & Cooper C (2000) *Destructive Conflict and Bullying at Work*. Report Sponsored by the British Occupational Health Research Foundation, University of Manchester, Manchester.

Hoel H, Cooper CL, & Faragher B (2001) 'The experience of bullying in Great Britain: The impact of organizational status', *European Journal of Work and Organizational Psychology* 10: 443–465.

Jones KP, Peddie CI, Gilrane VL, King EB, & Gray AL (2013) 'Not so subtle meta-analytic investigation of the correlates of subtle and overt discrimination', *Journal of Management* doi:10.1177/0149206313506466

Kivimaki M, Elovainio M, & Vahtera J (2000) 'Workplace bullying and sickness absence in hospital staff', *Occupational and Environmental Medicine* 57: 656–660.

Kreiner B, Sulyok C, & Rothenhausler HB (2008) 'Does mobbing cause post-traumatic stress disorder? Impact of coping and personality', *Neuropsychiatry* 22(2)112–123.

Lee R & Brotheridge C (2006) 'When prey turns predatory: Workplace bullying as a predictor of counter aggression/bullying, coping and well-being', *European Journal of Work and Organisational Psychology* 15(3)352–377.

Lee RT & Brotheridge CM (2011) 'Sex and position status differences in workplace aggression', *Journal of Managerial Psychology* 26(5)403–418.

Leung K, Bhagat RS, Buchan NR, Erez M, & Gibson CB (2005) 'Culture and international business: Recent advances and their implications for future research', *Journal International Business Studies* 36: 357–378.

Lillemor R, Hallberg M, & Strandmark MK (2006) 'Health consequences of workplace bullying: Experiences from the perspective of employees in the public service sector', *International Journal of Qualitative Studies on Health and Wellbeing* 1: 109–119.

Lutgen-Sandvik P (2003) 'The communicative cycle of employee emotional abuse: Generation and regeneration of workplace mistreatment', *Management Communication Quarterly* 16: 471–501.

Lutgen–Sandvik P, Tracy SJ, & Alberts JK (2007) 'Burned by bullying in the American workplace: Prevalence, perception, degree, and impact', *Journal of Management Studies* 44(6)837–862.

Martin S & Klein A (2013) 'The presumption of mutual influence in occurrences of workplace bullying: Time for change', *Journal of Aggression, Conflict and Peace Research* 5(3)147–155.

McDonald, S. & Ahern, K. (2002), 'Physical and emotional effects of whistleblowing', *Journal of Psychosocial Nursing and Mental Health Services* 40(1) 14–27.

McTernan WP, Dollard MF, & LaMontagne AD (2013) 'Depression in the workplace: An economic cost analysis of depression-related productivity loss attributable to job strain and bullying', *Work & Stress* 27(4)321–338.

Mikkelsen EG & Einarsen S (2002) 'Basic assumptions and symptoms of post-traumatic stress among victims of bullying at work', *European Journal of Work and Organizational Psychology* 11: 87–111.

Near JP & Jensen TC (1983) 'The whistleblowing process. Retaliation and perceived effectiveness', *Work and Occupations* 10(1)3–28.

Parzefall MR & Salin DM (2010) 'Perceptions of and reactions to workplace bullying: A social exchange perspective', *Human Relations* 63(6)761–780.

Rhodes C, Pullen A, Vickers MH, Clegg SR, & Pitsis A (2010) 'Violence and workplace bullying: What are an organization's ethical responsibilities?', *Administrative Theory and Praxis* 32(1)96–115.

Rothschild J & Miethe TD (1994) 'Whistleblowing as resistance in modern work organizations. The politics of revealing organizational deception and abuse', in Jermier JM, Knights D, & Nord WR (Eds) *Resistance and Power in Organizations*: 252–273. London: Routledge.

Rothschild J & Miethe TD (1999) 'Whistle-blower disclosures and management retaliation. The battle to control information about organization corruption', *Work and Occupations* 26(1)107–128.

Samnani A (2013) ' "Is this bullying?" Understanding target and witness reactions', *Journal of Managerial Psychology* 28(3)290–305.

Skogstad A, Einarsen S, Torsheim T, Aasland MS, & Hetland H (2007) 'The destructiveness of laissez-faire leadership', *Journal of Occupational Health Psychology* 12(1)80–92.

Stark E (2007) *Coercive Control: The Entrapment of Women in Personal Life.* Oxford: Oxford University Press.

Strandmark MK & Hallberg LRM (2007) 'The origin of workplace bullying: Experiences from the perspective of bully victims in the public service sector', *Journal of Nursing Management* 15(3)332–341.

Taylor SE, Sherman DK, Kim HS, Jarcho J, Takagi K, & Dunagan MS (2004) 'Culture and social support: Who seeks it and why?', *Journal of Personality and Social Psychology* 87(3)354–362.

Treadway DC, Ferris GR, Duke AB, Adams GL, & Thatcher JB (2007) 'The moderating role of subordinate political skill on supervisors' impressions of subordinate ingratiation and ratings of subordinate interpersonal facilitation', *Journal of Applied Psychology* 92: 848–855.

Treadway DC, Shaughnessy BA, Breland, JW, Renmin JY, & Reeves M (2013) 'Political skill and the job performance of bullies', *Journal of Managerial Psychology* 28(3)273–289.

Watson TJ (2000) 'Ethnographic Fiction Science: Making sense of managerial work and organisational research processes with Caroline and Terry', *Organisation* 7(3)513–534.

World Health Organization (WHO) (2001) *World Health Report 2001: Mental Health, New Understanding, New Hope*. Geneva: World Health Organisation.

Zerubavel E (2006) *The Elephant in the Room; Silence and Denial in Everyday Life*. Oxford: Oxford University Press.

Section 3

Aspects of Other

The chapters in the previous section focused on self, asking, what is meant by 'self'? What of the future self? And, what of the effects on self of a hostile environment? Taken together they present a picture of self that emerges through the relationship with other. The self cannot be fixed, measured, or defined, or at least can only be done so for one moment in time. It is changeable and composed of preferences, not fixed attributes. It is open to introspection, and preferences can change in accordance with how we view our past and future. However, we cannot create our self out of nothing.

Theory and practice show that the self is co-created. Our current selves, where we are now, are like this because of our experience of the relationships we have had with others. Co-creation of such relationships strengthened the self, but the self is also vulnerable to the other. The idea of identity and situation-specific multiple identities can be seen as a cocoon around the core of self, as an interface with the other. The chapters in this, the third section of the book, focus on that opposite end of the archetypal structure, the 'other'; however, as in the previous section, discussing the other also necessitates discussing self and identity.

Chapter 10 is based in Central Europe shortly after the Velvet Revolution of the late 1980s and early 1990s, in which the rhetoric was dominated by notions of freedom and change. This was a time in which there was so much buoyancy and enthusiasm for the idea of freedom for the self, alongside visions of the entrepreneurial free-market economy. This chapter explores one small part of that time, and questions whether it is ever possible to be 'free' in this way.

The second chapter in this section (Chapter 11) follows the notion of decision-making and the collective appetite for risk-taking, this time located in the boardroom and focused upon negotiating the group appetite for financial risk. This chapter exposes the idea of a hidden culture associated with farming and the countryside that has cooperative values more akin to the storytelling future described in Chapter 8, than to the heroic cut and thrust that one would expect to find in most boardrooms.

Chapter 12 focuses on difference in ways of asserting self against other by exploring differences in the approach to conflict and suggesting that the

nature of the conflict differs according to the extent to which the participants interpret the conflict as an attack on their core values. For those who
see their idea of their self to be under attack the conflict is personal, bitter,
and hard-fought. When notions of self are not implicated in this way the
conflict is seen as a matter of negotiation. The chapter also documents times
when managerialism has unwittingly attacked notions of self and turned
negotiation into bitter conflict.

10 Freedom and Choice

'*For to be free is not merely to cast off one's chains, but to live in a way that respects and enhances the freedom of others*'.

(Nelson Mandela 1995: 544)

The previous section focused on 'self', the central core of the individual, carrying with it ideas of individuality, uniqueness, and freedom to be one's own person. This is the sense one feels when thinking about buying something and saying 'no, that is not "me", but this one is "me", I will buy that' (Presskorn-Thygesen & Bjerg 2014). However, this single sentence carries a lot of baggage with it. The act of consumption, choosing one thing over another, citing preference for something that enhances the sense of me, becoming part of the collective bargaining around identity, marketing schemes, and the tangled web of finance: That act is all part of the individual interacting with others. In this chapter I explore the complexity of this chimera of individual freedom and choice as it is compounded by the wider envisaged future of the free market and economic choice that emerged during the Velvet Revolution in central Europe.

This account arises from the time when I was working with deans, senior academics, and government ministers from central Europe, helping them establish management schools in their countries during the Velvet Revolution. The central Europeans were embracing the Western rhetoric of freedom and democracy, of the free market and entrepreneurship, with open arms. Freedom of choice and management teaching were held to be underdeveloped at that time. I shall put this in context by first saying a little bit about the Velvet Revolution and action learning.

THE VELVET REVOLUTION

After World War II central Europe was characterised by control through the central fiat: almost 100% state ownership of industry. Managers were expected to follow centrally imposed rules and regulations without question;

their career progression was largely related to their links with the party hierarchy and depended on obedience and conformity to such centralised decision-making. The threat of force against workers and managers who tried to evade commands resulted in a reluctance to take responsibility and a lack of initiative or innovation (Skuza et al. 2013). Creativity and original thinking were not valued, management style was bureaucratic and authoritarian, and education, throughout the school system and right up to university level, was largely limited to received knowledge. In Poland significant social discontent was led by Solidarity, who won the first free elections in 1989, leading to major reforms that helped lower inflation, opened the Polish market to foreign companies, and allowed the private business sector to expand (Weinstein & Obloj 2002).

The work that I present here started in Poland just as people were finally starting to believe the dream of being able to live their lives freely and to be able to choose their way forward. I designed it to cascade into other central European countries as they also sought to realise the dream. This, the Central European Management Teacher Development Programme (CEMTDP), was funded jointly by the European Commission (EC) under TEMPUS, and by the Austrian Ministry. I pulled together a collaborative international partnership comprising Lancaster University, UK; Erasmus University, Rotterdam, The Netherlands; Copenhagen University, Denmark; Wirtschaftsuniversität Wien, Austria; Adam Mickiewicz University, Poznan, Poland; and Slovak Technical University, Bratislava. The central European partners each coordinated a network of institutions from their own country working within the programme. All partners played equal, though differing parts in the programme, and I coordinated and directed CEMTDP from Lancaster University, UK. Each 'Western' institution provided one or two tutors, and up to three researchers. The yearly variation in numbers was caused by the level of funding received for that year. Overall, the programme linked more than 45 institutions across Europe, 14 nationalities, and 130 management academics (many of whom also held government positions and/or managerial positions in small and medium-sized enterprises). It was seen to be very successful, and, on behalf of the EC, I presented the programme as an exemplar of the European TEMPUS initiative to the Swedish Council of Ministers.

ACTION LEARNING

I include a brief description of the programme later in this chapter (a fuller description can be found in Lee, 1996), but before I do so I shall say a few words about action learning to explain why it was so important for the programme. In establishing CEMTDP it became clear that our central European partners were looking to the West to provide best practice and homogenized learning (Clegg & Ross-Smith 2003). They were expecting an ex-cathedra approach by which they learnt from the experts in a way that mirrored their previous practice under the command economy, and 'distanced them from a sense of responsibility for their learning' (Pfeffer & Fong 2002: 85). In order to break from that cycle it was essential that they experienced, heart and soul as well as head, a way of encountering learning that encouraged them to challenge and critique the received wisdom that they were being handed by the many 'experts' that were flooding into central Europe.

Action learning, incidental learning, and, project-based learning each assume that learning and knowledge are derived from and are integral to everyday tasks and experiences at work. Action Learning is generally group based, and can be seen as a way by which the (normally) facilitated group helps individuals to review their experiences by non-evaluative exploration of the issues, as presented by the individual, leading to deeper reflection about the learning inherent in these experiences; the creation and incorporation of a wider understanding of the import of this learning in relation to other's experiences, theories, and models; and the building of possible future ways of working, and evaluating and modifying these approaches (see Chapter 3). Successful action learning is rooted in a belief that we can do something about our situation—a positive view to life—and is based upon trust and confidentiality (McGill & Beaty 1992). Although focused on the individual, the 'learning' is derived from a collective enquiry into actual and current organisational projects and projections, enabling a critical questioning of a specific situation from several perspectives. This facilitates reflexive questioning, and political, emotional, and ethical components as well as its conceptual or technical aspects (Reynolds & Vince 2004). Such collective questioning helps challenge power relationships (Elliott & Reynolds 2002), which were such a key part of the old command economy.

Freedom of choice is an essential element in the ideology of action learning. The individual is seen to have free choice in defining the issue to be focused upon. Others in the group collectively address the stated problem, but the ways and methods of approaching this issue are related to the individual's understanding and experience of this and similar issues and thus cannot be dictated by others. The individual has a choice about the degree to which he or she wishes to accept others' views and the relevance of others' experiences to the issue. Finally, it is only the individual who can choose, commit themselves to, and carry out a course of action that they believe best suits their needs, and who can fully evaluate and modify this approach in the light of their revised understanding of the parameters of the issue.

When, as educators, we adopt an action learning approach, we also proclaim adherence to the individual's right to freedom of choice. Ideologically, this sits relatively easily with the Western focus upon individualism, experience, entrepreneurship, free-market economies, intellectual freedom, and freedom of speech. Central Europe, in so far as it was looking to the West for the development of the post-communist era, was moving away from collectivism, socialism, and centrally planned economies towards freedom of choice and all this entails. This presented a timely opportunity to work with freedom of choice within the educational arena.

CENTRAL EUROPEAN MANAGEMENT TEACHER DEVELOPMENT PROGRAMME

Action learning therefore appeared to be the appropriate methodological approach for CEMTDP. I hoped this would avoid the imposition of culturally inappropriate Western 'know-how' whilst creating an atmosphere of open academic investigation, networking, and the sharing of experiences.

The programme ran for three cycles, each fellow (30 fellows per year) experiencing it as a two-year engagement during which, as part of a small group, they evaluated their current practice in the light of their experiences in the first year—developing an implementable project designed to meet the needs of themselves and their institution. The majority of these projects focused upon the generation of alternative approaches to existing provision, or the creation of new provision, and ranged across the full spectrum of management education provision.

In their first year on the programme participants met formally at three workshops. The first, held in Central Europe, was introductory and exploratory—designed to be flexible and responsive to participant needs, whilst providing a framework by which to understand Western practice. In the second workshop a third of the group went to Copenhagen, a third to Rotterdam, and a third to Lancaster, and each workshop was designed to meet fellows' stated hopes—making use of in-company visits, and specialists and technology more readily available in the West. The third workshop was held in Vienna each year, and focused upon a shared exploration of the experiences and learning generated by the programme, the planned projects, and their future implementation.

Regular informal group meetings were encouraged, and were at times attended by Western partners in the form of monitoring meetings. Each year of the programme was followed by researchers from each partner institution who had also spent some time with fellows in their home institutions under their 'normal' conditions, and who provided invaluable feedback upon the applicability (or otherwise) of much that occurred. The working language was English, and there was no facility for translation as such, but each year the programme was supported by what I termed 'cultural catalysts': people who were much more than interpreters. They were bicultural and able to act as a bridge between the cultures, being seen as trustworthy by both sides, and thus diminishing the potentially dangerous clustering of them-and-us.

The use of ex-fellow co-tutors reinforced the catalytic process, as they had the added advantage of having already lived the (often) highly confusing experiences of the programme in the previous year (particularly those experiences associated with the workshops and company visits situated in the West). They reported gaining deeper insight into the objectives and methods of the programme, and linked this heightened awareness to their direct involvement in tutor discussions about the progression of the programme and the management of issues as they arose.

Fellows were expected to implement their projects in the second year of their involvement. Whilst all partners were clear that this was not an assessed programme, there was a strong belief that the value of the programme (and our time/effort/emotional debt) might best be judged by the extent to which the projects were implementable and helped to create the conditions for stable and long-term change.

Results, apparent from the first year in Vienna, were the degree to which cross-school networking took place; the publication of a series of books of Polish materials, the first of which contained a variety of Polish case studies springing directly from the programme (Bednarski 1991); and the early implementation of whole projects or parts of the projects, and the effects those had on the respective institutions and their staff and students. By the end of the second year of each intake the majority of projects had been implemented, some of which had a dramatic effect upon the culture of the particular subsection of the participant's institution.

In principle this sounds like a nice clean design—organisationally complex, but offering the opportunity for collaborative learning and exploration whilst avoiding some of the pitfalls of educational imperialism. Each of the tutors was committed to the principles of action learning and willing to expend the time and energy necessitated by working cross-culturally on a flexible and needs-responsive programme. However, this account is not intended to present the glossy picture—rather, the intention is to look under the surface at the dilemmas, contradictions, and challenges to the espoused philosophy.

DIVERSITY AND EMPOWERMENT

Perhaps what typifies the West most, within the realms of management education, is the wide diversity of views, approaches, and understandings of the implications of both management and of education (Snell & James 1994). As was evidenced in CEMTDP, each Western institution understood these differently—for example, although we all agreed on the principles of action learning, we were unable to achieve a clear consensus about how we should translate these into practice. Debates about the appropriateness of a particular sub-method at any one instance or about administrative procedures were normally held between tutors, researchers, and co-tutors, but became (at times) deliberately integrated into the programme. This was in order to facilitate the exploration and application of a multiplicity of views and theories generated by the meeting of different cultures, and in order to stimulate a dialogue between all participants, thereby attempting to reinforce the concept of a coalition of equals. If anything, open discussion of cultural differences between the tutors caused some initial disquiet for the fellows, but they increasingly engaged in such debate, noting that such openness was part of the learning process being advocated.

I previously suggested that successful action learning requires (within the ambit of freedom of choice) equality, trust, the ability to appreciate and work with diversity, a positive approach to life, and the perceived and actual ability to implement the chosen action. These qualities, however, were suppressed in central Europe. This suppression can, of course, also be found in the West—as I discuss in Chapter 2. An evaluation of a similar programme I co-directed in the UK showed that some of those new to management education feel that there should be a single and clear definition of what management is; a unitary body of knowledge that should be taught; a best method of delivery; and that the tutor, as expert, should be able to deliver these accurately and without hesitation (Swan et al. 1993). This drive for definition and clarity has deeper roots than 40 years of suppression; however, the central European situation acerbated the dilemmas we faced.

DILEMMAS OF ACTION LEARNING

a) Equality and Expertise

Our espoused philosophy was that of a coalition of equals creating learning partnerships. The extent to which we managed this in practice is debatable. Each of us, as tutors were, at times, less than willing to listen to other tutors' views of areas in which we considered ourselves to have some expertise. It seems to me, however, that we were more open to challenge by fellows— possibly because they tended to collude with us in respecting our views of our own expertise. Our difficulty, initially, was in encouraging challenge and debate. We tried to do so, both by challenging each other and by attempting participative decision-making. This, however, posed a dilemma. The major decisions tended to be made at the tutors' meetings in the evenings—which were also attended by researchers and co-tutors, but not by the fellows.

We thus, in some sense, created a form of second-class citizen—in that where decisions were to be made by the whole group we tended to present clear-cut choices that we had previously discussed, rather than the full range of possibilities. Why did we do this and how legitimate was it? Was it because decision-making with 50 people was just too unwieldy, or was there an element of 'decisions are best made by those who already have some understanding of the "Western" approach'?

Given that we, as tutors, were not fully open to being challenged, and that, implicitly, we colluded with clear power differentials within the programme, what right did we have to preach a doctrine of equality? Perhaps I am judging this by Western expectations. Evaluations have indicated a perception of openness and equality—citing this as a shock, a powerful learning point, and an example for the fellow's own practice. However, I think it is the power differential, itself, that created this impact. Would such a practical challenge to the expected way of working have been as successful if the fellows had been unwilling to give us the status of experts? Was it only by failing to act fully within our espoused philosophy that we were able to convert fellows to this philosophy?

One of the more persistent tensions (to which I will return later) was around the degree to which we should accede to the request for a clear knowledge-based programme focusing on the content of management disciplines at the expense of methodology and the design of curricula. Many fellows were not only concerned with finding the right view as given by the Western expert, but also with obtaining up-to-date information on their subject area. The charge of hypocrisy could be levelled at the way in which we handled this. In practice we were saying, 'In our professional opinion effective management is interdisciplinary and based around experience, and effective management education occurs when you work creatively within the choices open to you— as experts we tell you that you will gain more benefit from finding your own routes than listening to experts, therefore we will ignore your requests and your opinion'. We came to a compromise—providing specialist input in the second workshops—and called it 'meeting participants needs'!

b) Trust and Confidentiality

This was a particularly delicate issue for central Europeans—even in a non-assessed programme in which we explicitly stated our independence from the system and created opportunities to discuss it. The ability to trust us seemed to go through several stages. In general, when we met initially at the first workshop, the fellows felt to me to be friendly, but deferential and reserved. Increasingly over the week some would come out with what might previously been seen to be dangerous views, challenged each other, and, occasionally, queried us. However, this tended to be done at an intellectual level. Perhaps they were believing our statements about open and confidential discussion but not trusting us with the personal side of their lives—with the exception of a few late-night conversations around the bar.

The monitoring meetings and second workshops tended to provide a different view. We visited each other's homes, made friends, and swapped personal histories and scandal—some fellows remain personal friends of mine from this process. I suspect that this relaxation of barriers was, in part, related to moving the contact away from the work setting—in which the more traditional collusion of teacher and student in establishing a clear power differential reasserted itself. This became more apparent in the third workshops when fellows' behaviour appeared to differ—some were relaxing, challenging, and enquiring, whilst others returned to being more passive recipients of perceived wisdom.

I am reminded of a powerful dynamic that occurred on one workshop. The workshops were intense, draining, and held in places 'new' to many of the fellows. By midweek fellows were feeling exhausted and at one session a large number failed to appear. This is only to be expected and is not an unusual occurrence; however, I decided, given the reflective nature of the programme, to turn it into a 'live case' of 'how should we handle the situation, given the stated educational philosophy?' I have been successful with this approach before. I elicit a variety of different behavioural options, and work with the group in exploring their implications for future behaviour and the way in which they are embedded in different educational approaches.

This time it didn't work. As soon as I commented upon the missing people the atmosphere changed—becoming quiet and heavy. As I presented the dilemma people started avoiding eye contact and it became almost impossible to elicit a response. I tried to re-establish contact by emphasising that it is a problem we all face as we create participant power—with no success. I resorted to trying to elicit their feelings about the situation, resulting in total loss of contact. The following day everyone turned up, smartly dressed, formal and sullen.

I felt effectively ostracised from the group for about a day and a half until I made a total fool of myself, balancing precariously upon a pile of furniture so that I was visible to the whole group whilst trying to direct a group-sculpt. The atmosphere suddenly changed towards me and people came up to me, individually, throughout that evening and the following day to talk with me of their feelings—the question I had posed earlier that had gone completely unanswered. People commented that because I was perceived to be in authority they thought I was telling them off; they thought that this punishment should have been aimed at those who were missing, not them, and was therefore unjustified and unfair. Anyway, we had said the programme was to help them meet their needs and that we were of equal power—so what was wrong with going their own ways? They said that, initially, they could not get past the barrier of perceived censure to hear me say that I was not cross and that I was using it as an example of a decision point for teachers who have choice in how they respond and in which the chosen response effects the philosophy in practice. They felt that whole situation was alien to their way of working—students turn up or get into trouble. Their faith in action learning as an enjoyable and relevant method had been shattered if it really meant working with this diminution of power.

They reported that the change in their attitude came about because my jumping around on tables demonstrated to them, at the emotional level, that I really meant what I said about the relaxation of authority and the impact of change of style. They felt that I would not have done it if I had cared about my authority and status—and the whole exercise had been sufficiently hilarious to emphasise that there was motivational benefit in treating students as equals.

This leaves me with a series of observations. Once they were able to see me again as an 'equal' almost the whole group came to talk to me, individually, about their personal experiences and feelings—yet it never felt to me to be a safe issue to return to it in plenary. It seemed very hard to build trust in the wider arena. Secondly, I had thought we had already established a trusting climate—yet the response to perceived authority quickly shattered the trust, which could only be regained by de-powering the authority at the emotional level. Thirdly, fellows appeared to have a reasonable theoretical grasp of action learning; they had experienced this and other methods as participants and had explored the implications these have for working with experience, student involvement, and motivation—yet they reported not realising some of the implications for themselves as teachers until that moment. At the emotional level the idea of choice of methodology impacting upon practical outcomes had not been addressed, and I am not sure of the extent to which we could have addressed it (with impact) in a rational way. Finally, I would like to note for later discussion the strength of the emotional reaction against perceived hypocrisy in an authority figure.

c) The Ability to Appreciate and Work with Diversity

The programme helped to create a wider understanding and appreciation of the benefits of working with diversity, at least for some. As tutors we worked hard to change the climate from an academic debate to empathetic listening, and appear, at one level, to have succeeded. The subsection of the group we failed with was ourselves (and, to a certain extent, the researchers).

Each tutor was committed to action learning, but, in working with the learning sets, demonstrated different views of the theory in practice. Some tutors could be seen working with an 'academic' style of tutor-led direction and confrontation, whilst others approached the set with a 'laid-back' facilitative style. The fellows commented, discussed it between themselves, and appeared happy to see these differences as further examples of choices of methodology open for use. The tutors commented, whispered in tight conversations, and judged the other style as evidencing a failure to fully understand action learning. The researchers, as protégés of different tutors, tended to be as evaluative and as unwilling to accept difference as the tutors.

We felt able to preach the need for acknowledging and working with diversity, yet unable to acknowledge openly to each other that we held different views, that it was appropriate to discuss this difference, or even that there was no right way. Further, we tacitly accepted that the open face presented to the fellows should not be allowed to crack sufficiently to allow deeper debate about issues we might find threatening. As 'parents' we censored what we wished our 'children' to see, and subconsciously colluded to protect our power.

d) A Positive Approach to Life

It was noticeable that some fellows got a lot more out of the second work-shops than did others. Some fellows, who were perhaps more vocal or who perhaps had a stronger grasp of the language, and/or were more deeply along the route of self-development, were able to ask searching questions on company visits, find subject specialists and arrange visits and meetings, and use the facilities of the library provided. Other participants who were perhaps more reticent and more closely tied to their own cultural views of education and their previous ways of working felt it unusual that they personally had to go the library to get books, rather than have a secretary get them, or that they would be expected to cross-examine board members of companies rather than accept what they were told.

Those fellows who demonstrated such proactivity also appeared more willing to accept the existence of a multiplicity of choices, the freedom and responsibility associated with the act of choosing, and the fact that mistakes are inherent in learning from experience. These qualities are, of course, all subjective and it might be that those people who came close to the tutors were more willing to show these qualities—or that the tutors were more able to identify them in their closer friends. In either case, however, it raises several issues.

Self-motivation is a stated need, yet how do we, as tutors, create it? Is it not the sort of need that a self-motivating person can only see in another? What right do we have to expose someone to the need for it if they have not personally identified this need? If they have identified it are they not already self-motivating? It appears to be a value integral to the individual's view of life and linked to an appreciation of freedom of choice. Is it possible to generate it by talking about it? Can it be fostered by opening the notion of a multiplicity of choices or would that create confusion and withdrawal (as in the example given above) without the pre-existence of a proactive approach to choosing?

We took the easy route and noted a positive approach to life as a desir-able prerequisite for entry into the programme. Were we making an educa-tionally valid decision—trying to achieve maximum benefit for the effort we expended—or were we biasing participation sufficiently to enable us to 'preach to the converted'? As tutors talking of equality and freedom of choice, does this also mean equality of regard? If so, then we can be accused of holding ourselves separate/not acting equally or freely—as, if we were free to choose, we would naturally develop stronger friendships with some than with others. If not, what equality are we giving to others?

e) The Perceived and Actual Ability to Implement the Chosen Action

Having made it clear that the fellows would not be assessed we proceeded to agree that the success or otherwise of the programme would best be judged by the quality and implementability of the projects, and the long-term effect these had upon the cultures of the home institutions. In other words we established a form of assessment for ourselves, and then transmitted it (second-hand) to the fellows. It is arguable that any form of action learning tacitly contains assessment—how else could one evaluate the implementation of the action? Our hypocrisy was in imposing externally defined criteria as integral to the programme without attempting to clarify whether, given freedom of choice, the fellows would have decided upon similar measures.

As providers of the programme we patrolled our right to call the shots—implicitly saying that 'we know best'. Nearly all the fellows went back to a political and educational culture in their own institutions, which were likely to be highly resistant to change; they faced challenges from their Institutional hierarchy, colleagues, and students. Further, at a purely functional level, they were tied by time slots and by having to fit into previous curricula that had not been altered. Some projects were particularly far-reaching, thus presenting additional problems. Long-term evaluation indicated that some fellows addressed these issues; they implemented part or all of their projects, and received a great deal of support from their institutions in this. Their activities created a domino effect within their institutions, facilitating large-scale change. Success was linked to one or all of the following: position within the hierarchy; political acumen; scale, detail, and planning of project; support from colleagues, ex-fellows within the institution and fellows from other institutions; and general enthusiasm. Would these fellows have attempted such dramatic change without a clear mandate for it from the 'Western experts'?

Some fellows left the programme knowing that, because of external circumstances, they would be unable to implement their projects. It could be argued that they should never have been admitted to the programme—though we then meet the dilemma of appropriate entrance criteria for action learning that was broached above. Other fellows left the programme enthused by the possibility of change only to meet a succession of barriers. Were we not, in the long term, inspiring in some the opposite of our intentions—disillusionment and demotivation? Perhaps if they had been able to define their own assessment criteria their projects would have been more realistic—and achievable.

CHOICE—WHOSE RIGHT IS IT ANYWAY?

Earlier in this chapter I suggested that freedom of choice is an essential element in the ideology of action learning—to what extent did we respect this?

a) Freedom of Access?

Even before the start of the programme we faced choice-related issues. The fellows were selected (from quite intense competition) on subjective criteria linked to our understanding of the sort of person who might benefit most from the programme. What legitimacy did we have to suggest that this was a necessary part of the educational process? Fellows reported change and benefit from the programme—would those who were not selected also have benefited? Some fellows appeared to have been selected for political reasons—this helped the programme, but how legitimate was it?

b) Freedom of Participation?

How could we run an action learning programme without allowing people freedom to decide the level of their participation—yet how could we run it with a shifting and non-committed population? This question extends from the physical absence to sullen attendance. What right did I have to assume (and enforce) enthusiastic participation at all times? Was my covert message one of 'as the expert I believe that you need to know/experience this, and as long as you pretend you are interested I will pretend that there is no pressure on you to participate'?

To what extent do we, as educators, ever really allow full participation in group decision-making? Do we not collude with hidden structures that reinforce in-groups and out-groups? Yet, if we impose our authority and insist upon equal voice are we not, by that very intervention, destroying equality?

c) Choice of Content?

We came along as 'Western experts' and said, 'We believe that this is what you will need in the future'. The fellows said, 'We need something that will help us now—we know the constraints we are under'. We replied, 'We understand how you feel, but can assure you that Western provision is becoming increasingly interdisciplinary and experientially based, and there is no agreement about core content—we are trying to remedy our mistakes and don't want to see you repeat them'. They replied, 'We are not children. Stop patronising us—we can see your mistakes, but our situation is not the same as yours and we reserve the right to make and learn from our own mistakes'.

What do we do? The situation is made more complex by our espoused philosophy. If we meet their stated needs fully we can see that we will be providing a formal, content-driven programme that mirrors existing provision—we will be following the theory we espouse but in practice we will no longer be working with action learning. So we compromise. We impose the philosophy of action learning without following it fully in practice.

d) Choice of Perceived External Forces?

We said to the fellows, 'The world is your oyster—if you take a different view of life. Proactivity involves freedom of choice and the managing of external forces. Of course you can implement your project—how about persuading colleagues to alter strict timetables? You say you need more equipment, but equipment is largely props—you and your methodological choices are the most valuable resources. You are enthused about working participatively, but know that your students will find it hard to accept—convert them! Listen to what we say and have faith'.

At the same time we said, 'Only 10 minutes for coffee'; 'Your session overran by 20 minutes and it has totally ruined what I wanted to do'; 'How can I work without the overhead projector—I need flip charts, where are they?'; 'It is such a large group—I had better give a lecture'; 'We don't want to be too challenging—let's work with the methods they are used to'; 'I know you want to go there but the budget won't allow it'; 'You must do a project—it is expected' . . . and so on. We are well versed in creating external forces and presenting them as ways of limiting choice, and in rationalising them as part of the educational process.

e) Choice of Project?

We say that the project should be designed to meet the needs of the individual and the institution—but that it should be a group project, implementable, and with a focus upon curriculum development and methodology. Once again, we are allowing choice within clearly defined parameters. What right do we have to predetermine needs and ways of working in this manner? As noted above, for some, the hurdles we presented as a necessary part of the programme might be too high—an individual might work on a group project knowing that the possibility of implementing it at their own institution is minimal. As tutors, we were flexible about this, accepting individual and modified projects where we felt it was appropriate—but in doing so we maintained the role of authority figure, expecting and getting requests to deviate from the prescribed pattern rather than working through these issues as equals within the group.

DILEMMAS OF SELF-OTHER

I have presented, at several levels, a range of dilemmas associated with the provision of an action learning programme in central Europe. I have tried to demonstrate how attempts to work with these dilemmas have consistently opened us up to charges of hypocrisy. The fact that, in most cases, these charges were not levelled at us, and that a variety of forms of evaluation of the programme consistently showed it to be exciting, innovative, of high impact, creating long-term change, and central to the development of networks focusing on both research and applied issues, does not remove the need to explore the conflicts between theory and practice that we experienced.

As discussed in the introduction, I do not see these dilemmas as unique to either action learning or working with central Europeans. They occur in most educational provisions of any sort—including parenting! They are, perhaps, more poignant here because of the clear tensions between expertise and equality, freedom and control, and trust and suspicion, which are highlighted by our presuppositions about the other cultures; the fact that we were working with our opposite numbers (academics of equal standing); and the fact that we were working within an educational ideology that, in my belief, is incapable to being translated, truthfully, into practice.

These tensions are also core to the negotiation of self amongst others. The ideals of freedom and choice have been held as a rallying call in many recent uprisings, some more violent than others. They sing to the centre of our nature, to the ability to be 'me'. Yet actually they are about negotiating with the other, finding compromise, working together. However seductive the notion of freedom, the words do not easily transcribe into reality. Take the developments in Poland as an example.

In economic terms, Poland advanced well after the transition, and by 1995 the number of foreign businesses operating in Poland grew to over 10,000 companies (CSOP 2009). By 2008, this figure had reached over 21,000. However, this led to increased competition for managerial and professional talent, and management development did not keep pace with market demands (Rozanski 2008). The Velvet Revolution might have brought freedom to the decision-making process, but Polish managers lacked the skills required to lead a company in the free-market economy (Hardy 2007). For example, many senior managers remained autocratic and highly centralised, leading to middle- and lower-level managers' increased alienation, limited initiative, and decreased willingness to participate in changes. Despite the emergence of a capitalist market many managers did not see the need for change, leading to management practices being embedded in a socialist framework that failed to converge with Western models (Vaiman & Holden 2011). Polish management practice faced the problem of a constant interplay between deeply rooted survival patterns developed under communism and superficial values 'hastily imported from the West' (Kozminski 2008: 188).

Poland had previously been reasonably egalitarian, but the sharp decline in real wages in the early 1990s brought increasing poverty, the new free-market focus brought inequality, and the process of privatisation started being perceived as exploitation, betrayal, and theft (Skuza et al. 2013). Feelings of cynicism, social injustice, and low trust quickly emerged. In 1989, almost 65% of Poles felt that most people could not be trusted, increasing to 81% by 2005 (World Values Survey 1989–2005).

Consumption

The rhetoric of freedom of self does not easily marry with the needs of others. This is emphasised in the debates around consumption that I mentioned at the beginning of this chapter. According to Holt (2002: 88), it is the market that now produces 'the experiential and symbolic freedom' that others argued could only be achieved by emancipation (Firat & Venkatesh 1995). The social side of our selves, our many identities, are created and recreated through marketing and consumption. Our social identities impact upon our perceptions, emotions, and behaviour, sometimes to the detriment of our self. Dittmar (2000: 106) suggests that consumer goods are seen to be an important route towards success, identity, and happiness, and people purchase these goods to bolster their self-image, drawing on the symbolic meanings associated with products in an attempt to bridge gaps between how they see themselves, how they wish to be, and how they wish to be seen. In this way, shopping functions as a form of identity repair (Dittmar 2005: 856). Our fantasies are bolstered by advertising, branding, and the ideology of consumption in general and teach us how to desire (Schroeder & Zwick 2004).

As we move from a form of self-centred freedom in early childhood, we develop an understanding of other, we adopt multiple social identities, and we learn to negotiate what freedoms and responsibilities might be available to us. The move from a command economy to market economy illustrates this on a grand scale; however, it is much more nuanced and complex than the words suggest. Friedman (1970) argued that a firm's only responsibility is to maximise profits, but that maxim, though still followed by some, seems very dated now. The market economy, with its focus on profit, the creation of consumption, and the generation of hyperreal social identities, is coming under question. Egan-Wyer et al. (2014) suggest that there is a fundamental incompatibility between ethics and capitalism (see also Chapter 17) such that major philanthropists today see themselves as 'liberal communists', by which the success of capitalism allows the promotion of classic goals of communism, such as the eradication of world hunger through the charity of the wealthy (Beverungen et al. 2013).

Conclusions

In this chapter I have looked at issues of freedom and choice within action learning situated in central Europe just as it was moving from the command economy to the market economy. I have tried to open up some of the dilemmas faced within each of these areas, and also to explore the core similarities between them, all of which hinge upon the relationship between self and other and the mediation of social identities. The form of national economies is more normally viewed in terms of structure, and the creation of entrepreneurship in terms of agency. Later sections of this book do look at these issues in terms of structure and agency, but I have chosen to raise them here in order to emphasise that the very personal issues of self and other also play out on a much wider canvas.

REFERENCES

Bednarski A (1991) *Materialy pomocznicze do cwiczen z organizacji i zaradzania.* Toruń : Uniwersytet Mikołaja Kopernika.

Beverungen A, Murtola A, & Schwartz G (2013) 'The communism of capital?', *Ephemera* 13(3)483–495.

Central Statistical Office of Poland (CSOP) (2009) *Statistical Yearbooks of Poland, Yearbook of Foreign Trade Statistics.* Warsaw: Statistical Publishing Establishment.

Clegg SR & Ross-Smith A (2003) 'Revising the boundaries: Management education and learning in a postpositivist world', *Academy of Management Learning and Education* 2: 85–98.

Dittmar H (2000) 'The Role of Self-image in Excessive Buying', in Benson AL (Ed) *I Shop Therefore I Am:* 105–132. Lanham: Aronson.

Dittmar H (2005) 'A new look at "compulsive buying": Self-discrepancies and materialistic values as predictors of compulsive buying tendency', *Journal of Social and Clinical Psychology* 24(6)832–859.

Egan-Wyer C, Pfeiffer A, & Svensson P (2014) 'The ethics of the brand', *Ephemera* 14(1)1–11.

Elliott C & Reynolds M (2002) 'Manager-educator relations from a critical perspective', *Journal of Management Education* 26: 512–526.

Firat AF & Venkatesh A (1995) 'Liberatory postmodernism and the reenchantment of consumption', *Journal of Consumer Research* 22(3)239–267.

Friedman M (1970) 'The social responsibility of business is to increase its profits', *New York Times Magazine,* September 13(32–33)122–124.

Hardy J (2007) 'The new competition and the new economy: Poland in the International Division of Labour,' *Europe-Asia Studies* 59(5)761–777.

Holt D (2002) 'Why do brands cause trouble? A dialectical theory of consumer culture and branding', *Journal of Consumer Research* 29(1)70–90.

Kozminski AK (2008) *Management in Transition.* Warszawa: Difin.

Lee MM (1996) 'Action Learning as a Cross-Cultural Tool', in Stewart J & McGoldrick J (Eds) *Human Resource Development:* 240–260. London: Pitman.

Mandela N (1995) *Long Walk to Freedom. The Autobiography of Nelson Mandela.* London: Macdonald Purnell.

McGill I & Beaty L (1992) *Action Learning: A Practitioner's Guide.* London: Kogan Page.

Pfeffer J & Fong CT (2002) 'The end of business schools? Less success than meets the eye', *Academy of Management Learning and Education* 1: 78–95.

Presskorn-Thygesen T & Bjerg O (2014) 'The falling rate of enjoyment: Consumer capitalism and compulsive buying disorder', *Ephemera* 14(2)197–220.

Reynolds M & Vince R (2004) 'Critical management education and action-based learning: Synergies and contradictions', *Academy of Management Learning & Education* 3(4)442–456.

Rozanski A (2008) 'The educational orientation of participants in Postgraduate Managerial Study Programs in Poland,' *Human Resource Development International* 11(1)91–99.

Schroeder JE & Zwick D (2004) 'Mirrors of masculinity: Representation and identity in advertising images', *Consumption Markets & Culture* 7(1)21–52.

Skuza A, Scullion H, & McDonnell A (2013) 'An analysis of the talent management challenges in a post-communist country: The case of Poland', *The International Journal of Human Resource Management* 24(3)453–470.

Snell R & James K (1994) 'Beyond the tangible in Management Education and Development', *Management Learning* 25(2)319–340.

Swan J, Aspin T, Holloway J, Lee MM, & Perica, L (1993) 'The Future of Management Education and Development: An Evaluation of the ESRC Management Teacher Fellowship Scheme in the UK', in *The Crafting of Management Research:* 231–232. Proceedings of the British Academy of Management Annual Conference: Milton Keynes.

Vaiman V & Holden N (2011) 'Talent Management Perplexing Landscape in Central and Eastern Europe,' in Scullion H & Collings DG (Eds) *Global Talent Management:* 178–193. London: Routledge.

Weinstein M & Obloj K. (2002) 'Strategic and environmental determinants of HRM innovations in Post-Socialist Poland,' *The International Journal of Human Resource Management* 13(4)642–659.

World Values Survey Years 1989–2005 (2008) (www.worldvaluessurvey.org) Accessed 12/2009.

11 Decision-Making and Hidden Others

This chapter follows the thrust of the previous chapter in looking at self in relation to other, but in this case the 'other' has two forms. The initial focus of this chapter is the management of risk in a UK livestock market; however, the reality of life and death permeates the mart, and the way in which rumour is used indicates that the hill farming community has a way of being that is different to, but largely hidden beneath, the sanitised, Westernised norm.

I suggest in Section 1 that words are momentary signifiers—come and gone. Yet, even in passing, those signifiers trap the moment into a particular time and space—interpret it from particular viewpoints—pin it onto the board for observation and dissection. Storytelling, rumour, and innuendo offer multiple disparate levels of meanings—meanings that are hidden in the play of words and that are hard to dissect. They are a vehicle for symbolism and metaphor; they can be unattributable and a powerful force for changing perceptions. I use 'rumour' here, however, to indicate those times when a story is, at least initially, hidden from the object—sometimes circulating behind the person's back in a way that they cannot contradict.

In contrast the worlds of accounting and financial risk management are commonly partnered with notions of accuracy and the control of data. Pelzer (2007) explored the management of risk in the banking industry by which the 'potential excess of the markets is met by an excess of controlling'. He presented a fascinating insight into the amount of data processing and rule development that is involved, leading to a hyperreal quality of accounting figures. He pointed to the need to interpret the data and assess cases individually rather than blindly following the figures and applying standardised rules—but the need for formulae sensitive to individual cases creates further excess of data. He concluded that the dual expansion of risk and regulation links to an unachievable striving for completeness and perfection, but that it is only in hindsight that we can ever know whether the actions that were taken were appropriate.

This chapter offers a strong contrast to the practices described by Pelzer, though the conclusion is similar. I shall describe the workings of a successful livestock mart that carries severe financial risk, which it largely manages through rumour and speculation. In this I am both active participant and reflective observer. My experience and observations of working within the agricultural community and in the livestock mart serve as my 'research data' and my analysis of these inform the points I wish to bring out for examination.

THE FARMING COMMUNITY

Over the last 25 years I have become deeply involved in the agricultural community. I am a smallholder and my holding stands alongside two farms in the hills of rural Lancashire, in the northern end of the UK. We are part of a small community, living and working beside other small communities that have been in place since the earliest maps were drawn—my house dates from 1651 and was built on the remains of previous dwellings. When meeting someone for the first time it is usual to spend hours first talking about which bits of land they came from and where they now farm, and to cross-check family relationships. It is not unusual for this enquiry about family to go back seven generations, and to cover the details of the many distant family members—some of whom are likely to be found to be common to both. The feeling of living in a timeless environment is heightened by the nature of hill farming—which has little changed for several centuries. There are tractors instead of horses, milking is by machine instead of by hand, but the vast majority of the local farms remain tenanted—vestiges of the feudal system in which almost the entire population works on or as part of a large estate. Moss (2015) quotes James Rebank, a hill farmer: 'people lead lives devoted to something bigger than themselves—the landscape, the flocks and their continuation. Somebody like my father wouldn't have thought his life was particularly meaningful or significant in its own right, but he saw himself as part of a community and way of life and tradition. I deeply admire that in an age when most things are about the individual and about instant gratification and consumption'.

I have become involved in the community in several different ways (see Chapters 14 and 19) and was invited to become a director of the local auction mart (which I shall call M&M) in the late 1990s. This was a rare honour for someone from 'off' (not born to the community) and particularly for a woman—I was most definitely entering a man's world. I had previously bought and sold stock through the mart, and am good friends with various families in the community, but it was not until I took up my directorship that I realised, firstly, quite how alien the rural community is to urban conceptions of existence, or to 'best management practice' as preached by the Western gurus, and secondly, quite how hidden this difference is—the modern floats on top of the rural, like oil on water; neither is really aware of the other, nor is fully able to understand the other.

Each mart is the social nexus of the rural community. Farmers spend a lot of time alone and value meeting others at the marts. Old and young go there—whether they have stock in that day or not—to catch up on the news, make deals, and discuss trade and genealogy. Whilst trade, and thus money (or lack of it), is a major topic of conversation, money is not a metaphor for status as it often is in urban communities. Money lends security, but status does not necessarily follow wealth, qualifications, class, race, or religion. Some people are valued more than others, but 'status' is the wrong word for this. Precedence, or a (slightly) louder voice, is awarded by others for contribution to the community, from oneself, from family, and secondhand via friends. In my experience the rural community is more accepting of strangeness and eccentricity than the urban, yet much less accepting of self-aggrandisement.

That this way of being is alien to many also helps explain some of the tension and rejection felt by non-farming newcomers who bring with them their self-worth measured by achievements and money (especially as it is normally the rich who move to the countryside)—to find that their badges carry little of importance. There are those in the hills with high academic and professional qualifications, high positions and gongs, and/or lots of money, but these achievements are normally not made apparent—though are not particularly hidden. Instead, they are generally treated as irrelevant.

News travels from mart to mart and is mulled over thoroughly. Phones and information and communications technology (ICT) do facilitate the economic side of things—but the social still requires the deep consideration of all sides of whatever the issue is. There is much use of silence and reiteration—something that can only be done in person (Lee 2000). Much of the conversation is around relationships, either directly or by implication. Who helped whom, who 'borrowed' without returning, who to trust, who to rely on in an emergency, who is having problems, who to visit in hospital and why, and so on. It is said that if you kick one farmer then all the others in the area limp—there is an ethos of support and accepting difference. People are incredibly generous with their time, attention, and possessions, but if that generosity is abused the news will travel quickly.

Whilst I am rooted in the hill farming community of Lancashire, what I say is relevant to some degree to farming communities across the UK. Certainly, when I meet farmers from other regions the conversations follow similar patterns, and I have been told (and have found it to be true) that one farmer, on meeting another, a stranger from the other side of the country, can probably within about 10 minutes find some common relations, joint friends, and so on. I have had similar conversations with French and Irish farmers, so although it would be presumptuous to generalise about 'the farming community' it seems to me to be probable that there is some commonality of culture or in the 'way of being' that spans national boundaries and is associated with working the land. It is interesting to note that farmers make a clear distinction between the farming community (themselves) and the wider rural community.

Nearly all farms are classed as small and medium-sized enterprises, and farmers look to care for the land (which requires thinking 30 years to the future or longer—creating an environment and making plans for their children that they are unlikely to live to see come to fruition) as well as make a living and running a business with very little profit margin and very long hours. Although the social and economic concerns of the farmer are largely local, the tendrils of the agricultural community are global. Political and climatic conditions on the other side of the world influence trade and the cost of keep, and mart directors quite regularly go on fact-finding missions to far-flung places. The agricultural community is becoming more vocal and the marts, in conjunction with the National Farmers' Union, are increasingly acting as a mouthpiece for this. As was seen several years ago in the news coverage of foot-and-mouth disease and bluetongue, the public are starting to become more aware of the profound problems caused by shifts in the export market, in legislation and funding regimes, and in stock movement.

THE UK MART SYSTEM

Whilst the buying and selling of livestock, and thus debt, might seem quite simple, there are actually many different factors in play, so I shall explain those briefly before looking more closely at the management of risk in M&M. North-west England mainly supplies sheep and cattle (dairy and meat). Both are sold throughout the year, but the sale of sheep also has a strong cyclical element. There are three main types of stock. Firstly, for both sheep and cattle, there are breeding and society sales, which are of great importance for maintaining good quality stock and attract buyers from many countries—but which do not particularly impact upon my story here.

Secondly, stock is also bred in the hills for fattening in the more lush lowland climes. It is here that the annual sheep breeding cycle impacts, as the stock grows over the summer until it is big enough to move, and as the grass loses its goodness and dies back in winter, so there are only a few weeks in autumn in which the stock can be sold. Farms in the north-west sell many thousands of sheep through the mart at this time and make the vast majority of their income during these few weeks. Marts generally make a loss in the early parts of the year and rely upon this period for much of their income, which is in the form of commission. Both the farms and the marts are particularly vulnerable to the imposition of movement restrictions at this time.

Finally, stock is also bred to go directly to the slaughter market. It is this area of commerce that I wish to focus upon here, and trade in this is pretty steady throughout the year. About 40% of the stock for slaughter goes 'dead weight'—not through the mart system but directly to the abattoir or buyer (both normally working for supermarket chains and export). The farmers are paid for this in arrears and have to rely on the buyer to both weigh the animal accurately and to give them a decent rate per kilo. Stock that goes through the ring is weighed as it goes through, the sellers get paid promptly by the mart, and the rate is set by market forces. All the statistics from mart sales are published and the Livestock Auctioneers Association produces an indicative price—which influences dead weight payments. This provides a small incentive for farmers to put some decent stock through the marts, otherwise the indicative price would be depressed.

Some farms are tied into the dead weight system, with long-term agreements with particular abattoirs and buyers, but most decide where to take their stock based upon the condition of their stock at the time and where they think they can get the best price for it. In the Lancaster area there are several marts within an hour's drive, so farmers can choose between these as well as whether to go dead weight or not. Farmers study the statistics, talk to their neighbours, listen to the rumours, and judge; the criteria often comes down to where their friends are going, whether or not they respect the auctioneer, and whether they think there will be a good trade—that is, lots of buyers eager to pay a high price.

The problem for the marts is that to get a good trade, and so attract sellers and commission, they need the buyers there and buying—three big buyers round the ring makes for good trade and the buyers know their value. They look for marts that can produce the quantity and quality of beasts that their end customer requires. The buyers' agents will travel the length of the country, buying as they go, to satisfy their needs—which usually include an attractive deal for the agent, and good financial terms for the buyer. Buyers seek reduced commission where they can, but mainly look for extended terms of payment. Marts effectively act as banks, ensuring that the sellers get paid, and carrying the risk of the buyers not paying them promptly, if at all.

Buyers are normally on terms of payment within 14 or 21 days. Competition with other marts, and the need to attract and retain buyers, means that renegotiation of terms is difficult. Marts constantly face the risk of bad debt, and several have been brought down by it in the last few years. Insurance is only available, possibly, on those with decent assets, sound finances, and a good track record. Only a few fall into this category, and even if there is insurance it is capped. If Buyer X is going under, they can start buying heavily at several sales a week, delay payment, and sell elsewhere. Within a couple of weeks, if unchecked, they can be well outside their insurance limit and can present a serious bad debt (easily in the region of £100,000). The mart can stop a buyer trading, and risk not only good trade (and the rumours of bad trade and problems) on that day, but risk offending the buyer, and thus trade, for some while. Similarly, if the buyer won't or can't pay, then the mart can always initiate the legal route, but it is often in the better interests of the mart to allow the buyer to continue trading and so pay back some of the debt, than to lose it all in bankruptcy proceedings.

THE LIVESTOCK MART (M&M)

M&M comprises several agriculture-related companies. At the time of writing, it has 18,000 clients on its books, many of these are local, and others from across Europe. Many clients are also shareholders. As well as seeking profit for the shareholders M&M is committed to helping the farming community that it emerged from. M&M has grown steadily in the last few years—it is now the leading mart in the area, and even manages to pay dividends. The majority of M&M's income is derived from commission, which is normally around 3%. In 2006 the income was in the region of £1.5 million (turnover of about £60 million), yet M&M was very pleased to be able to produce a profit of around £32,000, as most marts consider themselves lucky if they break even. Only £20,000 was lost to bad debt in 2006, making it a good year.

The management of risk associated with debt is a key enduring focus for M&M—there are daily and weekly meetings about it, very many phone calls, visits, and legal letters chasing it—we have heard every excuse under the sun (the meat trade is not known for its delicacy), and it takes up an inordinate time at board meetings. The challenge is that not only does each account have unique circumstances and not only does the board establish formulae sensitive to individual cases as Pelzer discusses, but the circumstances of each transaction are dependent upon who the other buyers and sellers are that are in the ring, and the contribution that they are making to the trade at that particular moment. The auctioneers need some discretion about when to let someone buy more than they should, in order to keep the trade going. The administrators need to have flexibility to offer reduced commission to keep an agent coming. The managers need to be able to negotiate terms according to people's circumstances. The directors need a crystal ball.

The actions of many employees can minimise or enhance the risk, and all have to make snap decisions at times—normally under great pressure. Sometimes these decisions take them outside the 'rules', as laid out by the board. That this is accepted (normally) and occurs regularly is an interesting phenomenon in its own right, and is at odds with the infantilisation of the workforce (Sievers 1996). Although the actions of the employees influence risk management, the directors hold ultimate responsibility for it and do question actions and data. The board sits there with sheets and sheets of figures in front of them and consider them deeply, but these figures are rarely used as the criteria for formulaic judgements. Instead—they provide a shorthand route to highlighting which actions and which debtors the board should be most concerned about.

Then comes the long part—in which several hours can be spent sharing rumours and accumulating a common picture. Family circumstances, history, trading patterns, and liquidity of the debtor are discussed, as is the reaction of other marts to their trade. Have they been buying heavily elsewhere? Was that because Mr Y lost some stock on the other side of the country and asked the buyer for more—or was the buyer getting desperate? Who did the buyer normally buy for—would they back him? Who are his friends? Will they stop buying? Which of our competitors would they go to? What would be the long-term effect on future trade if the buyer were stopped tomorrow? For how long? Can the board trust him when he says a cheque is in the post?

The board sit with mugs of coffee and cakes from the mart cafeteria and swap speculation and rumour. They pull apart the multiple meanings and implications. They appreciate the cleanliness of making decisions upon neat financial criteria and regularly agree policy and formulate generic debt management regulations—but in practice these are more a statement of aspiration and come to nothing. Each time, the board revert to a case-by-case discussion. These discussions are within the confidentiality of the meeting, so (should) go no further and only the decisions are noted, which means that there is no way to query a decision—either by a board member or by that person whose business is threatened.

This is most definitely not what would be considered as a good meeting by any MBA student . . . and it came as a great cultural shock to me when I joined the board. To an outsider it looks like a total shambles, and to someone used to weighing up figures and criteria the idea of making such decisions based upon rumour seems (at the least) foolhardy. It is easy to see this process as a problematic legacy from the outdated way in which the farming community operates, and this is how I saw it at first—particularly as an outsider, lacking the knowledge of the farming community acquired and transmitted across the generations that was displayed by the other board members. Through this process the board make decisions that can close abattoirs, can put farms out of business, could force the closure of M&M, and could ruin lives.

Yet I have come to see that this is not a failure of the management process, but a different way of working. Unlike in the sanitised environment of quantification, such potentially life-changing decisions are not taken lightly—or from a distance. This method of working seems to balance best the needs of buyers and sellers—people continue to trade and the mart benefits. M&M should look to shareholder profit as the driver in making such decisions, yet the majority of shareholders are also farmers and M&M has not shrugged off its benevolent conception and remains rooted in support for the farming community that formed it many years ago. If we take Sievers's (2006) description of unconscious dynamics as socially induced, then I do not think this method of decision-making would work in a different sort of community—the long and detailed tendrils of knowledge and speculation about others that are part of the farming community are an essential part of this process. Though time consuming and largely unmanageable, decision-making by rumour seems to suit the needs of the community as well as the business.

RUMOUR AND WAYS OF BEING

I want to be clear here that I am not referring to the sorts of rumour or idle gossip that seem to pervade most communities—the chit-chat and speculation that people share to foster friendship and alliances. Nor am I talking of the sort of exchange in which we can say so much without saying anything at all, and pass it on in a deniable but knowing way. The multiple meanings and weasel words of innuendo. The betrayal and sacrifice of others on the altar of one-upmanship, accompanied by the handmaidens of suspicion, contempt, and assertion of power (Sievers 2007). This form of rumour permeates the halls of the aspiring upwardly mobile—and can be associated with power play, self-aggrandisement, and status seeking (the biggest gold card, the smartest car, the most expensive design), with its roots in covert competition.

The use of rumour in risk management at the mart is different: constructive, despite the occasionally destructive results. This difference is in part due to the reason behind the use of rumour—invoking confidentiality and clarity, unpicking the multiple meanings, rather than aggression or status seeking. I do see potential ethical problems with making decisions that can influence someone's future in a way that is not open to external scrutiny. The words are not intended to hurt; however, they are used to discuss every single bit of information we can get in order to build as complete a picture as possible, though such a picture can never be fully complete. Much of what is classed as rumour behind the closed doors of the board meeting would be openly told as stories within the community, and thus most tales would be open to inspection and challenge. There are few secrets in such a community.

Constructive rumour is also rooted in different ways of being. Each farm is a small community in its own right, and even the young children are given responsibility—for example, to collect the eggs each morning. Children grow up with a sense of responsibility, knowing their family history and their place within it, knowing how to manage machinery, stock, and themselves in what the normal urban parent would consider to be dangerous situations. People within the community often work alone, but also drop everything and help each other when necessary. They also know all about life and death. Even as a smallholder I spend most of April birthing and caring for lambs—and yet, by September I am examining them to decide which ones should be kept and which killed (Lee 1998). Farmers make life and death decisions daily, working towards a future that they actively think of, and talk of, extending beyond their own lifespan— moulding the farm, the environment, and the bloodlines of the stock for generations to come. They are aware of, and embrace, their own mortality, discussing their own life and death and that of others around them in a matter-of-fact way that in my experience rarely occurs in discussions between healthy urbanites.

Indeed, the closeness of the rural community (and the livestock mart) to the imminence of birth, the messiness and chaos of life and finalities of death, are rarely accounted for in our literature. For example, in much of the literature death and the death instinct are seen as destructive and to be avoided (Carr 2003). As Sievers (1990: 321) says, it 'is obvious that through our common neglect of death and mortality our life is losing its frame'. Yet for farmers death is another aspect of life, one they deal in on a daily basis. As a hub of the farming community a mart has a similar way of being—its activities are directly and inevitably about life and death.

Management and decision-making are emergent. The relative lack of infantilisation of the workforce is due at least as much to the nature of the employees as to the actions of management. The employees are committed to the workplace and the community it serves. There is a strong sense of collaboration, but employees are rarely subservient. In contrast, they have a sense of responsibility and self-reliance that can make leadership of the workforce problematic. Employees are generally aware of the financial risks that are taken by the mart, and certainly the more senior staff are aware of the effect their actions can have on these. They are freely asked, or give their opinions, about potential risk, and seek to coordinate their 'on-the-spot' decisions in a way that supports the community aims. Their relative autonomy, however, carries its own risk, both to the more immediate financial health and control of the company and to the nature of the company itself.

As indicated earlier, a single bad decision, made under pressure at the point of sale, can put the company seriously in debt. How that debt is collected is a problem that can settle at board level—so, to some extent, the management and the board are playing catch-up with the actions of the employees. Whatever rules are established, they are really only guidelines, and however much the board might think it is setting policy, it is only doing so in collaboration with the community (see Chapter 13). Decisions cannot be imposed upon employees without removing the value of their relatively autonomous contribution. Similarly, as marts are derived from and serve the rural community they cannot impose policy changes without the engagement and support of that community. The board are not entirely led by external factors—they do make decisions and expect these to be implemented. At times these decisions can be very hard, but the discussion is extensive and is around what would be in the best long-term interest of the farming community (this presupposes that the longevity of the Mart would advantageous to the community), not just about how profit can be maximised.

TWO WORLDS IN ONE

This way of being necessitates frequent, open, and opportunistic flows of information. It parallels the interconnectedness of life and death evident in the rural community with the interconnectedness of knowledge and information about that community: with rumour. The mart uses rumour as a part of its decision-making resources because that is part of its way of being. This way of being has strong similarities to the Chinese concept of Guanxi, which Hammond & Glen (2004) describe as a form of social network theory that contextualises individuals within a highly collectivist society and defines one's place in the social structure, providing security, trust, and a prescribed role. Guanxi developed as a form of gift economy (Mei-hui 1994) in the Chinese marketplace, and 'refers to the concept of drawing on connections in order to secure favors in personal relations. It is an intimate and pervasive relational network in which Chinese culture energetically, subtly, and imaginatively engage' (Luo 1997: 2).

As with the farming community, Guanxi distinguishes between insiders and outsiders who are treated with mistrust (Chu & Ju 1993) and lack of moral obligation (Hwang 1987). Insider relationships are family, colleagues, and classmates and are offered some degree of automatic trust, including the sharing of important, even secret, information (Gu 1990). Scallon & Scallon (1991: 471) say 'discriminating a boundary (between insider and outsider) is not only a localized and descriptive activity, it is a regulative and moral activity. . . . What is outside the boundary is not relevant in any way to what is inside'. Guanxi is tied to reciprocity. Favours are always remembered and returned, but not always quickly. People who don't return favours are seen as poisoning the well (Graham & Lam 2003). Guanxi is transferable. If Person A knows Person B and C, then B and C are socially obligated because they are part of the same network, even if they only have a common friend in Person A (Watts 2003). These kinds of additive relationships are also stabilising because they bring new information into the system without disrupting the system, leading to a long-term vision and relationships that are seen as permanent (Hammond & Glen 2004). Guanxi has been described as a cultural remnant of a feudal society, an artefact of particularist cultures in which relationships are more important than rules (Triandis 1995) and that the forces of globalisation will eliminate the need for Guanxi. I suggest, however, that whilst the name might change, the sort of collective, supportive culture that is described as part of the Chinese heritage remains alive and well in Lancashire.

I am not trying to present this way of being as a form of utopia: There will always be the rich and the poor (in monetary or other terms), the good and the bad, heroes and villains, and for some life (and death) can be very hard indeed. What I am trying to assert is that the underlying way in which others are assessed and evaluated is different. The judgements made about self and others are rooted more in community and collaboration, and less in individuality and self-worth. In Chapter 8 I look at two main types of projected society which I termed the heroic (strong Western-type free-market competitive) and the symbiotic (collaborative, community-focused, storytelling). Perhaps the future visions of Chapter 8 and past rural cultures meet up somewhere here? (See also the rural initiative described in Chapter 19.)

It is often felt that one needs to compete aggressively to succeed in the world; however, based upon theoretical and practical evidence, Wilson & Wilson (2007) firmly support Darwin's (largely overlooked) insight that in evolutionary terms 'groups containing mostly altruists have a decisive advantage over groups containing mostly selfish individuals, even though selfish individuals have the advantage over altruists within each group'. The shunning of selfish members of a rural community looks very much like an unconscious control mechanism of an altruistic group.

The vast majority of literature and research around organisations focuses upon those organisations and communities that are part of the usual Western academic orbit. Rural communities represent a hidden way of being that is largely unacknowledged by research and is not understood by the Westernised world of 'best management practice', 'competitive advantage', and the search for status, riches, and power. Similarly, that the rural way of being permeates many farming businesses explains the difficulties that some business experts have in attempting to address the apparent needs of the farmer through the blind application of free-market principles.

On one side, as described by Pelzer, we have a highly sophisticated hyper-real system by which to manage financial risk, with sets of algorithms tailored to smaller and smaller sets of circumstances, overseen, controlled, and applied with little need to brush against the messy reality of people. On the other side we have a system that is only too deep in that reality, one which is on the concrete level of very real trades, buyers, and sellers. Both face the same type of financial loss based upon lack of knowledge. Both try and gather as much information as possible to minimise that potential loss. The first world relies upon figures for that information, the second upon discussion.

In the first world the decision-making has become distant from the problem, the workers infantilised and the hierarchy emphasised. Employees are concerned with power structures and thus social climbing, and the tendency is to misbehave subversively. In the second, the decision-making is directly related to the circumstances and agonised over, the workers can be difficult to manage, and misbehaviour tends to show as direct disagreement. The difference between the two worlds, therefore, is not just about the mechanisms of decision-making—it is about different approaches to organisation and life (and death). It is also about size—the figures involved in the management of the mart are of a very different order to those of the financial industry.

The size and reach of the financial industry has become more evident since the global financial crisis—spearheaded by bad risk management in the sub-prime market has made concrete the effects of hyperreal financial decision-making. Pelzer (2007) warned of the effects of the dual expansion of risk and regulation—and hindsight supports his concerns. To date, decision-making by rumour seems to work for the marts. It is problematic and alien to Western notions of good business practice, but it serves the marts and the rural community. Indeed the case of M&M holds out a valuable hint for the general development of risk management in relation to the infantilisation of the workforce. Perhaps there is something to be gained by bringing back the responsibility of deciding about the risks a company faces to concrete people rather than relying overmuch on the seductive apparent objectivity of figures. Perhaps there is something to be gained by these people sitting for hours on end with coffee and cakes discussing rumours. This approach, in which the senior management is reacting to the external knowledge and circumstances, accords well with the discussion in Chapter 13, in which I suggest that the agency and authority of senior management to 'drive' the organisation may just be a chimera.

REFERENCES

Carr A (2003) 'Thanatos: The Psychodynamic Conception of the 'Death Instinct' and Its Relevance to Organizations', in Biberman J & Alkhafaji A (Eds) *Business Research Yearbook: Global Business Perspectives*: 803–807. Michigan: McNaughton & Gunn.

Chu GC & Ju YA (1993) *The Great Wall in Ruins: Communication and Cultural Change in China*. Albany: State University of New York Press.

Graham JL & Lam NM (2003) 'The Chinese negotiation', *Harvard Business Review* (October): 82–91.

Gu YU (1990) 'Politeness phenomena in modern Chinese', *Journal of Pragmatics* 14: 237–257.

Hammond SC & Glenn LM (2004) 'The ancient practice of Chinese social networking: Guanxi and social network theory', *E:CO Special Double Issue* 6(1–2)24–31.

Hwang KK (1987). 'Face and favor: The Chinese power game', *American Journal of Sociology* 92: 944–974.

Lee MM (1998) 'Sheep and the Consumptive Identity'. In Hopfl, H proceedings of *'Production of Consumption' Conference*, Bolton, 2, 3 April.

Lee MM (2000) 'The art of silence,' *Human Resource Development International* 3(3)271–272.

Luo Y (1997) 'Guanxi: Principles, philosophies, and implications', *Human Systems Management* 16: 43–51.

Mei-hui Y (1994) *Gifts, Favors, and Banquets: The Art of Social Relationships in China*. Ithaca: Cornell University Press.

Moss S (2015) 'James Rebanks, Twitter's favourite shepherd: Sheep farming is another form of culture, just like Picasso or punk', *The Guardian* (@StephenMossGdn) Accessed 27/3/2015.

Pelzer P (2007) 'The futility of excess or the displaced world of rules and regulations', *Culture and Organisation* 13(2)157–169.

Scallon R & Scallon SW (1991) 'Mass and Count Nouns in Chinese and English: A Few Whorfian Considerations', in Blust R (Ed) *Currents in Pacific Linguistics: Papers on Austronesian Languages and Ethnolinguistics in Honor of George W. Grace*: 465–475. Canberra, Australia: Pacific Linguistics.

Sievers B (1990) 'Thoughts on the relatedness of work, death, and life itself', *European Journal of Management* 8(3)321–324.

Sievers B (1996) 'Participation as a collusive quarrel', *Ethical Perspectives* 3(3) 128–136.

Sievers B (2006) 'The Psychotic Organisation: A socio-analytic perspective', *Ephemera* 6(2)104–120.

Sievers B (2007) ' "It is new and it has to be done!" Socio-Analytic thoughts on betrayal and cynicism in organisational transformation', *Culture and Organization* 13(1)1–21.

Triandis H (1995) *Individualism and Collectivism*. Boulder: Westview.

Watts DJ (2003) *Six Degrees: The Science of a Connected Age*. New York, NY: W.W Norton and Company.

Wilson DS & Wilson EO (2007) 'Survival of the Selfless', *New Scientist* 196(268)42–46.

12 Difference and Conflict

In this chapter, two understandings of 'conflict' are derived from a multicultural East-West experience: As *fundamental threat* to a core view of self in which conflict is normally avoided, and as *competitive games* in which conflict is associated with the adoption of social identities as part of confrontation and negotiation with the other. These understandings are rooted in traditions developed prior to the Velvet Revolution, and represent polar opposites on a continuum. It is argued that it is the view of conflict as *competitive games* that is promoted through managerialism and that it is this view that is largely being transferred to post–Iron Curtain countries, despite the fact that conflict as *competitive games* does not lend itself easily to HR and management practice in cross-cultural situations. The chapter finishes by echoing the end of the previous chapter—questioning the impact that the others and the individual have on each other in the work environment.

> '*Normally,*
> *I kill for money,*
> *but you, my friend,*
> *shall be for free*'
> Graffiti in a Parisian toilet.

VIEWS OF CONFLICT IN THE LITERATURE

Managers on average spend 20–42% of their total work time in dealing with conflict (Thomas 1991), and the understanding and management of conflict plays a central, but contended, role in HR practice and theory. Senge talks of the successful executive who 'is used to tearing down other people at the office' and carries this behaviour home (Senge 1990: 312); many writers on cross-cultural management talk of ways of minimising cross-cultural conflict and as early as 1945, Roethlisberger was talking of the need to address problems associated with role conflict. In contrast, conflict can be seen as an accepted and important part of organisational life, and a necessary part of change and development—for organisational learning (Stacey 1993), in which visible conflict is a sign that a team is learning (Senge 1990), as well as for individual learning (Vasilyuk 1984) and Pascale's (1990) notions of the need for creative tension.

The concept of conflict is often broken into three main types. *Task conflict* involves differences of opinion about the goals or content of the work and is around facts, data, or evidence; *relationship conflict*, or personality conflict, is around differences in values or personal style; and *process conflict* is around the delegation of responsibilities and resource allocations (De Dreu & Weingart 2003). Task conflict is often seen to be good for performance, whereas relationship conflict is generally seen as detrimental (Jehn 1995), although meta-analyses do question this distinction (De Dreu 2008). Loughry & Amason (2014) point out that little multilevel research has been done, that task conflict can lead to relationship conflict, and that diversity tends to increase conflict.

A diverse team comprises individuals with different ways of thinking, expertise, disciplines, and backgrounds. Compared to homogenous groups, diverse groups are more creative, innovative, and perform better (Ely & Thomas 2001). They are also slower at making decisions and have more conflicts (Jehn & Techakesari 2014). Varala et al. (2008), however, found that this increase in conflict did not hold for deep-level diversity such as in national culture, and Ayub & Jehn (2014) found that, when there is national variety, task conflict increases while relationship and process conflict decrease, despite differences in social distance and negative stereotypes. The inclusion of just one team member of a different nationality (or moderate variety, as termed by Harrison & Klein 2007), was found to increase both task conflict and group performance.

Surface-level differences are seen to be associated with a greater degree of conflict, but also to be more able to change through cooperative debate (Nemeth et al. 2004) in national and organisational cultures that support open constructive criticism (Elbanna et al. 2011). Political or self-serving behaviour can result in lower team performance, particularly at lower levels of the organisation (de Wit et al. 2012), and Rognes & Schei (2010) suggest that an integrative approach is best applied to such conflict. By this they mean the creation of values or areas of joint gain as opposed to the employment of distributive subprocesses, which are about claiming values at the expense of the other party. Cultures that have a good history of managing conflict appear to be better able to keep task conflict from developing into relationship conflict (O'Neill et al. 2013). This slide from task conflict into relationship conflict seems to be moderated by the degree of trust, possibly because people who trust each other may be better able to disagree without feeling personally threatened (Simons & Peterson 2000). Similarly, people with more confident sense of self are likely to be more comfortable with task conflict and more able to deal with it (Judge & Bono 2001). However, objective and subjective outcome measures do not always converge

(Galinsky et al. 2002) and feelings of threat are moderated by individual differences and personal egos (Bono et al. 2002).

There has been a lot of research on conflict, and this is only a very brief outline of the main points; however, much of the literature focuses upon task conflict, and much of the research has been done in university settings. Poitras (2012) suggests that such research is likely to have underestimated the impact of conflicts on satisfaction and performance, because participants will have a lower vested interest in manufactured settings. The accounts I present here are different. They are very much part of real life and offer a messy mix of task, relationship, and process conflict in which individuals affect the group and vice versa. In particular, this account is about such differences in the understanding of 'conflict'.

THE CASE: CROSS-CULTURAL CONFLICT ON A SENIOR-LEVEL PROGRAMME

I led the team from Lancaster as part of an international partnership funded by the EC and created to help Slovak academics design and disseminate culturally specific case studies focusing upon organisational development and quality management. This was similar in nature, though slightly different in practice, to the CEMTDP discussed in Chapter 10. Exploratory work was carried out in organisations in Slovakia by multinational academic/student researcher teams. Findings from this were then fed into programmes for the Slovak academics. The programmes included theoretical input; Western organisational placements; and preparation, presentation, and feedback on cases developed from the Western experiences. The Slovak academics were split into two groups, one going to Rotterdam in Holland, and the second coming to Lancaster in the UK. In order to maintain continuity and coherence, the learning from each stage was fed into the design and content of the following stage. Staff and students involved in the previous activities came to Lancaster's workshop to share their findings.

The Encounter

We sat there, in a state-of-the-art training suite, clean, tidy, air conditioning humming gently, waiting to hear what they said. We worked together, but there were subgroups; people speaking the same language and who had similar backgrounds tended to gravitate towards each other. At this time we consisted of 'learners' (namely myself, a true Brit; a Taiwanese/British researcher; and 12 academics from institutions across Slovakia), and presenters (namely a Dutch academic with Canadian roots; a Dutch researcher on short-term loan from the US; and a rather nervous student, who was true Dutch). The Dutch student presented the findings of the initial investigations in Slovakia. He stood up and gave an upbeat, competent, and interesting analysis (with lots of coloured graphs and tables) of the team's findings about the present situation of Slovakian organisations, and the need for quality management. There were problems, but they could be solved—with the application of appropriate techniques.

Next, the Dutch academic and researcher gave their analysis of the learning from the workshop that had just been held in Rotterdam (the sister to the Lancaster workshop). They talked of content and design, learning objectives and achievements—and then moved into an analysis of their wider perceptions. They stated that their abiding impression when in Slovakia, and with Slovaks on the Rotterdam workshop, was that Slovaks feared and avoided conflict. They said that if a Slovak was challenged he or she would try to turn the subject; if that failed, he or she would agree with something they disliked rather than take a stand. They said that years under the command economy had led Slovaks to become subservient, but that Westerners valued conflict and fostered it—that business was done by conflict—that Slovaks would never be on equal terms with the West unless they grew to appreciate the value of conflict. They concluded that despite the traditional forms of organisational analysis that produced a positive view of Slovakia's future as an equal player in the market, Slovakian engagement in the global economy was doomed unless the Slovaks learnt (individually and organisationally) not to avoid conflict.

The Unravelling

A stunned silence developed. One person went to open a window, one went to get books out of a bag, another went to make a coffee, and several went to the loo. The rest sat and waited, and were slowly joined by the others until the group was complete again. The presenters remained standing at the front, and, tacitly, through eye contact and the clearing of throats, we, the seated ones, decided to face this challenge and started to nibble away at the edges.

I shall now try and condense several hours of urgent debate into a few short paragraphs. I initially played the host, trying to ease the situation and shift the discussion into gear. I asked whether this wasn't a gross simplification of national culture, of 'West is better than East', of lumping all Slovaks together under an inferred national characteristic. Some of the Slovaks started to engage, but others were clearly deeply offended by the whole thing and non-verbally withdrew. The presenters alighted on this withdrawal, citing it as proof that Slovaks would not engage in a conflictual situation. Others held the different responses in the group as evidence that not all 'Slovaks' were the same. After a brief spat, the group relapsed into confused and offended silence.

Trying to facilitate, I questioned the extent to which conflict was the rule in the West. I pointed out that I was a Westerner, but that, as I was doing in this instance, I would seek to avoid conflict where possible. I did not think that the West could be characterised in such bald terms and suggested that the presenters were wrong in assuming that their personal preferences could be generalised as Western. I questioned whether, despite the organisational rhetoric, most people in the West would prefer that conflict did not exist. Some of the Slovaks labelled the presenters' approach as 'American'. The presenters were offended by the thought that they could be seen as American and, once again, we shifted briefly into active discussion (composed largely of overlapping monologues) about stereotyping before returning to sullen silence.

I was fed up with rescuing the group, so I sat there, observing. Eventually, the Taiwanese researcher spoke out. Usually quiet and reserved, she spoke with a passion normally associated with the breaking of barriers. She explained that she was caught between two styles. Being a product of the American MBA culture, she knew about the use of conflict as an educative tool, and about the acceptance and fostering of conflict in organisational settings. As a product of her own culture, however, she also knew about avoidance of conflict, respect for seniority (that was equated with wisdom), and the need to keep face; and she pointed out that the Taiwanese economy had not been hindered by collectivism. One by one, others joined in and we talked personally about our individual approaches to conflict.

It became apparent that, for this group, if there were national boundaries on the issue then they were blurred and situation specific. One Slovak described how he worked in an environment that he described as 'Americanised' and in which there was often conflict. He added that if he, as a Slovak, experienced conflict of that sort at home, then it would be grounds for divorce. Another person explained that he sought compromise and a happy working environment. A third person built on this, saying that for Slovaks, conflict meant a fight to the death—it was much more than a minor altercation. The Dutch academic talked of how he looked for integrity and confluence in his actions, how he did not like the idea of different behaviours at home and at work, and how he saw conflict as an honest and beneficial encountering of the other. He said that Dutch culture was based upon negotiation and renegotiation—arguing with someone meant that you respected them, whilst lack of argument was a sign of disquiet, and turning your back on them (metaphorically) was the ultimate insult. I, as the Brit, talked for all Brits (as I saw it) and said that the work/home split was a common aspect of UK life: conflict at home was generally avoided whilst at work it was often seen as an unavoidable but unwelcome part of organisational life.

Afterwards, I talked to each of the people privately. These discussions revealed that, despite the fact that all the individuals involved in this experience had worked together well beforehand and continued to do so afterwards (some establishing or building on firm friendships), people felt that the group rapidly split into two sides (the Americanised presenters vs. the rest). The presenters were described by the others to be insensitive, culturally imperialistic, domineering, and inflexible. The others felt that the presenters' arguments were based upon financial motivation (conflict brings profit) and that they disregarded the cost to the individual and the society. The presenters described themselves as being honest, straightforward, and trying to work towards a truth of existence that others hypocritically avoided. They felt that the others hid conflict to the extent that they were untrustworthy, manipulative, and dishonest, and that they hid dubious motivations under a disingenuous rhetoric.

The Aftermath

This description, pared to the bone, does little justice to the charged emotion of the afternoon; to the way in which the group went round and round—repeating themselves many times in attempts to be heard; to the way in which people's emotions and attention was focused on the interaction, even whilst they were deeply engaged in trying not to be involved; to the way in which even the silences were alive and tense. I have left it here unfinished (though at a much more rational level than the group left it) in order to reflect the way in which all participants eventually left feeling a lack of closure. For the remainder of the workshop, and during meetings afterwards, conversations slid back to that afternoon—with people engaging briefly in undertone discussions about points that had occurred to them since—things they wish they had said, musing on others' behaviour, attempting to make sense of what had gone on.

To a large extent this account is my own attempt to make sense of what was going on. Despite being highly charged, the session was not particularly traumatic for me. I did not, personally, feel under threat, though there were several times at which I (as did others) responded as if something important to me was being attacked. My response was protective of a way of life and was similar to how I respond if I see a group of children bullying another in the streets—an immediate reaction to stop the bullying, followed by an attempt to talk it through and establish the roots of the issue in order to prevent further occurrences. For all of us, it was our cultural assumptions—our roots—that were being attacked by stereotyping, yet by the end of the afternoon, having initially reacted against that stereotyping, we were each using it as owners of our cultures (i.e., 'in Britain . . .', 'in Slovakia . . .' and so on) in order to lend force to our words. Furthermore, the presenters were labelled as 'American' and, by tacitly refusing to engage in that part of the debate with them, the rest of the group colluded in managing part of the conflict by shifting the ground and ignoring the protestations of the presenters—thereby engaging in the very act that the Dutch academic had said would be seen as a serious insult, and one that in retrospect could be seen to match the apparent insult of trying to force a form of individualised conflict upon people who espoused collectivism (see Pruitt & Rubin 1986 for avoidance as a conflict management strategy).

Whilst never stated explicitly, a basic premise evolved from the group experience and later discussions. This was that in conflictual situations different cultures adopted different behaviours and attributed different emotional valence to the whole collection of qualities and meanings that the word 'conflict' brought to the surface in their culture. Subsidiary understandings developed from this—namely, that there was national, individual, and situated difference in how conflict was managed, and in its perceived benefits and problems; that conflict might be an integral part of the functioning of certain organisational structures and managerial levels, but this was not universal in practice; and that differential understandings of, and behaviour towards, conflict was an important issue for local and national organisations, as well as those operating in international arenas. This last point was based upon the one totally unchallenged view that pervaded the experience—that American theory and practice promoted conflict, and that all organisations, wherever they were based, were increasingly having to engage with Americanised approaches. The remainder of this account explores these understandings in more detail.

Before moving on, however, I wish to emphasise that the shorthand of 'Americanisation' as reported here does not mean that I think all my many American friends are of that ilk. This cultural stereotype arose during discussions and is as questionable as all such stereotypes. However, it was something that nearly all the participants voiced freely and agreed on, and so it developed a life of its own. As it was seen to be an important part of the process it must be explored further.

EXPLORING THE ROOTS

During the presentation the presenters attributed the Slovakians' (apparent) avoidance of conflict to their years behind the Iron Curtain—they said it was years of enforced cooperation that led to subservience and a blame culture, such that, despite the Velvet Revolution, undue authority (and thus compliance) is still given to those who appear powerful. This analysis is tempting in its simplicity and in the way in which it accedes to the common practice of blaming a range of ills upon the Iron Curtain. It seduces us into seeing those who have lived behind the Iron Curtain as suffering from a kind of illness that is therefore curable. It follows from this that these 'ill' people should take the medicine prescribed by the doctors, and that the doctors are those who are wiser and remain well, as they have avoided the infection (Kostera 1996).

'Slovakian conflict avoidance', as the presenters called it, might also be attributed to slightly longer historical roots. For the past 150 years the Slovaks have faced the possibility of conflict with the Hungarians, and it is a long while since they have had exclusive responsibility for their own national fate. Now, having established the Slovak Republic, they face political conflict within the Slovak society, and around Slovak integration into Europe. It could be that the majority of people will avoid conflict that they consider to be unnecessary—and that the Slovaks, at present, are tired of confrontation and so have developed a high tolerance of what others might consider to merit a conflictual response.

Neither of these explanations, however, fit the reactions described above. Not only did each individual ascribe their approach to conflict to their individual stance and deep cultural roots (as opposed to recent history), but the major divide in approach seemed to include the Brits and Taiwanese in the group that would otherwise be derived from 'behind the Iron Curtain'. In addition, whilst there was certainly avoidance of open conflict in this group, there did not appear to be in compliance with the view that was being proposed—instead disagreement showed itself in more subtle ways. This could be seen in the way in which the debate was turned away from open conflict, and by the way in which individuals used group pressure (through, at times, withdrawal or ignoring other's agendas) in order to assert their own views and place their own agendas onto the proceedings. For example, the interpretation of conflict as confrontation was linked with management theory and 'Americanisation', and then attributed to the presenters, who were classed as 'Americanised' by association. In effect, in order to promote the idea of conflict as confrontation, the presenters had to accept the label they had been given; however, it then became almost impossible for them to backtrack and explore the negative connotations in more depth. The donation of the label meant that the non-presenters could reject the presenters' line of argument as 'culturally inappropriate'. In doing so the majority of the group not only sidestepped the initial confrontation, but also made the reopening of that issue a difficult task. The labelling was done in a way that was virtually unchangeable and legitimised the rejection of the idea that conflict was effectively minor confrontation. In this example, conflict was not avoided. It was recognised and managed collectively, but not by the obvious means of direct confrontation.

I will argue later that the emergence of different understandings of conflict is not limited to multicultural experiences, nor is approach to conflict necessarily a 'national' trait. Clearly each individual perceives the situation in the light of their interpretative frameworks, and for some, as suggested previously, a history of conflict has led them to label as 'non-conflictual' situations that others might consider to be highly conflictual. In the experience outlined above, however, all participants perceived the situation to be conflictual in nature. The variation in this perception appeared to be based upon the ways in which the confrontation was recognised and managed, and was split along rough (self-described) national lines—the Slovaks, Brits, and Taiwanese versus the Dutch and Americans.

If difference in understanding of the meaning of 'conflict' is not a direct product of the Iron Curtain, then where does it come from? It might be rooted much more deeply in our cultural psyche. Obeyesekere (1990) proposes that "the work of culture" is the process whereby symbolic forms existing on the cultural level get created and recreated through the minds of people'. He suggests that one of the mechanisms for this creation and recreation is the 'family myth', and that the family myth derives from some form of deep motivation which gets transformed into symbolic forms that produce a historical dialectic or 'debate', which in turn yields alternative myth versions, and so on. The patterns of this development can be explored through the way in which myths exhibit 'family resemblances' within or across cultures. In other words, in the same way that it is said that history is written by the winners, perhaps current preferred mythology is a reflection of current cultural values.

Following the experience outlined above, I questioned people individually about their cultural myths, and about those that they were attracted to as children. In brief, the Slovaks and Brits talked of myths and stories from pre-Christian eras (those of powerful deities, heroes and dragon slayers, virgins and witches) and of Christian descent (martyrs, saints and the sacrifice of self or worldly goods for the benefit of others and/or for transcendence). Similarly, Taiwanese myths were reported to be linked to the Chinese cultural heritage and appear to focus upon negation of self in support of the collective, the lack of importance of the flesh, and the transcendence of spirit for those who have achieved 'perfection'. For each of these backgrounds, conflict is normally between reified good and evil—in which man can become more 'perfect' through association with, or aspiration towards, good. In addition, the 'perfect' is presented as something outside of and above the self, and requires the willingness (if not the actuality) to sacrifice self in order to work towards perfection.

The types of myth that the Dutch and the American participants recounted contrasted strongly with this. The myths they gave to me were all from more recent history and focused on conflict between people (as of those derived from the founding of America, or the American Civil War) or boy and nature (as of the Dutch boy who saved the town by keeping his finger in the dike and so prevented a flood). There was little allusion to ultimate good or evil, and little sacrifice of self for transcendence. The myths involved 'good' qualities (bravery, honesty, probity, etc.), and the striving for a better life, and were located in the here and now—more the building of a better reality (that assumes the maintenance of self in order to enjoy the benefits) and less the aspiration towards a greater self-less spirituality (in which self is sacrificed as too basal for the higher planes).

This research can be interpreted through Obeyesekere's notions to show that the British and Slovakian myths show some family resemblance—they are derived from similar roots. Taiwanese myths, whilst different in content, have an import that is more similar to the British and Slovak myths than to the Dutch and American myths. In contrast, the mythological heritage of the Dutch and American nationals, as reported to me, has been truncated. If we maintain the family metaphor, they have left the family and established lives of their own, and in doing so they have rejected both the extensive historical roots and the long-term aspirations of the family (with its attendant slow cultural movement, resolution of difference through unstated cultural pressure, and subjugation of self to higher things) in favour of a concentration on the here and now and assertion of self (which is coupled with personalised short-term reward and loss, and resolution of difference through confrontation and negotiation).

TWO MEANINGS OF CONFLICT

The group functioned as if there were two forms of 'conflict'. The first form, termed 'American' by the group, appeared similar to a *Competitive Game* in which winners and losers are determined by open confrontation and negotiation, and in which there can always be a return match; as such, it is similar to the idea of task conflict described earlier. Conflict as a *Competitive Game* is relatively short-term and resolvable, and does not really threaten an individual's view of themselves or of their life. This ties in with a mythological heritage that truncates history (and vendettas?) and concentrates on the here and now, and upon the assertion of self. A difference of view is not worth dying for.

In contrast, the second understanding of conflict appeared to represent a *Fundamental Threat*. Although conflict as a competitive game can be equated with notions of task conflict, conflict as a fundamental threat does not equate directly with relationship conflict. Relationship conflict is seen to be deeper than task conflict, but is also seem to be negotiable, albeit with some difficulty. *Fundamental Threat* is long-term and irresolvable. It strikes at the individual's way of being, such that, if it were to be made explicit, then the importance of opposing it would have to be placed above the value of life and property. 'Conflict' was therefore seen to represent a situation that had gone too far: attempts to sidestep it had failed and it could no longer be resolved equitably. This resonates with a mythological heritage of sacrifice of self for the achievement of higher ideals. If higher ideals are threatened, a fundamental threat is perceived, and then the mythological heritage requests the ultimate sacrifice. I suggest that it is from this route that we get suicide bombers and kamikaze pilots. Personal stakes are much higher, and thus self-survival would suggest a policy of deflecting confrontation or attempting to avoid explicit acknowledgement of 'conflict'.

Fundamental Threat

Those who interpreted the word 'conflict' as a *Fundamental Threat* were clearly well able to appreciate and manage situations in which a difference of view was apparent. The two groups, however, managed difference of view in different ways, and each group had problems understanding the approach of the other—such that the 'conflict' escalated. Those who saw conflict as a *Competitive Game* also saw the different perspectives to be malleable such that direct negotiation would lead to people changing their views and reaching agreement on the issues, and, therefore, to one side 'winning' the argument. They felt that, because the other group was unwilling to try and negotiate or to consider the possibility of relinquishing their perspective, then they were unwilling to work towards a common solution. They therefore said that they felt that this indicated hidden agendas and lack of honesty—leading to lack of trustworthiness, loss of respect, and inferred personal insult.

In contrast, those who saw conflict as a *Fundamental Threat,* and thus something to be sidestepped, saw the differences as reflections of fundamental difference in approach and thus not appropriate for negotiation or change. Instead they felt that resolution could only be achieved through an agreement to differ that preserved individuals' perspectives whilst allowing a way forwards. They felt that the other group's attempts to seek conformity trivialised and undervalued their feelings and beliefs. They inferred that insistence upon negotiation indicated that the other group believed that all values were negotiable, and that insistence upon pushing direct confrontation indicated insensitivity, cultural imperialism, and lack of ability or willingness to appreciate another's viewpoint—leading to lack of trustworthiness, loss of respect, and inferred personal insult.

The apparent confrontation in the group revolved around words, and verbalised differences of opinion—but the real confrontation was being played out on a different stage . . . that of attitudes, values, and inferred motivation. The questions both sides asked of themselves were: 'Is this person I am talking to trustworthy? Do they value me and my difference? What is really motivating them? How can I trust them if I don't understand them? They say they don't intend to insult me, yet continue to do so—how can I respect them? How do I protect my 'self' as their insults negate me and my way of life?' I will return to this focus on trust later in the chapter.

Multiple Understandings

It would be wrong to take from this a generalised statement about national outlook or cultural heritage. The idea of national stereotyping has many holes, and even if it were acceptable the few people discussed here are distinctly non-representative. We can, however, explore whether there is anything in this experience that might be generalisable to others in which people from different cultures are thrown together and have to interact. The experience described here demonstrates that although people might be using a common language, this surface commonality is likely to mask a wide range of *'understandings'* of what the words mean (Jankowicz 1996). *Understanding* is used in a broad sense here, to include the concepts, values, and emotions that each of us attach to words—the word is a symbol form that is a carrier for the meanings we attribute to our life. I suggest that the more common our heritage the greater the commonality of our experience, and thus, the less obvious the differences between us. The other side of the coin, as demonstrated here, is that the more the apparent commonality, the more the mutuality of wording, the easier it is for us to assume (often erroneously) that appearance is 'reality' and that the differences in *understanding* are minimal.

A recent situation exemplifies this. The proportional funding for UK Higher Education (HE) dropped significantly over a few years, such that many people believe that the quality of HE (and, indeed, the HE systems) was seriously threatened. This belief resulted in a well-supported one-day national strike by UK staff and students in HE institutions. In all institutions, management were trapped in a role conflict: their job was to keep the institutions up and running, whilst their sympathies (in most cases) were with the ideals of the strike—to attempt to protect the future of HE in the UK. Many management teams found compromise solutions—for example, officially closing the institution for the day, or allowing staff to place their docked pay into bursary funds. One institution wrote a letter to staff prior to the strike that (due to poor choice of wording) implied that the 'management' believed that staff who were proposing to strike were only interested in short-term personal gain—seeking more pay at the expense of an institution that was already short of money, and that staff would be in breach of contract as they would be working for less than the 'contracted' number of days. In contrast, staff felt that they had responded to the poor financial circumstances of HE by consistently working well beyond their contractual requirements in a way that, in other occupations, would have merited extensive overtime payments. The recipients of the letter were so incensed by the apparent misunderstanding of their motivations that the strike action became almost unanimous. Staff felt that they had been deeply insulted—and the letter had the opposite effect to that which was (presumably) intended.

In this example an insult was inferred on both sides. The management clearly felt that they were doing the best they could under difficult financial circumstances. They saw the strike for more funding as an immediate short-term threat that could be 'negotiated'. They felt that negotiation would be best served by a confrontational letter implying that those who went on strike were working against the good of the institution for personal gain (in the vein of 'you are either with us or against us, and if you are against us you are not a very nice person'). The majority of staff saw it as a long-term structural and ideological issue that went much further than the bounds of the institution—one which they were willing to promote through personal sacrifice (the loss of pay). They were injured by the confrontational tone of the letter and insulted by their 'higher' motivation being misinterpreted as basal drives and a search for immediate gratification. They felt that a very serious issue (of future development and historical injustice) was being handled (badly) by short-term 'managerialism'.

This difference of understanding developed rapidly in the few hours following a single action. More usually, escalation develops through a series of stages, in which the path back from an event is more difficult than the path to it (Pruitt & Nowak 2014). Alternatively, it cascades as a contagion in which other people get drawn into a single point of conflict (Jehn et al. 2013). The circulation of the letter, however, divided managers and staff into two coherent groups that were now apparently separated by black-and-white views on the issue and on each other (despite the fact that, contractually, there is little difference between the two—managers are staff and vice versa). Both began to see the other as morally excluded, 'as outside the community in which norms apply' (Opotow 2000: 417). It seems hard to understand how a single act can have such a deep divisive influence upon a large 'rational' organisation such as an HE institution without bringing the 'soft' aspects of people into the equation—their value bases, deep-seated motivations, their sense of self, and their expectations of the other. It is these aspects that turn a minor incident into a major conflict, and it is these aspects that managerialism appears to ignore (or in this example, incite).

In addition, this difference of understanding occurred in one institution—in which everyone spoke the same language, had similar cultural roots, and supported the same organisation. Despite the fact that people had similar backgrounds, it divided them into those who saw the situation as a *Fundamental Threat,* or as a *Competitive Game.* Clearly evident in both examples is the way in which those who appear to understand conflict as a *Fundamental Threat* label the others as working from a '*Managerialist*' or '*Americanised*' perspective.

Managerialism (Americanisation)

In a detailed analysis Boyacigiller & Adler (1991) suggest that the majority of early research was done on (and in) white American bureaucratic organisations; that our understandings of management theory and practice are derived from this culturally specific and non-representative sample; and that this focus is self-fulfilling. Early American research was assumed to apply to all management—carrying with it the assumption that management was a singular global concept without national or situation-specific boundaries—thus that there were right and wrong ways of 'managing' and that it was possible to provide a singular global view of 'best practice'. Subsequent research generally accepted this assumption and thus compounded the bias by ignoring it (see Chapter 16). 'Managers' have moved from being parts of a large Tayloristic bureaucracy and are now seen to be part of the processes of re-engineering organisations—creating the 'lean machine' through flatter structures and internal (and external) entrepreneurialism. I suggest, however, that the deeper attributes remain.

In other words, the central mass of theory and practice is 'Americanised' and continues to carry, and thus to promote, the view that management is about organisational structures and systems in which people are subsidiary elements; in which managing HR is about short-term negotiation and confrontation designed to mould the people to the needs of the organisation; in which these needs are determined by the senior management; and in which organisational development is the process of moving towards best practice in aligning the people with the organisation. More particularly, everything focuses on the bottom line—money. Economic exchange is impersonal and does not entail investment in the relationship by either the employee or the organisation. Fundamentally this approach acts as if the people are the tools of the organisation, and thus, that their underlying motivations and higher aspirations are irrelevant to (or detract from) the efficient functioning of the organisation. Taylorism has been replaced by the search for the free market, but the basic elements have not changed—if anything, the free-market myth and attendant business process re-engineering relies upon seeing conflict as competitive games. Trust between employer and employee is treated as an anarchic concept—who needs trust when there is a contract!

The common assumption that people who are paid more will work harder has entered organisational mythology and is rarely questioned, despite there being a raft of information to the contrary. However, a range of studies have shown that employees reciprocate good organisational treatment with positive attitudes and higher levels of performance (Rhoades & Eisenberger 2002). Good treatment is seen as social exchange (involving trust and mutual investment, diffuse and open-ended obligations between the employee and the organisation, and a long-term orientation) as opposed to economic exchange in which 'transactions between parties are not long term or ongoing, but represent discrete, financially oriented interactions' (Shore et al. 2006: 839). Social exchange creates trust and a high degree of mutual obligation between exchange partners, and the fostering of common values (ideological exchange) may help enhance trust in the employer (McLean Parks et al. 1998).

Perhaps conflict as competitive game was explicated in America, perhaps it is based upon one subsection of one nation's historical view of the fundamentals of human interaction, perhaps it is inherent in much of the management literature—but if so, why are we all rushing forwards begging for it (let alone passively colluding with it)? Perhaps it is because this approach, one that assumes that a set amount of money equates with a set amount of benefit, carries with it a beauty of simplicity, clarity of purpose, and impression of control that promises the 'person in charge' that all will be well. Regardless of whether or not the promise is met, the message is seductive and becomes increasingly so as the situation that needs to be controlled becomes more complex (Lee 2003; see also Chapter 13 for discussions of agency and the need to control).

MANAGING CONFLICT

It could be that conflict as a *Competitive Game* is inherent in the managerial role—any manager, whatever their nationality or heritage, will seek the surety of clarity and control and the minimisation of the value of individual difference, and will act in ways that establish this. There are two reasons why this is unlikely to be the case universally. Firstly, the Slovaks, Taiwanese, and Brits each felt that viewing conflict as *Fundamental Threat* (thereby avoiding confrontation and seeking recognition of difference) was a legitimate way in which to manage. Secondly, both the examples given above question the extent to which approaching conflict as a competitive game might really be successful—they both illustrate the depth of feeling and strength of reaction engendered in those who were expecting to be managed through process skills but were, instead, confronted with the message of *Competitive Game*. Further, in both examples the situation became more complex and less controllable as the view of conflict as a competitive game was enacted and trust was lost, yet in both, the response was to increase the intensity of the confrontation rather than to question its validity.

It is possible that this escalation was due to the environment or the people involved. For example, once conflict has started and the environment has become oppositional it is more likely to develop, particularly where there is prior exposure to aggression (Brees et al. 2013). Similarly, personal judgements of acceptable behaviour, social norms, and aggressive cultures influence the level of aggression shown (Douglas & Martinko 2001). Managers with high self-esteem and belief in their own ability are less likely to exhibit aggression (optimistic attribution style, see Martinko et al. 2002). In contrast, the management style of those with hostile or pessimistic attribution is associated with anger and aggression (Aquino 2000).

It is my belief, however, that this escalation in both cases centred around a lack of trust that the other party understood, or even cared, about the core values of the relationship. The concept of trust has many different levels (Kiffin-Petersen 2004); however, for the purposes of this chapter I will focus on integrity-based trust, which concerns the degree to which one expects another to adhere to a set of principles that are acceptable and seen as fundamental to the fostering of interpersonal relationships (Kim et al. 2006). Trust is seen as vital for innovation, creativity, cooperation, high performance, and conflict management (Dirks & Ferrin 2002) and trust is seen to be crucial in gaining the benefits of task conflict without suffering the costs of relationship conflict (Simons & Peterson 2000). Conversely, conflict is also seen to foster trust, as does communication (Zeffane et al. 2011). Indeed, Dijkstra et al. (2014) emphasise the role that workplace gossip plays in easing conflict. Much of this research, however, is focused upon task conflict. The sort of conflict I have described above, that of fundamental threat, is about the need to support the core sense of self in the light of the other. Self-regard, dignity, and respect are very important for close social relations, but are harmed by feelings of injustice and misrepresentation and actions that impair one's self-worth (Cropanzano et al. 2001).

At the beginning of this chapter negotiation was seen as an integral part of task conflict, and a more difficult but necessary part of relationship conflict. Negotiation skills are generally considered essential for both personal fulfilment and professional success (Lewicki et al. 2009). They are linked to creativity (Wilson & Thompson 2014), and play an important part of everyday life (Volkema & Fleck 2012), but can present great personal challenge (Miles 2010). So the question is—how do we negotiate around a fundamental threat to our sense of self when we have lost all trust?

It is probably fair to say that if difference of view is managed in a way that all parties expect and are comfortable with, then it will probably be managed better than in the two cases above, in which the two sides adopted polarised and different understandings of how to deal with conflict. It is unlikely, of course, that each 'side' adopted a particular view of conflict as if it were an absolute category. Similarly, there is no intention within this paper to imply that they do represent absolute categories. The categories of *Competitive Game* and *Fundamental Threat* have been derived from the way in which people were talking about conflict in a limited and specific situation. The application of mythological and national roots to the categories, and the association between these and approach to management, is speculative and circumstantial. It is, perhaps, most appropriate to see the two categories as representing different poles of a continuum. At one end we have short-term managerialism, which knows the 'cost of everything and the value of nothing', and at the other end we have visionary ineffectiveness, which 'seeks the value of everything and the cost of nothing'. These poles appear similar to those presented across a wide range of the literature—from personal preference through managerial style to the nature of government. It is therefore, perhaps, not surprising to see these polar opposites rematerialise when looking at conflict. It is also, perhaps, not surprising to find that if one side in a conflict feels unappreciated, then it is likely to place the antagonistic label on the other side and polarise the debate.

Perhaps the management of (rather than the resolution of) conflict as if it were a fundamental threat requires the development of personal qualities that enable the manager to manage the communicative climate through process skills and in a way that recognises difference and inspires and influences (rather than confronts) others. The manager must learn to control by seduction instead of repression (Reed 1992): persuasion and social enabling, rather than negotiation and economic enabling. These soft qualities are harder to identify and harder to transmit to others (Lee 1996). In the concluding section of this chapter I want to return to the beginning—so what are the implications of these thoughts for HR practice and theory, and why the initial quote?

Implications for Organisational Practice

Most of us know when we get on with people and when we don't. We know that some people might appear very different to us, yet we can have stimulating and valuable interactions with them; others, who superficially appear similar to us, raise our hackles because, underneath the surface, we see them as representing something that threatens our sense of self. We make friends with those we like, and steer clear of the others. At work, however, we often don't have the luxury of avoidance. When working internationally, the problems of difference can be accentuated. In these situations the role of HR is often to find ways of managing and developing people who would not naturally form into friendship groups outside work. The potential for (and actuality of?) conflict is a frequent part of our organisational life. The management of conflict—how we learn and develop together—is central to the maintenance (let alone the development) of the organisation.

In the polar opposites of conflict as *Competitive Game* or as *Fundamental Threat* we have two very different views of the role of the people within organisations (either cogs in wheels and therefore to be controlled explicitly, or potentially problematic and to be seduced); how people can or should be managed (through confrontation, or consensus); and thus, of how organisations should operate (short-term and task-focused, or long-term and processual). If all the people who are involved adopt the same approach to conflict, then attempts to understand and manage the difference of view can more easily stay focused upon the issue at hand. If, however, people are adopting fundamentally different views of the situation itself and of how it should be managed (as well as different views about whatever seeded the situation) then the confrontation can escalate quite quickly—against the best intentions of all parties, and each in the belief that it is the other party who is not acting appropriately and is forcing the issue.

The problems of the HR role are likely to be accentuated as managers are expected to take on increasing responsibility for HR, as much of the literature seems to assume will happen. In Chapters 16 and 18 I explore the sorts of qualities that might be expected in the 'new' manager if he or she is to successfully embody the team player, accepted by colleagues and able to work flexibly across traditional organisational boundaries (in which) he or she is a manipulator of organisational symbols (Johnson 1990) who can inspire and influence others by managing the communicative climate through process skills, whilst maintaining a core of ethicality and strong self-concept. However, it might well be that the apparent clarity of streamlined organisational structure is foundering on the rocky, complex, and chaotic shores of HR—the individual motivations and histories that cannot easily be managerialised; the individual qualities and process skills that cannot easily be taught.

Clearly, each organisation or individual adopts their approach as part of a feedback system that is sensitive to what is occurring around them and their intentions towards it . . . as illustrated in the first example, response to (and interpretation of) conflict is situation specific, but tends to fall into one of these two approaches. As illustrated in the second example, these differences of approach can appear within one organisation and one nationality. The link between conflict as *Competitive Game* and managerialism that is evident in both examples, however, raises particular issues for cross-cultural working. As indicated above, this approach is being actively promoted, requested, and embraced across the world. It might have emerged from America, but it is now much bigger than that. The idol of the free market (the short-term entrepreneurial vision and quick riches at the expense of long-term social support) has become core to our work. The problem is that, whilst the approach is about confrontation and negotiation, it is not, in itself, open to negotiation. The ethnocentricity is in the assumption that there is a winnable solution—that there is a right way of doing things, and of being, and that conflict is about finding this (Said 1993).

This right way of being is so strong within organisational life that individuals expect to have to change behaviour, to work in a different way, to change nature as they walk through the doors of their workplace each day. Of those who saw conflict as a *Fundamental Threat*, not one person interviewed in this study felt that it was unusual, or even slightly odd, that they should *expect* to act like a different person (someone who was not really 'them') when at work—though there was some worry about the way in which it became hard to change back at the end of the day, and the effect that this had upon family, friends, and self!

This brings me to my final point—and the initial quote. In promoting 'learning organisations' based upon the idea that managers adopt developmental and supportive HR responsibilities, we need to train them to manage this. In, by necessity, providing them with a quick fix of tool-kit people skills to help them with their new responsibilities, we empower them to act quickly and well. In encouraging them to sacrifice the long and problematic job of valuing difference in favour of resolving conflict through negotiation, we encourage them to 'kill' themselves and their organisations. How can the organisation or the manager work with dissimilar others (people from other teams, functions, and nations) in a way that promotes appreciation and learning of the previously unknown (the unanticipated, the entirely different mind-set or approach to life) if they are being expected (and are themselves expecting) to adopt the 'right' way of 'doing' HR? Learning becomes the ethnocentric extension of previous knowledge and unique self becomes lost amongst the clones of others: all this from an approach that offers the chimera of individuality and freedom.

REFERENCES

Aquino K (2000) 'Structural and individual determinants of workplace victimization: The effects of hierarchical status and conflict management style', *Journal of Management* 26: 171–193.

Ayub N & Jehn K (2014) 'When diversity helps performance', *International Journal of Conflict Management* 25(2)189–212.

Bono JE, Boles TL, Judge TA, & Lauver KJ (2002) 'The role of personality in task and relationship conflict', *Journal of Personality* 70(3)311–344.

Boyacigiller N & Adler NJ (1991) 'The Parochial Dinosaur: Organisational science in a global context', *Academy of Management Review* 16(2)262–290.

Brees JR, Mackey J, & Martinko MJ (2013) 'An attributional perspective of aggression in organizations', *Journal of Managerial Psychology* 28(3)252–272.

Cropanzano R, Byrne ZS, Bobocel DR, & Rupp DE (2001) 'Moral virtues, fairness heuristics, social entities, and other denizens of organizational justice', *Journal of Vocational Behavior* 58(2)164–209.

De Dreu CK (2008) 'The virtue and vice of workplace conflict: food for (pessimistic) thought', *Journal of Organizational Behavior* 29(1)5–18.

De Dreu CKW & Weingart LR (2003) 'Task versus relationship conflict, team performance and team member satisfaction: a meta-analysis', *Journal of Applied Psychology* 88(4)741–749.

De Wit FRC, Greer LL, & Jehn KA (2012) 'The paradox of intragroup conflict: A meta-analysis', *Journal of Applied Psychology* 97(2)360–390.

Dijkstra M, Beersma B, & van Leeuwen J (2014) 'Gossiping as a response to conflict with the boss: Alternative conflict management behavior?', *International Journal of Conflict Management* 25(4)431–454.

Dirks KT & Ferrin DL (2002) 'Trust in leadership: meta-analytic findings and implications for research and practice', *Journal of Applied Psychology* 87(4) 611–628.

Douglas SC & Martinko MJ (2001) 'Exploring the role of individual differences in the prediction of workplace aggression', *Journal of Applied Psychology* 86: 547–559.

Elbanna S, Ali AJ, & Dayan M (2011) 'Conflict in strategic decision making: Do the setting and environment matter?', *International Journal of Conflict Management* 22(3)278–299.

Ely RJ & Thomas DA (2001) 'Cultural diversity at work: The effects of diversity perspectives on work group processes and outcomes', *Administrative Science Quarterly* 46(2)229–273.

Galinsky AD, Mussweiler T, & Medvec VH (2002) 'Disconnecting outcomes and evaluations: The role of negotiator focus', *Journal of Personality and Social Psychology* 83(5)1131–1140.

Harrison DA & Klein KJ (2007) 'What's the difference? Diversity constructs as separation, variety, or disparity in organizations', *The Academy of Management Review* 32(4)1199–1228.

Jankowicz D (1996) 'On "resistance to change" in the post-command economies and elsewhere', in Lee MM, Letiche H, Crawshaw R, & Thomas M (Eds) *Management Education in the New Europe*: 139–162. London: International Thompson Publishing.

Jehn KA (1995) 'A multimethod examination of the benefits and detriments of intragroup conflict', *Administrative Science Quarterly* 40: 256–282.

Jehn KA & Techakesari P (2014) 'High reliability teams: new directions for disaster management and conflict', *International Journal of Conflict Management* 25(4)407–430.

Jehn KA, Rispens S, Jonsen K, & Greer LL (2013) 'Conflict contagion: A temporal, multi-level perspective on the spread of interpersonal conflicts within teams', *International Journal of Conflict Management* 24(4)352–373.

Johnson G (1990) 'Managing Strategic change: The role of symbolic action', *British Journal of Management* 1: 183–200.

Judge TA & Bono JE (2001) 'Relationship of core self-evaluations traits—self-esteem, generalized self-efficacy, locus of control, and emotional stability—with job satisfaction and job performance: A meta-analysis', *Journal of Applied Psychology* 86(1)80–92.

Kiffin-Petersen S (2004) 'Trust: A neglected variable in team effectiveness research', *Journal of The Australian and New Zealand Academy of Management* 10(1)38–53.

Kim PH, Dirks KT, Cooper CD, & Ferrin DL (2006) 'When more blame is better than less: The implications of internal vs external attributions for the repair of trust after a competence- vs integrity-based trust violation', *Organizational Behaviour and Human Decision Processes* 99(1)49–65.

Kostera M (1996) 'The manager's new clothes: On identity transfer in post-1989 Poland', in Lee MM, Letiche H, Crawshaw R & Thomas M (Eds) *Management Education in the New Europe:* 194–211. London: International Thompson Publishing.

Lee MM (1996) 'Competency and the "new" manager in Central Europe', in Lee MM, Letiche H, Crawshaw R, & Thomas M (Eds) *Management Education in the New Europe:* 101–116. London: International Thompson Publishing.

Lee MM (2003) (Ed) *HRD in a Complex World.* London: Routledge.

Lewicki RJ, Barry B, & Saunders DM (2009) *Negotiation.* Boston, MA: McGraw-Hill/Irwin.

Loughry ML & Amason AC (2014) 'Why won't task conflict cooperate? Deciphering stubborn results', *International Journal of Conflict Management* 25(4)333–358.

Martinko MJ, Gundlach MJ, & Douglas SC (2002) 'Toward an integrative theory of counterproductive workplace behavior: A causal reasoning perspective', *International Journal of Selection and Assessment* 10: 36–50.

McLean Parks J, Kidder D, & Gallagher D (1998) 'Fitting square pegs into round holes', *Journal of Organizational Behavior* 19: 697–730.

Miles E (2010) 'The role of face in the decision not to negotiate', *International Journal of Conflict Management* 21(4)400–414.

Nemeth CJ, Personnaz B, Personnaz M, & Goncalo JA (2004) 'The liberating role of conflict in group creativity: a study in two countries', *European Journal of Social Psychology* 34(4)65–374.

Obeyesekere G (1990) *The Work of Culture: Symbolic Transformation in Psychoanalysis and Anthropology.* Chicago: The University of Chicago Press.

O'Neill TA, Allen NJ, & Hastings SE (2013) 'Examining the "pros" and "cons" of team conflict', *Human Performance* 26(3)236–260.

Opotow S (2000) 'Aggression and violence', in Deutsch M & Coleman PT. (Eds) *The Handbook of Conflict Resolution:* 403–427. San Francisco, CA: Jossey-Bass.

Pascale R (1990) *Managing on the Edge.* London: Penguin.

Poitras J (2012) 'Meta-analysis of the impact of the research setting on conflict studies', *International Journal of Conflict Management* 23(2)116–132.

Pruitt DG & Nowak A (2014) 'Attractor landscapes and reaction functions in escalation and deescalation', *International Journal of Conflict Management* 25(4)387–406.

Pruitt DG & Rubin JZ (1986) *Social Conflict: Escalation, Stalemate, and Settlement.* New York, NY: Random House.

Reed MI. (1992) *The Sociology of Organisations.* London: Sage.

Rhoades L & Eisenberger R (2002) 'Perceived organizational support, a review of the literature', *Journal of Applied Psychology* 87: 698–714.

Roethlisberger FJ (1945) 'The industrial foreman: Master and victim of double-talk', *Harvard Business Review* 23: 283–294.

Rognes JK & Schei V (2010) 'Understanding the integrative approach to conflict management', *Journal of Managerial Psychology* 25(1)82–97.

Said EW (1993) *Culture and Imperialism.* London: Chatto and Windus.

Senge PM (1990) *The Fifth Discipline.* New York: Doubleday/Currency.

Shore LM, Tetrick LE, Lynch P, & Barksdale K (2006) 'Social and economic exchange, construct development and validation', *Journal of Applied Social Psychology* 36: 837–867.

Simons TL & Peterson RS (2000) 'Task conflict and relationship conflict in top management teams', *Journal of Applied Psychology* 85(1)102–111.

Stacey R (1993) *Strategic Management and Organisational Dynamics.* London: Pitman.

Thomas KW (1991) 'Conflict and negotiation processes in organizations', in Dunnette MD & Hough LM (Eds) *Handbook of Industrial and Organizational Psychology:* 651–717. Palo Alto, CA: Consulting Psychologists Press.

Varela OE, Burke MJ, & Landis RS (2008) 'A model of emergence and dysfunctional effects of emotional conflict in groups', *Group Dynamic: Theory, Research and Practice* 12(2)112–126.

Vasilyuk F (1984) *The Psychology of Experiencing.* English translation 1991. Hemel Hempstead: Harvester Wheatsheaf.

Volkema RJ & Fleck D (2012) 'Understanding propensity to initiate negotiations', *International Journal of Conflict Management* 23(3)266–289.

Wilson ER & Thompson LL (2014) 'Creativity and negotiation research: The integrative potential', *International Journal of Conflict Management* 25(4)359–386.

Zeffane R, Tipu SA, & Ryan JC (2011) 'Communication, commitment & trust: Exploring the triad', *International Journal of Business and Management* 6(6)77–87.

Section 4

Aspects of Agency

The first section of this book put forward the idea of holistic agency, and presented a complex view of life, a life of becoming, structured around two great archetypal constructs that dominate the way in which we perceive and interact with the world. The second and third sections focused on the first great archetypal construct: self-other. The section on 'self' looked at the emergent self, aspirations for the self, and the self as changed by interactions with others. A distinction was made between self and social identity, and it was suggested that the way in which we manage multiple aspects of self in the face of the other, our social identity, acts as an interface between self and other. The section on 'other' focused more on interacting with others, looking at freedom and choice, decision-making and ways of working, and difference and conflict. These sound like neatly categorised and focused areas of self and other, but actually, on reading the chapters you will have found that none are uniquely focused on any one particular area, or indeed able to be so.

The next two sections of this book explore the second archetypal construct: namely, agency and structure. I suggested earlier that the agency-structure divide is similar to that between the individual personal approach or world view of becoming that permeates phenomenological research and the structured, defined, and canonological world view of scientific research. If social identity is the interface between self and other, then the way in which we manage our many aspects of agency in the face of society, the rules of interaction that we develop, can be seen as the interface between structure and agency. Just as we cannot see self without considering other, so we cannot neatly separate agency and structure. Both this section, on agency, and the next on structure, might appear to be neatly segregated, but as I have tried to emphasise throughout this book, such segregation is a conceptual tool that barely applies to reality. The three chapters that I present here in this section on agency focus more on the agent than the structure, though whether it is the agent influencing the structure or the structure that is influencing the agent is hard to judge.

Simply put, 'agency' could be seen as the capacity of individuals to act independently and to make their own free choices, and 'structure' could be seen as those factors, such as social class, religion, gender, ethnicity, and customs, that determine or limit an agent and his or her decisions. Of course, the capacity to act is influenced by the full gamut of beliefs and perceptions that are held (by society and the agent) about the agent and the circumstances. There is a relationship of meanings between these elements as well as a material relationship. One way of exploring this is through Actor Network Theory (ANT). This holds parallels to the agency—structure archetypal construct discussed here. It sees the actor or agent as an element active within a network of relationships between material things and concepts (Latour 1987). Its focus is on exploring the relational ties within the network, rather than explaining how the network takes the form that it does, and thus it has resonance with ethnomethodology, grounded theory, and complexity theory (as discussed in the first section of this book). Agents within ANT can be human or non-human; the important element is the relationship between them. Exploration of the network assumes that it forms a coherent whole, though the relationships need not be coherent and might be in conflict. It also assumes that relationships are transient, needing to be reaffirmed if the network is not to dissolve. As an actor, be it man, animal, or machine, engages with an actor network it too is caught in the web of relations and becomes part of the potentiality. To some extent this concept is similar to that of the Gestalt, in which the sum is greater than the whole of the parts. If the network dissolves then each of the parts reverts to their own actuality (Latour 1999). ANT is largely descriptive rather than explanatory and does not account for pre-existing structures, such as power, but rather sees these structures as emerging from the actions of actors (Collins & Yearley 1992; Whittle & Spicer 2008). However, of interest here is the distinction that ANT makes between actors that transport the force of some other entity and so are intermediaries, and those whose output cannot be predicted by their input, who transform the situation and the network—what we would commonly call agents. The degree of their agency is measured through their effect on the network. This measure is thus external to the agent.

The first chapter of this section, Chapter 13, adds further complexity to the notion of agent. Within the terminology of ANT, despite the fact that the human, as agent, believes that they have an effect upon the network, and does have an effect upon the network, to what extent is that belief of their own agency justified? I access this by recounting aspects of my recovery from a cerebral haemorrhage in 1998. At the time it was considered that if I did survive I was very likely to be a vegetable. There is very little academic or medical research on a recovery of this nature. I use this experience to look at consciousness and question the extent to which we are conscious agents in our lives. We talk of ourselves as if we were the agents of our destiny—we seek control of our environment and others, believe ourselves to be superior because of our consciousness, attribute luck to our good traits—but is 'I' the conscious me, or is it my brain that that is really running the show? Who, or what, is the agent here? I suggest that, in the same way that our brain makes many of our decisions prior to our awareness of them, so the leaders of organisations have a retrospective 'leadership' role.

The idea of the agent as someone in charge and driving the team forwards is further questioned in the second chapter (Chapter 14) with a look at what is meant by power and empowerment. In this I am exploring the dislocation between an agent who clearly does have an effect upon the network and that agent's self-perceptions of efficacy as measured by the effects upon them. In so far as the agent is also part of the network then the effects upon the agent are a legitimate area of measurement. This chapter tells the story of the individual fighting against several bureaucratic structures and the power that is wielded by them. The question of who had the power, and the nature of that power, remains. This extends the notion of power to include aspects of the individual's interpretation of the situation and of themselves—what might be termed agency.

The final chapter in this section, Chapter 15, presents a picture of the agent carefully picking their way through cultural boundaries as they attempt to achieve their goals, and explores the isolation associated with agency. The rhetoric of the structure is contrasted with the reality of agency, thus, in part, exploring practical existential aspects of holistic agency. This is important because although the notion of holistic agency is related to many of the important typologies and theories that we use in the literature, without agency it is little more than a meta-typology. The practical examples of real-life situations given in this section, and throughout the book, balance the holism of structure with the necessity and immediacy of agency.

REFERENCES

Aquino K (2000) 'Structural and individual determinants of workplace victimization: The effects of hierarchical status and conflict management style', Journal of Management 26: 171–193.

Collins HM & Yearley S (1992) 'Epistemological Chicken', in Pickering A (Ed) *Science as Practice and Culture*: 301–326. Chicago: University of Chicago Press.

Latour B (1987) *Science in Action: How to Follow Scientists and Engineers through Society*. Cambridge, MA: Harvard University Press.

Latour B (1999) *Pandora's Hope: Essays on the Reality of Science Studies*. Cambridge, MA: Harvard University Press.

Varela OE, Burke MJ, & Landis RS (2008) "A model of emergence and dysfunctional effects of emotional conflict in groups", Group Dynamic: Theory, Research and Practice 12(2)112–26.

Whittle A & Spicer A (2008) 'Is actor network theory critique?', *Organization Studies* 4: 611–629.

13 Who Is the Agent?

'What a piece of work is a man, how noble in reason, how infinite in faculties, in form and moving, how express and admirable in action, how like an angel in apprehension, how like a god! The beauty of the world! The paragon of animals!'

Shakespeare (1604: Hamlet II/2)

The focus of this chapter is on the potent illusion that we are in control of ourselves. I relate some experiences of blind-sight during my recovery from a cerebral haemorrhage in order to illustrate a consideration of consciousness and will. I argue that consciousness is an evolutionary side effect, a form of real-time imagination, through which we have developed the symbolic attributes fundamental to humanity, but this does not provide control. In the same way that control of mind over body in the individual is an illusion, so is the control of senior management over the organisation.

We talk of the agent as the one who is driving the situation forward, the one with a plan, the target, the motivation, and the will. We assume intentionality and purpose, and like to think of ourselves in this way, and apply this perspective to proactive individuals and top-level management in organisations. I shall argue, however, that this feeling of agency is an illusion.

THE BACKGROUND

Following very stressful times at work I had the whole near-death 'black tunnel going towards a distant light' experience in the summer of 1998. I had a cerebral haemorrhage, and slipped into a deep coma. My family were told that I had less than twenty minutes to live, and I was put into a quiet room to die. Most people with injuries like mine have received them violently and so also have massive trauma elsewhere, so research on previous cases or understanding of my condition was limited. It took me several days to come out of my coma, then about six months of rapid improvement as the non-permanent damage to my brain mended, and slower improvement as my brain adjusted and found alternative ways of working. To all intents and purposes I am back to normal now.

My recovery was, in effect, a process of rebuilding my 'self'. Most of us are so tied up with our hectic lives that we have little opportunity to review what we are—indeed, it is probably a tautology to do so, because as we review we recreate. As I came from my coma I had no real memories, no past, no anticipations for the future. I heard and saw many sounds and shapes and colours, but I had no 'sense-making'—no import of language, vision, sound, or feelings. Looking back, I can now describe it, but I couldn't at the time. My first memory, or notion that contained a sense of 'me', was in reacting to what I saw as funny in something that my husband said. My sense of 'me' developed from there—as I interacted, as I influenced and was influenced by my own thoughts and the people and the things that were happening around me. I wonder whether I would now be a different person if I had been re-acculturated under different circumstances. I was actively rebuilding my identity—but I was not doing so purposefully, nor was I aware of it.

One of the things I became aware of was my inability to speak coherently—initially I thought I was saying exactly what I meant, and failed to realise that people misunderstood my words. Among other things, I also had problems with distinguishing sounds and interference from lots of background noise and 'replaying' of conversations (like a radio that is on all the time and which switches channels at random), and sometimes hearing distant conversations perfectly, but being unable to hear what was being said next to me. I also had severe problems with my vision. I can talk about it now in terms that mean things to other people, but at the time I had no comparators and no way to link into other people's understandings. Initially, if I was asked how I felt I couldn't really say—I just knew that I did feel. Similarly, if asked whether my vision was any better, I was not really sure what constituted 'better'—just that I experienced it in the here and now.

As I rebuilt patterns of understanding, I did become aware of change. I had past states and a present state. I developed sufficient expectation of my current state to be aware of possible correlations in what was happening to me, and I started to develop hypotheses involving causal links. For example, I started to attribute the odd things I was hearing to my brain trying to rewire and practise different sounds. I became more able to talk about my condition—needing not just the words but the underlying logical structures and patterns of our communicative society before I could converse on par with others. Eventually, as there seemed to be no more variations on sound that could be experienced, my hearing reverted to 'normal'—first on one side, and then the other. Gradually, though not until well after I had left hospital, my vision started to settle from a confusing display of multiple images, after-images, flashing lights, and 'odd' bits, into patterns of meaning and deficit.

The main effect of the haemorrhage was on the visual centre in my left hemisphere. As I became aware of the patterns of deficit I went through an unsettlingly weird stage during which, when I moved my head, my brain could not keep up with the computations necessary to 'map' the changes in my visual field in relation to my movement (something that involves enormous computational power, but that is normally managed smoothly by our brain and without our noticing). This meant that if I moved my head it felt as if I was staying still, and that the room was twisting and distorting and moving around me. Standing still in the garden, especially when the trees blew in the wind, became a particularly scary challenge. Walking was even worse! Gradually my brain sorted itself, my vision became more normally 'multiple', and then, slowly, I became able to focus—initially on distant things and then, once again, more normally. I interpreted these changes as my brain attempting to regain its spatial, binocular ability.

Dyslexia

One extremely frustrating problem I faced was dyslexia of the written word. I was able to write, but then completely unable to read what I had just written. I couldn't use my computer (either to use the keyboard or read the screen) and I wasn't even able to telephone, because I just couldn't make out the numbers on the keypad—I could see the shapes, and I knew what they were meant to mean, but I couldn't work out which symbol represented which number. I gradually re-learnt to read, first with big letters (advertising slogans and logos), and slowly finding myself more able to read the smaller stuff. After more than 15 years I am pretty much back to normal now, although I still have occasional problems with subtitles on films, and other small text that moves quickly. This is not just due to the dyslexia, but also because as I get tired my brain chooses to ignore the right-hand side of words—so I have to keep on checking and cross-checking. I have learnt to be more meticulous.

Sense of Self

My sense of 'I', as 'me', was odd—'I' would wake up in the morning and lie there trying to work out what had changed in my brain/body. It changed as it needed, and certainly without any conscious purpose on my part. 'I', my mind, reviewed such changes as if they were entirely separate from 'me'. Perhaps the distance helped me cope with the whole thing—but I am not sure . . . it didn't feel like a coping mechanism, just that I had no control or way of influencing what was going on. My 'mind' seemed to be completely divorced from changes in my 'brain'. At that stage my mind was only involved in my recovery in so far as it kept an inventory of the changes that it noticed.

For much of the time during my recovery, I felt 'childlike' again—so dependent upon the development of my body/brain; no longer subject to the myth of adult control and purpose. As my brain changed and developed, I slept a tremendous amount, and dreamed the vivid, all-engaging dreams of the child attempting to make sense of the world. I am not sure whether my 'self' has changed. People gave me labels—told me how brave, determined (and so on) I was—which in some ways is nice. The labels, especially early on, gave me something to hang on to—but I don't think they were really 'me'. My family and those around me had a tremendous shock, and had to cope with an awful lot. They knew what was going on and what the consequences might be. As the childlike, unknowing, and reasonably passive recipient I was blissfully unaware of the drama I caused, and it was several months before this changed.

'I' am in the centre of living my life, and remain, to a certain extent, at the mercy of the continuing development of my 'body', but not entirely. I have relearnt a great deal, and find it easy to forget how far I have come, as one of the things I did relearn is my sense of purpose. Despite my best efforts, I stopped just taking an inventory of the developments in my brain, and started trying to influence it. I had goals—I wanted to go outside again, to move around, to learn to read, to compute, to drive, and so on. I needed to rediscover myself through acting upon or influencing my world (internal and external) in some way; to set myself tasks and goals, points of achievement. I am sure this has helped me recover to the extent that I have done. Many a time I have felt that if I stopped after a particular achievement I would stay there—competently doing what I was capable of—but then another possible goal arrived and I developed further.

Blind-Sight

I now have some permanent damage on the right-hand side of my left visual field—which means that when I look at something both eyes see the left-hand side of it, but for one part of the right-hand side, one of my eyes sees it, whereas the other claims that there is nothing there—my brain has to make a choice. At times there can be objects in plain sight to everyone that I just don't see. This is problematic when things are left on the floor, for example, as I suddenly fall full length over something that, as far as my brain is concerned, doesn't exist. At other times my body will react as if I have seen something, though I am not aware of seeing it—a case of blind-sight. An example of this would be when a ball is thrown to me and I not aware of the thrower or the ball—yet to my surprise my hand reaches out and catches the ball accurately. In blind-sight experiences like this, the body acts in a complex and accurate way, yet entirely independently of awareness.

My brain is now much more accurate about choosing what is, and isn't, there. It is only when I am tired that it compromises—showing the right-hand side of what I am looking at as squeezed up into half the size of the left-hand side—rather like in a 'Hall of Mirrors' (a fairground attraction that distorts everybody's image). This affects my perception of three dimensions in a variable manner, such that I am never quite sure whether I am judging the depth of something accurately, and thus, for example, going down stairs or walking around new places can be nerve-racking.

Much of my recuperation involved managing, or living with, the tension between ideas of self-control (mind over body) and the letting go of control, thereby trusting my body to manage without my interference. If I think a ball is being thrown to me, but I can't see it, I fail to catch it. Similarly, I still get fed up of falling over things I can't see—but those times are much less frequent if, instead of determinedly walking across the room, I relax my attention on where I want to get to and instead let my body take me there. It is hard to describe—it feels as if my mind is playing trust-games with my body.

What I want to emphasise here is the high degree of immensely complex operations that the body can undertake without the mind being aware of them. Another example can be seen in the experience reported by a few soldiers in the Vietnam War. These soldiers, when under threat of capture, apparently ran silently through the jungle at dead of night for about 40 miles, navigating their way to friendly encampments, whereas normally, in the same amount of time, they would only be able to hack their path for a few miles in full daylight. In each case they reported having no awareness of the journey and no understanding of how they did it.

Learning to ride a bike has similar aspect. Consider a bicycle being ridden in a straight line along level ground and then the rider executing a turn to the left. Elementary mechanics, or a little experimentation, shows us that the handlebars must first be rotated to the right when starting this turn. This destabilises the bicycle and enables it to lean into the corner and so turn left. Without such destabilisation the rider would fall off. Few bicycle riders are aware that they know this, and neither are they aware of learning it. Bringing a subconscious skill to attention results in repeating the errors that were made when were first learning to ride a bicycle.

Similarly, research into heroic altruistic acts in which people risk their own lives to save others who are often complete strangers shows that the vast majority of heroic acts are impulsive, unpredictable, and unexplainable (Bond 2015). People find they have done the act without any conscious decision to do so. Their body has completed the task before they fully realise what they have done. If they had stopped and thought they might not have done anything. Such people tend to espouse values of fairness, compassion, and personal responsibility towards strangers, and are unusually tolerant, by which they identify their 'in-group' as the whole of humanity, not just their own kind (Oliner 1992). Altruists and those high in empathy are adept at recognising fearful facial expressions and have larger and more responsive right amygdalae than normal (Marsh et al. 2014). Altruistic behaviour is also learnt through the early social interactions young children have with adults (Barragan & Dweck 2014). It would appear that people need an underlying tendency towards altruism if they are to show heroic behaviour, but not all altruists are heroic. In other words, the body can move around, make decisions, and manage complex tasks that we normally assume require some level of awareness and higher control—and the application of that higher control can actually hinder successful completion of the task.

MIND AND CONSCIOUSNESS

By higher control I am referring to mind and consciousness; however, these are concepts that are highly contested in the literature, with different levels of discourse surrounding the notion of 'consciousness'—ranging from the theological to the functional. As with the Shakespearian quote at the start of this chapter, for Polanyi (1962) consciousness represents a peak of evolution and is linked directly with sentience, responsibility, personhood, and humanity. It is seen as a fundamentally different state of being; one that separates us from animals. Polanyi suggests that different states of being follow different ordering principles and identity, and that consciousness represents an entirely different operating principle to that which was working before.

This sort of view is often associated with a sequel, which holds that because of the way in which each system is self-perpetuating and stable, development from one to the other cannot be accounted for, and thus attempts to account for the beginnings of consciousness form a philosophical challenge which can only be resolved by invoking an outside agency (such as a God). From this perspective consciousness is seen to raise us above the 'animals' and many would argue, as does Polanyi, that 'so long as we can form no idea of the way a material system may become a conscious, responsible person, it is an empty pretence to suggest that we have an explanation for the descent of man. Darwinism has diverted attention for a century from the descent of man by investigating the *conditions* of evolution and overlooking its *action*. Evolution can be understood only as a feat of emergence' (Polanyi 1962: 390).

In contrast, other writers suggest that consciousness develops through social interaction. 'Consciousness, while always embodied and constituted and expressed through the action of the body, is formed, I stress, through its engagement with other human beings in the world . . . to put it another way, individual consciousness emerges in a field of consciousness. It arises in a world of other conscious human beings who participate in the process of consciousness of any human being' (Kapferer 1995: 134). From the postmodern perspective 'consciousness' becomes a system of relations between strata, or, 'what is particularly significant about postmodernism is the replacement of belief in the power of *the* rational explanation by belief in the *subjectivity* of rational explanation' (Carter & Jackson 1993: 87). By implication, the notion of consciousness shifts away from that of self-directed agency towards nodality within the social discourse, in which 'the role of language in *constituting* "reality" is therefore central and all out attempts to discover "truth" should be seen for what they are—forms of discourse' (Parker 1992: 3).

This discourse, however, still places trust in the notion of rational explanation—albeit a subjective rationality—and it replaces notions of individual agency with a form of societal agency or social consciousness. In this interpretation, the apparent qualities of individual 'consciousness' such as rationality, intention, and the sense-making that gives meaning to life are substituted by a wider sense of rationality in which 'reality' is constituted through discourse, and in which discourse is a process of creating common meaning—or a common rationality: the collective consciousness (Shore 1995). There are elements common to both these views of consciousness that set them apart from the interpretation, which I shall discuss later.

In each of these accounts of consciousness, 'thinking' and 'thought' are privileged over practical knowledge. 'The Cartesian notion of consciousness . . . privileges a socially decontextualised mental state in search of an object. But mental states do not seek objects: they are only ever already inscribed in the materiality of bodily form, action, and encountered objects. If we are to transcend Cartesian dualities, we have to say that consciousness is not to do with abstract cognition but with intelligent . . . materiality' (Parkin 1995: 199). Similarly, Bourdieu (1990: 25) claims that the distinction between objective or absolute understanding and subjective or relational knowledge is ruinous to social science, as both are theoretical modes of knowledge, 'equally opposed to the practical mode of knowledge which is the basis of ordinary experience of the social world'. Hastrup (1995: 193) articulates this as: 'Theoretical knowledge implies an understanding of its own condition, as well as its possible impact upon practical knowledge'. Individuals are not only defined by their space but are also its defining consciousness (Ardener 1987: 40). People are never just victims of social forms, because social forms owe their shape partly to the fact that they are inhabited by people thinking about social forms (Hollis 1985: 232).

According to these accounts, therefore, consciousness is not just about thinking of our thinking, nor is it just about acting on the world, but it is about *knowingly* acting on the world. 'I know who I am because I know how I feel. The key to consciousness is in the knowing, not in the ability to speak fully of this knowing' (Kohn 1995: 50).

This stops slightly short of implying that consciousness is necessarily causal—instead, knowing is linked to intentionality, which 'refers to the direction of all action, that action has a trajectory. This is not driven by any necessary or essential reason or value. In the distinction of intentionality from motivation, while all motivated action is intentional action all intentional action is not motivated action' (Kapferer 1995: 135). Talking of 'knowing' in this way, then, carries with it a sense of intentionality and latent action—and it does assume that there is something to be 'known'. Whether consciousness is seen to be a God-given advancement, or to develop through contact with the social world, these accounts include notions of consciousness as directed and intentioned knowledge, the exercise of which gives meaning to a person's life, and the existence of which places humanity above animals (and nearer to God?).

Problems With These Accounts

The first problem is that it is hard to reconcile this notion of superiority of the mind with the way in which the body behaves. Without being aware of the trigger, our bodies are able to make complex computations and act, to all purposes, as if we are conscious of it. In the example of blind-sight above, I am awake and conscious in the normal sense and have the feeling of agency as I interact with the world, yet at the same time I am not aware of part of what my body is thinking and doing, other than by looking at the results of my actions. Though conscious, I am not always fully aware.

The second problem is that whilst my experiences do lend support to the (re)building of my idea of self through interaction with others, through the stories I was told, through my actions, and through a gradual (re)appreciation of time and the relationship between things, as soon as I came out of the coma I was more than a tabula rasa. I was just not able to make much sense of the social world before I had (re)learnt its patterns. I needed these skills and understandings to be able to communicate and be part of society—but was fully conscious and aware without them.

I can see that my experiences show how consciousness as a social activity (consciousness of self and self-consciousness) develops through other social activities, and, in the same vein, I can see how we can talk of collective consciousness. I can see why, when we talk of consciousness, we talk of the contents of consciousness. But—are we really saying that without 'society' or without 'content' the phenomenon that we call consciousness would not 'be'? Are we saying that the newborn child is without consciousness?

Normally when we talk of consciousness we talk of the dynamic *products* of our consciousness, or the *state* of being conscious—either in terms of the *act* of consciousness, or else the phylogical or teleological positions that possession of the *attribute* of consciousness might place us in—but we rarely talk of the *systems* of consciousness themselves.

The next section of this chapter concentrates on what the system of consciousness might entail—not with any intention of identifying it uniquely or of defining it, but in the hope of understanding better the nature of consciousness. The system of consciousness influences the form of the content, yet it is normally ignored, or assumed, and thus conceptions of consciousness that are current in the social sciences are rarely challenged. It is worth noting that some of the references in the following section date back to the 1930s, yet the import of their findings has not filtered through to some areas of social science. We could question why that is so. Why do we find it hard to challenge the supremacy of consciousness? Why do we cling to this despite powerful evidence to the contrary?

Because it is so hard to accept that our reason is not 'noble', nor our faculties 'infinite', I shall take a diversion to look more deeply at the evolution of consciousness. This line of thought is based upon theoretical work done by CW Lee in 1984, and it is interesting to find that it is now being discussed in various different fields and supported by empirical evidence. We descend, therefore, from considering consciousness as a link to the gods, to considering consciousness as just another evolved mechanism.

MECHANISMS FOR CONSCIOUSNESS

As illustrated by blind-sight and other examples, the information-processing functions of the brain necessary for day-to-day survival can all be performed without the involvement of consciousness. Obviously, sometimes we are aware of aspects of them, but we do not have to be conscious of them for them to occur. For example, there is plenty of evidence that mechanisms for extracting information from the external environment can proceed subconsciously (Lackner & Garrett 1972). Similarly, the operation of long-term memory is largely independent of consciousness (Underwood 1979), as is that of short-term memory (Spelke et al. 1976). Motor control is often managed better without conscious interference (Englekamp & Zimmer 1995) and it can be learnt, practised, and conducted with no awareness of the actual movements being performed (Rosenfeld & Baer 1969). The degree of involvement of consciousness in problem solving is well documented and it has been known for a long time that the solution to problems of the most complex and abstract types will often appear when the consciousness is engaged in some completely separate activity (Maier 1931). Nisbett & Wilson (1977: 240) state that 'creative workers describe themselves almost universally as bystanders, differing from other observers only in that they are the first to witness the fruits of a problem-solving process that is almost completely hidden from conscious view'. Complex decisions can be made subconsciously, and when people are consciously aware of the decision-making they are often unable to report accurately the reasons for reaching the decision. Furthermore, in a deceptively simple investigation Libet (1985) showed that there is neural activity in preparation for movement prior to the conscious decision to make that movement.

Attention is sometimes held to be almost identical to consciousness because one of the principal properties of consciousness is that it is always attending to something; however, consciousness does not appear to be a necessary part of any mechanism of attention. When driving a car we can switch our attention from one mirror to another without any conscious decision, and we can attend to several apparently incompatible tasks simultaneously with no loss of efficiency (Lachman et al. 1979).

It would appear, therefore, that the majority of our day-to-day functioning could occur perfectly successfully without requiring us to be conscious.

Indeed, our consciousness could be seen to reduce our evolutionary fitness: interference by consciousness in some of these processes (particularly motor control) generally results in degradation of performance, and when activity is unnecessary, consciousness often initiates the expenditure of energy on activities with zero, and sometimes negative, survival value.

Consciousness As an Operating System

It is these points that argue against the idea that consciousness functions in the manner of an operating system controlling the various parallel process of the brain, as suggested by some writers (Johnson-Laird 1983). This idea would certainly explain why consciousness is always active and why it appears to be concerned with the results of information processing and not the actual processing itself. It could also explain why it is mostly occupied with daydreaming, the forming of plans and the rehearsal of actions, and the resolution of unfinished business, given that the human brain is not an entirely real-time machine. However, it is some of the inabilities of the consciousness that cannot be explained so easily by the analogy with an operating system. Consciousness does not actually control the operation of the brain. It appears to be more concerned with the content of the task being performed rather than the administration of the various subsystems of the brain necessary to achieve the task. Indeed, the administrative abilities of the consciousness are almost non-existent. We do not consciously direct pieces of processing to various parts of the brain. We find great difficulty in forcing the consciousness to concentrate on a task where there is a small processing requirement but the need for constant vigilance (Antrobus et al. 1966). This is an unlikely feature to find built into the operating system of a machine mostly intended for real-time work. It would be quite simple for an operating system to be able to forbid all except urgent processing at times when vigilance was required, and if there is an operating system within the human brain we have no evidence that it is unable to do this. It is only the consciousness that appears to find difficulty in concentrating on tasks which it itself deems important.

So what does consciousness offer?

Parameters of a Mechanism of Consciousness

Simple organisms operate with real-time control. If we were to describe a robot, or indeed a fly as if it were a mechanism, all the processing that the system does is concerned with monitoring and controlling the operation of the robot or fly. The system is dedicated to the environment external to itself. The information it processes is generated by the environment outside of it, or by devices monitoring its internal state. When there is no stimulus to trigger the monitoring devices, then the system is quiescent. Information processing is real-time and aids immediate survival.

Lee (1984) argued that at some point in the evolutionary chain the otherwise real-time machine has acquired an additional mechanism—one which allows for the internal provision of material to be processed. This must allow:

a) processors to be shared between internal and external sources of information, through an interrupt mechanism, without significantly degrading real-time performance. A side effect would be that internally generated material might intrude on the processing of externally generated problems.

b) monitoring and ensuring the relevance of at least some of the internally generated material. This would require the recovery from memory of old problems through chaining, such that the retrieval of old problems from memory could, in itself, trigger the generation of further material from memory. This would also allow processing that was aborted due to pressing real-time problems to be continued later. Such chaining would need very delicate control mechanisms in order to maintain relevance to the external environment, and one side effect might well be occasional or progressive failure to maintain relevance.

c) the extra processing to have some effect upon behaviour by allowing the internally generated processing to have some share in the motor control. One side effect would be potentially inappropriate behaviour, and the other, the perceived quality of intentionality (using Kapferer's distinction between intentionality and motivation, and in which the, albeit complex, layers of non-conscious survival-based behaviour might be seen as generated by motivational drives).

CONSCIOUSNESS AS AN IMAGINARY-TIME MECHANISM

This is an imaginary-time mechanism that evolved where there already existed an embedded real-time system (that itself was embedded within a physical system). The purpose of this mechanism is to utilise spare processing capacity at times when the system is not needed for real-time work. To be of value, this mechanism must only marginally degrade real-time performance, and it must share motor control and goal definition with the real-time component. 'It is this imaginary-time mechanism that gives rise to human consciousness. That is, the function of human consciousness is the productive utilisation of the idle capacity of an embedded real-time machine' (Lee 1984).

This fits with our experience. Except during periods of sleep our consciousness does appear always active. It is involved in some sort of information processing whether there is any need or not, and, indeed, a substantial proportion of conscious thought is devoted to daydreaming (Singer 1975). We can be, and often are, conscious of our real-time information processing, despite the fact that, as discussed above, there is no need for our consciousness to be involved. There is ample evidence of perceptual systems, representational systems, and so on, being accessible to both real-time control and conscious control—and of interference between these. We can, and do, consciously recall old memories, review problems, and so on . . . and we do sometimes suffer from lack of control over this, going into fugues: getting 'lost' in our thoughts and daydreams. Finally, we do have conscious control over behaviour, and this can lead to inappropriate behaviour.

Phylogenic Perspective

The existence of an imaginary-time processor also fits the phylogenic and evolutionary evidence. The differences in the intellectual capabilities of young apes and young children have been shown to be remarkably small considering the great differences in brain size and behaviour, and there seems to be general agreement that the marked superiority in human intellectual accomplishments arises not from large scale differences in ability at, for example, solving problems, but instead from greater application of abilities of similar magnitudes (Gallup et al. 1997). The intelligence quotient of the great ape is difficult to ascertain, but appears to be slightly less than the human average (90 IQ, as opposed to 100 IQ: Hall et al. 1980). A human is considered to be educationally subnormal with an IQ of 70. IQ, therefore, does not appear to be the defining factor of difference. Neither is the use of tools and weapons. Great apes can make and use a wide variety of tools, and use them as weapons (Lethmate 1982), and the ability to use tools is not confined to primates (Gallup et al. 1977). Similarly, apes can be taught to communicate using a non-verbal language, with a vocabulary in excess of 100 words (Sebeok & Umiker-Sebeok 1980).

The concept of self is important here, because of the link between self-awareness and consciousness, and the possibility that the emergence of self-awareness (rather than consciousness) was the evolutionary leap. Gallup (1983), however, has shown that chimpanzees and orangutans share self-awareness with man, and that gorillas and other primates do not. Also, Mason (1976) has shown that so far as the conceptual structures that represent the external environment are concerned, the brain of man does not differ significantly from those of the great apes. There are some differences between the brains of a young child and an ape, but these are small enough to indicate that there must be another reason to account for the gross differences in brain size and behaviour.

That difference was the development of an imaginary-time processor. There is evidence that chimpanzees and gorillas cannot internally generate topics of conversation, and that 'apes in nature . . . are not given to extended reflections on the past, or elaborate speculations about the future' (Mason 1976). The notion of externally driven real-time processing does not necessarily require that processing be of *immediate* benefit to the organism, and thus primate 'play' and exploration could be accounted for by a real-time mechanism—in that during 'play' the primate is still reacting to the environment. In contrast, the sort of human play that is not observed in animals is the very common 'make-believe' type, in which external reality is ignored in favour of some internally generated pretence (Fagan 1981).

Evolutionary Perspective

An examination of the evolutionary perspective provides additional supporting evidence for the notion of consciousness as an imaginary-time mechanism embedded in a real-time processor. There are very strong evolutionary pressures against larger brains. The brain is the most delicate of all organs and suffers irreparable harm if its blood supply is interrupted for more than a few minutes. It has a massive consumption of energy in relation to its size, accounting for 20% of the body's total energy consumption whether or not it is itself working, whilst only accounting for 2% of the body's weight. In an infant it may take more than 50% of the body's energy consumption (Dunn & Bondy 1974). Not only is each extra gram of brain tissue exceptionally expensive and troublesome for the body to maintain, but the presence of the protective skull causes difficulty at birth in a large-brained animal. This results in evolutionary pressure for small brains.

In response to this evolutionary pressure the brains of human babies continue growing after birth—indeed the newborn infant brain is only a quarter of its final size (Passingham 1982). The cranial capacity of mankind has increased considerably since 3 million years (Ma) before the present (BP). Not only is the increase in size of interest, but also, and in particular, is the way in which 20,000 years ago man's cranial capacity was 10% *larger* than it is now, as can be seen in Figure 13.1. Lee (1984) points out that this pattern of change in cranial capacity is exactly what would be expected from the evolution of a *new* brain function, rather than an expansion of existing cognitive abilities. An increase in existing functions would lead to an increase in cranial capacity, but not to the subsequent decrease, unless the decrease was matched by a decrease in ability. 'This seems unlikely in view of the absence of behavioural evidence that the brain of man was any more competent during the Wurm glaciation than it is today' (Lee 1984: 19). This indicates the evolution of one or more new brain functions, commencing between 2 and 3 Ma BP, with the achievement of a capability equivalent to that found in modern man occurring between 50,000 and 10,000 years BP (at the top of the hump in Figure 13.1). As a new mechanism capable of achieving a specific function evolves it must initially require a significant increase in the total number of neurones, and the functioning of that mechanism is likely to be crude and relatively inefficient. Once the new brain function is being performed satisfactorily, however, pressures of survival will be towards the evolution of increasingly sophisticated methods for achieving

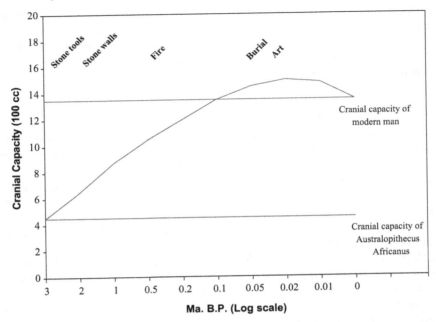

Figure 13.1   Average Human Cranial Capacity From 3 Ma BP to Present Day (After Lee 1984)

the same results with fewer neurones—as can be seen in the decrease in cranial capacity over the last 20,000 years.

The behavioural changes associated with this rise in cranial capacity are what might be expected if the developing new brain mechanism were an imaginary-time mechanism. The first cluster of behavioural changes would be those with immediate evolutionary survival value: namely, an expansion in the range of problems which are solved—including making stone tools, making walls, and developing the use of fire. The first innovation, because it is the simplest, might be a mechanism for the recovery from memory of problems on which processing had been stopped due to more urgent business. The second development might be 'open-ended' processing, not restricted to solving specific external problems, past or present. The costs of this would come principally from the additional memory required to store the work of such a mechanism, whether useful or not. The benefit would be an increase in the stored range of solutions to problems available to the real-time component of the brain. A long period of development of controls to such open-ended processing would probably be necessary. The final innovation might be the granting of direct control over behaviour to the new mechanism, giving the opportunity of physical activity to support its operations. This would bring about a major change in behaviour and several side effects, which would themselves continue to develop. The side effects would be behaviour that we might associate with a brain that is constantly searching for material to process, including the reprocessing of old material, and the remaking of meaning, such as painting and sculpture, and burial of the dead.

SIDE EFFECTS AND SYMBOLISM

Consciousness As a Side Effect of an Imaginary-Time Processor

The main side effect of all of this, however, seems to be consciousness. I call consciousness a side effect because although it seems of great importance to us (the recipients of it) it seems to be very unlikely that it is, indeed, the *'peak'* or even the *'intent'* of evolution. Evolution is not some *'thing'* that has a *'goal'* in mind, it is a term that we have given to a blind process, and it is hard to see why this process should have engaged in 'the sheer, apparently nonsensical, incongruity of an organism whose conscious mind appears so loosely coupled to its information processing capacity' (Dixon 1981) if what was being 'developed' was a form of overseer. Instead we are left with the idea that it is constant activity that was developed and which gives the system its evolutionary advantage over non-conscious systems that are dependent upon external input for the initiation of information processing. What was being 'selected' alongside the constant activity was the sharing of processors, the monitoring of material, and the ability for this new system to affect behaviour—which together just happen to allow for time-independent symbolism, language, and consciousness. Consciousness, as knowledge of *'self'* in the environment and self *'in'* the environment, seems to be (in evolutionary terms) a side effect.

We talk as if consciousness is a 'thing' that we now 'have', but it is much more likely that our systems are continuing to be refined (though developments in medical science mean that 'evolution' is no longer directly about survival of the fittest). Although consciousness and language are side products, having developed them we are now 'conscious' agents in their further development (though the time-scales are hard to image). Apes might be on the verge of language as we are on the verge of consciousness—and what we possess now might be a poor imitation of what our descendants might possess in thousands of years to come.

An understanding of the physical limits and possibilities of our functioning influences how we construe our world . . . for example, as each development in the understanding of how we manage our 'information processing' is made, so we realise, again and again, that the ideas of 'brain' as computer and 'awareness' as operating system are simplistic anachronisms. As Edelman (1988: 182) says, 'Although the brain looks like a vast electrical network at one scale, at its most microscopic scale, it is not connected or arranged like any other natural or man-made network. . . . It is an example of a self-organising system. . . . If one numbered the branches of a neurone and correspondingly numbered the neurones it touched, the numbers would not correspond in any two individuals of a species—not even in identical twins or in genetically identical individuals'. As we come to realise the full complexity of human functioning, so we need to refine the metaphors and similes with which we represent that functioning to ourselves. Our evolved capacity for consciousness not only enables us to monitor what is going on about us in the interests of survival and reproductive success but makes us aware of the *meaning* and *quality* of events as they occur. 'In the words of Saint Augustine, we both exist and know that we exist, and rejoice in this existence and this knowledge. It is commonly observed that we are the only animal that knows that it must die. But we are also, as Robin Fox has said, the only animal that knows that it is alive' (Stevens & Price 1996: 238–239).

Automacity and Intentionality

It can be argued that the more automatic the basic cognitive functions become, the less attentional resource is required for their execution, and therefore the more use can be made of workbench space—therefore, the more automaticity, the greater engagement of workbench space, and the greater ability to deal with complex cognitive processes. Broadly speaking, the more we rely upon our automaticity the better we function in our daily lives (Gray & Mulhern 1995). We seem to want the majority of our functioning to be as automatic as possible, and at the same time reassure ourselves that our functioning is fully under our 'aware' control. As Gazzaniga (1988: 234) says, people 'view their responses as behaviours emanating from their own volitional selves, and as a result, incorporate these behaviours into a theory to explain why they behave as they do'. Confabulation happens even when they know that as a split-brain subject one hemisphere does not have access to the information of the other, and therefore, they might be acting on information provided by the other hemisphere—instead they construct a plausible reason for their action (see Chapter 4).

Obviously, we can, and do, have access to aspects of our unconscious self—and the power of the unconscious complex self is evident in the whole arena of psychosomatic illness and healing, shamanism, and 'faith' healing. (Finkler 1994). There are, however, many ways in which we demonstrate our 'mind over matter'. Relaxation and biofeedback techniques rely upon this ability. Take, for example, our perception. People who use microscopes, including myself, can develop the trick of 'perceiving' through each eye separately, so that we can both 'see' what we are looking at under the microscope through one eye, and, simultaneously, 'see' what we are drawing or writing with the other eye. Similarly, as all artists experience, we can influence what we 'perceive' by concentrating on what we want to 'see'. The behaviour of animals indicates that they understand intention—a form of loose causality described above—yet it is only humans that appear to have a 'belief' in causality sufficient to see themselves 'in charge' when they are not, and sufficient to make confabulation (and suspicious behaviour) an everyday natural occurrence. This need to be able to explain what our bodies and brains do as if we were in charge of them, as if all that we do has intentionality, is common to us all, but is particularly prevalent in the 'logical' West and less prevalent in cultures that have a stronger notion of predestiny.

As well as trying to control our inner world, we also seek ways of coming to terms with it—the creative act is often described as 'letting go', and courses on creativity focus on standing outside oneself. Many major advances in understanding have come about by loosening our grip on current reality— through noticing and fully observing something that had previously been 'seen' but not questioned, and thus had been ignored. Our consciousness, our ability to live in imaginary time, to forget and to confabulate, therefore, help us create a false reality that accords to our expectations, one in which we are in charge of ourselves, and of many aspects of our life. Instead, our conscious self is a by-product of evolution, and is a bystander to our complex functioning that can observe, feedback, and initiate, but does not control. Our mind is largely the observer, not the agent of our body.

The Processing of Time

I have called consciousness a side effect of an imaginary-time processor; however, as I indicated in Chapter 4, our sense of time is complicated. Our different senses physically distinguish one event from another at different times: for example, two sounds can be distinguished just two milliseconds apart (Lotze et al. 1999), whereas two events need to be 20 to 60 milliseconds apart if we are to be able to tell which came first (Szymaszek et al. 2009). Our brains appear to physically adjust signals to synchronise events that they think should belong together (Kösem et al. 2014) and the brain creates atemporal system states during which incoming information is treated as co-temporal. This is called a 'functional moment', a snapshot of perception that has no perceivable duration (van Wassenhove 2009). In contrast, the 'experienced moment' has duration and relates to the experience of an extended now.

The experienced moment forms an elementary unit of a temporally unified experience of presence called the 'mental presence'. In phenomenological terms, what we perceive at present is strongly intertwined with what has just happened and what is about to happen, and the ability to perceive temporal order is of great importance for things like the perception of speech (Kiverstein 2010).

The working memory provides a temporal bridge between events— both those that are internally generated and environmentally presented— thereby conferring a sense of unity and continuity to conscious experience (Goldman-Rakic 1997). This gives a sense of a perceiving and feeling agent ('my self') acting in its environment, remembering the past, and planning the future. Our mental presence, therefore, is derived from the integration of activity from multiple distributed and specialised brain areas (Dehaene & Naccache 2001) supplemented by visuospatial, episodic, and phonologic storage systems, which holds information for temporal storage and manipulation (Baddeley 2003) and emerges from separate short flashes of timeless experience. In effect, our brain takes small snapshots of jumbled sensations, and then puts these snapshots together in some sort of order, that may or may not be accurate, but which we, going around our daily lives, perceive as smooth 'reality'.

DUAL PROCESS ACCOUNTS OF THOUGHT

More recent physiological research has shown that there are two entwined types or systems of thought, thus providing support for the idea of consciousness as an imaginary-time processor. The finer details are hotly contested (Kahneman 2011), so I will only give a broad-brush explanation here. Type 1 processes are fast, unconscious, automatic, of high capacity; they are more likely to assign appropriate weights to decisions criteria, are unable to follow one certain rule, and are more divergent and can operate in parallel. Type 2 processes are slow, conscious, of low capacity; they have a top-down focus, place inappropriate weights on decision criteria, are more focused and convergent, and are able to follow one specific rule, operating sequentially.

Type 1 processes involve those that control behaviour directly and those that provide representations for Type 2 processing. For example, the dorsal visual system is autonomous whilst the ventral visual system is a support system; habit and procedural learning are autonomous, but the hippocampal memory system is support; language modules are directly involved in the production of speech but also pass representations into the working memory. In each case Type 1 processing is involved in all cognitive acts that contribute to Type 2 processing. Similarly, there is no single unique Type 2 process that does all the things that involve higher cognitive functions. Neural imaging studies (Tsujii & Watanabe 2009) implicate many brain areas that differ greatly from study to study; however, each Type 2 process needs to engage the single process of working memory, such that only one Type 2 process can function at a time, whereas many Type 1 processes can operate in parallel. It is the recently evolved and distinctively human symbolic areas of cognition, such as language and theory of mind, that are key support systems for Type 2 processing.

Where is the control in this? Automatic processes can be goal driven, and controlled processes are just as determined as automatic ones; however, some mechanism must exist for allocating the resources of the working memory. The focus of Type 2 processing is constantly changing according to which current task or goal has priority, and although the working memory is always active it does not 'choose' its own function. Cognitive control and achievement of goals must be an emergent property of the interaction between the two types of processing into which we have no self-insight at all, and thus the control is preconscious and preattentive. So, from a very different field of study, we return to the idea that the feeling of conscious will is illusory (Bargh 1994).

Development of Language

The development of language can be seen as an additional side effect. Although non-human primates like chimpanzees or extinct hominid species such as *H. neanderthalensis* have or had the ability to hear and produce speech-like sounds, this does not mean that they could understand or produce language (Martinez et al. 2012). The anatomical ability to express language through speech necessitated the descent of the larynx, and posed the risk of adults choking to death, as simultaneous breathing and swallowing became impossible (Lieberman 2011). This evolutionary step is linked to adaptations acquired as early-Pleistocene archaic *Homo* populations became littoral omnivores, following coasts and inland rivers diving to collect food, leading to voluntary breath control not seen in other hominoids, but clearly present in diving mammals (Vaneechoutte et al. 2011). However, the descent of the larynx was already in place before symbolic language was acquired and there is evidence that the faculty for language is distinct from the evolution of vocalization or auditory-vocal learning or the evolution of communication (Bolhuis et al. 2014).

Language is a computational cognitive mechanism that has hierarchical syntactic structure at its core (Berwick et al. 2013). This can be seen in online brain imaging experiments (Pallier et al. 2011) but is absent in non-human species (Bolhuis & Everaert 2013). Many other species can communicate but no non-human species has the hierarchical syntactic structure of humans (Geschwind & Rakic 2013). For example, chimpanzees taught sign language demonstrably lack combinatorial ability (Yang 2013). Paleoanthropological evidence suggests a rapid genetic change occurred during which the hierarchical syntactic structure developed alongside the appearance of symbolic thought, around 100,000 years ago, and significantly after the appearance of anatomically distinctive *Homo sapiens* around 200,000 years ago (Tattersall 2008).

'By this reckoning, the language faculty is an extremely recent acquisition in our lineage, and it was acquired not in the context of slow, gradual modification of pre-existing systems under natural selection but in a single, rapid, emergent event that built upon those prior systems but was not predicted by them' (Bolhuis et al. 2014: 4). It is likely that language was not selected for directly by evolutionary pressures, but developed through secondary effects, such as cooperative problem solving and the transmission of culture. It is likely that increased use of language, verbal and non-verbal, came initially as a side effect of having something to say. A body of language, at the level that can be achieved by the great apes, could have been developed and transmitted culturally as a result of this. The existence of this core of language, and the prior occupation of an evolutionary niche involving specialisation in cognitive problem solving, would have facilitated the operation of the selection pressures required to drive the genetic changes necessary for the production of a sophisticated verbal language.

Interestingly, Inomata et al. (2015) found that the first builders in the Maya Lowlands (about 950 BC) were nomads who gathered periodically for community rituals and the construction of ceremonial buildings. The first architecture was symbolic, and it was only six centuries later that permanent homes (and farming lifestyle) became common. Therefore, the collective activity of building temples and worshipping eventually encouraged integration of the diverse traveller groups and the growth of an urban centre, rather than the other way round: Symbolism is at the very core of our development.

Rationality and Ritual

As I indicate in Chapter 2, Western society, in particular, places great belief in rationality, and our accounts of life and of management reflect that focus. There are many accounts of how managers should be enlightened, deliberate, rational, and always in full control; there are many accounts of how this does not concur with management practice. I address this further in Chapter 16, but what I want to focus on here is the assumption that our rationality is one of the aspects of humanity that places us at the pinnacle of evolution.

Our focus on conscious control blinkers us to our blithe lack of awareness of the power of the unconscious in our daily lives. For example, in a series of studies Frumin et al. (2015) found that we often subconsciously sniff our own hands. We significantly increase our depth of inhalation and the number of times we do this and after a handshake, thereby unconsciously receiving and acting upon the social chemosignals squalene and hexadecanoic acid obtained through contact with the other person's hand. If questioned about our behaviour we offer some rational response for bringing our hands to our face that ignores the subconscious root.

In fact, it can be argued that humans behave in a less rational manner than do non-human animals (Stanovich 2013). 'Our choices are laced with symbolism. It is symbolically important to us that not all of our activities are aimed at satisfying our given desires' (Nozick 1993: 138). It 'is of profound importance—that humans often feel alienated from their choices. This feeling of alienation, although emotionally discomfiting when it occurs, is actually a reflection of a unique aspect of human cognition—the use of the meta-representational abilities of the analytic system to enable a cognitive critique of our beliefs and our desires' (Stanovich 2008: 111–112).

These meta-representational abilities include the ability to decouple our mental representations from the world so that they can be reflected upon and potentially improved. We can therefore contemplate and evaluate second-order desires that are in conflict with first-order desires. We are able to mark a mental state as not factual. This ability to separate a belief or desire from its coupling to the world is of critical importance to human mentality (Carruthers 2006) and the development of our cultures (see Chapter 3 for a discussion of memes), and appears to be uniquely human (Penn et al. 2008). These meta-representational abilities make possible the higher-order evaluations that determine whether we are pursuing the right aims.

Meta-representational abilities infuse our lives with symbolic utility but they also disrupt our instrumental rationality. Non-human animals, without the drive to contextualise the various options that are available, and without the symbolism that permeates our world view, make much more direct functional and rational choices that we do. We might think and feel that we are being rational but, as discussed in Chapter 4, our intentions and reasons are frequently post hoc confabulations.

Our flight from instrumental rationality is demonstrated by use of rites and the rituals. Rituals are complex and nonsensical yet permeate every culture. A ritual involves several discrete specific steps that follow a defined script and is causally opaque: The actions are often hard to make sense of in terms of cause and effect, unlike other multistep behaviours such as changing a tyre or baking a cake (Jones 2015). Rituals appear useless to an outsider yet they build a sense of community. More intense rituals build stronger communities, as do those with synchronous movements (Fischer et al. 2013). Synchronous movement also produces a greater sense of shared sacred values among participants, which appears to motivate other prosocial behaviours such as generosity and trust (Valdesolo & DeSteno 2011). Similarly, the more complex the ritual the more people believe in its efficacy (Legare & Souza 2014).

Interestingly, children copy sequences of actions much more faithfully if they are apparently aimless than if they have a particular goal, and more so if more people are doing them (Herrmann et al. 2013), or if they feel ostracised from a group with which they identify—even merely one that they have been assigned to for the purposes of the experiment (Watson-Jones et al. 2014). Rituals don't just signal group membership; they also help bind people into groups. They are important for our sense of involvement in group and society yet they are predominantly non-rational; they are symbolic and emotional and their effect is largely subconscious.

CONSCIOUSNESS AND ORGANISATIONS

The points I make in this chapter are addressed in one form or another throughout the rest of this book, so I do not want to spend too much time following through one by one here. However, I shall pick them up in general terms in order to round off this chapter. From Morgan's (1986) metaphors to discussions of the embodied organisation, theorists have frequently linked aspects of the organisation to the human body. Notions of organisational consciousness abound and it is almost universally assumed that the top management team are in charge of, direct, and lead the organisation. I suggest that our understanding of organisations is as problematic as our understanding of our own agency.

Monitor, Not Control

The first point I want to emphasise is the way in which I experienced the separation of mind and body whilst recovering, thus providing personal empirical support for the idea of consciousness as an imaginary-time processor, and not as a control mechanism. My mind was able to review how I was recovering—what I could do now—but it clearly did not control it. I didn't lie in bed thinking 'tomorrow I will be able to do this or that'; instead, I would develop a desire to do something (for example, I went through a phase of doing jigsaw puzzles), and wake up one morning and notice that I could now do something (identify shapes) that I had been struggling with previously. Similarly, my experiences of blind-sight illustrates that the body is quite capable of managing real-time occurrences, and that the consciousness does not control this, but performs a different function, that of reviewing, auditing, evaluating, and overseeing progress and creating an environment that challenges (re)learning.

A parallel can be drawn with the executive of the organisation. Is it really in control or is it an 'illusion of control' (Fast et al. 2009)? Such illusion can foster mental health (Taylor & Brown 1988) and is linked to physical health, especially in older people (Plous 1993), although it can be maladaptive (Whyte et al. 1997). Whilst illusory beliefs about control may promote goal striving, they are not conducive to sound decision-making, and may cause insensitivity to feedback, impede learning, and predispose towards greater objective risk-taking (since subjective risk will be reduced by the illusion of control) (Fenton-O'Creevy et al. 2003). Given that the appropriate feedback mechanisms are in place, the body of the organisation, the workforce, can continue quite happily with its real-time day-to-day tasks. What the executive does is monitor activities and set in place the necessary feedback mechanisms—in other words, it monitors the environment (which includes the nature, activities, and output of the workforce) and seeks to establish one that is suitable for development of the company. This less aggressive, and more realistic, view of leadership has been around for a while yet gets crowded out by more strident voices (Armstrong & Lilley 2008; Chapter 18).

Need for a History

The second point of emphasis is the distinction between the content of consciousness, self-awareness; the mechanism, an imaginary-time processor;

and the real-time processing of the body. As I was (re)learning myself I was conscious and aware, and my body was working well (and healing itself) in real time, but it was as if I was having to rebuild links between my awareness of self, the past, present, and future, and the social world, through interaction. Extending the analogy above suggests that the organisation knows itself through interaction with its environment, the stories that are told of its past, and its anticipations of the future. In the same way that I needed a sense of past and future in order to be able to contextualise my 'now', so an organisation needs its work myths, tales of heroes and villains, and rites and rituals, in order to contextualise and know itself, and to create a sense of belonging. By implication, that knowing, in so far as an organisation can have an identity, is understood, or given meaning, by the executive and management, yet the rites in the rituals and the underlying history develops through the workforce.

Knowledge and Action

This brings me to my third point—that of middle management and access. The knowing described above is not the unique privilege of the senior staff. As I (re)learnt myself, the different parts of my understanding came together, but my understanding was rooted in the parts—as the organisational knowing is rooted in the actions of the workforce and interpreted by management, and reinterpreted for the needs of the executive. It is as if the executive and, through them, the management, set the shape and size of the hole in the net that catches the information that passes back and forth. It is easy to imagine the sort of person (and, following the simile, organisation) who has such a strong belief in a particular world view that they reject any information that casts doubt upon that world view. Despite what it might believe or choose to tell itself, the executive cannot control the workforce, but what it can do is control the parameters under which organisational knowledge is filtered—control the body image, as it were. The greater the need for control, the more the organisation becomes a lean mean fighting machine (or anorexic, depending upon your point of view), the less creative and flexible it becomes at the same time (Lee 1999). In such a way are 'yes men' and groupthink developed.

Knowledge Management and Aberrations

Finally, these points lead me to question the use of organisational learning and knowledge management literature and teaching that assumes that development and knowledge have similar properties across all parts of the organisation, and privileges the mind of the organisation over and above the practical knowledge of the body.

Conscious 'control' threatens interaction and development, so shouldn't the executive and senior management be exhorted to focus on relinquishing illusions of control in favour of a monitoring and imaginary-time role? This requires a different view of information—the information of key importance is no longer the normative standardised data about everyday functioning; instead it is the aberrations, the things that stand out as unusual. The things that disconfirm the organisation's world view, rather than the things that add to it. Knowledge management, therefore, is not about accessing all knowledge at the highest level—it is as much about forgetting the common and leaving that to be managed below the level of executive awareness by the massive parallel processing of the workforce.

Learning and Education As Interference

This entails a wider focus from the organisational learning literature, which typically addresses senior management at the expense of the workforce. To some extent, this is justified by the ideas presented above: Learning interferes with the smooth running of routine functions, so do all parts of the organisation need to learn? If people are indeed cogs in the mechanism, to be born and die in a particular job, then clearly not, but unlike body parts, people do move around and have independent aspirations. Organisational learning avoids the dilemma of how to address the needs of the cogs, either by focusing on the executive, or else by assuming the workforce are proto-management and thus should be addressed in the same manner as management—just at a lower level. What I am suggesting is that the workforce has developmental needs, but that they are of a different nature to those of the executive. Part of this difference is reflected in the typical differentiation between training and development. It is also, however, located in the climate surrounding the learning.

These arguments point to the need for a climate in which practical and tacit knowledge is valued and in which individuals are given time and opportunity to learn from each other, without the strict overseeing of immediate observable outcomes and cost effectiveness. Is this a call for the revival of the apprentice system?

REFERENCES

Antrobus JS, Singer JL, & Greenberg S (1966) 'Studies in the stream of consciousness: Experimental enhancement and suppression of spontaneous cognitive processes', *Perceptual and Motor Skills* 23: 399–417.

Ardener E (1987) 'Remote areas: Some theoretical considerations', in Jackson A (Ed) *Anthropology at Home:* 38–54. London: Tavistock.

Armstrong P & Lilley S (2008) 'Practical criticism and the social sciences of Management', *Ephemera* 8(4)353–370.

Baddeley A (2003) 'Working memory: Looking forward and looking back', *Nature Reviews Neuroscience* 4: 829–839.

Bargh JA (1994) 'The Four Horsemen of automaticity: Awareness, Intention, Efficiency, and Control in Social Cognition', in Wyer R & Srull T (Eds) *Handbook of Social Cognition:* 1–40. Hillside, NJ: Lawrence Erlbaum.

Barragan RC & Dweck CS (2014) 'Rethinking natural altruism: Simple reciprocal interactions trigger children's benevolence', *Proceedings of the National Academy of Sciences* 111(48)17071–17074.

Berwick RC, Friederici AD, Chomsky N, & Bolhuis JJ (2013) 'Evolution, brain, and the nature of language', *Trends in Cognitive Sciences* 17: 89–98.

Bolhuis JJ & Everaert M (2013) (Eds) *Birdsong, Speech, and Language. Exploring the Evolution of Mind and Brain.* Cambridge, MA: MIT Press.

Bolhuis JJ, Tattersall I, Chomsky N, & Berwick RC (2014) 'How could language have evolved?', *PLoS Biology* 12(8): e1001934: 1–6.

Bond M (2015) 'We could be heroes', *New Scientist* 3005: 36–39.

Bourdieu P (1990) *The Logic of Practice.* Cambridge: Polity Press.

Carruthers P (2006) *The Architecture of the Mind.* New York: Oxford University Press.

Carter P & Jackson N (1993) 'Modernism, postmodernism and motivation, or why expectancy theory failed to come up to expectation', in Hassard J & Parker M (Eds) *Postmodernism and Organisations:* 83–100. London: Sage.

Dehaene S & Naccache L (2001) 'Towards a cognitive neuroscience of consciousness: Basic evidence and a workspace framework', *Cognition* 79: 1–37.

Dixon NF (1981) *Preconscious Processing.* New York: Wiley.

Dunn AJ & Bondy SC (1974) *Functional Chemistry of the Brain.* Flushing, NY: Spectrum.

Edelman GM (1988) *Topobiology: An Introduction to Molecular Embryology.* New York: Basic Books.

Englekamp J & Zimmer HD (1995) 'Similarity of movement in recognition of self-performed tasks and of verbal tasks', *British Journal of Psychology* 86(2) 241–252.

Fagan R (1981) *Animal Play Behaviour.* Oxford: Oxford University Press.

Fast NJ, Gruenfeld DH, Sivanathan N, & Galinsky AD (2009) 'Illusory control: A generative force behind Power's far-reaching effects', *Psychological Science* 20(4)502–508.

Fenton-O'Creevy M, Nicholson N, Soane E, & Willman P (2003) 'Trading on illusions: Unrealistic perceptions of control and trading performance', *Journal of Occupational and Organizational Psychology* 76: 53–68.

Finkler K (1994) *Spiritualist Healers in Mexico. Successes and Failures of Alternative Therapeutics.* Salem, MA: Sheffield.

Fischer R, Callander R, Reddish P, & Bulbulia J (2013) 'How do rituals affect cooperation? An experimental field study comparing Nine Ritual types', *Human Nature* 24: 115–125.

Frumin I, Perl O, Endevelt-Shapira1 Y, Eisen A, Eshel N, Heller I, SheMesh M, RAvia A, SeLa L, Arzi A, & Sobel N (2015) 'A social chemosignaling function for human handshaking', *eLife:Neuriscience* 4: e05154: 1–16.

Gallup GG (1983) 'Towards a Comparative Psychology of Mind', in Mellgren RL (Ed) *Animal Cognition and Behaviour:* 473–570. New York: North Holland.

Gallup GG, Boren GL, Gagliardi GL, & Wallnau LB (1977) 'A mirror for the mind of man, or will the chimpanzee create an identity crisis for Homo Sapiens?', *Journal of Human Evolution* 6: 303–313.

Gazzaniga MS (1988) *Mind Matters.* Boston: Houghton Mifflin.

Geschwind DH & Rakic P (2013) 'Cortical evolution: Judge the brain by its cover', *Neuron* 80: 633–647.

Goldman-Rakic P (1997) 'Space and time in the mental universe', *Nature* 386: 559–560.

Gray C & Mulhern G (1995) 'Does children's memory for additional facts predict general mathematical ability?', *Perceptual and Motor Skills* 81: 163–167.

Hall AD, Braggio JT, Buchanon JP, Nadler RD, Karen D, & Sams JB (1980) 'Multiple classification performance of juvenile chimpanzees, normal and retarded children', *International Journal of Primatology* 1: 345–359.

Hastrup K (1995) 'The Inarticulate Mind: The Place of Awareness in Social Action', in Cohen AP & Rapport N (Eds) *Questions of Consciousness*: 181–197. London: Routledge.

Herrmann PA, Legare CH, Harris PL, & Whitehouse H (2013) 'Stick to the script: The effect of witnessing multiple actors on children's imitation', *Cognition* 129(3)536–543.

Hollis M (1985) 'Of Masks and Men', in Carrithers M, Collins S, & Lukes S (Eds) *The Category of the Person: Anthropology, Philosophy, History*: 217–233. Cambridge: Cambridge University Press.

Inomata T, MacLellana J, Triadana D, Munsonb J, Burhama M, Aoyama K, Nasu H, Pinzóne F, & Yonenobu H (2015) 'Development of sedentary communities in the Maya lowlands: Coexisting mobile groups and public ceremonies at Ceibal, Guatemala', *Proceedings of the National Academy of Sciences USA* 112(14)4268–4273.

Johnson-Laird PN (1983) *Mental Models*. Cambridge: Cambridge University Press.

Jones D (2015) 'Rite reasons: Why your brain loves pointless rituals', *New Scientist* 3004: 36–39.

Kahneman D (2011) *Thinking Fast and Slow*. New York: Farrar, Straus & Giroux.

Kapferer B (1995) 'From the Edge of Death', in Cohen AP & Rapport N (Eds) *Questions of Consciousness*: 135–152. London: Routledge.

Kiverstein J (2010) 'Making sense of phenomenal unity: An intentionalist account of temporal experience', *Royal Institute of Philosophy Supplement* 85: 155–181.

Kohn T (1995) 'She Came Out of the Field and into My Home: Reflections, Dreams and a Search for Consciousness in Anthropological Method', in Cohen AP & Rapport N (Eds) *Questions of Consciousness*: 41–59. London: Routledge.

Kösem A, Gramfort A, & van Wassenhove V (2014) 'Encoding of event timing in the phase of neural oscillations', *NeuroImage* 92: 274–284.

Lachman R, Lachman JL, & Butterfield EC (1979) *Cognitive Psychology and Information Processing*. Hillsdale, NJ: Lawrence Erlbaum.

Lackner JR & Garrett MF (1972) 'Resolving ambiguity: Effects of biasing context in the unattended ear', *Cognition* 1: 359–372.

Lee CW (1984) 'Human, Animal and Artificial Consciousness' circulated but unpublished at the time, published within Lee MM (2003) 'Blind sight and consciousness, Culture and Organisations', in *Organisational Wellness*. Proceedings of 21st Standing Conference on Organisational Symbolism (SCOS). Cambridge.

Lee MM (1999) 'Leading at the edge of chaos: a review', *Emergence* 1(2)123–127.

Legare CH & Souza AL (2014) 'Searching for control: Priming randomness increases the evaluation of ritual efficacy', *Cognitive Science* 38: 152–161.

Lethmate J (1982) 'Tool-using skills of orang-utans', *Journal of Human Evolution* 11: 49–64.

Libet B (1985) 'Unconscious cerebral initiative and the role of conscious will in voluntary action', *Behavioural and Brain Sciences* 8: 529–566.
Lieberman DE (2011) *The Evolution of the Human Head*. Cambridge, MA: Harvard University Press.
Lotze M, Wittmann M, von Steinbüchel N, Pöppel E, & Roenneberg T (1999) 'Daily rhythm of temporal resolution in the auditory system', *Cortex* 35: 89–100.
Maier NFR (1931) 'Reasoning in humans. The solution of a problem and its appearance in consciousness', *Journal of Comparative Psychology* 12: 181–194.
Marsh AA, Stoycos SA, Brethel-Haurwitz KM, Robinson P, VanMeter JE, & Cardinale SM (2014) 'Neural and cognitive characteristics of extraordinary altruists', *Proceedings of the National Academy of Sciences* 111(42)15036–15041.
Martinez I, Rosa M, Quam R, Jarabo P, Lorenzo C, Bonmatí A, Gómez-Olivencia A, Gracia A, & Arsuaga JL (2012) 'Communicative capacities in Middle Pleistocene humans from the Sierra de Atapuerca in Spain', *Quaternary International* 295: 94–101.
Mason WA (1976) 'Environmental models and mental modes. Representational processes in the great apes and man', *American Psychologist* 31: 284–294.
Morgan G (1986) *Images of Organization*. London: Sage.
Nisbett RE & Wilson TD (1977) 'Telling more than we can know: Verbal reports on mental processes', *Psychological Review* 64: 231–259.
Nozick R. (1993). *The Nature of Rationality*. Princeton, NJ: Princeton University Press.
Oliner SP (1992) *Altruistic Personality: Rescuers of Jews in Nazi Europe*. New York: Simon and Schuster.
Pallier C, Devauchelle AD, & Dehaene S (2011) 'Cortical representation of the constituent structure of sentences', *Proceedings of the National Academy of Sciences USA* 108: 2522–2527.
Parker M (1992) 'Postmodern organisations or Postmodern Organisation Theory?', *Organisation Studies* 13(1)1–17.
Parkin D (1995) 'Blank Banners and Islamic Consciousness in Zanzibar', in Cohen AP & Rapport N (Eds) *Questions of Consciousness*: 198–216. London: Routledge.
Passingham RE (1982) *The Human Primate*. Oxford: Freeman.
Penn DC, Holyoak KJ, & Povinelli DJ (2008) 'Darwin's mistake: Explaining the discontinuity between human and nonhuman minds', *Behavioral and Brain Sciences* 31: 109–178.
Plous S (1993) *The Psychology of Judgment and Decision Making*. New York: McGraw-Hill.
Polanyi M (1962) *Personal Knowledge: Towards a Post-Critical Philosophy*. London: Routledge and Kegan Paul.
Rosenfeld H M & Baer DM (1969) 'Unnoticed verbal conditioning of an aware experimenter by a more aware subject: the double agent effect', *Psychological Review* 76: 425–432.
Sebeok TA & Umiker-Sebeok J (1980) (Eds) *Speaking of Apes*. New York: Plenum Press.
Shakespeare W (1604) 'Hamlet, Prince of Denmark', in Thompson A & Taylor N (Eds) *Hamlet, (Second Quarto), The Arden Shakespeare*, 3rd revised edition (1 June 2005). London: Arden Shakespeare.

Shore C (1995) 'Usurpers or pioneers? European Commission bureaucrats and the question of "European consciousness"', in Cohen AP & Rapport N (Eds) *Questions of Consciousness*: 215–236. London: Routledge.

Singer JL (1975) 'Navigating the stream of consciousness', *American Psychologist* 30: 727–738.

Spelke E, Hirst W, & Neisser U (1976) 'Skills of divided attention', *Cognition* 4: 215–230.

Stanovich KE (2008) 'Theoretical note: Higher-order preferences and the Master Rationality Motive', *Thinking & Reasoning* 14(1)111–127.

Stanovich KE (2013) 'Why humans are (sometimes) less rational than other animals: Cognitive complexity and the axioms of rational choice', *Thinking & Reasoning* 19(1)1–26.

Stevens A & Price J (1996) *Evolutionary Psychiatry: A New Beginning*. London: Routledge.

Szymaszek A, Sereda M, Pöppel E, & Szelag E (2009) 'Individual differences in the perception of temporal order: The effect of age and cognition', *Cognitive Neuropsychology* 26: 135–147.

Tattersall I (2008) 'An evolutionary framework for the acquisition of symbolic cognition by Homo sapiens', *Comparative Cognitive Behaviour Reviews* 3: 99–114.

Taylor SE & Brown JD (1988) 'Illusion and well-being: A social psychological perspective on mental health', *Psychological Bulletin* 103(2)193–210.

Tsujii T & Watanabe S (2009) 'Neural correlates of dual-task effect on belief-bias syllogistic reasoning: A near-infrared spectroscopy study', *Brain Research* 1287: 118–125.

Underwood G (1979) 'Memory Systems and Conscious Processes', in Underwood G & Stevens R (Eds) *Aspects of consciousness Vol 1: Psychological Issues*: 91–112. New York: Academic Press.

Valdesolo P & DeSteno DA (2011) 'Synchrony and the social tuning of compassion', *Emotion* 11: 262–266.

Vaneechoutte M, Munro S, & Verhaegen M (2011) 'Seafood, Diving, Song and Speech', in Vaneechoutte M, Kuliukas A, & Verhaegen M (Eds) *Was Man More Aquatic in the Past? Fifty Years after Alister Hardy*: 181–189. Ebook: Bentham Publishers.

van Wassenhove V (2009) 'Minding time in an amodal representational space', *Philosophical Transactions of the Royal Society, B, London* 364: 1815–1830.

Watson-Jones RE, Legare CH, Whitehouse H, & Clegg JM (2014) 'Task-specific effects of ostracism on imitative fidelity in early childhood', *Evolution and Human Behaviour* 35(3)204–210.

Whyte G, Saks AM, & Hook S (1997) 'When success breeds failure: The role of self-efficacy in escalating commitment to a losing course of action', *Journal of Organizational Behavior* 18(5): 415–432.

Yang C (2013) 'The ontogeny and phylogeny of language', *Proceedings of the National Academy of Sciences USA* 110: 6324–6327.

14 Agency and Impotence

This chapter is an exploration of agency and structure, power and empowerment. The arguments here are based upon a description of the circumstances surrounding the investigation of a complaint against the governors of a small rural primary school in the UK. This is an empirical study of a local struggle in which the role of the researcher as a prisoner in a web of power is highlighted. The case is first analysed using structural and functional understandings of power; however, the voluntary nature of the individual engagement of the actors in the case highlights the role of the individual's interpretative frameworks—both in operation and as explanatory mechanisms. Structural and functional analyses of power do not appear to fully account for aspects of this situation, and therefore a distinction between the poetic and the rhetoric is considered as part of the explanatory mechanism. This account suggests that 'power' can be seen as an individually interpreted quality, and highlights the tension between individual agency and organisational structure.

Hardy & Clegg (1996: 636–637) suggest that there exists confusion around the understanding of power:

> Power requires understanding in its diversity even as it resists explanation in terms of a single theory. A theory of power does not, and cannot, exist other than as an act of power in itself. . . . One way out of this impasse is to explore the (hermeneutic) circle more completely and to investigate the relations and meanings that constitute it, by listening more carefully to the voices that normally populate it (e.g. Forester 1989) and unmasking the researcher that enters it. This approach advocates more empirical study of local struggles, focusing not on a monolithic conception of power, but on the strategic concerns raised by Machiavelli (1961) or the war of manoeuvre highlighted by Gramski (1971). . . . In so doing, we may privilege certain discourses . . . but, nonetheless, a space is claimed for voices that might otherwise be lost. . . . We must also acknowledge the researcher's arrival within the circle, not as a neutral observer, but as an implicated participant. . . . By exposing ourselves to this kind of genealogical analysis (e.g. Knights &

Morgan 1991), we become more aware of how we are also prisoners in a web of power that we have helped to create.

My intention is to follow Hardy and Clegg in examining power from the empirical and personal. My vehicle is a case, given below, in which Mrs Mulberry was chair of a complaints committee for a primary school. She found the school to have been seriously failing children for at least the last 10 years. This particular complaint was just the last in a series presented over that period, yet nothing had been done about the situation. All stakeholders knew of, or at least suspected, the situation, yet they became increasingly impotent in their attempts to deal with it. This chapter explores how the shifting patterns of power lay, and the lies that these patterns promoted, before taking a more personal look at the state of 'prisoner in a web of power that we have helped to create', in which feelings of empowerment become little more than self-told lies—the rose-tinted glass through which we justify our impotence to ourselves. Empowerment is, itself, a symbol of oppression.

SHENANIGANS AT TREESIDE

It all started one fine summer's day at a country fair. Over the previous months, the community local to the fair had been preparing their animals and produce for showing. The children had been working on their scarecrows, their pictures, and their miniature gardens. The smell of baking was everywhere. Would Jim win with his onions again this year? What about young Tom's lamb—had it learnt to lead properly yet? And so on. Mrs Mulberry joined in the spirit of the event and competed for the award of 'six best eggs' and the winnings of 50p. She paid the entrance fee (of 10p), dashed to the henhouse, and entered six eggs. Her entry reflected her haste—the eggs

---

CHARACTERS, IN ORDER OF APPEARANCE:

Mrs Mulberry:	Chair of the Complaints Committee
Mr Beech:	Second member of the Complaints Committee
Mr Larch :	Head teacher
Mrs Oak:	Part-time Special Educational Needs teacher
Mr Sycamore:	Head teacher's union representative
Mr Willow:	Inspector/advisor for the Local Educational Authority
Mr Chestnut:	Chair of the Governing Body
Mrs Tree:	Complainant
Sapling:	A child, about whose progress the complaint was made

Figure 14.1   The People Involved at Treeside

were a bit dirty and oddly shaped. The other competitors offered perfectly matched sets of clean eggs that had been carefully compiled over the previous weeks. In a break from tradition, the eggs were judged on freshness and not presentation. To her surprise (and that of the whole community), she won. The money involved was immaterial, but she was told of long-standing feuds that had developed from just such a break with tradition. The following year she donated a cup to the fair in an attempt to make amends, and in reply she was invited to become a governor of the local school. This proved, however, to be more of a Trojan horse than a peace offering.

A couple of months after her appointment to the Governing Body, she was made chair of the Complaints Committee, with the task of investigating a comprehensive complaint against the Governing Body. The Governing Body, as overseers of the functioning of the school, are ultimately responsible for effective provision of the National Curriculum. Mrs Mulberry was chosen because the recency of her appointment meant that she was the least 'tainted' person available to serve. In this context, 'tainted' is a technical term. Any governor with prior knowledge of the issue cannot serve on an investigatory or disciplinary committee and is called 'tainted'. Exactly what constitutes 'prior knowledge' is debatable, especially in a close community. Normally there are three governors on any committee of this sort. At any one time, the Governing Body needs to be able to place untainted governors on four different committees (complaints, grievance, disciplinary, and appeals). In this case, the small size of the school, and thus of the Governing Body, meant that, even if all governors were untainted, the Governing Body could only just cover each committee so long as only two people were on each of the first three committees. The other member of the Complaints Committee was Mr Beech: a local farmer, a parent governor, and someone whose integrity inspired trust from all sides. Working intensely over the next two and a bit months, Mrs Mulberry and Mr Beech interviewed nearly 100 people in depth; Mrs Mulberry produced a report of over 160 closely argued pages, an additional 100 pages of confidential appendices, and 44 detailed recommendations; and they both attempted to hold down their day jobs, and tried to pay some attention to their families. Mrs Mulberry's involvement did not finish with the submission of the report—she was left with the need to work through the implications of her recommendations.

Where the Power Lay

Treeside is a small traditional rural primary school. At the time described here, it had a head teacher, Mr Larch, who was responsible for the management of the school and for teaching the Junior children (7 to 11 years old), and one other full-time teacher responsible for the Infants (4 to 6 years old). In addition, there were two part-time teaching staff, and two non-teaching support staff. The need for Special Educational Needs (SEN) provision (and thus additional funding) is evaluated when the children move up from the Infants, and no child in the school had been judged to merit it at that stage. However, continued parental concern about the standards reached by the children in the Juniors had resulted in the additional employment of Mrs Oak for additional teaching and SEN provision.

Prior to the Local Management of Schools (LMS) legislation in 1989, the head teacher was effectively the sole manager of his or her school. The introduction of LMS resulted in a diminution of the head teacher's power by making the Governing Body responsible for overseeing the management of the school and ultimately to blame if this management was at fault. The mechanism by which governors were expected to do this was through the construction of Policies that covered all aspects of school life. It was the Policies that specified the governors' expectations about the running of the school, and the governors were responsible for ensuring that the Policies were being followed.

The boundary between the Governing Body and head teacher was complicated further by the responsibilities of the Local Education Authority (LEA). Despite being responsible for overseeing the school, the governors did not actually employ the staff. Staff were employed solely by the LEA. In addition, the governors were all voluntary workers and could not be assumed to have much knowledge of what might be expected by 'good educational practice'. The LEA was responsible for maintaining standards, and did so through an inspection/advisory service. An advisor was attached to each school (Mr Willow in this case) and made regular inspection visits. He or she advised the head teacher, and reported back to the LEA as the first stage in mobilising additional resources if they were felt to be necessary. In addition, formal inspections were conducted nationally, and had already resulted in the closure of one school and severe modifications to others that were found to be failing.

Treeside was anticipating a formal inspection in the next year or so. In addition, under LMS, the boundary between the responsibilities of a head teacher and the Governing Body were ill-defined, and Mr Larch's union was keen to recoup the power of its members. It had a reputation for seeking to do this by fighting 'test-cases' in the courts, and Mr Larch made sure that governors knew that he was in close contact with Mr Sycamore, his union representative.

To an outsider, the school appeared small and happy. Much of the background given below was pieced together during the investigation and was not apparent to the casual observer. During the investigation it became apparent to Mrs Mulberry that she needed a wider understanding of the functioning of the school, and that this could best be obtained by talking to the parents. She drafted some questions and obtained confirmation from the LEA that the questions were appropriate for a governor to ask (see Lee 1999 for details of the questionnaire). She then practised interview techniques with Mr Beech, and conducted a couple of pilot interviews with him such that both he and she adopted a non-leading, free-flowing, key points style, in which the interviewee was told that the governors were interested in their views on school provision, and their acceptance for recording the conversation was obtained. An open conversation was then held with each of the interviewees and, if key areas of interest were not covered spontaneously, then the interviewee was asked directly about that area using the pre-approved words. Over sixty semi-structured interviews were conducted (each taking between one and a half to four hours), with the vast majority of them done with parents who either had children at the school, or who had over the previous ten years. The second group were interviewed in order to obtain a longitudinal view of the school and to minimise the possibility that interviewees were merely passing on a collective mind-set. Their findings were stark. With only about four exceptions, each interviewee catalogued (often with detailed and vivid description of particular incidents) a series of deep concerns about their child's education at the school, particularly focused on Junior provision and what they saw as Mr Larch's failings as a teacher, as a manager of the school, and as a member of the community.

According to the parents, Mr Larch seemed unable to organise or administer, unwilling to put in any more effort than the absolute minimum, to have favourites, and to bully and victimise those children he classed as 'thick'. Parents reported that he was quite open in his statements about the farming children (and parents) being 'thick'. In addition, the parents reported him as lying his way out of problems, seriously misleading them about their children's ability and progress, and generally being almost impossible to talk to. These allegations were supported by accounts from the majority of the parents whose children had left the school. Children were often placed in remedial classes when entering secondary school, but progressed very rapidly, excelling in subjects that they had been told that they were hopeless at, and clearly evidencing that they were not 'thick'. Several parents said they had been refused access to their child's records by Mr Larch (despite that access being a legal right), and a few parents said that they had explicitly requested that their child be assessed by outside agencies, and had been refused this by Mr Larch on (they asserted) the grounds that it might make the school 'look bad' if people like psychologists were brought in. About 50% of parents were so concerned about their child's standards that they provided extra education for their children outside school hours (over and above 'homework'); approximately 20% of parents had submitted complaints or had taken legal advice about doing so, and a few had removed their children from the school. This pattern was consistent across each of the 16 years of education at the school that was covered by the interviews with parents.

The general feeling appeared to be that the problems really started when the children reached the Juniors. Several parents were clear that they would not have been so upset by poor educational standards as long as they could offer support outside school, but that they were very concerned about their child's emotional well-being. The majority of parents reported that their child had been bullied, either by other children or by Mr Larch, and that whilst this was dealt with effectively in the Infant class (so that bullying was only a problem for the infant children at break times), it appeared to be ignored (or, as some parents suggested, encouraged) in the Juniors. The majority of parents reported that as children entered the Juniors they developed an increasing lack of confidence and dislike of 'education'. Several parents reported that their children became withdrawn, antisocial, tempestuous, and often near to tears or sobbing themselves to sleep at night. Learning became a chore, and parents were concerned about the lack of self-discipline and increasing 'cheek' that spilled over into the home environment, and the disrespect that children appeared to develop for Mr Larch.

Parents also talked of why they felt they could do little to improve the situation. The majority believed that the severity of their problems with the school was unique to them, and that other parents and children were reasonably happy—so it wasn't worth making a fuss. They and others also reported that they believed that if they complained directly to Mr Larch, he would ignore their complaint (unless they were very insistent) and take it out on the child at school, either emotionally, or in the opinion of some parents, physically. Physical action was believed to be applied either by Mr Larch himself, or indirectly through his blind eye to (or encouragement of) selective bullying. Not all parents reported this happening to their own child, but nearly all volunteered in their interviews that they were concerned that it would if they complained. In addition, the small size of the school meant that it had been seen as a candidate for potential closure by the LEA several times over the previous few years. This presented parents with an additional fear (and one that they said that Mr Larch had been explicit about)—if complaints went further, then the school would be seen to be failing and the LEA would close it. The LEA had no power to close the school in such a unilateral manner, yet the majority of parents and governors firmly believed the opposite. With no other meeting place or any shops in the village the school was the hub of the community, and parents said that if they caused closure of the school through their complaint, they would destroy the community.

Over the years several parents were sufficiently concerned to take the risk of going further, either by complaining to the Governing Body or to the LEA. In each instance the normal procedures were applied. Some of the complaints that were made directly to the LEA were accompanied by a request for confidentiality to prevent anticipated victimisation of the child concerned. In each case, however, parents were convinced that Mr Larch quickly became aware of the origin of the complaint. The LEA would ask the advice of their inspector, Mr Willow, who would assure them that in his opinion everything was satisfactory. Mr Larch would contact Mr Sycamore, who would represent him in the discussions/hearing. No complaint appeared to improve the situation. For example, a relatively serious complaint that went to a full hearing was (in the opinion of the parents and of the governors involved) minimised into irrelevance. Those involved reported that it resulted in censure for the Governing Body over the technical issues, and the suggestion that Mr Larch might try to improve communication with the parents. They felt aggrieved that the body of the complaint (the welfare of the child concerned) was ignored.

The Governing Body had had a series of chairpersons, each of whom voiced their feelings of impotence about the situation they found themselves in. Mr Chestnut, the incumbent chair of the Governing Body, was a very direct sort of person. He was clearly becoming increasingly frustrated and demotivated by what he saw as his inability to fulfil his main goal—that of helping the school and the community. Equally clearly, Mr Sycamore saw the apparent problems within the school as nothing more than a clash of personality between Mr Chestnut and Mr Larch: a clash that symbolised the shifting power of head teachers and Governing Bodies nationally, and in which Mr Chestnut was overstepping his power as chair of governors and was transparently trying to interfere, personally, with the internal management of the school.

Mr Chestnut and the Governing Body saw things differently. When LMS was introduced they agreed with Mr Larch that he, not they, had the educational expertise. They had therefore agreed that Mr Larch should be responsible for formulating the Policies by which the school was to be run. Mr Larch was given additional time off from teaching in order to do this. Despite repeated requests Mr Larch was particularly slow in writing the Policies, and those that he did produce were vague and specified (often by omission) that the majority of management decisions, and checks on these, were to be made at his discretion. In accepting that Mr Larch was the expert, the Governing Body also accepted a dramatic diminution in their power to oversee that expertise. In addition, as came to light during the investigation, there were times and issues around which Mr Larch misled the Governing Body—by implication, by omission, or by mistruth.

The Story

Mrs Tree had taken informed advice and put forward a wide-ranging case that (in effect) claimed that the governors were failing because her child (whom I shall call Sapling) was not being provided with the full National Curriculum. Within two weeks of the complaint being made, and before the establishment of a Complaints Committee, Mr Sycamore initiated a grievance against Mr Chestnut (on behalf of Mr Larch). If the complaint had been against Mr Larch this would have served three functions. First, the grievance would have had to be investigated prior to the complaint. Second, investigating the grievance would have involved further governors, who would then be 'tainted' and unable to serve on any committees that might have to enact recommendations made by the Complaints Committee. Third, as described below, it enabled Mr Sycamore to threaten the Complaints Committee with legal battles if they continued to investigate the complaint.

Because the complaint was against the Governing Body (and the Complaints Committee had to be very careful that they continued to investigate it as against the Governing Body and not as against Mr Larch), Mr Sycamore had no formal ingress by which to influence their investigation. For the same reasons, however, they had no power to access the inner workings of the school. Mrs Mulberry discovered later that the normal mechanism employed to investigate this sort of complaint was to ask the LEA inspector to make a report. As the LEA themselves commented, it was fortuitous that she did not adopt this route as the result might well have been very different. Instead Mrs Mulberry and Mr Beech attempted their own investigation.

Within a couple of days of her appointment as chair of the Complaints Committee, Mrs Mulberry received a phone call from Mr Sycamore lasting nearly an hour. By the end of the phone call she had been made aware of several facts, though they had been impressed upon her by what she felt to be the use of innuendo and fatherly patronisation rather than clear statement. Mr Sycamore made it clear that he had 25 years of experience in these matters and he was trying to help her. That the complaint was against Mr Larch and not the Governing Body. That the complaint was the result of collusion between Mr Chestnut and Mrs Oak and was designed to continue their personal vendetta against Mr Larch. That there was no basis for the complaint and that she was wasting her time. That, on behalf of Mr Larch, he had initiated a grievance against Mr Chestnut. That if she continued to investigate the complaint she would be an unwitting victim of Mr Chestnut's vendetta and would be implicated in subsequent legal proceedings. And, that anything she said, did, or wrote would be scrutinised in detail by the national lawyers employed by the union and that these legal proceedings would have the full weight and finance of the union behind them.

At the time, Mrs Mulberry had no knowledge of the details given above, or of the people involved. It could be that Mr Sycamore's interpretation was correct and she certainly did not want to get involved in any legal battles. However, she did want to make her own decisions, and was extremely annoyed by his approach and veiled threats. She felt as if he were trying to subvert the investigation and that his actions would have been illegal if this had been a court of law. In a knee-jerk reaction to feelings of being patronised and manipulated, she was driven to question whether or not Mr Sycamore's allegations were true.

One aspect of the complaint revolved around SEN provision, so it was natural that Mrs Mulberry interview Mrs Oak. Mrs Oak was quite forthright in her analysis of the situation and made several points about lack of cooperation and victimisation on the part of Mr Larch towards her that were relatively easy to check through analysis of externally held official records and that proved to be true. Additional interviews with officials supported other aspects of Mrs Oak's account. To reduce two months' work to a few sentences, it became clear that there was no foundation for allegations of collusion or vendettas. Instead, much of the evidence pointed to 'irregularities' in the running of the school. The majority of these were minor, but together they painted a problematic picture. Mrs Oak had been consistently critical of what she saw as Mr Larch's unwillingness to accord with 'good practice', but appeared to be justified in her position.

Despite this, the rumours of collusion were pervasive. Within a couple of weeks of initiating the investigation, officials and outside agencies who had previously been very helpful started to clam up. Records of interviews and correspondence show that Mrs Mulberry was told, again, that they had heard that there was no justification to the complaint and that it was a personal vendetta. Her motives were questioned—it was rumoured that she was part of the conspiracy and was being paid to cause trouble. Mrs Mulberry's contact with the LEA hierarchy increased and records show that whilst being absolutely correct and helpful towards her, they had a close relationship with Mr Sycamore and they preferred to believe his view of the situation. It became clear that Mr Willow was less than impartial, had been misinformed by Mr Larch on several key points, and had either not bothered to check this information or had colluded with its promulgation.

The investigation became a game of strategy. In order to overcome the rumours and prejudgements, Mrs Mulberry deduced that her report would have to be watertight and overwhelmingly convincing. She felt that there was no option but to engage in serious detailed work late into the night for weeks on end. There was also no flexibility. The longer the report took, the deeper the tensions at the school became, and the greater the number of additional complaints that were received, both from Sapling's parents, and from other parents who were reacting to their own children's accounts of their 'day at school', each of which accused Mr Larch of venting his frustration on particular children. These complaints were passed on to the LEA, who appeared to discount them as chimera of the 'vendetta'. Shortly after this Sapling was withdrawn from the school, alleging physical abuse by Mr Larch. At the same time, a complaint about children being scared to go to school was received from a parent who knew nothing of the affair described here, but who was very concerned by the tales that her children were telling of Mr Larch's treatment of Sapling. Complaints continued to be made about the way in which Mr Larch was treating some of the other children. Mrs Mulberry, Mr Beech, and Mr Chestnut were starting to become deeply concerned about Mr Larch's state of mind and possible harm to the children in his care. The LEA, Mr Willow, and Mr Sycamore had effectively blocked any way forward, and as chair of the Complaints Committee and writer of the report Mrs Mulberry was becoming increasingly attuned to the urgent need for an early completion.

Mr Sycamore requested that the Complaints Committee interview Mr Larch in his presence, suggesting that Mr Larch must be given the opportunity to refute the falsehoods in the complaint—otherwise he would feel that he had not had a fair hearing. This was complex because the complaint was not specifically against Mr Larch, and the committee did not wish to give any indication that they thought it might be. However, Mr Larch was implicated in many of the interim findings of the investigation, and they wanted to develop a balanced picture of the issue. All four people did meet, and had a long discussion that was largely driven by Mr Sycamore. Mr Larch was emphatic that he was doing an extremely good job, that there was no basis to the complaint, other than a personal vendetta, and that whilst there might be the odd problem with Sapling, Sapling was thick and the parents would not support the school in helping the child. Mr Larch also made several statements (for example, about there not being a need to keep records in a small school) that Mr Sycamore would clearly have preferred not to have been made. Mr Sycamore explained (from, as he pointed out, his many years of expertise in testing children) that Sapling's apparent ability in Infants was a spurious side effect of the tests and procedures employed and did not reflect Sapling's real, rather poor ability.

Several of these points were directly contradicted by Mrs Mulberry's interim findings. She had obtained expert evidence externally that Sapling was of significantly above-average ability, that the parents were highly supportive, and that the problems cited in the complaint were widespread. In addition she had expert evidence that there was nothing untoward in either the tests or the procedures employed. Mr Sycamore's raising of this issue, backed by his 'expert' knowledge, appeared to her to be little more than a deliberate attempt to mislead the Complaints Committee.

Almost since the beginning of the investigation, and on Mr Sycamore's recommendation, Mr Larch had been unable to attend any governors' meetings or sports/community fixtures that occurred outside the core teaching hours of 9:00 a.m. to 3:15 p.m. due to ill health. The Governing Body did question how Mr Larch could be fit for teaching whilst unfit for any activity outside class contact, particularly as this meant that information vital to the duties of the Governing Body was not forthcoming. This was particularly worrying for the governors at a time when they were anticipating notification of a school inspection from Offsted. As the investigation progressed Mr Larch spent portions of teaching time talking with Mr Sycamore, who was a regular visitor to the school, and during those times they were known to meet in the School Office, so preventing any school administration occurring, and occasionally a supply teacher was used as additional cover. Shortly after the meeting described above, Mr Sycamore heard that the majority of parents had been interviewed. Mr Sycamore recommended that Mr Larch go off sick due to stress, and school staff reported that within a couple of hours he had cleared his desk and left. The replacement staff could find no curriculum plans, no schemes of work, no accurate timetables, and no children's records of any sort. The governors were advised that all communication with Mr Larch had to go through Mr Sycamore, who initiated further grievance proceedings on behalf of Mr Larch. The first of these were personally against Mrs Mulberry and Mr Beech. Some weeks later, on advice from his headquarters, Mr Sycamore initiated a collective grievance against the Governing Body.

Mrs Mulberry believed that Mr Larch was genuinely very stressed—in fact she suspected that many of his reported actions (over the 16 years that were covered by the interviews) could have been attributed to an inability to handle stress and criticism, let alone confrontation. It was also, however, a highly strategic move. No potential action could be taken against Mr Larch whilst he was ill, and his illness could be cited in an industrial tribunal for constructive dismissal. In addition, there would be insufficient 'untainted' governors to handle an additional grievance (let alone possible disciplinary or appeals procedures).

The game of strategy was becoming more complex. The Complaints Committee had uncovered a range of evidence that suggested serious problems within the school, but the internal workings of the school were beyond their remit, and, without direct access, all their evidence was circumstantial. Their concern was for the well-being and progress of the children, but they felt as if these concerns were being lost amongst a morass of strategically placed correspondence. The only way to address their concerns was to convince the LEA that the issue was more than one of personal vendettas. Mrs Mulberry felt, even more strongly, that the outcome depended upon how convincing the report was—once again, she felt that she had no option but to follow it through.

The report was completed and submitted to the chair of governors as 'commissioning agent'. It found the complaint against the governors to be merited, and it recommended that the Governing Body 'consider initiating a comprehensive disciplinary/competence investigation against Mr (Larch) for the purpose of fully and fairly exploring the points made in the Report and in the Appendices'. It recommended suspension of Mr Larch during that period, and included a wide range of recommendations about the overseeing functions of the Governing Body. An additional copy of the report went to the LEA, who then sent a copy to Mr Sycamore. It quickly became apparent that neither was expecting such complexity or detail. In a genuine attempt at clarity (but also as a strategic ploy), Mrs Mulberry had included in the report her deliberations about the remit of the Complaints Committee and her conclusions about the allegations against Mrs Oak and Mr Chestnut. These points led to implicit questioning of the efficacy and impartiality of the LEA and of the degree of pressure brought to bear on the Committee and the Governing Body by Mr Sycamore.

The report reached the higher echelons of the LEA and the evidence presented was sufficiently detailed and documented to be incontestable and led to acceptance of the report. The attention of the LEA shifted away from questioning whether there was a case to answer towards working out what could be done with the situation. The LEA were clearly concerned that the circulation of the report should remain highly restricted.

Mr Sycamore was obviously influenced by the LEA's acceptance of the report. He was, naturally, unhappy about the inferences that could be drawn about him from the detail of the report, and threatened separate legal action to protect his reputation, once again stating that he had the weight of the union lawyers behind him. Whilst this reflected a genuine concern on his part, it would have also had the effect of burying the report (and thus any actions that might result from the recommendations contained within it) until the matter had been resolved in the courts. Mrs Mulberry stood firmly behind the report, and remained concerned that the recommendations of the report be acted on as soon as possible in order to alleviate continuing disruption of the school. After meetings and correspondence with senior LEA staff it was agreed that she would move the offending details to the confidential appendix, but reserve the right to refer to them if it became necessary at a later stage. During this process it also became clear that the union lawyers had pored over every sentence of the report, but could not find any loopholes or inconsistencies, and they also accepted it. Despite repeated 'threats', or statements of 'fact' (depending upon one's viewpoint) by both Mr Sycamore and Mr Larch, stipulating that the behaviour of the Governing Body would lead to legal action by the union, no such action was taken. Clearly, the union's lawyers did not feel that it could be used as a test-case in determining the power of the head teacher. New threats of legal action (of one form or another) diminished, and the old ones were not enacted (though they were also not withdrawn). Mrs Mulberry suspected that a factor in this was the embarrassment to both the LEA and the union that might result if the report were to be examined publicly.

Several months after submission of the report, Mr Larch remained off school sick, and the Governing Body, the LEA, and Mr Sycamore were waiting for him to make a firm decision about his future. If he decided to leave it was still possible that they would face an industrial tribunal. It was indicated that he was unlikely to return to the school, which was operating very successfully under a supply teacher. In the short term, therefore, Mrs Mulberry's concern about the progress of the children was minimised. The report, however, remained restricted. The governors knew that there was a complaint and that grievances have been lodged against each of them individually as part of the Governing Body; they knew that Mr Larch was off sick and that Mr Sycamore and the LEA were involved. They knew that a report was written but that they could not read it until the whole matter was finalised, for fear of becoming 'tainted'. Some knew that the LEA would prefer them never to read it. Only some of the recommendations could be fed to the Governing Body, and even this had to be done in a sanitised manner—without any explanation of the reasoning behind them, and thus without the detail that 'untainted' governors felt they needed to justify a change in their practice. They were being forced to place a lot of trust in someone who had only recently joined them, and, quite naturally, some of them were unhappy about this.

Despite it being potentially embarrassing to them, the LEA praised the report, suggesting that little would have happened without Mrs Mulberry's involvement. The hollow joke is that she followed this route through ignorance, not knowing that there were recognised mechanisms for investigating this sort of complaint, and through a short-sighted reaction to being patronised by Mr Sycamore. Without Mr Sycamore's early involvement she might not have sought the detailed and extensive information that was necessary to check on his allegations. Similarly, without that spur to action, little information (albeit circumstantial) would have come to light about the inner workings of the school. I shall leave this story here, abandoning the characters in mid-air, in order to unravel some of the threads.

THE LIES OF POWER

Each of the characters in this story had problems with power. In the previous section, all assertions and statements were based upon data collected from official documentation, minutes of meetings, correspondence, and the people concerned. I shall now go beyond the 'facts' and create interpretative pen pictures in order to explore my suppositions about 'power'. These pen pictures are based upon detailed discussion with the people involved and analysis of supporting documentation, but remain my 'best guess' at what was happening and might not fully reflect how the characters saw their situation.

Mr Larch

Rumour has it that upon appointment Mr Larch made it clear that he would only be at the school for a year or two, as this was yet another step in an illustrious career. He certainly applied for other jobs, but did not get them. I can imagine that he became increasingly frustrated at what he saw as lack of recognition, and so began to feel that the community owed him a favour. This, in turn, led to cutting corners and taking the apparently easy way out. He was helped in this by his presentability and sensitivity to the hierarchy of power. He was adept at presenting a good impression to those whom he thought mattered, and at glossing over difficult areas. If something went wrong he would explain it away as a result of circumstances outside his control or someone else's (deliberate) fault. I suspect that he fully believed that this was the case and that he was doing a good job. Mr Larch acted as if he fully believed that he was better than any who criticised him or appeared to challenge him. When he felt challenged in any way (whether by parents, governors, or children), he would rapidly become highly and defensively aggressive.

Unfortunately, his unwillingness to spend any more time than was absolutely necessary on school work, and his inability to operate in the give-and-take environment of collaborative development of Policies and management of the school, became more noticeable with the introduction of LMS and the increased administrative, information gathering, and reporting burdens it entailed. Parents reported that problems had occurred over the last 10 years, and the nature of these remained similar over that time. What did change was that governors began to attempt to exercise their increased power, and therefore began to question. Parents and governors continued to believe, however, that their concerns were isolated incidents, that Mr Larch might have only minor problems, and that the LEA might close the school. They did not interpret the situation as one of a power struggle, so much as one of trying, individually, to meet their own needs for information. Mr Larch, as the focus for many individual questions, reacted as if it were a struggle for power, and increasingly interpreted isolated events as a coherent attack against him. I suspect that he genuinely came to believe that parents, governors, and eventually Mrs Oak, were colluding against him, and was thus very persuasive when he passed on this interpretation to Mr Sycamore or to the LEA.

The Governing Body

Mr Larch was unwittingly helped in this by Mr Chestnut (and by some of the other governors), whose increasing frustration at the lack of information necessary for the effective functioning of the Governing Body led to forthright statements of dissatisfaction. Whilst intended as open and honest, they were taken as hostages to fortune by Mr Larch, Mr Sycamore, and the LEA, who employed more subtle tactics. The governors increasingly allowed themselves to be boxed into a highly frustrating and defensive position, one from which their concerns were neither heard nor believed, and one from which they could be construed as collusive, disruptive aggressors.

The governors were clearly aware that there was a problem. They had agreed to provide extra supply teaching to 'cover' for Mr Larch whilst he undertook his administrative duties, in the understanding that he had problems with this. Due to parental pressure, they had also agreed to the increased employment of Mrs Oak and another teacher to help bring the Juniors up to an acceptable educational standard. In addition, as several years of minutes from the governors' meetings show, a lot of time and energy was spent in trying to obtain basic information from Mr Larch, information necessary for the completion of their statutory duties. Finally, the Governing Body had already dealt with a series of complaints from parents.

Looking at it from a distance, it is hard to understand why the Governors could not cope with the situation. They had the ability—many of the governors involved in this story held senior positions elsewhere. It seemed as if, because the governors were living these problems on a daily basis, they never stood back sufficiently to see them as a whole—as a pattern of concerns that might be symptoms of something deeper. Governors give their time voluntarily for the benefit of the community, and the vast majority have little spare time to give. Despite being aware that there were problems, and despite becoming increasingly frustrated about their individual inability to resolve these problems, discussion with the governors showed that other pressures (external life, family, etc.) intruded and the easiest short-term response was sought. Governors tended either to minimise the extent of the problem; to tell themselves that the problems were irresolvable or the consequences of doing something would be even worse; or to assume that someone else would take responsibility for resolving them.

I imagine the situation would be different if the governors had interpreted the problems as a power struggle against the collective Governing Body. The structure of the situation, however, mitigated against that. Governors are chosen on an individual basis and reflect a wide spectrum of interests. They expect to work collaboratively with the head teacher and seek to minimise confrontation. To work as a collective against the head teacher would be to admit that the relationship was seriously amiss, to admit personal responsibility, and to move into games of strategy and what they repeatedly described as 'dishonesty' (collusive politics) that would be directly at odds with their reported reasons for becoming involved in the first place—those of helping the community and the school. In addition, Mr Sycamore's strategy of initiating grievance against selected individuals appeared designed to divide and conquer. Mr Sycamore's legalistic approach to people who were just attempting to 'do a good job' was very upsetting to those people. By the end of this, some, like Mr Chestnut and Mrs Mulberry, were sufficiently incensed (by what they felt to be personal slander) to welcome the opportunity of a fight in which people had to swear to tell 'the truth, the whole truth, and nothing but the truth'. At the start, however, it affected all governors alike—a sort of 'why me?' approach. Nearly all governors reported considering their own positions quite carefully, wondering about the possible personal costs and the effect it might have on their families, and the majority of them considered (at least once) resigning from the Governing Body.

Mr Sycamore

Mr Sycamore seemed, like the other characters, to be a victim of his interpretations of the situation. He consistently presented himself as someone trying to do the best for his members, and, to a large extent, I believe him. He had been involved in dealing with other complaints against Mr Larch, and over the years he had had several confrontations with Mr Chestnut. I can imagine that on being notified of this complaint he immediately assumed that there was a vendetta against Mr Larch and that the quickest (and thus least disruptive) way to deal with it would be to signal this view to Mrs Mulberry. I can also imagine that when he found that she wanted to question this, he assumed that she was part of a vendetta, that the collusion must be widespread, and therefore that the situation was clearly one of a power struggle between a head teacher and governors—a situation that the Union Headquarters would be interested in. Having the conviction of his beliefs, he went out on a limb (for example, being rather free with initiating personal grievances and making misleading statements about testing procedures), but I imagine that he continued to work in a way that he justified to himself as trying to break through a widespread and destructive vendetta against one of his members who was innocent of any wrongdoing.

The report shattered the basis for his conviction. It was obvious that the Union Headquarters was more objective about the situation and did not give him the full support that he had expected prior to their reading of the report. He shifted from individual attacks to issuing a collective grievance, and became less threatening. Despite his friendship with the LEA, he found that they, also, were now less willing to attribute the whole matter to personal conflict. He became increasingly concerned for his own professional reputation, and shifted from attacking the Governing Body to defending himself.

The LEA

The LEA underwent a similar shift. It had clearly placed a lot of trust in Mr Willow, who had, in turn, clearly placed a lot of trust in Mr Larch. Similarly, it was very sensitive to Mr Sycamore's point of view. This was, to a certain extent, only to be expected, and was a result of the wider circumstances. With the introduction of LMS, many head teachers had difficulty with changes in their role that entailed an increased administrative load and greater sensitivity to working collaboratively with the Governing Body. Equally, many Governing Bodies had problems in understanding their changing responsibilities, and overestimated their power (often through fear that they would now be held responsible for any failings, and thus they wished to ensure that no blame could be attached to them). As members of the LEA explained, the LEA was closely involved with Mr Sycamore (almost on a daily basis) in attempting to work through the ensuing conflicts. They, naturally, developed a sort of trading relationship in which the LEA and the union (as two monolithic bodies) adopted 'gentleman's agreements' about the situation in different schools. On the basis of a long-established (and effective) relationship, the LEA had many reasons for trusting Mr Sycamore.

Equally, the LEA had many reasons for trusting Mr Willow. Mr Willow made it clear in his interview that he believed himself to be doing a good job in supporting a head teacher who was being faced with unreasonable demands from the Governing Body. The LEA had little reason to doubt this analysis of the situation. The governors, as minuted in their meetings, had formally expressed dissatisfaction with the advice they had been given by Mr Willow over the handling of previous complaints, but it is quite likely that the higher echelons of the LEA never had access to those minutes.

Instead, they relied on Mr Willow's reports, and Mr Willow relied on what Mr Larch told him. For example, one complaint about the school went direct to the County Council, and, in response to the request for a report from councillors, Mr Willow stated (and clearly believed) that there were only two teachers at the school and that Mr Larch had no cover for his managerial activities. A glance at the LEA payroll would have disconfirmed these beliefs. Mr Willow's belief that Mr Larch was doing a good job under very difficult circumstances, and with no support from the Governing Body, was sufficient to prevent him making even the most simple of checks.

Clearly, the LEA advisors are expected to develop friendly relations with the schools and head teachers on their circuit. They are also, however, expected to develop a realistic picture of what is going on. Mr Willow was interviewed quite late in the investigation, and some of his responses were particularly ambiguous. I suspect, however, that he had developed a friendly relationship with both Mr Larch and Mr Sycamore. There were several reports of them being personal friends and they would regularly play golf together. It is likely that Mr Willow did not see the need to check what he was being told, nor to engage in his inspection duties in as full a manner as the LEA understood him to be doing, and it is possible he misinformed the LEA about this. Under normal circumstances this might have presented little problem. Normally, he could expect the head teacher to be honest and open with him, and he could expect to trust a personal friend. As it was, there is some circumstantial evidence that as the investigation progressed, his loyalty to Mr Larch increasingly drew him into mistruths. Possibly, having accepted a modified version of the situation to start with he then had to justify why he had not fully appreciated from the start that this view was significantly incomplete.

On the face of it, the LEA remained supportive of him; however, under the surface the LEA was seriously embarrassed by the mismatch between their own understanding of the situation as derived from Mr Willow, and the substance and findings of the report. The LEA were forced to question how a school under their jurisdiction was able to fail consistently over a number of years, despite repeated complaints and factual evidence that this was occurring. They were also forced to question how this could happen without their knowledge, and, moreover, how they could be sufficiently blind as to ignore the evidence and assert to councillors that everything was satisfactory.

Mrs Mulberry

Mrs Mulberry was described by the LEA and the governors as pivotal in the progression of events. She was undoubtedly seen as a middle-class, middle-aged, interfering busybody by some—an increasing irritant as the investigation progressed. Mr Sycamore and Mr Larch both made their frustration with her very clear. Some official sources of information shifted from being helpful, to openly and very directly questioning her motives. The Governing Body increasingly voiced their concerns as they (individually and collectively) became named in grievances and threats of legal action. Mr Beech, whilst remaining supportive of Mrs Mulberry, several times said that he would not have dared to take the actions she did. Mrs Mulberry's work and family life was severely disrupted—both leaving her with a backlog of favours owed and confused emotional relationships. After having started on the investigation with feelings of goodwill and the desire to contribute to the community, she rapidly started to feel beleaguered and isolated. These feelings were not an entirely accurate reflection of the situation. The Governing Body and her family continued to support her, and her workplace and the LEA remained neutral. She did, however, feel an increasing need to expend additional energy and care in maintaining her relationships with others—she no longer felt able to rely on their goodwill.

Her motives and role in the research are discussed in detail in the final sections of this paper. For completeness of this section, however, it is worth noting that her involvement in this was not initially by her choice—she acceded to (was flattered by?) requests showing her to be the logical person to chair the Committee. She need not have chosen to investigate so thoroughly—yet she did so largely as a reaction to Mr Sycamore. In other words, a search for the 'truth' played a part throughout, but the gut-level need to reassert her 'self' became an increasingly important motivator. She was able to convince herself that the search for truth gave her the moral high ground, and thus assertion of her 'self' was legitimate. This can be seen in her progression of the investigation against severe opposition—thereby proclaiming that her view of the situation and way forward was the right and only way to go, and thus that her view was privileged over others (despite the disagreements and problems it caused others). The nature of her actions made her feel 'heroic' (of the sort discussed in chapter single-minded, God-given 'hero' discussed in Chapter 8), and so her actions legitimated her 'self-sacrifice' . . . and her sacrifice of others around her.

Mrs Mulberry appears to have been both 'empowered' and a victim of the power. Regardless of her reasons for acting as she did, however, it remains that she succeeded in carrying the investigation to detailed completion where others had previously failed; that her report was accepted in its entirety and without challenge by two major 'institutions'—the union and the LEA—both of whom would have challenged it if they could have done; and that the union would have used it as the basis for legal action against the governors if it had been deemed possible.

THOUGHTS OF POWER

Before examining Mrs Mulberry's role in more depth, I wish to take a step backwards and examine what implications this story might hold for our understandings of power. In line with the Hardy and Clegg quote given at the start of this paper, the account given above is an empirical study of a local struggle. I suggest that this is perhaps better understood as a series of voices, each of whose individual story demonstrates a complex relationship with power, than through a monolithic conception of power. Whether we look at French & Raven's (1959) five bases of power (reward, coercive, legitimate, expert, and referent), or more recent analyses, power is normally represented as if it is an obtainable 'thing'. This approach imbues power with clearly defined roots from which it can be derived. For example, Figure 14.2 offers us three groups of sources of power. The first two groups are largely tautological: I am powerful because I have power (Group A); I am in control because I have control (Group B). The power has already been given by others and the mechanisms of control are

A) Formal existing 'power'	B) Existing 'control'	C) Informal existing sources
1) Formal authority; 2) Use of organisational structure, rules and regulations; 3) Structural factors that define the stage of action; 4) The power one already has	5) Control of scarce resources; 6) Control of decision processes; 7) Control of knowledge and information; 8) Control of boundaries; 9) Control of technology, 10) Interpersonal alliances, networks, and control of 'informal organisation'; 11) Control of counter-organisations; 12) Gender and the management of gender relations	13) Ability to cope with uncertainty; 14) Symbolism and the management of meaning

Figure 14.2 Sources of Power (Derived From Morgan 1986)

already embodied in the representation. Similarly, the sources of power given in Group C imply that one either has the ability to cope with uncertainty or to manage meaning, or one doesn't. These sources can account for the status quo in the story above—the way in which Mr Larch held on to power. Mr Larch steadily built upon the formal authority that he already had (Source 1) and his historical bases for power (his reputation with peers and allies; Source 4). He used this power to persuade the governors to give him expert status, and thus to create the school policies and to define the stage of action (Source 3). He maintained his hold on the structural factors by emphasising the rules and regulations (through regular citing of Mr Sycamore, Source 2). In establishing his right to create and manage the school policies he increased his control under all aspects of Sources 5 to 12, and obtained the right to manage meaning (as of Source 14).

This view of power, however, fails to account easily or naturally for two important aspects of the data presented here: namely, why this particular Complaints Committee succeeded in challenging the established power despite having neither formal existing power nor control, and despite the failure of previous Complaints Committees, who had been in very similar situations (the last one being less than a year before). The remainder of this paper examines alternative approaches to this view of power in order to better account for the empirical data. Although traditional conceptions of power differ in the details, there are two aspects of the way in which power is presented that are particularly pertinent here: namely, the way in which it is objectified, and the way in which it is seen as the product of two or more entities. I shall discuss these in turn.

Power As Relational

Power is frequently presented as a commodity, a 'thing' (Foucault 1981); as both an outcome of behaviour and as an instrumental means of action (Bass 1981; Cobb 1984); as a form of agency over others, with 'positive power' as the ability to initiate activity and 'negative power' as the ability to stop activity (Rus 1980). Another approach, still within the same framework, is to distinguish between power and influence, such that influence is the act of obtaining compliance from another whilst power involves inference or attribution (Calder 1977) and is therefore unobservable (Hinkin & Schriesheim 1990), or power as a store of potential influence through which events can be effected (Pfeffer 1981).

Townley (1994) suggests that the adoption of power as commodity is legitimised by the sorts of question that ask 'Who holds the power?' or 'Where is the source of power?'. She follows Foucault (1981), in arguing that 'power is relational: it is not a possession'—and thus that 'understanding power as a relational activity widens the scope of attention from the "who" and the "why" of power to the "how"' (Townley 1994: 9). It would seem that power, therefore, could be likened to something like electricity: It has the possibility of existence everywhere but is only identified as it flows from one thing to another—it is a potentiality, or 'the probability that an actor within a social relationship will be in a position to carry out his own will despite resistance' (Weber 1947: 152).

Certainly, a great deal of the 'how' was, in this case, about the managing of social relationships—about juggling the individual shifts that together made up a pattern. Self Categorisation Theory (Turner 1991) suggests that conformity to social norms is driven by the categorisation of others as similar to self, and influence occurs where there is disconfirmation of shared expectations within an appropriate reference group (the governors). Where an individual is outside of 'acceptability', then mechanisms of social influence no longer apply, and that individual has to enforce control—leading to increased coercive behaviour and alienation. Mr Larch was clearly behaving politically. He showed each of ingratiation, structure change, co-optation, and threat, as well as 'paranoid distortions', as described by Kumar & Ghadially (1989), with attendant negative consequences for interpersonal relations and performance. However, whilst the governors clearly exhibited groupthink (as explored by Janis 1972), they did not form a cohesive group and appeared unable to generate or evaluate alternatives. Instead, in accordance with Moorhead & Montanari's (1986) findings, the governors were insular and this led to increased vulnerability and over-reliance upon perceived experts. Mr Larch was able to influence the groupthink sufficiently such that each individual failed to appreciate or acknowledge any group cohesion. The governors' susceptibility to this was not due to lack of ability, education, or training, as evidenced by their work and private lives. By managing individualised personal relationships Mr Larch was able to manage the collective meaning or knowledge in a way that would not have been possible if he had addressed it in the collective arena.

Power As Knowledge

The interactions described above illustrate the truism that knowledge is power—that 'power is exercised by virtue of people being known and things being seen' (Foucault 1980: 154). 'Knowledge' is used in this context as the creation of meaning, not as a source of power (as in the withholding or giving of nuggets of information—Source 7 above). The creation of the report, the bringing together of all the individual views and the structuring of these into a whole that presented a coherent view of the world, was an act of knowledge/power that existed outside formal channels and sources of power, but was persuasive enough to overturn the status quo. As Townley suggests:

> Procedures for the formation and accumulation of knowledge, including investigation and research, are not natural instruments for presenting

the 'real'. A classificatory table, for example, operates as a procedure of knowledge, and as a technique of power, making an arena 'known' in a particular way and thereby rendering it amenable to be acted upon. The processes involved in the construction of knowledge—processes of classification, codification, categorising, precise calibration, tables and taxonomies—constitute an arena of knowledge, and, in constituting something as known, provides the basis for action and intervention— the operation of power. (Townley 1994: 7)

If we invoke the idea of knowledge creation as a 'how' of power shifts we can explain more about the way in which the Complaints Committee, with relatively few traditional sources of power, was able to work around much more powerful bodies and thereby address the complaint. Such invocation does not, however, address why or how this Complaints Committee succeeded where previous committees had not. There was something about this particular situation that enabled the ten-year-old deadlock to be broken.

Power As Individual

Analyses of power, including all those above, tend to assume that power play revolves around conflict (or the relationship) between two or more people (for higher status, more money, greater resources, etc.). Underlying this assumption is the notion that there exists a form of contract—an understanding between the players (either explicit or ratified through collusion) in which services are exchanged for financial, or other, recompense. In this view power play is about implicit renegotiation/redefinition of the terms of the contract or understanding. This assumes, in turn, that people look to external sources (those with whom they are relating) for systems of assessment/measurement, standards, or whatever, by which they can ascertain how well the contract is holding up.

It became apparent during discussion of motivations and conversations after the event that the people presented here were driven by the desire to do a 'good job' (within their own terms) and did not expect to get anything out of it personally. The governors worked voluntarily for the good of the children and the community, Mr Sycamore worked for the good of his union members, and it was part of the normal workload for the LEA, Mr Willow, and Mr Larch. Each person was measuring the success (or otherwise) of what they were doing against (largely) internalised criteria. This is in accordance with Shamir (1990), who found that whilst social rewards and sanctions are motivators in collectivistic work, other important factors are moral commitment and affirmation of identity. Similarly, Raven (1988) revisited McClelland's (1975) view that success provides its own intrinsic motivation and found that feelings of success result from a large number of cumulative and sustainable, but psychologically independent, competencies rather than on a single internally consistent variable. This led him to suggest that work in the area should adopt a more descriptive and analytic approach, and should focus more on the individuals involved.

The idea of a contract suggests that, if dissatisfied, the actors can express their views overtly, and if they remain unsatisfied, they can leave. Kolarska & Aldrich (1980) found, however, that in the voluntary sector managers and leaders can be highly unresponsive, leading to feelings of lack of voice, and 'exit' as the only response to an unsatisfactory situation. Very few parents, throughout the 16 years covered by the data, chose to exercise this option—to exit would be to move out of the community or to open oneself to charges of lack of loyalty. For the parents, loyalty became synonymous with lack of voice. Similarly, if Mr Larch or Mr Willow were to have chosen to 'exit' they would have lost their jobs—however, as voluntary workers, the governors and Mr Sycamore could have exited with little apparent cost to themselves. Despite increasing personal cost, which might be expected to lead to some resignations (Miller et al. 1990), no one left the Governing Body.

Each of the actors talked of the worth of their approach. In working voluntarily, the governors and Mr Sycamore had the strength of their convictions (the need to help others) behind them. Similarly, Mr Willow and Mr Sycamore were convinced that it was appropriate to trust their friendship with Mr Larch, and Mr Larch was convinced he was doing a good job in an adverse environment. Mr Sycamore and the LEA both felt that they could place their trust in the bureaucratic machinery they were part of. For any of the actors to review their behaviour would also be for them to question their convictions—their belief in their 'value-based' justification for their approach to the situation. They were buoyed by the sense of this worth. As Frost et al. (1983) suggest, the individual interpretation of the situation, associated with the belief the 'it needed to be done' and that no one else could do it, counterbalanced the personal cost and was a powerful intrinsic motivator.

'Power as individual', therefore, extends the notion of power to include aspects of the individual's interpretation of the situation and of themselves—what might be termed agency. This is distinct from the idea that power is a commodity that an individual might 'have', because, here, 'power' is a situation-specific conjuration, possibly different for each actor, that walks beside the emergent reality. When talking of agency we need to take care to recognise the self as constituted by social relationships (Fogel 1993), belief systems (Rose 1990), and power relations (Knights & Willmott 1985). However, notions of agency provide a sense of unitary purpose—the intent. For example, other people told Mrs Mulberry that she appeared to be single-minded, focused, powerful, empowered, and so on—she was seen as a directed unitary entity. On the hidden side she felt that she knew what to do, but that she was seeing life from a multiplicity of viewpoints. This brings us back to the complexity associated with the presence of Mrs Mulberry in this story.

THE POWER OF THE RESEARCHER

I will explore the issue of unitary intent and multiplicity of view further below, but before doing so there is another factor to consider. This is Hardy & Clegg's (1996) unmasking of the researcher: 'We must also acknowledge the researcher's arrival within the circle, not as a neutral observer, but as an implicated participant'. You will by now perhaps have guessed that 'I' (the 'narrator' of this paper) am also Mrs Mulberry. (As an aside, I have altered additional identifying features in order to preserve confidentiality, but all other facts and impressions were as presented here.) Hatch (1996) suggests that 'in a main character narrative, the narrator is not restricted to discussing only what any outsider could observe, but is also allowed to speak as an insider who has privileged information. Evered & Louis (1981) defined the insider perspective as that of the actor psychically and psychologically immersed in the research setting. Immersion permits access to contextually embedded meaning, but also makes the insider conscious of his or her own embeddedness.' Certainly, as Mrs Mulberry, I was privileged in my ability to access contextually embedded meaning. I was a reasonably welcome outsider—someone with little past history to bias the understandings created, but also someone to whom the participants felt able to talk in, at times, elephantine depth. Elephantine, in the amount of data gathered, in the length of memories and extent of the detail in which the data were conferred, and in the way in which seemingly unrelated, and unreliable, parts of the elephant had to be meticulously joined, one by one, to create the whole.

As well as an observer of myself and of others, I was also an active participant and co-creator in the unfolding story. In writing this I have had to be very careful about abuse of confidentiality and the possibility of legal action. I had to try and understand my motives in multiple roles—as 'Mrs Mulberry', as 'researcher', and as 'narrator'. At least the first is chronologically separate from the last two, as it was not until a meeting with the LEA, after the report had been accepted, that I fully realised the quantity of well-documented data that I had gathered in a few months. Despite this, neither my interpretation of the data, nor my narration, is free from bias. Nearly all the data are text-based, but some interpretations are derived from my understandings of the reported perceptions of others—these have been cross-checked with the relevant people and others wherever possible. I have tried to distance myself by portraying myself as another person (Mrs Mulberry) and analysing her, as I have everyone else—essentially, however, the 'story' and its analysis is a chimera constructed from my/Mrs Mulberry's interpretations.

In this account I have tried to avoid the power of the narrator—I have tried to give each character a voice, and I have tried to talk for myself, rather than with 'authority'. This position, however, appears paradoxical. Hatch (1996) suggests that

> 'if ethnography represents anything at all, then it represents the ethnographer and his or her own cultural biases. All description, all ethnography, and all uses of language for that matter involve cultural projection and therefore are not "pure" or "true" representations in the traditional scientific sense of being objectively unbiased (Vidich & Lyman 1994). As reflexivity became the defining characteristic of the crisis of representation in postmodern ethnography, attention shifted to literary, political, and historical features of the research process itself. This is producing, amongst other things, a poetics of anthropology (e.g., Brady 1991), but it is a poetics with political overtones. The politics involved is the politics of (re)defining the role of the researcher . . . although research reports may demonstrate scientific achievement, the act of reporting is a narrative act'. (359–360)

Thus the acts of 'researching' and of 'reporting' are themselves acts of power.

It is this point that is central to my account and my discussion of power. I have tried to avoid power, but cannot. My exploration of the power play acted out in this story is interpretative—it reflects the scripts I was playing to myself as I attempted to manage the situation. It also reflects my unintentional reinterpretation of these scripts that I have made each time I return to my analysis of them, and it reflects my unthinking desire to present myself in a good light. Essentially, however, at some stage in the process I chose (possibly by retrospective acknowledgement of what was already occurring) to proactively impose my interpretation on the situation, on the story, and on this analysis. I imposed my own interpretation or tacit theory of power, which was an act of power in itself.

Hardy & Clegg suggest that a way out of this hermeneutic circle can be found by listening to the voices more carefully and by unmasking the researcher that enters the circle, yet I have tried to do this and, through the power of the narrator, have found myself back in the circle again. This time, however, the circle encloses my 'theories in action' rather than grand theorising about the nature of power. The local approach emphasises the interpretative nature of our reality of power.

Threads of Impotence

In essence the majority of studies of power look at how one person does or does not do what another asks of them. The power in the case above could be seen as an individual and interpretative quality such that individuals were as 'powerful' as the extent to which they colluded in giving or taking perceived power from themselves. In other words, perceptions of an individual's power were socially, and subconsciously, co-regulated (cf. Fogel 1993). However, we can take this line of argument further to suggest that this account shows that as they became empowered the individuals also each became impotent.

In theory, if power is taken and given between two people then if someone is dissatisfied with the bargain they can leave. In this case, it was the individuals who were putting the pressure on themselves. It was their belief in themselves, their view of self, that was at stake. Their belief in their interpretation of the situation empowered them to act, but also bound them. They were pulled in to support that belief, through gifts of self: integrity, additional work, or the ability to question the system. The justification of conviction turned into little more than impotence in the face of the chain of events. Self-empowerment turned into self-oppression.

Hopfl (1995) offers an alternative vehicle for exploring this situation. She distinguishes between rhetoric (as goal-oriented and concerned with the skills and strategies of manipulation), and the poetic (as an individualistic expression of lived experience). Rhetorical acts support the representation with authority and propriety—they are directed at persuading the individual to adhere to a wider belief. Rhetoric, therefore, can be coupled with a de-individuated, structured, symbolic, ordered, and strategic representation of the situation. In contrast, the poetic is more similar to Kristeva's (1984) view of the semiotic. It resists subjection; it disrupts and seeks expression through the subversion of the symbolic order. It creates uncertainty and ambivalence, and threatens disorder and lack of commitment to the collective. The poetic can be coupled to a local, centred, individualistic perception of the situation.

There have been, throughout this case, tensions between the individual and the collective; between effective agency (or lack of agency) and strategic games playing; between the poetic and the rhetorical. The art of management has been described as that of mediating between the goals of the organisation and those of one's subordinates; of interpreting organisational culture in a way that is accessible to one's team; of acting as a bridge between the wider structures and the localised desires. Perhaps, within these terms, the 'art' (or poetic?) of management is to balance the tensions between the rhetorical and the poetic. The empowered manager would be someone who embraced this role willingly. He or she would identify with the organisational climate, feel valued by it, and wish to pass it on. He or she would be happily proactive—working for the good of all (Lee 1991). It sounds good—but this is said tongue in cheek. Such 'empowerment' necessitates a coming together of the rhetorical and the poetic: a subsuming of the poetic within the rhetoric—a loss of self concurrent with the acceptance of a unitary identity.

Each of the characters discussed here mediated between, on one side, empowerment based upon their belief in the rightness of their interpretation of the situation and their convictions about the motivations of others (their rhetoric in tune with their poetic), and, on the other side, impotence—derived from an increasing realisation that they were little more than the tools of other people's interpretations; that their individual freedom was dominated by the constraints of the situation; that their rhetoric denied their poetic.

This point changes the emphasis of Hopfl's argument. Despite saying (pp 183) that the 'oppositions (she presents) should not be seen as counter constructions but rather as textures of experience which are defined in relation to each other and inextricably woven together in social experience', to a certain extent, her text embodies both the rhetorical and the poetic—likening them to objectified opposing sides (organisation/individual; man/woman; order/disorder). In adapting this approach to talk of empowerment, I am presenting them more clearly as a dialectic within a single body. In addition, I am suggesting that the switch between the two is self-determined—a function of how the individual perceives the situation. Banks (1990), within an entirely different context, describes this well. He is contemplating a snowstorm, and describes two ways of seeing it. One can either view the individual flake, see it drifting down and becoming clearer in its uniqueness, or one can look at the swirling mass of snow, and see the patterns and whorls within it. It is almost impossible to 'see' in both ways at the same time. One has to switch between the two, and one's whole perception, sense-making, or understanding of the situation switches at the same time. Louis & Sutton (1991) describe how individuals and groups can wilfully invoke different forms of thinking; however, the forms of thinking they discuss (automatic processing and active engagement) are not what I mean, and are, perhaps, more similar to Schon's (1983) 'knowing in practice' and 'reflecting in action' or the boundary shifts discussed in Lee et al. (1996). The situation described here was the same for all, but those who saw it as a game of strategy from the outset acted in a different way, and with different self-justification, to those who initially saw it as one of localised involvement. Both forms of operating had their strengths and drawbacks.

Those who saw it from a structural perspective as a game of strategy from the outset (Mr Sycamore and Mr Willow/the LEA) were able to justify actions (and inactions) through their need to achieve the end goal. Their personal responsibility for their own actions was minimised, or diffused, by their adherence to the corporate culture: their belief in the legitimacy of the systems and checks under which they operated; their belief in the validity of the organisation's past assumptions; their belief in the rhetoric, and of the value of employing rhetoric. In this case, their strategic interpretation of the situation was based upon false assumptions. In adopting a rhetorical approach they also adopted a macro-view of the situation, which blinded them to a mass of disparate micro-information that would have disconfirmed their interpretation. They believed in an inappropriate end goal, and thus their micro-actions were also (at times) inappropriate.

Those who saw the situation from an individual, poetic, perspective (Mr Larch, Mr Chestnut, and the rest of the governors) were each aware of different aspects of the disconfirmatory, but uncollated, chunks of micro-information. Individually the governors knew that the wider interpretations adopted by the union and the LEA were wrong, but were unable to transfer this knowledge for two main reasons. Firstly, each governor thought their own micro-information to be unique, and did not realise the wider relevance that their collated information might hold. Secondly, politics and strategy were seen as interchangeable, to be dirty, and to corrupt all that they touched. Governors did not want to become involved in the wider picture for fear of losing their affect-based self-told reason for being governors in the first place—that of helping. Governors became increasingly frustrated as the weight of strategic play overrode their individual positions. In only adopting a micro-view, governors were unable to work towards ensuring satisfactory development of the children in their care, however real, appropriate, or justified that was.

Mr Larch exemplifies the same approach, though his concerns were different. His actions at the school had caused problems (as reported by the parents) across each of the 16 years of educational provision that were examined. Because the LEA was not operating effectively as an overseeing body, Mr Larch was able to deal with each problem separately as it arose, and was thus able to act as if there was only ever one (minor) problem. He was, in each case, able to convince the other actors that the problem was individual, unique, a matter of affect, unimportant. He projected personability and sensibility—the (rather vulnerable) personal touch. He embodied the poetic, and others responded to him in like manner. The introduction of LMS brought a second overseeing body into play—that of the Governing Body. Because of its micro-approach, the Governing Body was, in reality, largely unable to operate as a strategic collective in response to the situation. Mr Larch, however, from a poetic perspective, clearly saw the threat that collective understanding and action might pose. He responded to that threat by invoking rhetoric (the union and the LEA) and interpreting the actions of the governors (to himself as well as his collectives) as a collective conspiracy. Despite being what I might imagine as an almost archetypal embodiment of the poetic, it was his power with rhetoric that, for many years, persuaded others to believe in him in the way that he presented himself to others (regardless of the mounting disconfirmatory evidence). He played, in a more typically feminine role, the sensitive, isolated, and downtrodden individual, desperately under attack from an antagonistic collective—one who needed the support of his friends (the LEA and the union) to protect him.

As an outsider I was not set in any one way of operating. Indeed, as Wilson et al. (1986) suggest, it might well have been my unique position as an accepted outsider that catalysed the bounded (and stagnant) situation. Initially, I was living the poetic: I was helping out and seeking affective confirmation. Mr Sycamore's intervention changed this. He passed on the wider rhetoric to me, expecting me to believe it. As it became clear that I wished to question it he did his best to force my compliance. Instead of achieving this, he signalled to me that he saw it as a game of rhetoric rather than an individual search for the facts of the matter. I thus acted in an empowered manner—here rhetorical and poetic sides were consonant. I was empowered by my belief in the need for a clear understanding of the situation, and my concern for the children. As an individual, I effectively took on two large bureaucracies and forced them to review their interpretation of events. I did so by adopting a strategic perspective; by weaving through the rules of the structures; by bringing the disparate elements of micro-information together in a way that presented a coherent macro-picture; by rhetorically influencing the rhetoric. I produced a macro-picture that, because of its wider nature, spoke the same language as those used to seeing life through structures and implications. My power was rooted in my ability to bridge the two approaches—to speak the two languages and to translate between the two cultures. This is the only major difference between this Complaints Committee and any of the other investigations that had occurred over the previous ten years. For example, I was given some formal authority to investigate, as other Complaints Committees were; and, as other investigators did, I used the rules and regulations in so far as I questioned the extent to which they were followed, and so on. This sort of investigation could have occurred at any time over the last ten years, and a traditional analysis of sources of power does not account for why it was I, rather than other investigative agents, that was able to influence the extremely powerful cross-organisational mind-set that had developed.

Nearly all parties concurred with the mind-set. Some explicitly believed it (such as the LEA, the union, Mr Larch, and outside bodies that were questioned); others believed in its overwhelming power, such that it could not be challenged (individual governors, teachers, and parents). If they did try to challenge (as did Mr Chestnut), they reactively challenged minor points from within the mind-set, rather than attempting to proactively challenge the mind-set itself. There were only three people who questioned the mind-set itself, namely myself, Mrs Oak, and Mrs Tree. Mrs Tree dared to challenge the prevailing view that complaining would force the closure of the school. Mr Beech, whilst working with me on the Complaints Committee, said several times that he would never, on his own, have dared to adopt the approach I took—instead he, as with previous complaints, would have taken a localised and minimalist perspective from within the prevailing mind-set. As described above, Mrs Oak had been consistently critical of what she saw as Mr Larch's unwillingness to accord with good practice. This had put her at odds with Mr Larch (and the power he wielded), and made her life extremely uncomfortable, yet she continued to challenge the mind-set from within the organisation. Mrs Tree, Mrs Oak, and I were all driven by the affective need to challenge the mind-set, and were all female.

This gender difference supports Hopfl's (1995: 183) gendered description of the poetic disruption of rhetorical structures:

> In terms of the social regulation of organisation (Clegg 1981), women constitute a considerable threat precisely because their commitment is problematic: they have difficulty presenting themselves 'as a full organisational member', as someone who 'fits in' as a 'committed person' (Hearn et al. 1989: 38) because they have commitments outside the organisation. Yet there is more to this than an acknowledgement of conflicting demands might suggest. Women are less able to yield their collectivity which is contained in the poetic dimension of experience. Organisations have sought to secure greater commitment via the appropriation of the poetic and heroic narratives. This is a transgression of experience and a simulacrum. In the face of such elaborate vacuity, the corporate actor is inhibited, anxious and alienated. Compliance eases the friction of dissonant experience and captures it via powerful transformational metaphors and representations. The trajectory of the discourse is affirmed by symbolic rewards which confirm direction, success and desired outcomes. That women bear the poetic, embody ambivalence, communicate condensed affect and preserve unconscious rhythms is a considerable challenge to the authority of the text. Women threaten disorder.

I am not suggesting in any way that it was male vs. female, or that it is only women who can be effective, nor that the women worked together on this—we knew of each other, but we generally moved in different circles and, if nothing else, it would have been highly inappropriate for us to have had any more than formal contact during the process of the investigation. Instead, I am pointing to a coincidence, and wondering whether, given Hopfl's argument, it might have been more than that. Perhaps what distinguished this from previous investigations was that I was the first female investigator. Perhaps, as a woman, I was more frequently placed outside the rhetorical structures; was more alert to the tyranny of the rhetoric; had more skill (born of hard practice) at moving between the poetic and the rhetoric; and was therefore more able to challenge the rhetoric than a man might have been.

Perhaps, as one reviewer of this account suggested, there is no need to invoke the poetic and rhetoric as explanatory mechanisms, as my success was because I was accepted in the stereotypical female role of mediator. In other words, I was helped in my task by being more socially acceptable as a mediator than a man would have been—my success was just because I was female. Certainly, in Western media at least, women are often portrayed as the mediators; however, this is not just because of their gender—society, as interpreted through the media, expects them to employ mediation skills akin to the ability to empathise with multiple viewpoints. It is possible, however, to accept that women are (in general) more skilled at dealing with multiple viewpoints without also accepting notions of the poetic and the rhetoric. In response to this, I suggest that the rhetoric is more like a filter overlaid upon the potential chaos of multiple viewpoints. It is the rules and mores to which the collectivity colludes in managing itself; it denies the individual. As the collectivity is a synthesis of multiple viewpoints, aware-ness of these points of order is an essential tool in the armoury of the stra-tegic influencer, and of the mediator who intervenes between the system (or the collective) and the individual. We could take this further, and question whether or not it is an essential tool in the armoury of every mediator, in so far as individuals are constructed by the collective, and vice versa. The point is that mediation requires contact both with the individual (and their unique [multiple?] viewpoint) and with that same individual as constituted by, and in light of, their contribution to and influence on the collective. The act of mediation then takes this and multiplies it with dynamic con-tact with other (complex) individuals—and so on. In each case there is a substantial difference between working with the individual, poetic, aspects of the situation, and working with the overarching laws of engagement. In organisational or academic terms, this could be seen as part of the distinc-tion between HRD and HRM.

Regardless of the terminology used here, I shall assert my power as par-ticipant researcher and narrator to say that this distinction must have some place in this account, as it is the distinction (or post hoc rationalisation) used by myself to account for my actions. This way of viewing the situation has validity in so far as it is, anyway, part of the explanatory mechanism from within the story.

Empowerment: A Symbol of Oppression

By exposing ourselves to this kind of genealogical analysis (e.g., Knights & Morgan 1991), we become more aware of how we are also prisoners in a web of power that we have helped to create. Other people said that they saw me as empowered—I was, however, also impotent. I could only act as a mediator by losing my 'self'. As with the poetic approach of the governors, I could justify my need to investigate through seeking coherence with my affective value base—it was important for the children. This justification became increasingly important to me as the investigation, at times, brought real pain to the other actors involved. None came through unscathed. Mr Chestnut and Mrs Oak faced serious personal allegations, which, if proved, could hold deep repercussions for them. In Mrs Oak's case, it would have destroyed her career as a supply teacher. Mr Sycamore and Mr Willow faced being judged as misguided if not, at times, incompetent. Mr Larch was already stressed, and faced further stress associated with an investiga-tion that might have vindicated his position, but left him with a serious, and potentially incapacitating, emotional legacy. I felt for these people and wanted to minimise their pain, but this was balanced against the possible pain of the children, who, if the complaint was to be believed, were being seriously hampered in their educational progress, some being physically or emotionally bullied. I felt I had no choice but to continue, and my sense of self, my 'I', became subservient to my belief in the validity of my value-based justifications. I worked day and night, ignoring my real work and my family, and threatening my health. I became an acolyte of my own rhetoric. By empowering myself through aligning my poetic and rhetorical justificatory mechanisms I had also made myself impotent—I was unable to do anything other than that which I had committed myself to do at a time when I was unaware of the costs it would entail.

I can tell my tale as narrator, construct the reality as a researcher, and influence the outcomes as a participant. The blurred distinctions between these means that, in effect, I have done all three—I have worked in the tradition of all researchers who each influence the emergence and realisation of their construction, perception, and representation of their research. I cannot say that this research is true or accurate, only that it reflects my own perceptions (as far as I know them) and my attempts to represent as fairly as possible the perspectives of each of the other players in the story. This story was based on a great deal of documentary evidence, but each datum still had to pass the filter of my judgement of its relevance.

Perhaps this case is unique and has little to offer the wider world than an account of what was a highly stressful time in my/Mrs Mulberry's life. I suggest, however, that despite being dissimilar to situations more normally presented in the mainstream analyses of power and empowerment (which revolve around the fight for status and financial recompense), this case fosters greater clarity in understanding the tensions at play in organisational life. I suspect that the tensions described here exist in the majority of organisations, but are masked by a focus on traditional sources of power. What is clear here is that power went to those who were able to persuade others to believe firmly in their particular interpretation of events and, thus, in their view of life. Power was about the ability to create belief. Traditional sources of power were an adjunct to, or derived from, that basic ability.

In addition, this case highlights the tension between individual empowerment and organisational structure. It suggests that one's empowerment is more a matter of personal belief than an externally measurable quality. From an organisational perspective, empowerment is about the ability to set and achieve goals that are valued by the organisation. An empowered employee would be one who proactively supports and furthers the organisation's activities—he or she believes. One loses one's self-responsibility to the needs of the organisation—one becomes impotent as a questioning, reflective, and potentially disruptive individual. Belief in the organisation begets impotence, such that empowerment becomes a symbol of organisational oppression. The twist in the tale is that the organisation is but a collection of individuals, so that belief in the organisation is really *lack* of belief of one's right to have an equal personal voice in the collective. Similarly, from an individual perspective, feelings of empowerment seem to stem from the ability to create a value-based justification or belief in what one is doing. In order to be effective in this one has to work strategically and adopt a macroview. This provides external justification for the overriding of individual concerns. One becomes impotent in the face of the self-imposed jihad. Belief in one's values begets impotence, such that empowerment becomes a symbol of self-oppression. In both cases, one can convince oneself that one is empowered (with all the good feelings that entails) so long as one believes in the rightness of the wider situation. The strength of that belief, however, carries impotence with it.

REFERENCES

Banks IM (1990) *The Use of Weapons*. London: Orbit.

Bass BM (1981) *Stogill's Handbook of Leadership*. New York: Free Press.

Brady I (1991) (Ed) *Anthropological Poetics*. Savage, MD: Rowman & Littlefield.

Calder BJ (1977) 'An Attributional Theory of Leadership', in Staw BM & Salanick GR (Eds) *New Directions in Organisational Behaviour*: 179–204. Chicago: St. Clair Press.

Clegg S (1981) 'Organisation and control', *Administrative Science Quarterly* 26: 545–562.

Cobb AT (1984) 'An episodic model of power: Toward an interpretation of theory and research', *Academy of Management Review* 9(3)482–493.

Evered R & Louis MR (1981) 'Alternative perspectives in the organisational sciences: "Inquiry from the inside" and "inquiry from the outside"', *Academy of Management Review* 6: 385–395.

Fogel A (1993) *Developing through Relationships: Origins of Communication, Self and Culture*. Hemel Hempstead: Harvester Wheatsheaf.

Forester J (1989) *Planning in the Face of Power*. Berkeley, CA: University of California Press.

Foucault M (1980) *Power/Knowledge: Selected Interviews and Other Writings*. New York: Pantheon.

Foucault M (1981) *The History of Sexuality. Volume 1: The Will to Knowledge*. London: Penguin.

French JRP & Raven B (1959) 'The bases of social power', in Cartwright D & Zander A (Eds) *Group Dynamics*: 150–165. New York: Harper and Row.

Frost DE, Fiedler FE, & Anderson JW (1983) 'The role of personal risk-taking in effective leadership', *Human Relations* 36(2)185–202.

Gramski A (1971) *Selections from the Prison Notebooks*. London: Lawrence & Wishart.

Hardy C & Clegg SR (1996) 'Some dare call it power', in Clegg SR, Hardy C, & Nord WR (Eds) *Handbook of Organisational Studies*: 622–641. London: Sage.

Hatch MJ (1996) 'The role of the researcher: An analysis of narrative position in organisation theory', *Journal of Management Inquiry* 5(4)359–374.

Hearn J, Sheppard DL, Tancred-Sheriff P, & Burrell G (1989) (Eds) *The Sexuality of Organisations*. London: Sage.

Hinkin TR & Schriesheim CA (1990) 'Relationships between subordinate perceptions of supervisor influence tactics and attributed bases of supervisory power', *Human Relations* 43(3)221–238.

Hopfl H (1995) 'Organisational rhetoric and the threat of ambivalence', *Studies in Cultures, Organisations and Societies* 1(2)175–188.

Janis IL (1972) *Victims of Groupthink*. Boston: Houghton Mifflin.

Knights D & Morgan G (1991) 'Strategic discourse and subjectivity: Towards a critical analysis of corporate strategy in organisations', *Organisation Studies* 12(3)251–273.

Knights D & Willmott H (1985) 'Power and Identity in theory and practice', *Sociological Review* 33: 22–46.

Kolarska L & Aldrich H (1980) 'Exit, voice and silence: Consumers' and managers' responses to organisational decline', *Organisation Studies* 1(1)41–58.

Kristeva J (1984) *Revolution in Poetic Language*. New York: Columbia University Press.

Kumar P & Ghadially R (1989) 'Organisational politics and its effect upon members of organisations', *Human Relations* 42(4)305–314.

Lee MM (1991) 'Spirituality in organisations: Empowerment and purpose', *Management Education and Development* 22(3)221–226.

Lee MM (1999) 'The lie of power: Empowerment as impotence', *Human Relations* 52(2)225–262.

Lee MM, Letiche H, Crawshaw R, & Thomas M (1996) (Eds) *Management Education in the New Europe*. London: International Thompson Publishing.

Louis MR & Sutton RI (1991) 'Switching cognitive gears: From habits of mind to active thinking', *Human Relations* 44(1)55–76.

Machiavelli N (1961) *The Prince*. Harmondsworth: Penguin.

McClelland DC (1975) *Power: The Inner Experience*. New York: Irvington.

Miller LE, Powell GN, & Seltzer J (1990) 'Determinants of turnover among volunteers', *Human Relations* 43(9)901–917.

Moorhead G & Montanari JR (1986) 'An empirical investigation of the groupthink phenomenon', *Human Relations* 39(5)399–410.

Morgan G (1986) *Images of Organisation*. London: Sage.

Pfeffer J (1981) *Power in Organisations*. Marshfield, MA: Pitman Publishing.

Raven J (1988) 'Toward measures of high-level competencies: A re-examination of McClelland's distinction between needs and values', *Human Relations* 41(4)281–294.

Rose N (1990) *Governing the Soul: The Shaping of the Private Self*. London: Routledge.

Rus V (1980) 'Positive and negative power: Thoughts on the dialectics of power', *Organisation Studies* 1(1)3–20.

Schon DA (1983) *The Reflective Practitioner*. New York: Basic Books.

Shamir B (1990) 'Calculations, values and identities: The sources of collectivistic work motivation', *Human Relations* 43(4)313–332.

Townley B (1994) *Reframing Human Resource Management*. London: Sage.

Turner JC (1991) *Social Influence*. Milton Keynes: Open University Press.

Vidich AJ & Lyman SM (1994) 'Qualitative methods: Their history in Sociology and Anthropology', in Denzin NK & Lincoln YS (Eds) *Handbook of Qualitative Research*: 23–59. Thousand Oaks, CA: Sage.

Weber M (1947) *The Theory of Social and Economic Organisation*. New York: Free Press.

Wilson DC, Butler RJ, Cray D, Hickson DJ, & Mallory GR (1986) 'Breaking the bounds of organisation in strategic decision making', *Human Relations* 39(4)309–332.

15 The Isolation of Agency

'To be truthful, probably 60% of the decisions I make are my decisions. But I keep my intentions secret. In discussions with subordinates, I ask questions, pursue facts, and try to nudge them in my direction without disclosing my position. Sometimes I end up changing my position as the result of the dialogue. But whatever the outcome, they feel part of the decision. Their involvement in the decision also increases their experience as managers'.

(A senior executive of the Sony Corporation: Pascale 1978: 154)

During my years as a process consultant I worked with all sorts of different organisations, from family firms to multinationals, from traditional bureaucracies to creative partnerships, from charities, not-for-profit organisations, and public bodies to organisations driven by the need to create money for their shareholders. Management theory, at the time, seemed very prescriptive and of little use to me in my day-to-day practice. My experience was one of almost daily change—working with different people, at different levels, with different espoused goals, and even wider difference in real goals. I was with people all the time yet I was isolated. As someone from the outside looking in and throwing light on what was going on, I expected to be on my own and that was part of my job. However, I also talked to the managers about their jobs and their day-to-day life, and I discovered that increasingly, and as management structures changed, many of them felt as isolated as I did.

Writers have been talking about the changing nature of management since the 1980s (Zuboff 1988) if not earlier. This might be a function of where 'management' was studied, as early research focused mainly on Westernised bureaucracies and manufacturing and associated trades. Such research into management and organisations generally ignored the myriad small family corner shops and non-traditional and not-for-profit organisations, and the vast amount of trade, bartering, and other forms of transaction that go on around the world and often under the radar. Researchers are finally acknowledging these alternative forms of management, including those involved in child labour and sex work, which perhaps present more blatant ethical dilemmas than do more traditional forms of management. These issues are discussed more in Chapter 16, but I mention them here to highlight the fact that they have been around for a very long time, but we have generally chosen to ignore them—we prefer to work with a sanitised view of 'management'.

Over the last 50 years Western economies have largely shifted from manufacturing to service industries, with a concurrent shift in the nature of work, forms of organisation, and career path (Chapter 16). Heimans & Timms (2014) argue that old-power organisations value managerialism, competition, and professionalism, and rely on the exclusive nature of what they own, know, or control. New-power organisations value self-organisation, collaboration, and a DIY spirit, and rely on sharing and fostering the activities of others. They see this as a shift away from a world defined by hierarchy to one shaped by mass participation: one that can be associated with the desire to make choices for ourselves and to have a say in our lives.

We are increasingly led to believe that we are agents of our own lives. Over the last century there have been major developments in individual freedom: from the suffragettes to birth control; from the abolition of slavery to anti-discrimination laws. Our views of freedom and agency have changed. '[I]n times like the present, when the individual is seen as the king of creation, it is difficult to convince the general public that an individual is a relatively recent invention of early liberalism, which had important political reasons for launching it' (Czarniawska 2014: 3).

EMPLOYABILITY

A shift in the focus of management and economics has mirrored this rise in individual agency, whereby the notion of employability and the responsibility of the individual for the development of their career has replaced the idea of long-term organisational career bargains. As organisations and governments become more flexible in order to compete in the global market they also make 'it possible for the individual to make necessary choices to become employable' (Fejes 2010: 99). Careers are now portrayed as boundaryless, with individuals moving from one job to another, constantly updating their skills (Arthur & Rousseau 2001). A loss of job security is presented as giving 'employability security' (Kanter 1989), thereby empowering the employees through choice in the labour market (Clarke & Patrickson 2008). The idea that the state and employers are responsible for providing lasting and secure jobs has disappeared, such that 'to be employed is to be at risk [and] to be employable is to be secure' Hawkins (1999: 8). However, employability is a condition that can never be truly fulfilled (Cremin 2010). Furthermore, it downplays the influence of structural issues on the labour market and individualises social problems (Holmqvist 2009). Employability engenders the need to conform, to continually strive more, to lie, and to hide issues such as disability or mental illness. Individuals are made responsible for their employment: Being unemployed is seen as the result of not trying hard enough (Chertkovskaya et al. 2013).

The enactment of employability engenders an idealised notion of the sellable, skilled, hard-working, disciplined, enterprising, employable 'self' (Williams 2005). Individuals are seen as responsible for their own marketability such that individual agency is predicated upon 'self-work' and 'self-management' (Beverungen et al. 2013) and the realisation of 'self' is a reflection of that of employability (Andersen 2007). Self-development has shifted to the search for an unrealisable, ideal 'employable self' (Southwood 2011). As Levitas (2005: 121) points out, '[T]he project of employability begins at the cradle, if it has not yet been extended to the grave'. The increasing focus on employability rather than education for its own sake is evident at school (Komulainen et al. 2009) and university (Beverungen et al. 2009). Chertkovskaya et al. (2013: 713) argue that our 'contemporary preoccupation with employability tethers questions of equality and human development to an instrumental capitalist obsession with growth and renewal that may aggravate marginalization, exploitation and stigmatization'. My focus on it here is because of the way in which ideas of employability are linked with those of agency, self-development, and individual responsibility. The rhetoric clearly states that we are the authors of our lives, we have no one to blame but ourselves if things go wrong.

In the same way that individuals are increasingly being seen and treated as agents of their own destiny, so it is with managers. The literature would have managers at the centre of a node of agency: efficient, effective, lucrative, strategic, team players, and above all good agents for the organisation. Effective managers are 'agents of change', not 'targets of change' (Hill 2003: xiii). In this era of agency the manager is someone who is expected to hold super-agency; however, we could question the reality of this view. 'Becoming a manager is not about becoming a boss. It's about becoming a hostage. There are many terrorists in this organisation who want to kidnap me. I used to love my job. People listened to me. People liked me. I'm the same person now, but no one listens and no one cares' (a manager's response, reported in Mintzberg 2009: 145). So what is so hard about being the super-agent?

AGENCY IN ORGANISATIONS

Battilana & D'Aunno (2009) discuss three dimensions of agency within organisations. The iterative dimension is linked to the reproduction of established, and often subconscious, practices (DiMaggio & Powell 1991); however, iterative agency is not effortless as it requires thought in order to recognise specific situations and behave accordingly (Jarzabkowski

2005). The projective dimension supports planning and future change and is thus linked to entrepreneurship and creativity (Battilana et al. 2009). The practical-evaluative dimension enables actors to exercise judgement and 'get things done' in the here and now (Tsoukas & Cummings 1997). Smets & Jarzabkowski (2013) emphasise the complex interactions between these directions. They highlight 'constellations' of logics and the way in which agents recast them as more or less compatible as they go through the normal working day (Goodrick & Reay 2011). They argue that most individuals are not grand entrepreneurs, but practical people doing practical work to get a job done, and they emphasise the importance of the iterative and projective dimensions of agency as the starting point of creative institutional work. Similarly, the use of stories shapes the organisation. The stories that are told focus on the remarkable or the unusual with routine aspects referred to in a cryptic or elliptical manner: 'Technicians' stories are work; they are part of diagnosis, and they help preserve the knowledge acquired for the benefit of the community' (Orr 1996: 143). Stories are modified to encompass the needs of outsiders, but storytelling is a situated practice: The reasons for telling stories are always local and occasioned in situ, and it is in this way that much of the implicit knowledge is passed on. In other words, the ideas of ritual and the unconscious explored in Chapter 13 have resonance with the mundane reinforcement of institutional order that is described here.

This presents a complex and situated view of agency (Battilana 2006) in which the 'everyday getting by of individuals' (Lawrence et al. 2011: 57) includes the need to encounter contradictory institutional practices, negotiate adaptations that facilitate task accomplishment, and reconstruct their underlying institutional logics (Smets et al. 2012), and connects the micro-level activities to the macro-level effects of what is more commonly seen as agency. The super-agency of management, therefore, seems to involve activity and influencing on many different levels at once in a situated and complex manner. The small day-to-day parts and rituals seem almost irrelevant, yet build into the whole bundle of efficacy. Despite the focus on managers as agents of change, Marshall & Stewart (1981a, b) found that many middle managers believe that their behaviour is largely fixed by external constraints: that they have little agency. *Within this context the quote from Pascale (given at the head of this paper) is presented as an example of good practice.*

EXPLORING ISOLATION

I interviewed 30 of the managers that I worked with, exploring in depth the skills they felt they needed to become change agents within their organisations (see Lee 1991; 1994 for more details of this study). The key skill they identified was that of coping with isolation and loneliness.

Reasons given for the perceptions of isolation can be classed as

- structural (I don't feel as if I have a home anymore, I'm always part of one group or another, but no group is 'mine');
- protective of role (I can't let off steam about X to Y, because I know that tomorrow they will be working together, comparing notes and looking for evidence of favouritism);
- protective of life balance (I seem to be at work all the time; I never get a chance to see my family—I feel like a stranger to them);
- protective of self (we all act open and friendly together, but I know that in the end it is results that count and that if I really show my weak 'human' side, the real me, I'd be finished); and
- communicative (I just don't seem to be able to find the language to explain what is really going on for me).

My exploration of this moves from the level of organisation (cultural identity and an isolating structure), through group issues (manipulation, trust, and protecting the role), through work and family issues (life balance, psychological contract, and misbehaviour), to the individual considerations (development, control, and protecting the self). The fifth category (process and communication) permeates the others. At each level feelings of isolation spring from the necessity to walk the boundaries that are inherent in the espousal of 'new' ways of working.

1. Structural: *Micro-Culture and an Isolating Structure*

Managers are increasingly required to work in flatter and more flexible organisational structures, to work cross-functionally and with high task interdependence. They are thus expected to engage in a multiplicity of different groups and micro-cultures—necessitating closer coordination, communication, and mutual adjustment with co-workers (Kiggundu 1981). The idea of micro-cultures harks back to the implicit group norms that developed in the communications exercise that I described in Chapter 3. The role of the individual manager within these micro-cultures is likely to vary from group to group, from customer to client, from leader to co-worker. In moving between micro-cultures managers are going through a continuous process of forming and re-forming relationships. In so far as the roots of self-esteem and identity are correlated with the ability to identify with place and group (Breckler & Greenwald 1986), the manager is, within the terms of the micro-culture, becoming stateless. The relatively stateless managerial role carries with it increased health problems associated with task interdependency; social readjustment; socio-cultural difference; and problems of adaptation, accommodation, and stress of change (Lee et al. 1991). These effects are moderated by individual difference in perception of agency: general self-efficacy and control over one's own life—locus of control, and level of social support received by the individual (Monroe et al. 1983).

The manager is, in effect, being expected to move into and work within alien subcultures, and thus to place him- or herself into a similar position to that of indigenous socially inadequate individuals (Trower et al. 1978), with the attendant need to learn the salient characteristics of each new micro-culture and to use them as necessary and discard them when inappropriate (Bochner 1982). It is usually those who are highly socially skilled within their own cultures that attain positions which enable them to interact with other cultures. However, Furnham & Bochner (1986) suggest that high levels of social skill in one culture, in that they are internalised and automatic, can mitigate against fluent cross-cultural work. A person skilled in the iterative dimensional of agency might find that to be a problem if they are crossing the boundaries of micro-cultures. The main attribute needed may thus be the ability to *consciously* adopt an extensive and flexible repertoire of social skills. However, the managers I interviewed were emphatic that gaining the ability to move skilfully between social situations did not ameliorate their feelings of isolation, but only masked the symptoms.

In summary, flatter organisational structures require the increasing mobility of managers. The managerial role becomes one of moving between micro-cultures, yet rarely staying long enough to become fully acculturated. Indeed, if the manager were to become fully acculturated (go native) he or she would no longer be fulfilling the role of the mobile manager. In itself, this mobility removes (in part) the manager from the social support systems that would otherwise help buffer social readjustment. Effective working across micro-cultures might benefit from social skills training that facilitates making conscious the subconscious processes of the group, thereby engendering the active choice of appropriate influencing behaviours. However, the removal of social support systems created by organisational structures that require frequent shifts of micro-culture means that the potential for isolation is an inevitable facet of the 'new' managerial role.

2. Protective of Role: *Manipulation, Trust, and Protecting the Role*

Roles provide a formalisation of co-created and regulated frames of reference, both for the individual and in locating the individual within the organisation. In the more traditional structured view of organisation, roles vary with managerial level, form of organisation, culture, and research methodology. Even within such a structured view, a continuing role for managers is seen to be in monitoring and influencing culture and managing meaning, in so far as organisations are systems of wholly or partly shared meanings (Pfeffer 1981). The managerial role, as described in the literature, has altered from the hierarchical position of responsibility and authority to one of a change agent in a flatter structure: someone who is a team player, accepted by colleagues and able to work flexibly and supportively. The isolation of the traditional manager is seen as a thing of the past, and the new manager is expected to nourish creative tension generated by a balance between a focus on human resources and personal well-being on one hand and a clear, hard management on the other (Pascale 1990). This involves the 'knowledge and acceptance of a wider repertoire of ways of being' (Kinsman 1990). These have echoes of Adler's vision of the multicultural man, as someone 'who is intellectually and emotionally committed to the fundamental unity of all human beings while at the same time he recognises, legitimises, accepts, and appreciates the fundamental differences that lie between people of different cultures' and whose identity is based 'not on a "belongingness" which implies either owning or being owned by culture, but on a style of self consciousness that is capable of negotiating ever new forms of reality. . . . He is neither totally a part of nor totally apart from his culture; he lives, instead, on the boundary' (Adler 1974: 24–25).

However, Hales (2002: 64) points out that organisations have only changed to a limited form of bureaucracy and that 'there is little change in the substance of managers' work activities . . . individual responsibility and a preoccupation with administrative action remain'. Raelin (2003) challenged the conventional view of leadership as one person out in front, suggesting instead that it could be collaborative, with all members of the community being in control of and able to speak for the entire community. Such patterns of leadership do exist across the world (Turnbull 2014), but are not yet common in large organisations. Mintzberg suggests that managers should see themselves as 'not on top of a hierarchy or at the centre of some kind of hub, so much as throughout a web of activities . . . the manager has to be everywhere, not drawing people into some centre so much as going out to where they are. This suggests a favouring of linking over leading, dealing over doing, and convincing over controlling' (Mintzberg 2009: 124–125).

Role conflict associated with being a 'leader' is the normal lot of the manager and has been recognised for many years. As Roethlisberger (1945) noted, the foreman must become adept at double talk, but may also become its victim. Messages transmitted by the leader need to be filtered and distorted to stand best chance of acceptance, but distortion of communication flows may lead both foreman and organisation into extreme difficulty. In filtering the organisational message the leader is neither at one with the organisation nor with subordinates. Over time, managers become polarised, liaising either with their superiors or subordinates, but not both, and polarisation becomes more frequent in times of rapid change (Smith et al. 1969). The ambiguity and conflict facing the manager, however, involves additional complexity. The crux of the dilemma is that he or she is expected to be both a leader (and thus a mediator and linchpin (Graen et al. 1978)), and engaged in lateral and hierarchical transformational transactions as an 'equal' collaborative colleague. The latter is described as a process by which 'one or more persons engage with others in such a way that leaders and followers raise one another to higher levels of motivation and morality . . . a process of mutual exchange where the function of leaders and followers is fused' (Burns 1978: 20). Superior-inferior relationships are eliminated (Samovar & Porter 1976), subordinates become colleagues and espoused equals, and the ex-leader's power (and perceived high performance) is more firmly located in personal ability to manage the processes of the interactions than in position or expertise (Martinko & Gardner 1987).

In practice, Ferlie & Bennett (1992) found that change agents need to have status or access to other sources of power to be effective. Furthermore, the leader still carries the organisational culture, and has the positional power conferred by the role (appraisal, dismissal, promotion, location of resources, and so on). It is unlikely, therefore, that a move towards 'equality' with subordinates is truly perceived to be just this. The leader might be perceived as developmental, supportive, and a mentor, but it is the leader who does most of the initiating (Bass 1985) and carries the responsibility. To imply to the subordinate that he or she has equal voice is to lie. Such lies can be told in the spirit of advancement, such as the condoned manipulation described by Pascale at the head of this chapter. Previously this has been given as an example of good practice; however, from a Western perspective it is also possible to interpret it as a clear account of a manager who chooses to conceal information about his own position in order to manipulate others into feeling that they have been part of the decision-making process.

There are clear cultural differences here. Rohlen (1974: 108) points out that 'the conclusions may be foregone, the fact that discussions have been held is most important, for a chief is expected to share his opinions, ask for advice, and permit dissenting voices [to be heard]. His trust and respect for the others and his acknowledgement of the group's importance, both symbolised by this [decision-making] process, are what counts'. Smith (1983) describes the circulation of memoranda, in which each recipient marks that they have read it and may comment on it, as a form of consultation. 'This system is so perplexing to Americans accustomed to a more dictatorial style of leadership from the top down that it has given rise to the myth that the Japanese have a mysterious bottom to top form of leadership called the "ringi" system'. Yet it simply shows that 'a decision preceded by this process deals with a problem with which all members of the group are familiar. They are therefore in a position to carry it out much more effectively than would be the case had the decision simply been announced' (Reischauer 1977: 188). To non-Westerners this is the traditional and highly preferable way in which managers and leaders should acknowledge and encourage the engagement of their staff. This way of working, however, does not remove problems of role conflict.

A similar argument can be made about cooperation with colleagues. Today's collaborative and 'equal' colleagues are likely to be tomorrow's competitors for promotion or resources. Thus 'the image of lateral relationships which emerges from almost all the studies we have reviewed is one of difficulty, complexity and cautiousness . . . because each party represents a separate series of interests' (Smith & Peterson 1988: 137). Perhaps, in a society in which everyone was content with their position in the organisation, and in which each person fulfilled expectations of them with excellence, then we would no longer have such manipulation. As it is, I suggest that *aspiring* managers collude with overt and covert manipulation as an essential part of both their managerial function and their attempts to reach what they perceive as fulfilment within the organisation. Furthermore, manipulation of others often goes hand in hand with working with process (certainly within the managerial context). This is almost tautological, in so far as working with or managing the process of interactions involves the exercising of agency based upon active choice in the use of social skills designed to influence the relationship to advantage as perceived by the manager. Managerial power still exists, but is hidden under the rhetoric of the inspirational team player.

The line between manipulation and influence is a fine one. Influence is a more socially acceptable word, and is an accepted part of building relationships. The difference between the two becomes more apparent when we examine whose needs the 'influence' is meeting. The notion of the manager as a change agent or transformational leader suggests a Rogerian approach, by which subordinates are helped to help themselves (Rogers 1959). This can be seen in the light of Bartunek & Moch's (1987) description of second- and third-order change. Second-order change attempts are designed to phase in particular frameworks in which events are understood (schemata) and phase out others, whereas third-order change attempts aim to help organisation members develop the capacity to identify and change their own schemata as they see fit. They argue that the two approaches present change agents with different roles and ethical dilemmas. In second-order change the agent would advocate a particular interpretation of events, whilst in third-order change the agent would help the organisation members develop the ability to determine for themselves when second-order change is required and then help them implement it. In these terms the influence is mutually beneficial, but is such change really achievable within the organisational setting? What the manager might call influence, the subordinate might term manipulation. From the subordinate's point of view, manipulation will be seen to occur when hidden agendas and knowledge, mixed motives, and personal ambitions of the manager are intuited, suspected, or experienced. Trust is lost, and all interactions will be viewed with a level of suspicion. As someone who moves between micro-cultures, has power over others, and uses personal power to influence others, the manager's actions will almost inevitably be misinterpreted by some, and will generate some lack of trust (see Chapter 16). Such trust might be around whether or not a particular manager can be believed, but it is also around whether or not the employee thinks that the organisation will treat them in a fair and legitimate manner and will not make inappropriate demands of them.

The more the manager feels that they can trust their colleagues and subordinates, the greater their job satisfaction (Knoll & Gill 2011), and the more subordinates feel able to trust colleagues and their superiors, the greater their work-related self-esteem and productivity. More importantly from the organisation's perspective, however, is that the greater the climate of trust, the more employees feel able to take balanced risks (Neves & Eisenberger 2014). Organisations with no appetite for risk tend to die (Wiseman & Gomez-Mejia 1998, Chapter 11). Employees are more willing to take risks on behalf of the organisation, to act as agents for the organisation, if they believe the organisation recognises their own good intentions and dedication, and it is the line managers who play a key role in communicating trust in the organisation and in subordinates (Zagenczyk et al. 2010).

Development in the stages of a relationship is reciprocal. In order to inspire trust the manager has to be seen to (or be believed to) trust the subordinate to an equal extent (Duck 1991). Thus the manager has to appear to be increasingly honest, open, communicative, authentic, and fully engaged in each micro-culture whilst maintaining a central core of hidden motives (necessary for the managerial role). However, true engagement and identification with each micro-culture is not only unrealistic, but positively dangerous for the individual's perceived role as a mediator of the organisational culture, and thus for their employability. The manager's role is also threatened by being too successful as a developmental change agent. There is an analogy here with education and training. If a course is truly successful and the learning fully integrated, then it is unlikely that it will be fully credited with effecting the change, as people are proud to believe that they are the force behind their own development. I suggest that the same principle holds for the manager as a change agent. Promotion prospects are not served well by invisibility.

To summarise, in order to protect his or her role, the developmental manager needs to inspire trust by generating the appearance of openness, whilst hiding the manipulative level of action inherent in management; and he or she needs to have sufficient process skills to facilitate the appearance of cooperative working, whilst maintaining a form of power that is hidden from subordinates but is apparent to superiors. In walking the boundaries of role the developmental manager treads a slippery path that is only wide enough for one.

3. Protective of Life Balance: *Work-life Balance, Heavy Work Investment, and Managerial Resistance*

For many managers achievement at work is not just about the possibility of promotion and their marketability; it is also about their organisation-based self-esteem associated with the achievement of challenging work experience, positive feedback from significant work colleagues, and feelings of value, importance, efficacy, and competence (Pierce & Gardner 2004). As a good manager, they may also wish to help others improve their self-esteem with challenges tailored to the individual and acceptance of the employee's self-direction and self-control (Swann et al. 2007). In order to help their staff develop, the manager also needs to trust them to develop their own agency, but there are several problems with this. As Vickers & Fox (2005) show, middle managers can covertly change organisational strategy, although working against the views of top management. How far does that trust go?

The sense of agency and self-esteem gained through achievement at work is important to many people and contributes to coping, job performance, and job satisfaction (Judge & Bono 2001). For some who make a heavy investment in work, this can become a compulsion (workaholics). Astak-hova & Hogue (2014) argue that it is important to consider the simulta-neous influences of biology, psychology, and social factors on heavy work investment, as such investment and its import changes with cultural values and circumstance. For example, counterintuitively, Snir et al. (2009) found that women devote more time to work after becoming parents and men devote less. Heavy work investment could be seen as 'an employer's dream' (Kiechel 1989: 50), but it is closely connected to problems with physical and mental health and overall well-being (Schaufeli et al. 2009). It is also disrup-tive for individuals, their families, and the organisation (Bonebright et al. 2000). A key source of stress for the agent is found in situations in which the demands of work and family roles are mutually incompatible. There are two distinct forms of conflict, when work interferes with family life and vice versa (Mesmer-Magnus & Viswesvaran 2005), but both are disruptive and require considerable effort from the agent in trying to meet competing role demands (Sonnentag & Zijlstra 2006), leading to a downward spiral of low resources, fatigue, and emotional exhaustion (Hall et al. 2010).

Glaser & Hecht (2013) found that all the individuals they studied, regard-less of their self-efficacy beliefs, viewed increases in work-to-family conflict as an increasingly harmful threat to self-esteem; however, in family-to-work conflict they found that it was those with the highest levels of self-efficacy that were most affected by high levels of conflict, and it was likely that they became frustrated by trying to control things that simply cannot be con-trolled. Individuals low in self-efficacy appear to be more accepting of things that they perceive as unchangeable or outside of their control and suffer less emotional exhaustion, possibly because they place less blame and less responsibility to resolve the conflict upon themselves (Moore 2000). The anticipation of conflict has similar effects (Brosschot et al. 2006), though if seen as a challenge rather than a threat the outcome is more positive, and challenging inter-role conflicts might be seen as an opportunity for growth (McNall et al. 2010).

The approach to work-family issues that is adopted by the organisation is key to the impact of conflicts upon the agent (Behson 2002). Supervi-sors play an important role, as does the implementation of family-friendly policies and enhancing worker autonomy (Valcour 2007). Wider cultural expectations also play a part. For example, Zhang et al. (2012) found that for Chinese managers, work-family conflict was positively associated with affective commitment and did not associate with turnover intentions, whereas the reverse was the case for Western managers. This appears to contradict the view that people who reside in countries with collectivist values, such as China, place more importance on family than on work pursuits (Yang et al. 2000). However, collectivism encourages the Chinese to work for the welfare of the family (Spector et al. 2007) and work is seen as adding to family benefits, rather than competing with them (Lobel 1991). Chinese families are said to see work as benefiting the whole family and require a strong commitment from the whole family to the work role (Lu et al. 2006). In contrast, Western workers view work as an instrumental means to enhancing their own careers (Yang et al. 2000) and so are less likely to gain family support in work-family conflicts.

The effects of work-family conflict mitigate against the idea that heavy work investment is good for the organisation. It is rarely good for the agent, and in attempting to resolve the conflict the agent may resort to behaviour inconsistent with the organisation's requirements. Organisational misbehaviour is, in itself, often conflicted (Dalton et al. 2007), leading to shirking, consumption of office goods, or other opportunistic behavior by managers (Fama & Jensen 1983). A common assumption is that with sufficient financial incentive an agent will support the needs of the organisation over and above their own preferences (Nyberg et al. 2010); however, wider issues such as family, but also personal values, broken psychological contracts, issues of conscience, and concern for social benefit, can intrude and cause the agent to question their commitment to their colleagues and the organisation.

4. Protective of Self: *Development, Control, and Protecting the Self*

The above discussion has focused upon inter-role conflict. However, with a move towards collectivity, managers are likely to experience a greater incidence of person-role conflict (Smith & Peterson 1988: 111). It is this dilemma, that of supporting the self within the demands of the role, that is explored below. As discussed in Chapters 9 and 16, a positive view of selfhood is correlated with high performance, increased ethicality and ability to relate to others, and a decrease in ethnic prejudice and polarisation, with reduced levels of anxiety. High self-acceptance is generated by open, authentic, and mutually risky communication with others (Duck 1991). This is hard to engender as a manager.

The traditional approach to relating to others (one of evaluation, competition, restriction in establishing warm personal relationships, routine activities, power-based monologue, and a focus upon the right answer) is correlated with low self-esteem, whereas a participatory approach (defined as active, other-centred, creating divergent thinking, and generating time for others to talk) is related to high self-concept (Burns 1984). Fey (1954) found that prototypic 'well-adjusted' people with high self-other acceptance are perceived not to 'need' friendships; their psychological robustness is resented, and they become isolated by those with lower self-acceptance who are able to meet each other's feelings of being needed. The withdrawal of friendship, however, is likely to lead to a lessening of self-acceptance, which in turn can be rewarded by increased friendship. If social support is not provided the individual increases the distance between themselves and others in order to protect their self-concept, thereby preserving psychological security by creating an out-group that can be classed by the individual as both alien and of lower social standing (Burns 1984). It is possible that this mechanism is co-regulatory, and thus level of self-acceptance becomes one of the norms of the micro-culture.

It is unclear to what extent different views of selfhood co-vary with the concept of control over self or others. The Japanese manager described by Pascale appears to have control over others as given by societal views of seniority and position, even though pragmatically appropriate limitations of the ego are seen as a virtue. We could infer that he is content to adopt an external locus of control in accepting societal definitions of his role as equivalent to his self-concept. Will his perception of his selfhood change as his role changes, and how does he cope with a multiplicity of roles presenting conflicting demands? In other words, when working in a collectivity of equals, as opposed to a hierarchical collectivity, will he experience more person-role conflict? Co-regulation negates the notion of control to the extent that behaviour and goals are not planned in advance but emerge creatively out of social discourse, in which individuals are prized for their intrinsic value as human beings. By contrast, a controlling relationship is rigid and acceptance is conditional upon meeting the evaluative criteria of others.

It is worth reflecting upon the discussion about individual differences in locus of control in the section about structure above. It was suggested there that a moderately internal locus of control was correlated with adaptation, cooperation, and the ability to work successfully across cultures. Approaches typified by consensual vs. rigid relationships seem to stand on either side of this. The notion of holistic agency (see Chapter 3), in which self-knowledge and the managing of one's boundaries replaces the need for control, can be seen as a fulcrum between these states, although the extent to which it is anything more than an unrealisable vision is debatable. A further aspect of both self-concept and development has been alluded to above—that of ethicality. This approach is one in which the individual is continually reanalysing their role in the creation and development of the processes they are part of. In doing so, they are confronting their own ideas, unsurfaced assumptions, biases, and fears (Argyris 1990), thereby addressing the development of themselves and others from an ethical standpoint. Yet the development of ethical awareness is an interactive process (Snell

1993) relying upon openness and understanding of others. The individual needs to be open with others for the sake of their own development, but their managerial and developmental roles prevent authentic openness.

Therefore, the role of the developmental manager largely precludes the possibility of true and open friendship with colleagues or subordinates. The manager is unlikely to find sufficient social support to maintain or generate a high level of self-acceptance, and is therefore likely to become increasingly isolated in order to protect his or her selfhood. In so far as developmental change is the process of elaborating, dissolving, comparing, and consolidating dialogical self-frames, this leads to lack of personal development and reduced ability to develop others. The self, or sense of self-cohesion, becomes barricaded behind a facade of openness and authenticity. The boundary becomes a wall.

5. Communicative: *Process and Communication*

It could be that the manager can find support outside the workplace, so the isolation described above is only felt by those whose life is their work. Indeed, one of the positive benefits of developmental courses is the ability to further one's self-development in a supportive and confidential arena. However, one of the essential differences between the traditional manager and the manager as a change agent is the increased need for working with process, influencing the process of groups, and rooting managerial power in processual ability. As was illustrated in the description of the debriefing of the communications exercise in Chapter 3, talking about the task is relatively easy in comparison to talking about process.

The words used to describe processual events represent a different, and difficult-to-define, language. As happened to me once, we could say something like: 'X said, "If you want promotion, you will need to dress more smartly" to Y, who replied, "I want to be promoted for my work, not your view of my dress sense"'; thus we could offer a factual description of who said what. This could be extended by contributing an observation: 'Y's tone of voice and body language indicated strong anger', and an interpretation: 'Y does not like being labelled as scruffy and therefore non-promotable by X'. However, even as observers, we are still part of the process. The deeper we go into the description the more we rely on our interpretation of our perception of the event. Our perception of the event will be coloured by our feelings towards X and Y, and our interpretation will be influenced by (amongst other things) our view of the managerial role, our own feelings of being labelled, and our own dress sense. The greater our experience of our own fallibility of interpretation (gained by openly discussing what was happening with X and Y, and other observers of the interaction) and the greater our self-knowledge (understanding our own hidden agendas and motivations), the more likely we are to be able to be flexible and realistic in our interpretation of the event.

This is not simple. Discussing the event with those who were there requires all participants to be able to talk the language of process, to mean the same things by that language, and to be able to surface their subconscious interpretations and the words to describe them. Perhaps most importantly, they must also be willing to open their interpretations, feelings, and blind spots to the scrutiny of others. Furthermore, the process of learning this language is difficult. Although there may be common words, their meanings may be individual. Joint experience of the event might allow the participants to develop some consensus in the meanings attributed to it and thus to start to define the language for themselves, assuming a reflexive and complementary view of the development of language and meaning (Whorf 1957). Experience of many events with different players might lead to a form of common understanding. Even so, knowing the words does not mean that they are easy to use, and voicing them too clearly might lead to reification of the word and subsequent loss of the import of the meaning for each individual (Lee 1995).

The managers as change agents, described at the start of this paper, gave examples of times when an event had affected them so deeply that they had severe physical reactions after the event (vomiting, etc.). They reported being unable to articulate the subconscious reasons for this or to find the words to describe what was happening to them or to rationalise it. This was the case even with colleagues who were working collaboratively with them at that event, and who had therefore been a highly supportive part of the process. To explain the personal implications of an event to someone who was not part of it was seen to be much harder. To explain them to a person who neither had the language nor was there was seen as almost impossible.

In order to become an effective change agent the individual needs to breach the wall they have constructed around their selfhood through communication with others at a processual level. This cannot be done at work because of the need to 'manage' others, and it is hard to do elsewhere because others will not understand the language or the events to which it relates.

CONCLUSIONS

This account is intended to open up a line of thought rather than present a clear directive overview. Much of the evidence I have drawn upon is correlational, descriptive, and open to interpretation. I have argued that the nature of management in organisations with flatter management structures, and with an attendant increase in the mobility of the manager across these structures, has similarities to working cross-culturally. However socially skilled the individual is, it is an inherently isolating organisational structure that exacerbates the personal costs of working as a developmental manager. Working as a change agent (whether internal or external to the organisation) exacerbates the personal costs of an inherently isolating structure. The role of manager of others and that of empowering and developing others (as in transformational leadership, manager as developer, and the learning organisation) are functionally mutually exclusive. In being asked to perform both roles managers are requested, in the first instance, to transmit the organisational mores, to take full responsibility for the work of their staff, and to evaluate and appraise their staff. At the same time, in the latter case, they are being asked to create a climate of trust, openness, and equality with their subordinates and colleagues. These two positions are reconciled by giving the appearance of openness whilst maintaining a central, hidden, core from which decisions to influence or manipulate are made. In hiding the inner self, the manager reduces the opportunities for 'true' contact with others and limits their own self-development, becoming increasingly isolated from those that might provide social support. Further, as managers are increasingly expected to use personal power in working with the processes of interactions, they need to gain the language of process. Processual language, however, is normally co-defined by actors in the experience. It is, by its very nature, hard to translate for those who are not intimately involved. Therefore potential for isolation can be seen as an integral part of working with process.

In so far as these effects are structurally derived (albeit that the structure itself is co-regulated), they cannot be avoided—they can, however, be ameliorated. This line of thought has two main implications. The first is the need to create opportunity for managers to communicate with others in an open and authentic way, in situations that will not be affected by their managerial or developmental roles. Some managers already develop networks and social support systems suitable for themselves. One way forward might be the generation of organisational support for internal and external networking that is focused upon personal as well as task development, and thereby the creation of an organisational culture that values social support for the whole person. The second main implication is the need to help managers develop the language of process, enabling them to both communicate and influence others more efficaciously. However, as with the learning of any foreign language, the organisational and educational systems need to develop a value base that creates an understanding of the need for an alternative language, supports its exploration, and provides the opportunity to practice.

Enhanced managerial ethicality, self-knowledge, communication, and processual language use all highlight the need for developmental workshops and training. This is at a time when competitive forces encourage the organisation to look to fast and measurable outcomes, conformity, and task orientation at the expense of longer-term learning and development (see Chapter 18). If the organisation cannot support 'development' of their developmental managers, it will be the individuals who pay the cost.

I have presented a bleak and provocative picture of isolation as an inherent part of agency. Not all change agents become isolated; some develop networks and social support systems suitable for themselves. They learn to manage the boundaries of the micro-cultures, protect their role, maintain their selfhood, and find ways of communicating with others. However, the thoughts presented here do have relevance at several functional levels.

If organisational norms are dynamically created, co-defined, and regulated (albeit subconsciously) by individuals, then research needs to incorporate an awareness of the underlying processes that drive organisational structure and individual agency. Research into each of culture, structure, strategy, managerial role and competencies, leadership, group behaviour, and individual agency (amongst others) has traditionally been conducted as if they were isolated areas of study. These thoughts pose a call to address the interrelationship between these areas from an interdisciplinary, multilevel, and dynamic approach that relates the findings from one area of investigation to the implications they have for other areas, and that recognises the underlying processes that help inform the rich picture.

The notions contained within this account also present a challenge to management educators. Management education takes a wide variety of forms, from short-cycle in-house skills training to long-cycle post-experience corporate master's programmes; from self-development to theoretically based education. All forms of provision are made easier to transmit (and test) by structuring and subdividing the learning. However, they all, at some stage, refer to individuals and organisations. If the above arguments have any validity, then educational provision will gain increasing relevance as it acknowledges the existence of underlying processes and the interrelationship between individual and structure.

Furthermore, whatever our management discipline, if we subscribe in any way to the view that a manager is also a change agent, then we need to take some responsibility for the implications this has for the managers and change agents who attend our courses and who are presented a vision of better ways of working, only to find that in attempting to put into practice what they have learnt they face the possibility of becoming increasingly isolated. Notions of transformational leadership, the developmental manager, and agents of change are all rooted in the development of personal power and the ability to work with process. These, in turn, are rooted in learning the skills and attributes as well as the language of process, in the making explicit of implicit processes, and in working towards continuing self-development, self-knowledge, and the exploration of the ethical core of Adler's multicultural man. None of these are traditionally found in management curricula. In addition, educational provision that explicitly addresses the personal costs of managerial working is rare, and that which attempts to develop personal resources to counter the costs is more normally classed as 'almost psychotherapy' rather than 'management'. For the vision to be implementable it needs to come in wrapping that helps engender the necessary attributes, and should carry both health warnings and suggestions for self-preservation.

REFERENCES

Adler PS (1974) 'Beyond cultural identity: Reflections on cultural and multicultural man', *Topics in Culture Learning: 2*. Honolulu: East-West Culture Learning Institute.

Andersen NÅ (2007) 'Creating the client who can create himself and his own fate: The tragedy of the citizens' contract', *Qualitative Sociology Review* 3(2)119–143.

Argyris C (1990). *Overcoming Organisational Defences*. Boston, MA: Allyn and Bacon.

Arthur MB & Rousseau DM (2001) *The Boundaryless Career: A New Employment Principle for a New Organizational Era*. New York: Oxford University Press.

Astakhova M & Hogue M (2014) 'A heavy work investment typology: A biopsychosocial Framework', *Journal of Managerial Psychology* 29(1)81–99.

Bartunek JM & Moch MK (1987) 'First-order, second-order, and third-order change and organisation development interventions: A cognitive approach', *Journal of Applied Behavioural Science* 23: 483–500.

Bass BM (1985) *Leadership and Performance beyond Expectations*. New York: Free Press.

Battilana J (2006) 'Agency and institutions: The enabling role of individuals' social position', *Organization* 13(5)653–676.

Battilana J & D'Aunno T (2009) 'Institutional Work and the Paradox of Embedded Agency', in Lawrence T, Suddaby R, & Leca B (Eds) *Institutional Work: Actors and Agency in Institutional Studies of Organizations*: 31–58. Cambridge: Cambridge University Press.

Battilana J, Leca B, & Boxenbaum E (2009) 'How actors change institutions: Towards a theory of institutional entrepreneurship', *The Academy of Management Annals* 3(1)65–107.

Behson SJ (2002) 'Which dominates? The relative importance of work-family organizational support and general organizational context on employee outcomes', *Journal of Vocational Behavior* 61: 53–72.

Beverungen A, Dunne S, & Hoedemækers C (2009) 'The university of finance', *Ephemera* 9(4)261–270.

Beverungen A, Otto B, Spoelstra S, & Kenny K (2013) 'Free work', *Ephemera* 13(1)1–9.

Bochner S (1982) 'The social psychology of Cross-cultural relations', in Bochner S (Ed) *Cultures in Contact: Studies in Cross-cultural Interaction*: 5–44. Oxford: Pergamon.

Bonebright CA, Clay DL, & Ankenmann RD (2000) 'The relationship of workaholism with work-life conflict, life satisfaction, and purpose in life', *Journal of Counseling Psychology* 47(4)469–477.

Breckler S & Greenwald A (1986) 'Motivational Facets of the Self', in Sorentino R & Higgins T (Eds) *Handbook of Motivation and Cognition*: 145–164. New York: Guildford.

Brosschot JF, Gerin W, & Thayer JS (2006) 'The perseverative cognition hypothesis: A review of worry, prolonged stress-related physiological activation, and health', *Journal of Psychosomatic Research* 60(2)113–124.

Burns JM (1978) *Leadership*. New York: Harper and Row.

Burns RB (1984) *The Self Concept: In Theory, Measurement, Development and Behaviour*. New York: Longman.

Chertkovskaya E, Watt P, Trame S, & Spoelstra S (2013) 'Giving notice to employ-ability', *Ephemera* 13(4)701–716.

Clarke M & Patrickson M (2008) 'The new covenant of employability', *Employee Relations* 30(2)121–141.

Cremin C (2010) 'Never employable enough: The (im)possibility of satisfying the boss's desire', *Organization* 17(2)131–149.

Czarniawska B (2014) *A Theory of Organizing*. Cheltenham, UK: Edward Elgar.

Dalton DR, Hitt MA, Certo ST, & Dalton CM (2007) 'Chapter 1: The fundamental agency problem and its mitigation', in Walsh JF & Brief AP (Eds) *Academy of Management annals* 1: 1–64. New York: Erlbaum.

DiMaggio P & Powell WW (1991) 'Introduction', in Powell WW & DiMaggio P (Eds) *The New Institutionalism in Organizational Analysis:* 1–38. Chicago, IL: University of Chicago Press.

Duck S (1991) *Understanding Relationships*. New York: Guildford.

Fama EF & Jensen MC (1983) 'Agency problems and residual claims', *Journal of Law and Economics* 26: 327–359.

Fejes A (2010) 'Discourses on employability: Constituting the responsible citizen', *Studies in Continuing Education,* 32(2)89–102.

Ferlie E & Bennett C (1992) 'Patterns of strategic change in health care: District Health Authorities respond to aids', *British Journal of Management* 3: 21–37.

Fey WF (1954) 'The acceptance of self and others and its relation to Therapy Readi-ness', *Journal of Clinical Psychology* 10: 266–269.

Furnham A & Bochner S (1986) *Culture Shock: Psychological Reactions to Unfa-miliar Environments*. London: Routledge.

Glaser W & Hecht DT (2013) 'Work-family conflicts, threat-appraisal, self-efficacy and emotional exhaustion', *Journal of Managerial Psychology* 28(2)164–182.

Goodrick E & Reay T (2011) 'Constellations of institutional logics', *Work and Occupations* 38(3)372–416.

Graen GB, Cashman JF, Ginsgurgh S, & Schiemann W (1978) 'Effects of linking-pin quality upon the quality of working life of lower participants: A longitudinal investigation of the managerial understructure', *Administrative Science Quar-terly* 22: 491–504.

Hales C (2002) 'Bureaucracy-lite and continuities in managerial work', *British Jour-nal of Management* 13: 51–66.

Hall GB, Dollard MF, Tuckey MR, Winefield AH, & Thompson BM (2010) 'Job demands, work-family conflict, and emotional exhaustion in police officers: A longitudinal test of competing theories', *Journal of Occupational and Organi-zational Psychology* 83: 237–250.

Hawkins P (1999) *The Art of Building Windmills: Career Tactics for the 21st Cen-tury*. Liverpool: Graduate into Employment Unit, University of Liverpool.

Heimans J & Timms H (2014) 'Understanding "New Power"', *Harvard Business Review* 92(12)48–56.

Hill LA (2003) *Becoming a Manager: How New Managers Master the Challenges of Leadership*. Boston: Harvard Business School Press.

Holmqvist M (2009) *The Disabling State of an Active Society*. Farnham: Ashgate Publishing.

Jarzabkowski P (2005) *Strategy as Practice: An Activity-based Approach*. London: SAGE.

Judge TA & Bono JE (2001) 'Relationship of core self-evaluations traits—self-esteem, generalized self-efficacy, locus of control, and emotional stability—with job satisfaction and job performance: a meta-analysis', *Journal of Applied Psychology* 86(1)80–92.

Kanter RM (1989) *When Giants Learn to Dance: Mastering the Challenges of Strategy, Management and Careers in the 1990s.* New York: Simon and Schuster.

Kiechel W III (1989) 'The workaholic generation', *Fortune* 119: 50–62.

Kiggundu MN (1981) 'Task interdependence and the theory of job design', *Academy of Management Review* 6: 499–508.

Kinsman J (1990) *Millennium: Towards Tomorrow's Society.* London: Allen and Co.

Knoll DL & Gill H (2011) 'Antecedents of trust in supervisors, subordinates, and peers', *Journal of Managerial Psychology* 26(4)313–330.

Komulainen K, Korhonen M, & Räty H (2009) 'Risk-taking abilities for everyone?', *Gender and Education* 21(6)631–649.

Lawrence TB, Suddaby R, & Leca B (2011) 'Institutional work: Refocusing institutional studies of organization', *Journal of Management Inquiry* 20(1)52–58.

Lee CP, Earley PC, Lituchy TR, & Wagner M (1991) 'Relation of goal setting and goal sharing to performance and conflict for interdependent tasks', *British Journal of Management* 2:33–39.

Lee MM (1991) 'Playing the Guru: Inequality of power in interpersonal relationships', *Management Education and Development* 22: 302–309.

Lee MM (1994) 'The isolated manager: Walking the boundaries of the microculture', in Westall O (Ed) *Proceedings of British Academy of Management conference:* 111–128. Lancaster, UK: Lancaster University.

Lee MM (1995) 'Action Learning as a Cross-cultural Tool', in Stewart J & McGoldrick J (Eds) *HRD: Perspectives, Strategies and Practice:* 240–260. London: Pitman.

Levitas R (2005) *The Inclusive Society: Social Exclusion and New Labour.* Basingstoke: Palgrave Macmillan.

Lobel SA (1991) 'Allocation of investment in work and family roles', *Academy of Management Review* 16(3)507–521.

Lu L, Gilmour R, Kao SF, & Huang MT (2006) 'A cross-cultural study of work/family demands, work/family conflict and wellbeing: The Taiwanese vs British', *Career Development International* 11(1)9–27.

Marshall J & Stewart R (1981a) "Managers' job perceptions: Part 1: Their overall frameworks and working strategies', *Journal of Management Studies* 18: 177–189.

Marshall J & Stewart R (1981b) "Managers' job perceptions: Part 2: Opportunities for and attitudes to choice', *Journal of Management Studies* 18: 263–275.

Martinko MJ & Gardner WL (1987) 'The leader/member attribution process', *Academy of Management Review* 12: 235–249.

McNall LA, Nicklin JM, & Masuda AD (2010) 'A meta-analytic review of the consequences associated with work-family enrichment', *Journal of Business and Psychology* 25: 381–396.

Mesmer-Magnus JR & Viswesvaran C (2005) 'Convergence between measures of work-to-family and family-to-work conflict: a meta-analytic examination', *Journal of Vocational Behavior* 67(2)215–232.

Mintzberg H (2009) *Managing*. San Francisco: Berrett-Koehler.

Monroe SM, Imhoff DF, Wise DB, & Harris JE (1983) 'Prediction of psychological symptoms under High-Risk psychosocial circumstances', *Journal of Abnormal Psychology* 9: 338–350.

Moore JE (2000) 'Why is this happening? A causal attribution approach to work exhaustion consequences', *Academy of Management Review* 25(2)335–349.

Neves P & Eisenberger R (2014) 'Perceived organizational support and risk taking', *Journal of Managerial Psychology* 29(2)187–205.

Nyberg AJ, Fulmer IS, Gerhart B, & Carpenter MA 2010) 'Agency theory revisited: CEO return and shareholder interest alignment', *Academy of Management Journal* 53(5)1029–1049.

Orr JE (1996) *Talking about Machines: An Ethnography of a Modern Job*. New York: Cornell University Press.

Pascale R (1990) *Managing on the Edge*. London: Penguin.

Pascale RT (1978) 'Zen and the art of management', *Harvard Business Review* 6(2)153–162.

Pfeffer J (1981) 'Management as symbolic action', in Cummings LL & Staw BM (Eds) *Research in Organisational Behaviour* 3: 1–52. Greenwich, CT: JAI Press.

Pierce JL & Gardner DG (2004) 'Self-esteem within the work and organizational context', *Journal of Management* 30(5)591–622.

Raelin JA (2003) *Creating Leaderful Organisations*. San Francisco: Berrett Koehler.

Reischauer EO (1977) *The Japanese*. Cambridge, MA: Harvard University Press.

Roethlisberger FJ (1945) 'The industrial foreman: Master and victim of double-talk', *Harvard Business Review* 23: 283–294.

Rogers CR (1959) 'A Theory of Therapy, Personality, and Interpersonal Relationships as Developed in the Client-Centred Framework', in Koch S (Ed) *Psychology: A Study of a Science, Vol. 3*: 184–256. New York: McGraw-Hill.

Rohlen TP (1974) *For Harmony and Strength: Japanese White-collar Organization in Anthropological Perspective*. Berkeley: University of California Press.

Samovar LA & Porter RE (1976) *Intercultural Communications: A Reader*. Belmont, CA: Wadsworth Publishing Company.

Schaufeli WB, Bakker AB, & Van Rhenen W (2009) 'How changes in job demands and resources predict burnout, work engagement, and sickness absenteeism', *Journal of Organizational Behavior* 30(7)893–917.

Smets M & Jarzabkowski P (2013) 'Reconstructing institutional complexity in practice: A relational model of institutional work and complexity', *Human Relations* 66(10)1279–1309.

Smets M, Morris T, & Greenwood R (2012) 'From practice to field: A multi-level model of practice-driven institutional change', *Academy of Management Journal* 55(4)877–904.

Smith PB & Peterson MF (1988) *Leadership, Organisations and Culture*. London: Sage.

Smith PB, Moscow D, Cooper CL, & Berger M (1969) 'Relationships between managers and their work associates', *Administrative Science Quarterly* 14: 338–345.

Smith RJ (1983) *Japanese Society: Tradition, Self and the Social Order*. Cambridge: Cambridge University Press.

Snell R (1993) *Developing Skills for Ethical Management*. London: Chapmann Hall.

Snir R, Harpaz I, & Ben-Baruch D (2009) 'Centrality of and investment in work and family among Israeli high-tech workers', *Cross-Cultural Research* 43(4)366–385.

Sonnentag S & Zijlstra FRH (2006) 'Job characteristics and off-job activities as predictors of need for recovery, well-being, and fatigue', *Journal of Applied Psychology* 91(2)330–350.

Southwood I (2011) *Non-Stop Inertia*. Washington: Zero Books.

Spector PE, Allen TD, Poelmans S, Lapierre LM, Cooper CL, Sanchez JI, Abarca N, Alexandrova M, Beham B, & Brough P (2007) 'Cross-national differences in relationships of work demands, job satisfaction and turnover intentions with work-family conflict', *Personnel Psychology* 60(4)805–835.

Swann WB, Chang-Schneider C, & McClarty KL (2007) 'Do people's self-views matter? Self-concept and self-esteem in everyday life', *American Psychologist* 62(2)84–94.

Trower P, Bryant B, & Argyle M (1978) *Social Skills and Mental Health*. London: Methuen.

Tsoukas H & Cummings S (1997) 'Marginalization and recovery: The emergence of Aristotelian themes in organization studies', *Organization Studies* 18(4)655–683.

Turnbull S (2014) 'Worldly Leadership: Uncovering Ancient and Indigenous Leadership Wisdom for a More Sustainable World', in Lee MM (Ed) *HRD as We Know It*: 115–126. New York: Routledge.

Valcour M (2007) 'Work-based resources as moderators of the relationship between work hours and satisfaction with work-family balance', *Journal of Applied Psychology* 92: 1512–1523.

Vickers D & Fox S (2005) 'Powers in a Factory', in Czarniawska B & Hernes T (Eds) *Actor-Network Theory and Organising*: 129–144. Copenhagen: Liber.

Whorf B (1957) '*Language, Thought and Reality*: Selected Writings of Benjamin Lee Whorf'. Cambridge, Mass: MIT Press.

Williams C (2005) 'The discursive construction of the 'competent' learner-worker', *Studies in Continuing Education* 27(1)33–49.

Wiseman RM & Gomez-Mejia LR (1998) 'A behavioral agency model of managerial risk taking', *Academy of Management Review* 23: 133–153.

Yang NN, Chen CC, Choi J, & Zou YM (2000) 'Sources of work-family conflict: A Sino-US comparison of the effects of work and family demands', *Academy of Management Journal* 43(1)113–123.

Zagencryk TJ, Scott KD, Gibney R, Murrell AJ, & Thatcher JB (2010) 'Social influence and perceived organizational support: a social networks approach', *Organizational Behavior and Human Decision Processes* 11: 127–138.

Zhang M, Griffeth RW, & Fried DD (2012) 'Work-family conflict and individual consequences', *Journal of Managerial Psychology* 27(7)696–713.

Zuboff S (1988) *In the Age of the Smart Machine*. New York: Basic.

Section 5

Aspects of Structure

For some, agency is about the conscious and deliberate expenditure of effort to achieve something specific. For others it is about the degree of influence the agent has upon the structure. Whilst accepting these are part of agency, in the previous section I widen the debate to question the role of consciousness, the impotency and the isolation of agency. In the previous section I presented agency as the other side of structure, as in the other side of the coin. A coin is not a coin without both sides. We can't look at both sides together and have to adopt either one or the other viewpoint, but we know they both exist. We would not have structure without agency or agency without structure. As we exist in the world alongside others we adopt a form of agency even if we feel pretty powerless about it or prefer not to be involved. Whether we do or don't do something has an effect upon others. This might not be deliberate, and it might not be the effect we were seeking, but the existence of that effect remains. ('All that is necessary for the triumph of evil is that good men do nothing', often attributed to Edmund Burke). We are agents by the very nature of our existence, and as such, everything we do or think is informed by structure and helps co-create new structures.

This final section, therefore, focuses upon the structured world we help create, the structures that support and hinder, confine and define us. We now live in the Anthropocene—an age created by man: a time in which humans have replaced nature as the dominant environmental force on Earth. The structures around us are physical and conceptual, geographic and symbolic, concrete and abstract; from the meme of the meme (Chapter 3) to the International Space Station and beyond, this world is of our making. For better or worse, richer or poorer, in sickness and in health, we are married to this world and what we do, the structures we create, will affect us now and in the future for (hopefully) many generations to come.

The first chapter in this section (Chapter 16) presents a global picture of human structures and shifting boundaries. This chapter presents a much wider view of HRD than is normally considered, locating HRD at the centre of global influences. It also looks at the way the world is changing, and the changing nature of HRD within this. This is the largest and most heavily referenced chapter in the book, but even so, I can only skim the surface here—to do more would be to write a second book.

Chapter 17 focuses on ethics, and thus the rules that we develop by which we can work together. Many of the rules and ways of working are subconscious—we are rarely aware of them or aware of following them—but several organisations are now actively specifying rules of ethics for their members to follow. The suggestion is that these rules, although well intended, are often chimeric. Despite the structures we build, our ethics boil down to on-the-spot decision-making, a case of self and other that is largely independent of wider societal rules. Indeed there is the danger that a rule might become reified such that people no longer think it is important to reflect or critically consider the situation because they 'know' they are following the rules.

The final chapter in this section (Chapter 18) builds on some of the threads in Chapters 8 and 16 in particular, and looks to the future—asking what sort of future we want to build. In a discussion of alternative ways of work I offer the example of a cooperative volunteer-driven start-up telecoms company, to consider as one (of many) possible futures. I then explore the role of management education: Are we empowering others, helping them to be agents of their own lives ('becoming' in a holistic world)—or are we fitting them into holes of others' design? Who are our masters and what are the consequences of our role?

I conclude the main arguments of this book with Chapter 19. In this I look back to the introduction to the book and explore the holistic view of HRD and the role of the agent within that (thus my model of holistic agency). I reiterate the way in which the sections of the book (self and other, agency and structure) pull together to provide a coherent whole, one that is based upon evolutionary principles and permeates our existence. I reinforce the idea of our existence as one of emergence and becoming—an agent alongside others, co-regulating and co-creating our past, present, and future.

Chapter 20 briefly outlines the antecedents to the chapters in this book. As I explained at the beginning of the book, I have largely failed in my attempts to be a 'good academic' and publish a consistent stream of papers around one topic in weighty, well-recognised journals. I have picked up topics that I found to be of interest and I have published in all sorts of strange places. This book is intended to bring some of these disparate sources together, and each chapter is based upon a previously published paper. This last chapter acknowledges those sources and tells some of the stories behind them.

16 Boundaries and Change

This chapter extends the argument for the adoption of a holistic perspective of HRD that I laid out in Chapter 3. In order to set the scene I first look at different views of management and their implications for HRD. I then step sideways to look at global changes and their impact upon us, before returning to the implications for HR at the end of this chapter. There are some issues, such as trust, that reverberate throughout this and are not easily pigeonholed; similarly, and as might be expected, the big four (structure, agency, self, and other) are constantly part of this account, in the same way that they are part of humanity.

This chapter establishes the archetypal notion of 'structure' as the polar opposite to 'agency'. Earlier in the book I explored how we develop structure in our thoughts and memories. We learn to identify what constitutes a cat through developing a representation of an idealised cat and through finding out what it is not. Our construct of the cat is structured in a way that accords with the structure of the physical world (Chapter 4). We operate through an imaginary-time processor, which we like to call consciousness, which mimics the structure of the world outside (Chapter 13). More than that, we interpret and structure our world to accord with our understanding of the past and present, and our hopes for the future (Chapter 5). We now live in the Anthropocene age, one created by man (Crutzen & Stoermer 2000), a time in which humans have replaced nature as the dominant environmental force on Earth (Ruddiman et al. 2015). As we create structures we also create boundaries, and manage them in a range of different ways (Kreiner et al. 2009). The erection of a boundary or 'mental fence' (Zerubavel 1991) is both a defence mechanism and a conceptual convenience. The physical and conceptual structures and boundaries of our existence are of our own making—as is their evolution.

UNDERSTANDINGS OF HRD

It might seem that many of those boundaries, such as geographical and political boundaries, are beyond the remit of HRD. In this chapter I shall challenge that view: I argue that in so far as holistic agency is applicable to our existence then the nature of HRD, as the glue that holds it together, is better understood by taking into account the boundaries that we create, and is better practised by taking into account the many changes that are happening across these boundaries. As I discuss in Lee (2015), HRD has a history of change. People have been 'doing' what could have been called HRD for many years, but these activities were not initially conceptualized as HRD—it is only we looking backwards who now call 'it' HRD. It rose to the fore alongside ideas of management, and if management includes employment situations in which one person directs and coordinates the work of others, then the history of HR goes back to the dawn of human civilisation, when the Egyptian pharaohs and Chinese emperors directed tens of thousands of labourers in the building of the Great Pyramid and Great Wall (Kaufman 2014).

I outlined four approaches to management in Chapter 3—namely, the classical, the scientific, the processual, and the phenomenological. Each entails a different view of HRD. In the classical approach, HRD is about selecting the right people, ensuring that they are fully conversant with past experience and current practice, and that they are committed both to their calling and to the organisations in which they will subsequently work. Most staff development occurs within the organisation, in what would best be seen as apprenticeships, with a focus on the teaching of good practice through the use of cases as exemplars. To a certain extent, externally accepted qualifications are seen as an inducement to job mobility and hence organisational instability. This approach is marked by 'obedience, application, energy, behaviour and outward marks of respect in accordance with agreed rules and customs; subordination of individual interest to general interest through firmness, example, fair agreements and constant supervision; equity, based on kindness and justice, to encourage personnel in their duties' (Morgan 1986: 26). From this perspective, the role of HRD is to ensure that all members of the organisation have the knowledge and skills necessary for the completion of their tasks.

The scientific approach is based upon the beliefs that human behaviour is rational; that people are motivated by economic criteria; and that managers, not workers, should hold all responsibility. The scientific selection of students, managerial staff, and academic faculty is trusted more than unscientific 'experience'. The focus is on the delineation of functional disciplines, departments within organisations, and compartmentalisation within business schools. It is here that HRD is labelled as a subset of HRM and called training; the development part of HRD is seen to be education and outside of the business school remit. This view remains the dominant paradigm, despite many critics (Lincoln 2012).

In the processual view of management it is the internal processes of the organisation that are re-engineered, rather than the individuals. The strict focus on strategy, efficiency, and technology is accused of leading to the dehumanisation of the workplace, and to an increase in managerial control. People manage their own employability, and the role of HR is to manage hiring and firing and to meet the organisation's strategic needs via the reworking of the organisation's internal processes.

The phenomenological perspective recognises that people are less motivated by economic rationality than by being given recognition and responsibility, and rarely have time to do any of the things textbooks rehearse, such as planning and analysing problems. The manager is seen as a stakeholder in his or her own education and development, alongside both the organisation and the provider. This is associated with the vision of multidisciplinary, flexible pathways of development and lifelong learning that benefit all the stakeholders, who together shape a learning organisation that is able to adapt and change in response to a changing environment. The role of HRD is that of supporting managers to develop their own ideas through tackling real problems in a work situation.

From this we can see that the normative academic view of HRD as 'training and development' and as a subset of HRM, in which HRM is seen as a subset of 'management', is rooted in the scientific approach to academic disciplines, management, and education, which emanated from the US (Boyacigiller & Adler 1991). It adopts the Western economic command and control paradigm of production lines and giant corporations, in which people are indeed seen as and managed as 'assets' or 'resources'. In this view, each organisation has clear boundaries, and each of the many little pegs that comprise the organisation knows its role within the organisational matrix. Each organisation also has a drive to expand and to profit (financially, metaphorically, and literally) from the destruction of its competitors. Bigger is better so long as all the pegs fit in their holes, so long as the environment remains static, and so long as resources remain unlimited (in other words—an endless supply of more pegs, more competitors to submerge, and more paying customers from which to profit).

However, if we look at different cultures we can see alternative approaches to HRD. Naturally, the whole project of tracing links through time and through cultures is much more complicated than I am presenting here, but, nevertheless, there are clear links. For example, in the 1990s there were very few management or HRD courses in German universities, because most managers received a long technical training followed by short bouts of skill-specific training within the organisation. Similarly, in Japanese companies on-the-job training was structured and systematised, job rotation was normal for most managers, and managers were expected to act as coaches/tutors for their subordinates (Storey 1991). In both, the onus was on the *organisation* to provide the education, training, and development. By contrast, in the US the first recorded case of a separate department for HR is from 1901 in the National Cash Register Co., which organised a unit dedicated to improving worker relations by properly handling employee grievances, discharges, and safety and other employee issues (DeNisi et al. 2014). The concern of the organisation was on people management, not development, and the onus was on the *individual* to progress via the gaining of qualifications. In addition, there was a split in HRD provision between *training* as a subset of HRM—part of the management function and provided by business schools—and *development,* which was provided through educational qualifications within schools of education.

In the UK there was a mixture of different schemes, alongside active government involvement, designed to improve that quality of management nationally (see Chapter 2, and also Stewart et al. 2009). Two groups, the University Forum for HRD (UFHRD) in the UK, and the Academy for HRD (AHRD) in the US, were formed independently within a couple of years of each other (Ruona 2009). A separate body also called the Academy of HRD was formed in India at about the same time.

In 1994 the European Council of Ministers decided to adopt measures to establish a common framework of objectives for community action (Lee et al. 1996). This influenced a wide range of Europe-wide initiatives, including the development of Euresform, a cross-national collaborative project that provided dual qualification (master's-level academic and professional recognition) to students from across Europe. The certificate recognised diverse master's-level HR courses in participating institutions alongside a common framework of professional attainment across all institutions, and was jointly awarded by all the participating institutions. This was the first multinational attempt to establish what HRD might be. It quickly became clear that we could not reach common agreement on what should be taught—but we could agree on what we expected an HR professional to be able to do at the end of the course, and so qualification was based on learning *outcomes,* not *input*—a novel approach at the time. This initiative finished in 2000 as European priorities and funding changed. Its influence, however, is still evidenced by the cross-European nature of UFHRD. Since then UFHRD and AHRD have been active in participation and sharing in each other's conferences, publishing activities, research collaborations, teaching initiatives, and so on. The AHRD expanded to support an Asian network, with its first conference in 2002, and a network in the Middle East and North Africa (MENA), whose first conference was in 2010. As HRD emerged from the mists of the last century, it was not as a single cohesive concept or field of study. Instead, it might be considered to have several interrelated dimensions.

This perspective harks to a structured, reasonably affluent world in which change is about competition and growth, mergers and going under, but all within known and manageable boundaries. However, the world is not like this for everyone, and the brief history of management given above, although generally accepted, is sanitised. For example, Cooke (2003a; 2003b) argues that American slavery has been wrongfully excluded from histories of management. He documents how current management theory derives from a time (the 1860s) when four million slaves were working in the US, controlled by 38,000 managers. Industrial discipline and capitalist rationalisation emerged from the plantations, and both classical management and scientific management were built upon infantilised slave consciousness rather than associating the development of management with the heroic myth of the frontier railway builders. The heroic myth gives management a broad social and cultural legitimacy, whereas association with slavery and institutionalised racism, post-colonialism, and imperialism carries less pleasant connotations. As Prasad (2014) points out, the vast majority of emerging economies are operating in neocolonial contexts—so as we study them, or work in them, we must engage with the colonial legacy in a way that lets us understand how discourses that emerge are manifest outcomes of colonialism, or how the forms of organising come from and maintain hierarchical power systems rooted in a (neo)colonial heritage (Banerjee & Linstead 2000).

The boundaries have been drawn around management and HR in a way that excludes the more questionable bits of our history. It is clear that the way in which we theorise and practise HRD has changed and continues to change. Our conception of it has moved from an organisational function within a stable bureaucratic environment to encompass settings such as not-for-profit organisations, family firms, high-tech environments, and SMEs (Stewart & Beaver 2003). We have come to appreciate that HRD occurs on the national stage (McLean 2004) and that for many nations and non-governmental organisations (NGOs) the profit-motive of the West (that has dominated academic conceptions of HRD) plays only a minor part in the equation. It is worth noting here, as well, the highly important area of critical HRD that has emerged over the last few years (Callahan et al. 2015; Elliott & Turnbull 2005). Critical HRD picks up the debates around the postcolonial and imperialistic heritage, and questions inequality and difference, seeking to understand more by looking through the cracks in the rhetoric of the mainstream portrayal of HRD. This book is one example of that approach.

In so far as 'HRD' is part of the core of the human condition, then, whether it is called 'HRD' or something else, it plays out wherever people are. HRD is there in the local family shop as well as the multinational corporation, and the nature and shape of HRD is influenced by a range of factors that embrace the political, cultural, technological, and economic. We need to adopt a holistic perspective—I can say this with confidence because HRD is about people, and people are influenced by wider politics and events, whether they are aware of it or not, whether they like it or not.

We are part of a global community and our thoughts and actions stem from response to wide philosophical, economic, and political concerns that impact upon our lives on a daily basis. The global interconnectedness of our lives has been thrown into focus by events such as the comprehensive disruption of global air traffic caused by a small volcano in Iceland; worldwide and profound economic effects catalysed by a couple of problems in the US banking system; a health threat of global potential forcing nations to work together, such as the Ebola crisis; or the need for a global response to support those facing aberrant climatic events, such as the floods in Pakistan.

The rapid rise of fundamentalist terrorism illustrates what can happen in a world of collapsing boundaries and conflict. I will briefly look at three main areas of global change (climate, technology, and the ageing population of the West) to argue that we are moving into a world of shifting boundaries, conflict, and change.

SOME GLOBAL CHANGES

There is insufficient space here to include much change theory (see Smith 2004), but the sorts of change I am focusing on here are unplanned and emergent—this is about the world, and humanity, in the process of becoming! Management is less about controlling and enforcing stability, but more about working with change as the norm, not the exception (Salem 2002). This approach recognises complexity in which systems are balanced between chaos and stability, where change is unplanned and without formulated goals or objectives, and where equilibrium leads to organisational death (Pascale 1999). This view of change accords with that of complexity science, which emphasises acausal, holistic interpretations in which nonadditive, non-linear behaviour emerges out of interactive networks, is unpredictably related to input, and is somewhere between predictability and non-predictability (Dent 1999)

A tropic cascade exemplifies this. For example, the reintroduction of grey wolves into Yellowstone National Park in the US led to the elk that used to browse and clear the valley bottoms moving to the hillsides. This resulted in significant regrowth of indigenous trees and plants, in turn providing more shelter and food for small animals and birds, and thus for larger animals such as bears and beavers. The regrowth slowed stream bank erosion and retained sediment, thereby increasing nutrient cycling, and this, along with the work of the beavers, impacted upon the river flow and the geography of the area. So, the introduction of a few wolves significantly enhanced biodiversity and altered the geography of the area (Ripple et al. 2014).

From this perspective we are awash in a world of shifting boundaries with unplanned and unpredictable change around us, always becoming but never quite there. What can we do to manage this? We cannot control or plan for exactly what the changes are or how they might affect us, but we can anticipate, and we can try to create social structures that help us accommodate change. In the final chapter of this book I look towards possible structures and futures; here, I take the first step towards that by looking at some of the ways that change already impacts upon us.

Climate Change

The Intergovernmental Panel on Climate Change (IPCC) published its first assessment report in 1990, and now, with prominent champions (Gore

2007), most people are aware that the climate is changing, though many find it irrelevant to their daily lives. Each subsequent report, the most recent in 2014, has emphasised that the risks are stronger, and of higher likelihood than identified previously. In essence the 2014 report finds that there are already unprecedented changes in which the atmosphere and ocean have warmed, the amounts of snow and ice have diminished, and the sea level has risen. This is directly attributed to human influence, leading to extreme weather and climate events, including a decrease in cold and an increase in warm extremes, and an increase in extreme high sea levels and heavy precipitation events.

Models predict that surface temperature will rise under all scenarios, with more frequent and longer heat waves and precipitation, and the ocean will continue to warm and acidify, and global mean sea level to rise. Risks for natural and human systems will amplify and new risks will emerge: these will be unevenly distributed and are generally greater for disadvantaged people and communities, but will impact upon countries at all levels of development. The risks of abrupt or irreversible changes increase as the magnitude of the warming increases, and current policies will lead to high to very high risk of severe, widespread, and irreversible impacts globally by the end of the twenty-first century. The impacts of climate change will continue for centuries, even if greenhouse gases are stopped.

The report points out that climate change can be influenced by a variety of options but no single one is sufficient. There needs to be cooperation on all scales, with an integrated approach that links adaptation and mitigation with other societal objectives. These include effective institutions and governance, innovation and investments in environmentally sound technologies and infrastructure, and sustainable livelihoods and behavioural and lifestyle choices. Successful implementation relies on relevant tools, suitable governance structures, and an enhanced capacity to respond (IPCC 2014: 2–31). It is well worth exploring the IPCC website, as there are a lot of interesting data there; however, it is all quite dry scientific stuff until you realise what this means in human terms. One in six of all species, regardless of taxonomic group, are threatened with extinction under current policies (Urban 2015). All large-scale predictions of the effects of climate change involve scarcity and shift in renewable resources such as water, fertile land, wood for fuel, and fish stocks. In some cases whole communities are at risk, particularly small island states (Hay & Beniston 2001). In others, the impact upon households within the same community can vary, in relation to wealth, gender, age, and ethnic origins.

Migration

In richer nations large-scale migration has not been used as an adaptive option since the 1930s, even though exposure to drought continues to this day; however, many vulnerable populations will be left with little option but to migrate (Myers 2002). For example, climatic changes in Pakistan would likely exacerbate present environmental conditions that give rise to land degradation, shortfalls in food production, rural poverty, and urban unrest. Circular migration patterns such as those observed in north-eastern Africa, punctuated by shocks of migrants following extreme weather events such as occurred in post-Mitch Honduras, could be expected. Such changes would likely affect not only internal migration patterns, but also migration movements to other countries such as Canada that host large Pakistani communities. Typically the most adversely affected will be landless people, the rural poor, the sick or elderly, those with little family support, whereas migration tends to be undertaken most often by young males. In other words, those most vulnerable are not necessarily the most likely climate-change migrants.

As migration (particularly of the young and fit males) increases so will conflict over resources, both within and across national boundaries. Furthermore, scarcities may act to strengthen group identities based on ethnic, class, or religious differences, most notably by intensifying competition among groups for ever-dwindling resources. At the same time, they can work to undermine the legitimacy of the state and its capacity to meet challenges. As the balance of power gradually shifts from the state to the challenging groups, the prospects for violence increase. Such violence used to be subnational, diffuse, and persistent. More recently, groups espousing fundamentalist principles, such as the Islamic State, have shown disregard of geographic and national boundaries in their formation. Waves of refugees fleeing conflict have joined the economic and climate-change migrants.

Climate change brings with it a maelstrom of social, political, behavioural, and ethical issues, and there are calls for the IPCC process to be extended to include insights into these (Victor 2015). Whilst some are vulnerable to climate change because of their location, for many it is our social systems that incorporate marginalised people in a way that increases their vulnerability, whilst creating relative security for others (Taylor 2013), and the issue is as much about the global use and distribution of natural resources as it is their scarcity. There are also issues around climate injustice, by which poorer nations such as Africa are suffering from the climate-altering actions of richer nations (Magrath 2010).

In summary, climate change is having an enormous effect upon the world, and this will increase. Geographical boundaries are submerged (literally in some cases); resource boundaries come into dispute; populations migrate and alter— however, the highly vulnerable do not have this option. Both migration and the search for, use, and distribution of scarce resources create potential sources of internal and cross-national conflict and refugees. These issues need to be addressed transnationally, as well as nationally and locally (Derman 2014).

Technological change: Biotechnology and nanotechnology offer the prospect of new ways to enhance our living conditions and longevity, and add to the adaptive strategies that can be employed in climate change by those who possess such technological advances. I shall, however, focus on new intelligence technologies, and particularly upon data management and communications technology. These areas have revolutionised the Western world. Not only can we handle, make sense of, and store more and more information, we can also structure it differently. It is no longer necessary to have long chains of command. In theory, anyone in an organisation can have access to senior management, and vice versa, and people can work from anywhere at any time. Teleworking can help the work-life balance and facilitate an atmosphere of trust (Brahm & Kunze 2012). Whilst there is increasing use of technology for governance (Shareef et al. 2014) and HR systems (Stone et al. 2013), it tends to be used more for business stabilisation than as an aid to organisational strategy (Schalk et al. 2013).

E-HRM is now common in Europe, with earlier adoption in large organisations (Strohmeier & Justus-Liebig 2009), though SMEs are benefiting from increasing availability of focused software and outsourcing (Keebler 2001). Interestingly, the political and economic collapse of former communist countries allowed and required a new design of organisation (as discussed in Chapter 12), facilitating speedy adoption of e-HRM in contrast to the inertia shown by established organisations (Autio et al. 2000). There have been warnings, however, about mixed results and unintended consequences from using e-HRM. For example, Payne et al. (2009) found that the use of electronic appraisal created greater involvement in the process yet was perceived to produce lower quality ratings than face-to-face. New systems might focus too heavily on efficiency and cost containment, and may disadvantage protected groups such as older job applicants, and invade personal privacy (Eddy et al. 1999). The expectations built around greater ease of information exchange exacerbate problems when information is unavailable, wrong, or late (Guenter et al. 2014). Rapid problem solving or further information helps, but additional delay can lead to a downward spiral, strengthened by expectations of speed (Blount & Janicik 2001).

Technological change is leading to increasing open access—with concomitant need for extra security of 'hidden' data. Information, facts, data, and knowledge are available to any who know how to look for them. With wireless technology, alongside reductions in size of equipment and increase in battery power and with alternative energy sources, we are able to work from anywhere, and at any time. We have also seen rapid change in mass media, with television and video phones revolutionising how we see the world. Small cameras and live data feeds mean that we can have minute-by-minute exposés of world news. We are voyeurs in the middle of conflict and catastrophe as it happens—and the fight for ratings means that news has also to be entertaining. The news and our information sources have become economic and political tools in which the news has become a form of live soap opera, played around sound bites. We learn to ignore the bits that don't interest us and we become hardened to the many tales of woe and the plights of other communities and people. To some extent, in having to be so selective, we also become more, rather than less, biased in the face of so much information.

Mobility and technological change bring us face-to-face with issues of personal freedom, traceability, and cyberbullying. Grigg (2012) makes a distinction between normal bullying (see Chapter 9) and cyberbullying. Cyberbullying offers a greater frequency of harassment and greater potential of exposing the personal to the public, leading to psychological harm and suicide. Victims can be targeted at any time and place and it can be difficult to identify or punish the perpetrator (Ford 2013). These difficulties arise in part because there is a lack of clarity about what exactly constitutes cyberbullying and thus how civil, criminal, and common law punishment and policies should be applied. Our social structures have yet to catch up with technological advances.

Low Technology Slums

Technology only benefits part of the population of the world. Large parts of the population do not have access to it, are unable to power it, have greater concerns than communication, and might not be able to use it—we the privileged assume worldwide literacy. Although I have concentrated on information technology here, the situation is the same with biotechnology and nanotechnology. The technological elite can benefit from the enhanced lifestyle and longevity that goes hand in hand with innovations in these areas. The technologically impoverished cannot. Moreover, the high technology populations tend to be those that have high power consumption needs, which have contributed to climate change. Agreements associated with the Kyoto treaty apply to all nations, and as indicated by the political storms around this, some nations feel that it is unfair that their attempts to join the technology enhanced world are taxed in this way by those who have already benefited from being members of the elite for many years.

These factors mean that the divide between the technologically elite and others is increasing steadily as technology advances. The technologically elite have the world in their hands—virtually crossing geographical and national boundaries as they wish. Their world and that of the technologically poor are separating at an accelerating rate—and this difference is around every aspect of their existence.

Population Change

Similarly, changes in the profile and speed of population growth are causing boundaries to shift. 'In 1950, worldwide the average woman had five children. Today she has just 2.7, and the continued collapse of fertility is set to become the dominant demographic feature of the 21st century' (Pearce 2002). The 2002 projection for the population of the world in 2150 is that in the best-case scenario (as of Sweden) it will be just over five billion, and thus below our current population of six billion, and in the worst-case scenario (as of Italy) it will drop to just over three billion. It takes an average of 2.1 children per woman of childbearing age to maintain the population at a constant level. The European Union has an average live birth rate of approximately 1.5, and Japan is hovering around a 1.3 birth rate: 'Japan and all of Southern Europe—Portugal, Spain, Southern France, Italy, Greece—are drifting toward collective national suicide by the end of the 21st century' (Drucker 1999: 44). The Australian rate is 1.9, with the population projected to rise from the current 24 million to about 38 million in 2060, and it is estimated that if born in 2012, the average woman will live for 94.4 years, and the average man for 91.6 years (Commonwealth of Australia 2013). The ageing population is only partly offset by Australia's relatively high rates of immigration of young people compared to those of other industrialized countries, and by 2050 a quarter of the population will be aged 65 or over (Compton et al. 2014).

The US, with a birth rate at 2.1, presents an anomaly because of its high migrant population (6 million in the 1970s to over 11 million in the 1990's). This is expected to have a compounding effect in future years as the fertility rate of non-Hispanic whites is slightly over 1.8 and that of blacks is 2.1, whereas the Hispanic fertility rate is nearly 3.0. Accordingly, US total population rate is expected to continue to grow; however, the balance of racial backgrounds within the population will change considerably. In poor countries with a traditional patriarchal society, the spread of television and other media has opened many women's eyes to a whole new world, and modern birth control methods have allowed them to turn those aspirations into reality. Not having children has become a statement of modernity and emancipation, and women are unlikely to give up their new freedom. Countries such as Sweden that have managed to stabilise their birth rates have done so because of their supportive child care policies, rather than because the women have different aspirations (Pearce 2002).

Most of this focuses on the technologically rich world, but it is worth noting that Rodal (1994) found that those in occupations with high probabilities of dying young marry earlier than those with a lower likelihood of dying young, and that higher expected child mortality encourages earlier marriage. He estimates that by 2025, only two of the industrialized democracies will be among the twenty most populated countries in the world. Nigeria will be more populous than the US, Iran will be more populous than Japan, and Ethiopia's population will be twice that of France.

Well-Being of Older People

The ageing population affects many aspects of society, governance, and the economy (Kulik et al. 2014). Fewer people in work means less economic productivity and less tax income as well as increased spending on healthcare. Despite an invisible and often abusive relationship with migrant workers, many nations in the Western world are coming to rely on a steady influx of young workers as their population ages. Socio-economic resources are less important for predicting life satisfaction in retirement than other factors, such as health and social support (Heybroek et al. 2015). Younger relatives and friends provide some of the healthcare and support that is needed; however, this impacts upon their work-life balance, well-being, and productivity (Coyne et al. 2003). As people age they are more likely to lose their partner and friends and become less mobile, leading to an increasingly smaller social network, and employment, as well as retirement, may become increasingly stressful with age (Bamberger 2015). The well-being of older people will be enhanced by policies that strengthen family support and existing networks, as well as those that improve the local social environment (Litwin & Shiovitz-Ezra 2011).

In summary, the population is declining sharply in the majority of the technologically rich world. It is also growing older as people delay having children. The reasons for the ageing population appear to be enhanced expectations of longevity and a stable environment. Those nations that have social support systems that enable caregivers to maintain employment are maintaining a low but steady birth rate. In contrast, in the technologically poor world, high child and male parent mortality are linked to early marriage and many children.

THE IMPACT OF GLOBAL CHANGES

I have outlined what I see to be three key areas of global change: the climate, technology, and the human population. From these spring challenges ranging from global commerce, the distribution of wealth and resources, and the spread of people and technology, to sustainability and social responsibility. In the next sections of this chapter I will explore how they interact with the idea of shifting boundaries before looking at that impact upon what might be seen as more traditional areas of HR in the final section.

Climate change will have a direct effect upon geographical boundaries, such as shorelines and floodplains, and in some instances whole areas (such as the Pacific Islands) are going to shift with climate change. Maps will need to be redrawn, and political boundaries revised. As populations shift, individual and national identity will be challenged. In a fair world resources would be shared equally across the emergent populations but, as we are already seeing, some collections of people, such as those looking to Russia in the Ukraine, or those looking to the Islamic State in the Middle East, have been tempted to take by force what they see to be theirs.

Global warming, changing weather patterns, and increased travel have all contributed to shifts in the global pattern of disease and health. Following the Ebola crisis, there is an increased understanding of the need for further study into the dynamics of infectious diseases, both old, such as measles, and new ones yet to emerge (Schuster 2015). Some global risks are becoming highly prevalent and will have consequences for generations to come, such as childhood (and adult) obesity in more developed nations (Ng et al. 2013). The global financial crisis has also led to reduced funding for health in many developing countries, and the need for international decisions on how to best direct what funding is available (Lu et al. 2010).

Shifting Populations

Refugees from war-torn areas place immediate strain upon surrounding areas and highlight the problems of migration, but economic migration and the associated issues of discrimination, workforce unrest, social justice, and government response are not new (McDonald 2014). Shifting geographical boundaries and changes in resources, technology, and work patterns, along with the destructive influence of major conflict zones, are resulting in large population shifts within countries and between countries. For example, in China since the late 1970s, 145 million people, including 39 million peasant workers or 12.5% of total urban employees in 2009, moved from inland provinces to the south-east coastal region of China. This rural to urban migration—the largest in human history—has transformed Chinese society by creating many large cities so that the urban population now exceeds its rural counterpart. Between 2001 and 2010 migrant workers contributed nearly 20% to economic growth (Economist 2012). Chinese migrant workers are defined as temporary residents. This restricts their access to public education and indirectly limits access to higher paid, permanent jobs and participation in local social insurance schemes, and it fosters discrimination. In general terms, however, the status of the migrant population in China seems to be shifting from a distinct, impoverished underclass to a working class that may be slowly integrating into party-state capitalism and becoming a force for social change (Frenkel & Yu 2015).

Cross-border migration presents similar issues. For example, domestic and care work counts for 4–10% of employment in developing countries and 1–2.5% in industrialized countries, and much of this is done by women migrating without their families (Kontos 2013). This sector is said to be one of the fastest-growing industries, although largely invisible and unregulated (Kontos et al. 2009). Such people are often vulnerable, isolated, and open to discrimination and abuse as domestic slaves, au pairs, and mail-order brides. Often migrant domestic and care workers have their own families at home, but seek to enhance their children's well-being and education. Some, such as German care workers, have developed a self-organised system of rotation in the workplace, working three months in the host country and then returning for three months to their own country, in an attempt to work abroad whilst meeting the care needs of their family (Metz-Gockel et al. 2008).

There are, of course, also myriad problems around who might be acceptable as a migrant or as an immigrant. Alongside the great complexity of rules and regulations designed to enhance national security, labour, and finance, there are other more discriminatory issues around the sort of person 'we' might want in 'our country'. For example, Wodak & Boukala (2015) highlight the hegemonic role of the EU/EC in the discursive construction of in-groups of 'Europeans' and out-groups of 'third-country nationals' through the shaping of immigration and language policies, by which the multilingualism of the EU is limited to the national languages of member states, in spite of the wording of official EU multilingualism policies. Implicit and explicit structures are in place to draw the boundaries around the sort of population deemed to be acceptable; however, these are leaky boundaries. As indicated above, the nature of national populations is changing from inside because of differential birth rates, and from outside because of increasing migration due to humanitarian concerns, and the shortage of skills and labour. Whether they want to or not, populations are becoming multicultural. The average age of each population is changing too, with those in the more developed countries getting steadily older. Each of these changes influences how people relate to each other, and taken together they drive and make major change in the way people live and work, and in their cultural identities.

Shifting View of National Culture

It is worth stepping aside for a moment to have a look at how these ideas impact upon our notion of culture. We increasingly live in a world of mass immigration, mergers and alliances, and worldwide corporations that span national boundaries—yet we continue to adopt a multicultural approach, one that sees different cultures as separated wholes of fixed belief and world view; sees cultural borders as permanent, coherent, and unified; and places culture at the core of social structure. Intercultural differences are assumed to be a fixed reality, such that we need to identify the differences (define the other—see Chapter 7) and to learn how to bridge them (Koot 1996). For example, Kets de Vries (2001: 597) say that the stable core of culture retains its 'significance regardless of place, time or regime', and Hofstede & Hofstede (2005: 13) hold that national values are 'as hard as a country's geographic position'. Though, the example of trophic change, above, might indicate that geographic position is not that fixed! Some uniformity is clearly identifiable within a country, such as the side of the road on which people drive, but the uniformity and stability by which culture is often presented is not consistent with the variety and variation found empirically or the 'evanescent bricolage' of cultures (Batteau 2000: 726) that we experience on a daily basis moving from one situation to another.

The notion that culture is stable is also challenged by the work of classical social theorists for whom the social is the core and culture is derivative or emergent (Peacock 1981). People experience structure through cultural frames and filters, such that 'structure' and 'symbolic systems' interact and persist as overlapping social phenomena: Social structure cannot exist without symbolic systems, which individuals use to make sense of, maintain, and change social structure, while symbolic systems cannot exist for long without 'plausibility structures, which root symbols in behavioural patterns' (Morrill 1991: 586). From this perspective culture is co-created and emergent and can be distinguished from the notion of ideology: Ideology implies the deliberate crafting of ideas and values towards a specific goal such as the generation of a 'corporate culture' (Kunda 1992).

Theories of hybridisation see cultures as constructs of history and discourse that flow into one another, producing something that is familiar but new (Papastergiadis 1997). Cultures are shaped and reshaped through interactions with other cultures in which people insert new meanings into their own (already hybrid) cultural understandings (Werbner & Modood 1997). Not all cultural change is slow, and to retain the elements of a particular culture it must be rehearsed and reinvented to prevent incipient change (Etzioni 2000). Multiculturalism's concern is with cultural multiplicity while hybridisation's concern is with interactions, negotiations, and mutual enrichments among these cultures, and thus 'culture' needs to be seen in plural and diverse terms. As an example of this Shimoni & Bergmann (2006) illustrate how local managers retain local managerial culture even as they are indoctrinated into the culture of the corporations. In the balance between structure and agency, the homogenizing force of globalisation might appear to subsume the smaller and less powerful elements in its path (be they people, organisations, or nations), yet the local cultures remain in hybridised form.

Whether we are aware of it or not, just by coming into contact with other histories and other peoples, our borders and boundaries are being redefined by cultural hybridisation. We might call ourselves one thing and say 'this is what we are' but in the process of doing so we are changing—we are very slightly becoming something else: This is the evolution of our culture and our social systems. This is fostered by travel and education, and now by the power of communication technology and the media.

Shifting Relationship Between Global and Local

Changes in technology also mean that, at least for the technologically rich, the world becomes a smaller place. This also erodes national boundaries as people relate more freely across them. The boundaryless cyber world is also part of a different form of erosion of national boundaries—the economic one. Global environmental changes and associated negotiations over global resources, responsibilities, and population shifts are going to require global political and economic responses, which in turn can already be seen to be eroding the legislative, political, and economic boundaries of nation states (Costea 1999). As Gore (2007) suggested with respect to climate change, if we are to do anything about it then there is a need for global action. Since the turn of the century we have seen more willingness between those in power to reach compromise on global issues, particularly around issues where the danger is obvious, such as climate change and pandemics.

Many large corporations have more economic power than do the nations whose boundaries they cross, thereby influencing the wider global economy, forming the 'international business elite' that is at the forefront of globalisation (Ferner et al. 2011). Globalising corporate strategy is, in part, a result of the introduction of international taxation systems (Mollan & Tennent 2015). The 'elite' seek increased harmonization of accounting techniques across borders, and professional service firms are happy to oblige, clothing naked economic interests in juridical justifications (Spence et al. 2015). Such organisations are establishing supranational governance structures that serve as a strong homogenizing force. For example, the International Financial Reporting Standards has been mandatory in the European Union since 2005 and is hastily being adopted around the globe—these standards reflect largely Westernised understandings of how to account for things, and impose a particular way of organising upon institutions that contains all sorts of sociologically unacceptable, and anthropologically deaf, assumptions about individual rationality, shareholder primacy, and market efficiency (Ramirez 2012). For example, I was party to a wonderful moment in St. Petersburg, shortly after the Velvet Revolution, when an American banker had carefully laid out how accounts should be prepared within the free market to the Russian managers and officials, after which a Russian manager quietly asked, 'Please, where are the columns we need for the 20% that we have to put aside for bribes?'. In providing global structures professional service firms are not a mere product of globalisation but key engineers of it; they are globalisation's hired guns (Dezalay & Garth 2004).

These global structures are superimposed on national regimes, but do not replace them, thereby generating paradoxes, contradictions, and competing pressures that prevent such firms from becoming truly global. For example, global audit methodologies are routinely distorted when appropriated at the local level (Muzio et al. 2013) and organisations do better if they adopt local HR practices (Fitzsimmons & Stamper 2014). Haley & Boje (2014) point to how the creation of stories helps ease the management of global-local boundaries by pulling together aspects of both; however, the overwhelming importance of economic capital dominates in the largest organisations despite the way in which both global and local effects combine to reshape institutions (Spence et al. 2015).

These are all large issues that appear to have little to do with the individual 'here and now'; however, these changes form a cluster of shifting boundaries through which our society and the nature of the world as we know it is changing—they cannot be dissected and addressed effectively on a singular basis, and though global, they have a direct local impact upon our understanding of ourselves and our relationships, our world of work, and how we conduct our lives. Global change has a personal impact.

THE CHANGING WORLD OF WORK

Changes are happening to all forms of social grouping, from family life and voluntary and social groups through to commercial organisations and nations. Much of the research is on commercial organisations and I shall concentrate on those here, but the wider picture is about how we structure our relationships and our societies, and that runs as a sub-theme throughout this chapter. I shall examine the impact of some of these changes to our organisational and working life before looking at the implications for HRD.

An early draft of this chapter had nearly 80,000 words, enough for a book in itself. I faced the problem of putting bounds on a chapter about boundaries! This is because each of the areas that I briefly touch upon here has its own large area of literature and debate. I have pulled out a few key points, but there is much more to be said about how we are changing from the world of the traditional organisation. In talking of the traditional organisation I am really referring to the sort that is most commonly researched and written about: namely, the medium- to large-sized bureaucratic profit-seeking organisation of the Western world. If we adopt a wider lens we can see the vast number of alternative forms of organisation, particularly medium and small, and the many not-for-profit, charity, government, and community collectives by which groups of people across the world manage their affairs. If we want to understand a community better we need to explore its structure: its processes of organising (Friedland & Alford 1991).

The birth, life, and death of organisations is influenced by the regulatory structures around them. In a series of studies comparing the regulatory frameworks of 85 countries, Djankov et al. (2004) found that more democratic countries have lighter regulation of start-up organisations and labour. Those with high levels of state control tend to have less consistency, less honesty, less fairness in judicial decisions, larger unofficial economies, lower participation from the labour force, and higher unemployment, especially of the young. High barriers to start-ups have a negative impact on employment growth and on the efficiency of small firms, whilst reforming regulations produces a large positive economic impact (Haidar 2012). Of course, the regulations are there to help balance the needs and wants of the individual with the needs and wants of society; however, a more affluent society as measured by GDP does not necessarily mean that everyone within it benefits equally. Public organisations are a good example of the problems associated with a regulatory environment. They typically operate in a complex political arena characterised by checks and balances, shared power, and divergent interests (Burnes 2009), which forces managers to adopt a planned, top-down 'one size fits all' approach to change, whilst the complex environment simultaneously limits the effectiveness of such an approach (van der Voet et al. 2013).

Daepp et al. (2015) found that the typical half-life of a publicly traded company in the US between 1950 and 2009 is about a decade, regardless of business sector and independent of the company's age. Many organisations, however, change form and become reanimated rather than die (Kelly & Riach 2014). Small local organisations are loosely banding together to reach international markets. Large bureaucratic organisations are facing the need for greater integration of their subsystems (Kidron et al. 2013) or are being replaced by cross-national network organisations and partnerships. Instead of talking about a bounded organisation within a particular society, we can see the relationship between organisation and society as similar to that between individual and organisation—interdependent, co-creational, and with fuzzy boundaries.

In a text like this the concept of 'partnership' is used as a neutral management tool that creates economic value or addresses social problems, and carries with it an explicit egalitarian agenda (Tomlinson 2005). On the ground, however, there can be a disjunction between the ideal of partnership and its reality. For example, Contu & Girei (2014) looked at the relationship between international and national non-governmental organisations in Africa, which are routinely described as partnerships, but found that they were characterised by inequality, subordination, and oppression. To some, 'partnership' in the aid and development arena is a de facto recolonisation of Africa (Murithi 2009). Power and politics are fundamental to partnership, in which organisations and people are constituted, and constitute one another, in competitive and unequal co-creation, and in which historical power relations cannot be dismissed or put 'on hold'. Such partnerships raise issues around trust and identity, which I shall explore later in this chapter.

Collaboration and Networking

Successful partnership and networking depend upon good knowledge management and rapid integration of new members and new knowledge (Gardner et al. 2012); however, this can be difficult in complex cross-disciplinary tasks and teams involving specialised knowledge that cannot easily be explained, or might be sensitive (Bruns 2012). Such knowledge needs to be reformulated in order to reach a shared meaning, highlighting both the importance of trust and reflexivity for the transmission of knowledge, as well as the development of shared beliefs through social interactions (Sankowska & Söderlund 2015). In other words, knowledge integration can be a process of co-creation.

There is a lot of research on multinationals and the role of expatriates: The organisation benefits from assigning key staff to foreign postings because they can make use of knowledge obtained across the world that the local competitors do not have (Mudambi & Swift 2012), both through the transfer of core knowledge to the subsidiaries, and from the subsidiaries to the core. Short-term assignments minimise problems with cultural adjustment and work/family issues, but they can limit knowledge transfer and the development of strong relationships. Better technology and virtual assignments, however, are helping them become more common (Tahvana-inen et al. 2005).

Consumption and Corporate Social Responsibility

Better technology and networking is also facilitating the media-based culture of exposure and rapid moral judgement, which in turn influences organisations and people that are 'in the public eye'. The nature of conspicuous consumption has changed with society and historical age, and can be interpreted from texts, common myths, and memories (Sharma & Grant 2011). In general, however, a life of luxury and excess has been seen as an assertion of power and social standing. More recently, signs of material excess by organisations and leaders across the world have often evoked public outcry (Riad 2014). Earlier I emphasised the overriding economic focus of multinational organisations; however, the increasing power of the media and the influence of activist groups, alongside increasing realisation of inequality and the desperate plight of some people, is highlighting the social responsibility of organisations. Corporate social responsibility is usually driven by external pressure (Aguinis & Glavas 2012), and is increasingly positively correlated with corporate financial performance (Ambec & Lanoie 2008).

There is an increasing tension in the capitalist world between consumption and ethical leadership (Gerde et al. 2007), which has led to a resurgence of interest in the 'new philanthropists' (Handy 2007): business and social leaders who use their acquired wealth in sustainable ways to help those in need, changing from conspicuous consumption to conspicuous philanthropy (Guest 2011). Organisations can also seek to achieve a good reputation through sponsorship of good causes that are not linked to the organisation itself, so that neither the organisation nor the employees directly benefit. Such sponsorship tends to attract better employees who become committed to the cause, and the organisation (Bingham et al. 2013).

Older Workers

The age profile of the organisation is also changing. An older population puts increased strain upon society's resources, as more people collect pensions and fewer earn wages and provide support (financial, physical, and emotional). More people will need complicated healthcare and specialist programmes of support. More community resources will be required along with educational provision designed for the needs of the elderly (Davis et al. 2013). Keeping older workers in employment helps economically, but also has health benefits for many who seek continuity in their life by maintaining routine, particularly those who are highly involved in their jobs (Kalokeri-nos et al. 2015). Similarly, partially employed or volunteer retirees report greater well-being than those forced to retire fully (Dingemans & Henkens

2014). This is, however, a complex issue, as the nature of the employment can shape the experience of ageing as well as the retirement process, and early preparation is important for life satisfaction (Zacher & Grifn 2015).

There are many stereotypes about older workers; however, Finkelstein et al. (2015) found little empirical support for these stereotypes, though older workers can demonstrate prejudice about how they think other people are stereotyping them as 'older'. This varies according to context and power, age and gender; for example, those without power have the greatest concerns about others' views, and this is particularly so for women and younger workers (Ryan et al. 2015). As people's life expectancy shortens they may be less motivated to engage in achieving knowledge-relevant and work-related goals, and focus instead on achieving emotional and social goals in transition or retirement-related roles (Griffin 2015). They start psychologically disengaging from their jobs in the years prior to retirement, particularly in jobs with high autonomy (Ng & Feldman 2015). Motivation may be influenced more by the way in which older people are treated at work than to age itself (Stamov-Roßnagel & Biemann 2012). They are less likely to act against the needs of the organisation than younger workers, and more likely to be more self-controlled in handling the negative side of work (Besen et al. 2013). Therefore, older workers might benefit from a shift in the nature of their work towards task-specific jobs that make use of their social skills; however, their deep engagement in complex knowledge-intensive or creative tasks seems to balance any effects of cognitive ageing (Zacher 2015).

Cahill et al. (2005) suggest that the idea of traditional retirement may be dying out. Organisations and older workers both benefit from workplace flexibility and the development of phased transition to retirement, by which employers retain the knowledge and experience gained by their older workers and employees avoid having to look for a job elsewhere whilst facing high levels of age discrimination in the labour market (Adair et al. 2013). An alternative is bridge employment, which usually involves part-time or temporary work following full retirement (Zacher & Bock 2014). Some countries such as Japan expect people to find bridge employment (Usui et al. 2014) whereas labour and pension laws in others, such as Poland (Zientara 2014), discourage it. Older people prefer bridge employment that furthers their skills and abilities and is consistent with their values and interests, and in which they can mentor others (Beehr & Bennet 2001: 5).

Shifting Patterns of Career

Until the 1980s the psychological contract promised job security, steady pay, and development opportunities (Karren 2012). As many organisations become more networked and flatter in structure, individuals and offices within such organisations are more likely to be multifunctional, or internal portfolio–centred. This fundamentally changes traditional notions of work and organisation and 'home' becomes a mobile concept. Wherever they are located, skilled individuals can work for several organisations from across the world at the same time, and similarly, wherever they are located, adept organisations can call upon the services of skilled individuals from across the world. Skilled workers need no longer be bounded by geography or loyalty—they can sell their human capital to those that offer the best packages of pay and benefits. The changing world of work is challenging people to reposition themselves, to reorganise their work activities, and to redirect their loyalties and identifications. This presents the worker as the independent agent, throwing aside the structure of organisation, able to choose where they want to go—in theory, anyway.

Mitra (2015) argues that career is a cultural practice that draws on both structure and action, and is both about objective aspects, such as pay and hours, as well as subjective aspects, such as meaningfulness, and that it accommodates the influence of such things as heroic identity scripts and everyday communication upon a person's career path (LaPointe 2010). There has been a focus on relatively privileged managers and expatriates from the global north, working in private sector companies (Dutta 2012); however, subaltern groups also have hierarchies of power and knowledge, and these fluctuate with context—for example, Pal & Buzzanell (2008) found that working in Indian call centres at night (rather than day) carries both social stigma in the local context, as well as a sense of pride of being upwardly mobile in the global economy. Similarly, a career that might seem to be privileged professionally might carry with it social stigma, or vice versa (Cheney & Ashcraft 2007). Thus an individual career is addressed through multiple discursive frames in which two people might receive the same message (e.g., 'you can succeed if you work hard') but interpret it differently (Bradford et al. 2001). Similarly, different cultures can view the same careers differently (see Berkelaar et al. 2012). Individuals need to negotiate their career within a complex web of cultural identity and maturity and associated tensions that cannot be investigated in linear terms (i.e., home or host culture) (Arthur & Popadiuk 2010). The idea of 'career' is expanding from a choice-driven, sequential pattern of work arranged by paid labour (Buzzanell & Lucas 2013) to include people who are in marginalised groups, such as immigrants and workers in the informal economy, as well as those with spiritual life paths and alternative work ethics, such as female priests, houseworkers and garbage-workers (Shenoy-Packer 2014).

The converse of the structured linear career path can be seen in the idea of the boundaryless career, where agency comes to the fore and people are able to (re)invent themselves periodically by experimenting actively with diverse roles and occupational identities (Ashforth 2001). Such people develop their identity around their skills and competencies, rather than upon their job or organisation, and are more prepared to be organisationally and internationally mobile. This applies most to knowledge-based economies, among highly qualified workers and in Western cultures (Roper et al. 2010). Even there, not everybody has the chance to follow a boundaryless career (Chudzikowski

2012) nor is it necessarily the best option (Biemann & Andresen (2010). The idea of the career script can be seen as a bridge between the traditional structured approach to careers and the ad hoc agency of the boundaryless career Valette & Culié (2015) in which the script is influenced by social position and institutional resources as well as individual skill.

Much of the risk related to employment has moved from the employer to the employee, along with increased mobility and greater uncertainty and discontent. In what Fraher & Gabriel (2014: 938) refer to as 'the limbo land' of employment, workers are expected to show loyalty to their employer and to identify strongly with the organisation and its cultural scripts whilst also maintaining their sense of self and adapting smoothly to organisational flux and to new work situations. One of the greatest changes is that of decreasing job security. Job loss impacts emotionally and physically upon the individual whose job is at risk, as well as their colleagues, whose jobs might be threatened or changed in the process. It also impacts upon the organisation that might be losing one or more valuable resources. Unemployment has a similar negative impact upon psychological and physical health, with extended unemployment leading to depression, the loss of relevant skills, and long-term effects upon the individual and their families (Classen & Dunn 2012). However, Zikic & Richardson (2007) argue that losing a job can actually have a beneficial outcome through catalysing career growth.

Downsizing and Justice

One of the factors in achieving a more positive job loss is the extent to which downsizing decisions are seen to be just. Older and minority employees often bear the brunt of downsizing with little performance-related justification (Dwyer & Arbelo 2012), and the sense of such injustice holds a high political cost for organisations both during the downsizing and with a demotivated workforce afterwards. Conversely, people are more likely to accept the lay-off, and talk positively about their organisation, if they believe they have been kept informed and treated fairly and with respect (Spreitzer & Mishra 2002). Ex-employees form self-defining attachments to their organisations, which can help preserve a sense of self-enhancement, belongingness, and prestige, and can also help the organisation avoid bad publicity (Tosti-Kharas 2012). In general re-employment appears to lead to improved well-being, including restoring the level of well-being that existed prior to the job loss (Krueger & Mueller 2011), although underemployment, when people take lower paying, less secure, and more temporary jobs than they expect, is linked to lower job satisfaction, organisational commitment, and trust (Feldman et al. 2002). Desirability of job, however, is a matter of perception and career intentions, and those who are more willing to adapt their career plans are more satisfied with their choice of employment (Koen et al. 2010).

LEADERSHIP AND THE CHANGING NATURE OF THE WORKFORCE

Embodiment and Physicality

Much of the research discussed above, as with that in the mainstream management literature, assumes people are logical, rational, conscious decision makers (though, see Chapter 13). It assumes that people can share information about other cultures and ways of working, and that with sufficient background and training people can be inserted into, or lead, new groups and workplaces without problem. This view has been challenged by researchers looking at psychodynamics and the subconscious, as well as the corporeal side of interrelationships. There is a great difference between knowing about something and experiencing it! For example Riach & Warren (2015) focus on the role of smell in the workplace, which highlights 'the interdependence of shared, personal, local and cultural elementals'. The mix of odours permeates the workplace and binds people together in a way that breaks through the assumption of workers who are ontologically separate or distinct. The use of smell and our other senses influences how we see our co-workers and can play a part in whether or not we trust them (Mason & Davies 2009). After shaking hands with someone we bring our hands towards our face and inhale more deeply than we would otherwise do. In doing this we are not aware of sniffing our palms, but our bodies act on the scent signals we receive (Frumin et al. 2015). The permeability of our bodily boundaries as we interact with others is similar to the co-evolving microbial community that I discussed in Chapter 3. How we interact with others is not just about 'who does what to whom' but is influenced by circumstances, memories, and anticipations, as well as looks, smells, sounds, and other sensual information that we might not be aware of.

Embodiment is integral to sense-making and sense-giving (Cunliffe & Coupland 2011). Abstract concepts (such as leadership) are embodied in the material world and are innately politicised by the nuances they carry with them (Hawkins 2015). We communicate beliefs, intentions, and emotions through movement, both purposefully and inadvertently, and embodied non-linguistic practices play an important role in the formation of identity. Their absence (as in people with impairments) influences the non-linguistic presentation of self, impression management, and the allocation of stigma (Kašperová & Kitching 2014). Issues of who we trust and how we form identity are much more than an isolated conscious decision—they are rooted in our psyche and our biology, and a part of our animal inheritance; part of our co-evolution with the people and the structures around us. Each of us becomes what we know of as our 'self' as we become part of the groups we are in. It is therefore no surprise that our sense of self often actively includes our workplace.

The notion of a leader and leadership is important in this debate and within the wider thesis of this book. A leader can be seen as a key agent within the world of structure: balanced between asserting their own view of what that structure should be and complying with the rules of the existing structure; balanced between imposing the rules of the structure upon others or allowing the co-evolution of new rules; balanced between working for the good of self or the good of other (though who determines what that good might be is a different question). In other words, the leader is the nexus of balance between structure and agency, and self and other.

Growing Narcissism

The increasing power of the media and the globalisation of news and views have helped foster corporate social responsibility, but have also fostered narcissism (Resick et al. 2009). Duchon & Burns (2008) suggest that Western organisations are now a breeding ground for a culture of narcissism because of the focus on individual achievement, professional prestige, and social celebrity. Similarly, Western educational systems and parental practices have contributed to the increasing levels of unrealistically positive views of the self (narcissism), through the promotion of a culture of rewards and entitlement (Twenge & Campbell 2009). Rather than serving the company, narcissistic employees use the resources available to them to attract the admiration of others as a way of confirming their feelings of superiority (Higgs 2009). Narcissistic employees are generally rated as poor on interpersonal performance and integrity, with difficulty learning from feedback, and show a proclivity for white-collar crime and the belittling of their fellow workers (Campbell et al. 2011).

Narcissistic leaders are also motivated by self-enhancement, and demonstrate a sense of entitlement and a strong charisma (Judge et al. 2009). They see themselves as more human than the 'Other' and have the potential to be abusive, authoritarian, and sadistic (Locke 2009). They tend to be manipulative and deceitful (Jonason et al. 2009) and whilst fostering a coterie, they exploit their employees. Typically they inhibit the contribution and development of their subordinates; bully, coerce, and cause damage to their psychological well-being; and generate a toxic work atmosphere (Benson & Hogan 2008). They favour strategic sensationalism (such as the impulsive acquisition of companies that are grandiose and guaranteed attention-getters) over strategic conservatism (such as incremental improvements of product quality that relegate the CEO to total obscurity). This leads to volatile and risky decision-making (Chatterjee & Hambrick 2007) and the degradation of organisational effectiveness and sustainable performance (Higgs 2009).

It seems strange to think that we might choose such people to be our leaders, yet narcissistic people tend to do well in interviews and give the appearance of a good leader as they are extroverted, socially exciting, and seductive (Brunell et al. 2008). In an emergency (whether real or managed through the manipulation of the media) there can be a need for strong and apparently heroic leadership and people are particularly receptive to the confident reassurance of a narcissistic leader who promises that they can control and can cure the situation (Padilla et al. 2007). In general then, narcissistic leaders come with a health warning. Ouimet (2010) shows how easily narcissists can get promoted into leadership positions, and the devastating effects narcissistic leaders can have on organisations. Narcissistic leaders are shaped by, and shape, the organisational culture, and if unchecked can become our despotic rulers—or, on a smaller scale, can lead to a toxic workplace and the death of the organisation (Duchon & Burns 2008). Stone-Romero & Stone (2002) warn that if the collectives that form the building blocks of societies become permeated by narcissistic leaders, then this will open the way to societal decline.

Humane Workplace

The sanitised view of HRD (the one that doesn't incorporate critical interrogation or invite ethical or moral responses) talks of roles and performance in ways that divest the organisations and the people within from responsibility for themselves, for their colleagues, or for the wider world. For example, the introduction of paternalistic 'humane management' (Pun & Chan 2012) is seen as a major factor in the phenomenal economic success, relative industrial peace, and high worker commitment in East Asia; however, it infantilises the workers—constructing them as irresponsible, spoiled children needing to be led, moved, touched, taught, and ruled (Choi & Peng 2015). As Hatcher & Lee (2003) argued, and as I document in Chapter 9, HRD can collude with some very nasty practices. Often the rationale for mistreatment of workers is the maximisation of profit; however, Sully de Luque et al. (2008) examined 520 firms in 17 countries and found that where leaders emphasise economic values, their leadership style is seen to be autocratic, whereas those who put emphasis on stakeholder values are seen as visionary leaders. Furthermore, employees of those perceived as visionary work harder, leading to increased performance by the organisation. No such relationship is found for autocratic leadership. It would appear that too strong a focus on profit maximisation may not help and may even hinder the firm's ability to maximise profit!

A recent large-scale survey of all sectors in the UK by the Chartered Institute of Personnel and Development (CIPD 2015) found that almost half the respondents remain satisfied with their jobs, and 23% are looking for a new job with a different employer. Overall 39% feel that they are engaged in their work (49% in the voluntary sector), with 59% feeling neutral towards it. Employees are most dissatisfied with senior managers (judged to be poor at involving and consulting employees in important decisions), work-life balance, and line managers. Respondents most wanted line managers who were fair, followed by open and honest, caring, and displaying trust.

Although 55% of employees specified that they would prefer to work in 'an organisation with a strong family feel, held together by loyalty and tradition', nearly 50% describe the culture of their organisation as a 'formalised and structured place to work, where procedures govern what people do and hold people together'. This finding might well have links to the evolutionary preferences, discussed in Chapter 3, for small family-based groupings of up to about 50 people.

Employees work better if they believe they are seen as people rather than profit-making resources. This is not particularly surprising, but it is sometimes easy to lose sight of this, the human aspect, within the myriad changes that we face. A wide range of studies describe how work environments that meet an employee's psychosocial needs (for challenge, support, autonomy, and feedback) are associated with positive outcomes—such as individual learning, development, satisfaction, and performance (Parzefall & Hakanen 2010). This also holds true in non-Western countries (Brough et al. 2015).

The literature frequently associates the humane workplace with transformational or change leadership. Change leaders typically develop a vision and a plan for implementation, communicate the vision, become a good role model, and motivate employees to contribute to the change (Fernandez & Rainey 2006). However, the context is important: for example, the pluralistic nature of the public sector requires leadership that is not about envisioning and making strategic decisions, or aimed at motivation and inspiration, but rather is about being in touch, lobbying and collaborating and working with power, interests, and coalitions (Crosby & Bryson 2005). The focus, therefore, is on achieving political consensus through skilled collaboration and networking (Kickert 2010). This harks to a more generic skill set, associated with intercultural competence, and, as Lloyd & Hartel (2010) suggest, it is almost guaranteed that individuals will work in culturally diverse work teams at some point in their career. The shifting nature of organisations increases the chance of mergers, between organisations and also in restructuring between parts of the same organisation.

There is a great deal of research on intercultural competence, and no space here to do it justice, but speaking generally, it is held to include dynamic management and leadership capabilities, the management and use of knowledge flows, and the ability to interact effectively with people who are culturally different; to deal with various competitive and political environments, and to see rapid change and uncertainty as an opportunity (see Bucker & Poutsma 2010). International managers also face culture shock, and transitional adjustment difficulties, and one of the key attributes, that I shall discuss later in this chapter, would appear to be cognitive hardiness. In almost any team we will come across people with different backgrounds and understandings to ourselves and intercultural problems can arise however much we look alike. This is less about leadership and its heroic accoutrements, and more about symbiosis: working together to reach towards a co-created vision (see, in particular, Chapters 8 and 18).

Implications for You and Me

I started this chapter by looking at the development of HRD, and moved on to looking at ideas around structure and boundaries. In doing so I explored global changes and how they might impact upon the world of people, how we construe our organisations, and what that might mean for our world of work. It is almost impossible to talk about management without the intrusion of a raft of subtext around economics and politics; performance and measurement; manipulation and conformity. In the closing sections of this chapter I bring the line of thought back to more traditional aspects of HR—namely, how these grand changes might impact upon the development of us, you and me, and our role in that. These changes, however, also impact upon how we think of work. For example, the dominant view is that people work for money (the more money the better) and would prefer not to be at work. For those of us working in traditional organisations, work life used to be separate from home life, and work identity separate from our sense of self. Of course, that never really applied to those in the very many small family-run organisations—but then the literature has only just started looking at them. Nowadays, there is a greater focus on how we influence our workplace and in turn how our workplace influences us—and at their co-evolution, or mismatch. As discussed above, our career paths have become more unpredictable. We develop different skills and interests, earn money on some things and spend money on others, volunteer our labour and resources for things that are important to us, travel and come across different peoples and ways of being; and, even though we grow older and stop being in paid employment, we still wish to work with and engage with others to follow our interests and dreams.

If we remove money or payment from the equation, do we still work? What are the overarching qualities that we look for when we engage with others to a common goal? The sort of systems and structures I am talking about here are often subconscious and not necessarily obvious to us, but they are key to how we work together. Systems of accountability can be as informal as the tacit norms established between friends or family up to formal performance evaluations and management structures. These structures of accountability influence behaviour by making people answerable to both themselves and others, and proffering reward or punishment according to peer evaluation (De Cremer & van Dijk 2009) with people modulating their behaviour based on its anticipated consequences. To a large extent, this depends upon trust, which is seen to play a core part in knowledge integration and creativity (Sankowska 2013) and team and individual performance (De Jong & Elfring 2010).

Trust

Both social exchange theories of leadership and relational leadership theories focus on factors that shape the interpersonal dynamics between a supervisor and a subordinate, and in which one person is dependent upon another for resources whilst the other can exploit those resources to gain leverage. It is possible to build safeguards into the relationship to minimise vulnerability, but they carry a transaction cost. Trust helps to minimise transaction costs and usually carries the belief that the relationship is reciprocated (Hopkins & Weathington 2006). The question of the necessary conditions for trust, and the belief that trust is reciprocated, are important, both for this chapter and this book. Before going further into that it is worth noting that 'trust' is a word frequently used without a qualifier, as, of course, we all know what it means, but trust to what? For example, I know soldiers who trust their mates with their lives, but wouldn't trust them enough to lend them £100. Trust seems to serve a complex role in identity work: to be fragile, temporary, and under construction (Alvesson 2010), and whilst the two concepts are not the same, they are inextricably linked.

We cannot easily say what 'identity' or 'trust' are, but we know when they break down; we know that violation of trust leads to a corroded sense of self (Driver 2015), that both are constructed in and through discourse, and that each person takes a different and unique sense of this discourse (Morrison & Macleod 2013). For example, Werbel & Henriques (2009) looked at trust within teams and found that though all the team members talked of trust, they were looking for different qualities by which they could judge whether to trust the other party—supervisors sought indications that they could safely delegate authority, whereas their subordinates sought indications that their supervisors would provide interactional justice. Trust is given more easily to those who appear to deal with the situation from the perspective of integrity, honesty, and transparency than those who appear to work on principles of expediency (Ayree et al. 2002). Furthermore, an expedient approach is likely to lead to a loss of trust, and this may be felt more deeply by subordinates than for supervisors (Lapidot et al. 2007). There are declining levels of trust in organisations (Caldwell & Dixon 2010); however, people clearly want to be trusted and may 'engineer' trust or communicate about its virtues despite its absence (Sievers 2003). Initial presumptions of trust can elicit reciprocal trust from others, leading to a virtuous cycle of trust reciprocity. Skinner et al. (2014) suggest a similar cycle in which trust is predicated on shared identifications, with greater identification leading, cyclically, to more trust and trust leading to a sense of identity; thus it is possible to create too much trust, where overly high levels of trust lead to reduced performance and reduction of agency (Molina-Morales et al. 2011).

An act of trust represents not only an assessment of the trustworthiness of another but is also an elusive phenomenon (Li 2011) whose absence and presence is influenced by systemic organisational issues as well as those around one's identity. The ability to reflect plays an important part in addressing whether to trust, especially around open-ended problems and situations (Tarrant 2013), as does the ability to understand and investigate alternative perspectives and see other people's points of view (Nederveen Pieterse et al. 2011).

Shifting Identities

Our understanding of ourselves shifts in concert with shifts in geographical, cultural, economic, and social boundaries (see Chapter 7) and the generation of collective identity often follows a similar pattern, via a discourse of differences and disparity between 'self' and 'other'. We like the comfort of smaller groups in which we can feel that our contribution to them is recognised and valued—in which we are trusted and belong. As the traditional boundaries shift we need to create others by which to know who we are. There are disagreements about how this might happen, with some looking at 'identity work' (see Alvesson 2010), and others focusing less on the shaping nature of the dominant discourse and more to the micro-level processes within events and experiences through which we seeking meaning (Ibarra & Barbulescu 2010). These different perspectives, once again, reflect bipolar notions of structure and agency. In either case people combine life experiences or insights into their multiple identities and thereby modify them according to the circumstances; thus identity is a social process but we also retain core or deeper identities that are more central to the self (Farmer & Van Dyne 2010).

The construction of meaning through narrative is normally considered a sociological approach to identity, but that, alongside the core sense of 'me', presents a powerful picture of how we interpret ourselves. We tell ourselves stories of what we are and what we would like to be, and how we fit in with the rest of the world; we reinterpret, we review other people's stories (explicit, and those carried through metaphor or by what is not said or done), and in doing so we make things happen. In using our imaginary-time processor (see Chapter 13) we ponder alternatives to social contexts and enact social realities that had not materialised prior to their telling. In this way people are in 'perpetual states of storied becoming' (Brown & Thompson 2013: 1153). Through this we replace fragments of tales that are incoherent or unacceptable and we tell the tale of our 'self' as a journey of transformation that makes sense of our lives and enables us to feel that we are making progress in our life story (Creed et al. 2014). As the audience and life events change, so do our stories, which are 'dynamically enacted in relation to pluralist, shifting landscapes' (Tams & Marshall 2011: 109). During times of change our stories transition, which Conroy & O'Leary-Kelly (2014: 67) describe as 'a liminal state between letting go of the old and moving on to a new identity'. People narrate themselves in both ambiguous and coherent ways as part of a balancing act between complexity and coherence (Chreim 2005), mediated by a thick layer of unconscious desires, emotions, and fantasies (Antonacopoulou & Gabriel 2001). Although painful, disruptive moments can simultaneously allow people to reorganise their experiences and emerge with a stronger sense of identity.

Finding Meaning and Commitment

Our stories can combine to create the group narrative, and a more inclusive story that cuts across the us-and-them divide can help build and maintain partnerships across social and cultural boundaries (Ybema et al. 2012). To some extent, the more congruence between our own story and the stories of those around us, the more likely we are to be happy (Sheldon & Schuler 2011), and the more meaning we find at work, the greater our subjective well-being. For example, Menard & Brunet (2011) found that if key aspects of the workplace and the person's identity are not aligned then their identity is devalued. Conversely, when they are aligned employees feel that their work is meaningful. The experience of meaningful work is positively associated with health and work benefits (Clausen et al. 2010) and increased commitment to work, particularly the more similar it is to their ideal culture (Meyer et al. 2010). Commitment is derived through unconscious, as well as conscious, bonds (Klein et al. 2012), and is influenced by a whole range of factors, including incidents at work and global influences. People can become committed to an organisation before they start working there, and remain committed after they leave for another job, as well as being committed to many other organisations within and outside of the workplace (Cohen 2007). I am talking here of affective commitment, which correlates with desired employee behaviour in general and reduced absenteeism in particular (Mathieu & Zajac 1990). In contrast, both normative commitment and the feeling that there is no alternative are experienced as being externally regulated or imposed, which leads to a lower sense of well-being, lower performance, and greater absenteeism (Sheldon & Schuler 2011).

HRM practices in organisations revolve around commitment because of its role in determining important individual outcomes, including job attitudes, motivation, performance, and retention, and because of its links to successful teamwork, organisational outcomes, and reduced turnover. From this perspective, however, commitment can no longer be seen to be based upon loyalty to the organisation itself, but is more often about commitment to goals, teams, projects, career, or values.

I discussed organisation-sponsored causes earlier in this chapter, and the way in which such sponsorship enhances loyalty to the organisation as well as to the cause itself. Approximately 72% of employees in the United States want their employers to do more to support a cause or social issue, and such sponsorship generates substantive benefits to employees and organisations (Grant 2012). This is in contrast to the predominant profit-motif of our times, which is leading us to a progressive increase in inequality driven by a sense of entitlement (Picketty 2014). In the UK, charitable giving by the rich is very low, with those earning above £200,000 annually giving just £2 for each £1,000 they earn (Philanthropy Review 2011). In contrast to this trend is that of the philanthropic entrepreneur—someone who seeks a large personal fortune and then actively invests their resources on non-profit-making social objectives (Harvey et al. 2011). Philanthropy is one route to the construction of desirable past and future selves and we have a wide raft of not-for-profit organisations (Villadsen 2007), voluntary groups, and people willing to volunteer, often working day in, day out for no financial reward (see Chapter 18). Conspicuous philanthropy offers legitimacy, influence, social investment, and enhanced connections (Bosworth 2011). However, not all philanthropy is conspicuous or about self-legitimation. Philanthropic self-narratives show solidarity with deprived communities (Johnstone & Lionais 2004) and the desire to give back and make a difference to their community of origin. Some might seek redemption (Creed et al. 2014) or a life-validating legacy of the self (Peredo & Chrisman 2006) as part of an ongoing narrative fostering a new identity that is both self- and socially oriented (Maclean et al. 2015).

Conflict and Well-Being

Interestingly, the way in which conflict is handled at work has an impact upon commitment to the organisation. As explored in Chapter 9, conflict can make employees genuinely ill and increase absenteeism. Supervisors have the greatest chance of influencing the outcome of conflict when it is in its early stages (de Reuver 2003), either by imposing solution or opening dialogue about the issue, or by delegation to another. The path they take helps define the relationship with their subordinates and impacts upon the subordinate's sense of trust and loyalty towards both their supervisor and the organisation, thus impacting upon the employee's sense of commitment (Eisenberger et al. 2005). A cooperative approach to the resolution of conflict is most likely to make people feel part of a sound relationship that the values the employee, and thus supports commitment to the organisation and reduced absenteeism. Supervisors who handle conflict in an oppositional manner tend to control through the misleading manipulation of information and veiled threat (Lewicki & Litterer 1985), thereby creating a competitive climate that reduces mutual trust and commitment, though the dislike created tends to be focused on the supervisor rather than the organisation. Supervisors that attempt to pacify the situation without seeking resolution are seen to be weak and absconding from their responsibility and not showing that they value the well-being of the employees (Yukl 2002), thereby reducing commitment. Managing absenteeism is a major issue for many organisations and de Reuver & van Woerkom (2010) argue that approaches such as focused attendance management, integrated disability management, benefit design, and wellness programs are not sufficient on their own. It is important that the organisation also adopts an integrative conflict strategy by which commitment to the organisation is primarily based on intrinsic reward, thereby establishing a fully engaged workforce. In this context an integrative conflict strategy takes on a wider meaning and can be seen as a form of prosocial (transformational or non-narcissistic) leadership in which leaders focus on the needs of the group rather than their own interests, thereby achieving higher levels of organisational commitment and lower absence (Lorenzi 2004).

To some extent, ideas of well-being at work (Spreitzer et al. 2005) pull together many of the threads that I have discussed here. As Gagné & Deci (2005: 353) suggest: 'When people are autonomously motivated at work they tend to experience their jobs as interesting or personally important, self-initiated and endorsed by relevant others'. In this way, job performance is associated with an experience of satisfaction and formation of positive attitudes towards work. Subjective well-being is associated with satisfaction and quality of life, the lack of which is linked to stress caused by organisational factors such as work-related demands associated with high levels of responsibility and obligations (Schieman et al. 2006; and see also Chapter 9). Psychological well-being is associated with the pursuit of meaningful goals and the achievement of true potential across lifespan (Ryan & Deci 2001) and is linked to personal factors, such as cognitive hardiness.

HRD IN A CHANGING WORLD

Through this we return, again, to the balance needed between agency and structure. We like to think of leaders as imposing their view of the world, making things happen, driving the organisation forward. Yet ideas of transformational leadership revolve around cooperation and integration, and the co-creation of the way forward. If we look at the literature around complexity and change management, however, it is clear that the path is not predetermined and we are all of us in a process of becoming. Whether or not they want to, leaders and managers increasingly need to be able to cope with the incipient chaos of a complex world. Instead of either setting out clear paths (as an agent) or developing cooperative groupings (building structure) they need to develop the conditions under which there is enough order for people to be able to feel a sense of predictability and consistency, but also enough looseness to allow new things to emerge and to minimise resistance to control. We need to work in the balance between rigid structure and unbounded chaos. From this perspective the manager builds the vision and focuses on the outcome, reiterating to all sections of the organisation what needs to be achieved, and promoting the conditions important for change to take place, but allowing the employees to determine how the change is obtained. From a co-evolving perspective, all stakeholders work together (negotiating consciously or unconsciously) to bring about the end result—these might be the employees, including the leaders, in a for-profit environment, but the same holds true for non-profit, volunteer, and friendship groups. This takes us away from the neocolonial infantilisation of the workforce to seeing all employees as potentially valuable contributors, able to think for themselves, and able to work with change in a positive and constructive manner. In this final section of the chapter, I shall first look at the sort of individual qualities that might be needed for such change, before looking at the implications for HRD.

In the changing, more mobile, world that I describe above, the sort of skills usually associated with entrepreneurs (such as a high level of tenacity and obstinacy, problem solving, social adaptability, ability to learn, social intelligence, negotiation skills, and coordination of social relationships) are becoming highly valued (Lamine et al. 2014). One of the key attributes is cognitive hardiness, which distinguishes those who do well in stressful situations from those who do less well, and is correlated with commitment, control, and challenge (Maddi et al. 2009). People higher in hardiness are more satisfied with their jobs, they see stressful situations in a positive way, and they also perform better (Cash & Gardner 2011). However, there are also problems with high cognitive hardiness—such people tend to self-rate their performance more highly than others would, and be overly self-reliant (Krizan & Suls 2008), particularly because they can then take on individual responsibility for managing stressful situations that might be a shared responsibility or the result of bad organisational processes and cultures, thereby hiding and possibly exacerbating the root cause of the problems (Dewe 1997).

Another key quality in a changing world is that of proactivity: self-initiated behaviour that is anticipatory or future-oriented and intended to constructively change current circumstances (Grant & Ashford 2008). This can range from expressing ideas for constructive change to making positive changes in work methods or procedures and preventing problems from occurring (Frese & Fay 2001). As Fuller et al. (2015) point out, this behaviour is very important to the organisation and proactive employees tend to have higher performance evaluations and greater career success. However, proactivity may be seen as criticism or a challenge to authority and the person may not be given any credit for the valuable contributions they make and can be given lower performance evaluations, reduced training opportunities, and less promotion, particularly if the manager does not feel responsible for the changes that have been proposed or initiated. This rather neatly illustrates the interplay between structure and agency. The entrepreneurial proactive employee, bursting with agency, may rapidly become demotivated and disillusioned if faced with a hierarchical structure in which, despite the rhetoric, the leadership does not value change and will not allow employees to take responsibility for change. Neither the agent nor the structure can progress this situation on its own.

Structures for Learning?

This brings me back to the role of HRD in our changing world. As I have explored in more detail elsewhere in the book, we can liken HRM to the structures that we establish in order to work together, and HRD as the relationships and processes between the structures: the glue that holds it all together. We can't really talk about one without the other. If we consider the need to foster proactive behaviour as an example, it is clear that we need to address structural issues (the current *rules* of our culture) such as job design, including access to resources; levels of autonomy; and active career management, including compensation and promotion practices. At the same time we need to look to personal qualities: helping individual employees become proactive whilst also developing leaders who feel responsible for constructive change, and are also willing to give responsibility and credit to employees.

We can give people knowledge and understanding, but we can't sit them down and 'make' them proactive or entrepreneurial; we can't give them cognitive hardiness or the ability to work easily across cultures. People are also expecting more from education and training. They are buying into the chimera of employability and want to learn about things that are important for their future—at a faster rate and with quick feedback (Bellanca & Brandt 2010). Educators (whether academic staff, trainers, mentors, or colleagues) are expected to have the learners' needs to heart, providing personalised support. This is resource intensive and demanding of the time, energy, and ability of the educators—most of whom do not have the experience necessary to manage students learning in the intense and ambiguous environments of non-traditional provision.

Obviously school, formal learning, exams, qualifications, and professional recognition play a part in this, but they more mark the way, indicate stages passed, than they are part of the passage itself. I have discussed action learning in Chapters 2, 3, and 10, and I hope I have made it clear throughout this book that I am convinced that what makes us who we think we might be becoming is much more than book learning or received wisdom: People learn (subconsciously as well as consciously) from trying things out, from seeing other people do things and the results of that. Therefore, rather than telling, we are better off setting the scene and establishing structures, and showing and doing. As the world changes, so must our understanding of 'education'. The process of becoming is about co-creating ourselves, alongside others, together facing tasks, challenges, and enjoyment. This is about making sense of, and developing from, experiences—these might be at work, at home, or in-between, but are rarely planned.

Experiential learning is a process of learning through reflection on experience and creating meaning from the encounter (Kolb 1984). It involves direct transforming experience rather than simply reading or thinking about the topic; the making conscious of, and reflecting on, tacit knowledge; and (within the work environment) focusing on the development of an individual's practical skills and attributes within real situations in which the learner is an active participant. I quibble that the Kolb cycle does not easily account for embodied or subconscious aspects of our learning; however, it does emphasise that what is learnt from a shared experience is individual to each person—the focus on social and contextual issues is important, as are situational factors such as age, ethnicity, technology, and learning styles (Chavan 2011). Experiential learning can occur through simulated experience (as with business games and case studies) but it is hard to simulate all aspects of the experience (Pittaway & Cope 2007), including feelings and emotions, and the effect of those embodied aspects that I discussed above. What experiential learning does is enable people to learn about themselves as agents within the structures that they and others create.

CONCLUSION

Although at an initial glance global issues such as climate change might appear unrelated to HRD, I hope I have illustrated that the effect of such supposedly non-HRD issues are likely to have a fundamental impact upon the nature of work and working lives (let alone our private lives). I have presented a picture of a world with less clear boundaries, a kaleidoscope of cultures and skills, in which HRD is the glue of processes and relationships that holds the myriad of perspectives together. This is a world of movement, tension, and conflict, balanced by rewards for the small, skilled, flexible, and technologically aware organisations that succeed by working in harmony and partnership with a wide and shifting selection of other organisations from across the world. This is a world of refugees, migration, and conflict for the technologically poor, and one of small cluster organisations, high skill and mobility, and longevity for the technological elite. This will impact upon us all, influencing our jobs and our security, our mortality—and also our morality. To do our jobs properly we must consider the wider picture.

Organisations are now able to manage their internal statistics and systems more fluidly, such that keeping track of flexible working and a wide system of varied benefits no longer presents the logistical problem that it used to do. However, they have been slow to realise the value of human capital, and slow to develop necessary evaluative skills. Organisations need to be able to manage high turnover, attract skilled staff, and retain those already employed. The presence of older employees in the workplace is prolonging workforce regeneration cycles and heightens the need for more flexible work patterns. HRD needs to be at the centre of creating an organisational environment that stimulates and values workers, that meets their needs such that it retains them in a marketplace where workplace benefits— as mundane as working with a nice supervisor—can outweigh the lure of a higher wage. HRD also has a part to play in balancing the structures of the organisation: overseeing how the rules of working together are developed and monitored; overseeing alternative forms of employee benefit; developing the organisation's culture in a way that balances the needs of all employees; benchmarking and making sound judgements about the comparability of qualifications, attainment, and provision; and taking a proactive part in the development of strategy, sustainability, and longevity.

This balancing role of HRD is likely to include the more traditional 'training and development' aimed at establishing the qualities and abilities required in successful employees. Promoting, developing, and assessing these remains essential, though the attributes that are sought are likely to shift towards those of the flexible portfolio worker. HRD will also increasingly need to pay attention to areas such as cross-cultural awareness, diversity, and conflict resolution. These areas will be needed both in terms of managing these within organisations and also as key skills that employees will need as they work with others across a range of situations: co-creating the future.

People are increasingly turning to their professional bodies to enhance their sense of identity at work and provide a sense of permanence. After all, an individual is likely to be a member of one or more professional bodies all their working life, but may only be with a single organisation for a few years. It is their profession that stays with them as they move from organisation to organisation, role to role, and nation to nation. Professional bodies, therefore, are likely to become a more vocal champion of their members' needs and rights. They are also in a position to collaborate with, or act as mediator between, the organisation, the individual, and the state. Perhaps it is the professions, also, which are able to adopt the broader view—to express their concerns about those who fail to bridge the increasing skills and technology gap. Perhaps it is the professions who can foster ways of helping those who lack the resources or are less able to adapt to change.

Some of the deeper questions that people and professional bodies need to face are moral considerations for themselves, but are also about the remit of HRD. As we think of HRD do we include child labour and sex workers, the self-employed, NGOs, or even virtual organisations? As we develop systems of flexible interrelated organisations that can draw employees from across the globe we need to establish some global understanding of what we expect such employees to be able to do—yet how do we avoid cultural imperialism? As ownership and identity become contested and conflict increases, where do we stand on war, armed forces, peacekeeping? As we work we are party to information on people and organisations—who do we trust and with what information? What liberties are we willing to give away in order to support the maintenance of power and order, or to prevent possible acts of terrorism? Where do we stand on the plight of others? How much tax are we willing to pay to support equality? How much are we willing to change to help reduce global warming? How much do we rely on the 'system' to take responsibility for us, or to take on our responsibility for others? What do we hold ourselves responsible for?

As we prepare our students to become HR professionals, academics, and managers we should be anticipating what their future needs will be: preparing them for the future, not the past (see Chapter 18). If HRD is to be an active and ethical agent in this new world in which the divide between the rich and the poor grows increasingly large, then HRD has to engage in areas such as politics and policy, law and economics, strategy and structures, philosophy and morality, and so on. HRD, itself, has to become a partner in the struggles of the world in order to promote core aspirations of fostering a sustainable environment in which the needs of people are balanced and in which no one group or interest takes precedence at the expense of another, and in which the value of each element to the whole is recognised.

In this changing world of shifting boundaries and global challenges HRD should no longer be seen as a bureaucratic subfunction. It can help create a better future: It is time for HRD to come of age.

REFERENCES

Adair T, Temple J, Ortega L, & Williams R (2013) *Age Discrimination in the Labour Market*. Melbourne, Australia: National Seniors Productive Ageing Centre.

Aguinis H & Glavas A (2012) 'What we know and don't know about corporate social responsibility', *Journal of Management* 38: 932–968.

Alvesson M (2010) 'Self-doubters, strugglers, storytellers, surfers and others: Images of self-identities in organization studies', *Human Relations* 63(2)193–217.

Ambec S & Lanoie P (2008) 'Does it pay to be green?', *Academy of Management Perspectives* 22(2)45–62.

Antonacopoulou EP & Gabriel Y (2001) 'Emotion, learning and organizational change', *Journal of Organizational Change Management* 14(5)435–451.

Arthur N & Popadiuk N (2010) 'A cultural formulation approach to career counselling with inter-national students', *Journal of Career Development* 37(1)423–440.

Ashforth BE (2001) *Role Transitions in Organizational Life: An Identity-based Perspective*. New York: Routledge.

Autio E, Sapienza HJ, & Almeida JG (2000) 'Effects of age at entry, knowledge intensity, and imitability on international growth', *Academy of Management Journal* 43(5)909–924.

Ayree S, Budhwar PS, & Chen ZX (2002) 'Trust as a mediator of the relationship between organizational justice and work outcomes: test of a social exchange model', *Journal of Organizational Behavior* 23(3)267–285.

Bamberger PA (2015) 'Winding Down and Boozing Up: The complex link between retirement and alcohol misuse', *Work, Aging and Retirement* 1(1)92–111.

Banerjee SB & Linstead S (2000) 'Globalization, multiculturalism and other fictions: Colonialism for the new millennium?', *Organization* 8(4)683–722.

Batteau AW (2000) 'Negations and ambiguities in the cultures of organization', *American Anthropologist* 102(4)726–740.

Beehr TA & Bennet MA (20015) 'Working after retirement', *Work, Aging and Retirement* 1(1)112–128.

Bellanca J & Brandt R (2010) *21st Century Skills: Rethinking How Students Learn*. New York, NY: Solution Tree Press, Bloomington.

Benson MJ & Hogan RS (2008) 'How dark side leadership personality destroys trust and degrades organisational effectiveness', *Organisations and People* 15: 10–18.

Berkelaar BL, Buzzanell PM, Kisselburgh LG, Tan W, & Shen Y (2012) ' "First, it's dirty. Second, it's dangerous. Third, it's insulting": Urban Chinese children talk about work and careers', *Communication Monographs* 79(1)93–114.

Besen E, Matz-Costa C, Brown M, Smyer MA, & Pit-Catsouphes M (2013) 'Job characteristics, core self-evaluations, and job satisfaction: What's age got to do with it?', *International Journal of Aging and Human Development* 76: 269–295.

Biemann T & Andresen M (2010) 'Self-initiated foreign expatriates versus assigned expatriates: Two distinct types of international careers?', *Journal of Managerial Psychology* 25(4)430–448.

Bingham JB, Mitchell BW, Bishop DG, & Allen NJ (2013) 'Working for a higher purpose: A theoretical framework for commitment to organization-sponsored causes', *Human Resource Management Review* 23: 174–189.

Blount S & Janicik GA (2001) 'When plans change: Examining how people evaluate timing changes in work organizations', *Academy of Management Review* 26: 566–585.

Bosworth D (2011) 'The cultural contradictions of philanthrocapitalism', *Society* 48: 382–388.

Boyacigiller N & Adler NJ (1991) 'The parochial dinosaur: Organisational science in a global context', *Academy of Management Review* 16 (2)262–290.

Bradford L, Buck JL, & Meyers RA (2001) 'Cultural and parental communicative influences on the career success of White and Black women', *Women's Studies in Communication* 24(2)194–217.

Brahm T & Kunze F (2012) 'The role of trust climate in virtual teams', *Journal of Managerial Psychology* 27(6)595–614.

Brough P, Timms C, Cook J, Siu O, Kalliath T, O'Driscoll MP, Sit CHP, Lo D, & Lu C (2015) Validation of the Job Demands-Resources model in cross-national samples', *Human Relations* 66(10)1312–1335.

Brown AD & Thompson E (2013) 'A narrative approach to strategy-as-practice', *Business History* 55: 1143–1167.

Brunell AB, Gentry WA, Campbell WK, Hoffman BJ, Kuhnert KW, & DeMarree KG (2008) 'Leader emergence: the case of the narcissistic leader', *Personality and Social Psychology Bulletin* 34: 1663–1676.

Bruns H (2012) 'Working alone together', *Academy of Management Journal* 56(1)62–83.

Bucker J & Poutsma E (2010) 'Global management competencies: A theoretical foundation', *Journal of Managerial Psychology* 25(8)829–844.

Burnes B (2009) 'Organizational change in the public sector', in By RT & Macleod C (Eds) *Managing Organizational Change in Public Services:* 111–132. London: Routledge.

Buzzanell PM & Lucas K (2013) 'Constrained and constructed choices in career', in Cohen EL (Ed.) *Communication Yearbook* 37: 3–31. New York: Routledge.

Cahill KE, Giandrea MD, & Quinn JF (2005) 'Are traditional retirements a thing of the past?', *BLS Working Paper:* 384.

Caldwell C & Dixon RD (2010) 'Love, forgiveness, and trust: Critical values of the modern leader', *Journal of Business Ethics* 93(1)91–101.

Callahan J, Stewart J, Rigg C, Sambrook S, & Trehan K (2015) (Eds) *Realising Critical HRD.* Cambridge: Cambridge Scholars Publishing.

Campbell WK, Hoffman BJ, Campbell SM, & Marchisio G (2011) 'Narcissism in organizational contexts', *Human Resource Management Review* 21: 268–284.

Cash ML & Gardner D (2011) 'Cognitive hardiness, appraisal and coping', *Journal of Managerial Psychology* 26(8)646–664.

Chatterjee A & Hambrick DC (2007) 'It's all about me: Narcissistic chief executive officers and their effects on company strategy and performance', *Administrative Science Quarterly* 52: 351–386.

Chavan M (2011) 'Higher education students' attitudes towards experiential learning in international business', *Journal of Teaching in International Business* 22(2)126–143.

Cheney G & Ashcraft KL (2007) 'Considering "the professional" in communication studies', *Communication Theory* 17(2)146–175.

Choi SYP & Peng Y (2015) 'Humanized management? Capital and migrant labour in a time of labour shortage in South China', *Human Relations* 68(2) 287–304.

Chreim S (2005) 'The continuity-change duality in narrative texts of organizational identity', *Journal of Management Studies* 42(3)567–593.

Chudzikowski K (2012) 'Career transitions and career success in the 'new' career era', *Journal of Vocational Behavior* 81(2)298–306.

CIPD (2015) *Employee Outlook: Spring.* London: CIPD.

Classen TJ & Dunn RA (2012) 'The effect of job loss and unemployment duration on suicide risk in the United States', *Health Economics* 21(3)338–350.

Clausen T, Christensen KB, & Borg V (2010) 'Positive work-related states and long-term sickness absence: A study of register-based outcomes', *Scandinavian Journal of Public Health* 38(3)51–58.

Cohen A (2007) 'Commitment before and after', *Human Resource Management Review* 17(3)336–354.

Commonwealth of Australia (2013) *An Ageing Australia: Preparing for the Future.* Canberra, Australia: Australian Government Productivity Commission.

Compton E, Brady H, Hetherington D, Howe B, Lewin G, O'Neill M, & Roach N (2014) *Blueprint for an Ageing Australia.* Sydney, Australia: Per Capita.

Conroy SA & O'Leary-Kelly AM (2014) 'Letting go and moving on', *Academy of Management Review* 39(1)67–87.

Contu A & Girei E (2014) 'NGOs management and the value of 'partnerships' for equality in international development', *Human Relations* 67(2)205–232.

Cooke B (2003a) 'Managing organizational culture and imperialism', in Prasad A (Ed) *Postcolonial Theory and Organizational Analysis:* 75–94. New York: Palgrave.

Cooke B (2003b) 'The denial of slavery in Management Studies', *Journal of Management Studies* 40(8)1895–1918.

Costea B (1999) 'International MBAs and globalisation: celebration or end of diversity?', *Human Resource Development International* 2(4)309–313.

Coyne B, Coyne E, & Lee MM (2003) *Human Resources, Care Giving, Career Progression And Gender.* London, UK: Routledge.

Creed WED, DeJordy R, & Lok J (2014) 'Myths to work by', *Religion and Organization Theory* 41: 111–156.

Crosby BC & Bryson JM (2005) *Leadership for the Common Good.* San Francisco, CA: Jossey-Bass.

Crutzen PJ & Stoermer EF (2000) 'The Anthropocene', *Global Change Newsletter* 41: 17–18.

Cunliffe A & Coupland C (2011) 'From hero to villain to hero', *Human Relations* 65(1)63–88.

Daepp MIG, Hamilton MJ, West GB, & Bettencourt LMA (2015) 'The mortality of companies', *Journal of the Royal Society Interface* 12(106). DOI: 10.1098/rsif.2015.0120

Davis HP, Klebe KJ, Guinther PM, Schroder KB, Cornwell RE, & James LE (2013) 'Subjective organization, verbal learning, and forgetting across the life span: From 5 to 89', *Experimental Aging Research* 39(1)1–26.

De Cremer D & van Dijk E (2009) 'Paying for sanctions in social dilemmas', *Organizational Behavior and Human Decision Processes* 109: 45–55.

De Jong BA & Elfring T (2010) 'How does trust affect the performance of ongoing teams?', *Academy of Management Journal* 53(3)535–549.

DeNisi AS, Wilson MS, & Biteman J (2014) 'Research and practice in HRM: A historical perspective', *Human Resource Management Review* 24: 219–231.

Dent E (1999) 'Complexity science: A worldview shift', *Emergence* 7(4)5–19.

de Reuver R & van Woerkom M (2010) 'Can conflict management be an antidote to subordinate absenteeism?', *Journal of Managerial Psychology* 25(5)479–494.

de Reuver RSM (2003) *Manager and Conflict*. Amsterdam: Dutch University Press.

Derman BB (2014) 'Climate governance, justice, and transnational civil society', *Climate Policy* 14(1)23–41.

Dewe P (1997) 'The transactional model of stress', *Asia Pacific Journal of Human Resources* 35(2)41–51.

Dezalay Y & Garth BG (2004) 'The confrontation between the Big Five and Big Law', *Law and Social Inquiry* 29(3)615–638.

Dingemans E & Henkens K (2014) 'Involuntary retirement, bridge employment, and satisfaction with life', *Journal of Organizational Behavior* 35(4)575–591.

Djankov S, Botero J, Porta R, & Lopez-De-Silanes FC (2004) 'The regulation of labor', *The Quarterly Journal of Economics* 119(4)1339–1382.

Driver M (2015) 'How trust functions in the context of identity work', *Human Relations* 68(6)899–923.

Drucker P (1999) *Management Challenges for the 21st. Century*. New York: Harper-Collins Publishers.

Duchon D & Burns M (2008) 'Organizational narcissism', *Organizational Dynamics* 37: 354–364.

Dutta MJ (2012) 'Critical interrogations of global public relations', in Sriramesh K & Vercic D (Eds) *Culture and Public Relations:* 202–217. New York: Routledge.

Dwyer DJ & Arbelo M (2012) 'The role of social cognition in downsizing decisions', *Journal of Managerial Psychology* 27(4)383–405.

Economist (2012) *'The largest migration in history'* (http://www.economist.com/blogs/graphicdetail/2012/02/daily-chart-17).

Eddy ER, Stone DL, & Stone-Romero EF (1999) 'The effects of information management policies on reactions to human resource information systems', *Personnel Psychology* 52: 335–358.

Eisenberger R, Jones JR, Aselage J, & Sucharski IL (2005) 'Perceived organizational support', in Coyle-Shapiro JA-M, Shore LM, Taylor MS, & Tetrick LE (Eds) *The Employment Relationship:* 206–225. Oxford: Oxford University Press.

Elliott C & Turnbull S (2005) 'Critical thinking in Human Resource Development: An introduction', in Elliott C & Turnbull S (Eds) *Critical Thinking in Human Resource Development:* 1–7. London: Routledge.

Etzioni A (2000) 'Toward a theory of public ritual', *Sociological Theory* 18: 44–59.

Farmer SM & Van Dyne L (2010) 'The idealized self and the situated self as predictors of employee work behaviors', *Journal of Applied Psychology* 95: 503–516.

Feldman DC, Leana CR, & Bolino MC (2002) 'Underemployment and relative deprivation among re-employed executives', *Journal of Occupational and Organizational Psychology* 75: 453–471.

Fernandez S & Rainey HG (2006) 'Managing successful organizational change in the public sector', *Public Administration Review* 66(2)168–176.

Ferner A, Edwards T, & Tempel A (2011) 'Power, institutions and the cross-national transfer of employment practices in multinationals', *Human Relations* 65(2)163–187.

Finkelstein LM, King EB, & Voyles EC (2015) 'Age Metastereotyping and Cross-Age workplace interactions', *Work, Aging and Retirement* 1(1)26–40.

Fitzsimmons SR & Stamper CL (2014) 'How societal culture influences friction in the employee–organization relationship', *Human Resource Management Review* 24: 80–94.

Ford DP (2013) 'Virtual harassment', *Journal of Managerial Psychology* 28(4)408–428.

Fraher AL & Gabriel Y (2014) 'Dreaming of flying when grounded', *Journal of Management Studies* 51(6)926–951.

Frenkel SJ & Yu C (2015) 'Chinese migrants' work experience and city identification', *Human Relations* 68(2)261–285.

Frese M & Fay D (2001)' Personal initiative: An active performance concept for work in the 21st Century'. In Staw B & Sutton R (Eds) *Research in Organizational Behavior*, Vol. 23. Oxford: Elsevier Science Ltd: 133–187.

Friedland R & Alford RR (1991) 'Bringing society back in', in Powell WW & DiMaggio PJ (Eds) *The New Institutionalism In Organizational Analysis*: 232–263. Chicago, IL: University of Chicago Press.

Frumin I, Perl O, Endevelt-Shapira Y, Eisen A, Eshel N, Heller I, Shemesh M, Ravia A, Sela L, Arzi A, & Sobel N (2015) 'A social chemosignaling function for human handshaking', *eLife* 4: e05154. doi:10.7554/eLife.05154.

Fuller B, Marler LE, Hester K, & Otondo RF (2015) 'Leader reactions to follower proactive behavior', *Human Relations* 68(6)880–898.

Gagné M & Deci EL (2005) 'Self-determination theory and work motivation', *Journal of Organizational Behavior* 26(4)331–362.

Gardner HK, Gino F, & Staats BR (2012) 'Dynamically integrating knowledge in teams', *Academy of Management Journal* 55(4)998–1022.

Gerde V, Goldsby M & Shepard J (2007) 'Moral cover for capitalism: The harmony-of-interests doctrine', *Journal of Management History* 13(1)7–20.

Gore A (2007) *The Nobel Peace Prize 2007*. Nobel Lecture. Oslo, Norway: Nobel Foundation.

Grant A & Ashford S (2008) 'The dynamics of proactivity at work', *Research in Organizational Behavior* 28: 3–34.

Grant AM (2012) 'Giving time, time after time', *Academy of Management Review* 37(4)589–615.

Griffin B (2015) 'Promoting the Work Adjustment of Late Career Employees', in Hartung PJ, Savickas ML, & Walsh WB, (Eds) *APA Handbook of Career Intervention: Applications*: 439–451. Washington, DC: American Psychological Association.

Grigg DW (2012) 'Definitional constructs of cyber-bullying and cyber-aggression from a triangulatory overview', *Journal of Aggression, Conflict and Peace Research* 4(4)202–215.

Guenter H, van Emmerik H, & Schreurs B (2014) 'The negative effects of delays in information exchange', *Human Resource Management Review* 24: 283–298.

Guest R (2011) 'Special report on global leaders', *The Economist* 22 January: 3–20.

Haidar JI (2012) 'The impact of business regulatory reforms on economic growth', *Journal of the Japanese and International Economies* 26: 285–307.

Haley UCV & Boje DM (2014) 'Storytelling the internationalization of the multinational enterprise', *Journal of International Business Studies* 45: 1115–1132.

Handy C (2007) *The New Philanthropists*. London: William Heinemann.

Harvey C, Maclean M, Gordon J, & Shaw E (2011) 'Andrew Carnegie and the foundations of contemporary entrepreneurial philanthropy', *Business History* 53: 425–450.

Hatcher T & Lee MM (2003) HRD and the democratic ideal: The conflict of democratic values in undemocratic work systems' in (Ed) Winterton, J., International, Comparative and Cross-Cultural Dimensions of HRD, Proceedings of UFHRD conference, Toulouse. ISBN 1-86220-149-8

Hawkins B (2015) 'Ship-shape: Materializing leadership in the British Royal Navy', *Human Relations* 68(6): 952–971.

Hay J & Beniston M (2001) 'Environmental change and migration', *Tiempo* 42 December: 17–41.

Heybroek L, Haynes M, & Baxter J (2015) 'Life satisfaction and retirement in Australia: A longitudinal approach', *Work, Aging and Retirement* 1(2)166–180.

Higgs M (2009) 'The good, the bad and the ugly: Leadership and narcissism', *Journal of Change Management* 9: 165–178.

Hofstede G & Hofstede GJ (2005) *Cultures and Organizations*. New York: McGraw-Hill.

Hopkins SM & Weathington BL (2006) 'The relationship between justice perceptions, trust, and employee attitudes in a downsized organization', *The Journal of Psychology* 140(5)477–496.

Ibarra H & Barbulescu R (2010) 'Identity as narrative', *Academy of Management* 35(1)135–154.

IPCC (2014) *Climate Change 2014: Synthesis Report*. Geneva, Switzerland: IPCC.

Johnstone H & Lionais D (2004) 'Depleted communities and community business entrepreneur-ship', *Entrepreneurship & Regional Development* 16: 217–233.

Jonason PK, Li NP, Webster GD, & Schmitt DP (2009) 'The dark triad: Facilitating a short-term mating strategy in men', *European Journal of Personality* 23: 5–18.

Judge TA, Piccolo RF, & Kosalka T (2009) 'The bright and dark sides of leader traits: A review and theoretical extension of the leader trait paradigm', *The Leadership Quarterly* 20: 855–875.

Kalokerinos EK, von Hippe C, & Henry JD (2015) 'Job attitudes are differentially associated with bridge employment and phased retirement among older Australian employees', *Work, Aging and Retirement* 1(2)129–132.

Karren R (2012) 'Introduction to the special issue on job loss', *Journal of Managerial Psychology* 27(8)772–779.

Kašperová E & Kitching J (2014) 'Embodying entrepreneurial identity', *International Journal of Entrepreneurial Behaviour & Research* 20(5)438–452.

Kaufman BE (2014) 'The historical development of American HRM broadly viewed', *Human Resource Management Review* 24: 196–218.

Keebler T (2001) 'HR Outsourcing in the Internet Era', in Walker A (Ed) *Web-based Human Resources*: 259–276. New York, NY: McGraw-Hill.

Kelly S & Riach K (2014) 'Monstrous reanimation: Rethinking organizational death in the UK financial services sector', *Culture and Organization* 20(1)7–22.

Kets de Vries MFR (2001) 'The anarchist within: Clinical reflections on Russian character and leadership style', *Human Relations* 54(5)585–627.

Kickert WJM (2010) 'Managing emergent and complex change: The case of the Dutch agencification', *International Review of Administrative Sciences* 76(3)489–515.

Kidron A, Tzafrir SS, Meshulam I, & Iverson RD (2013) 'Internal integration within human resource management subsystems', *Journal of Managerial Psychology* 28(6)699–719.

Klein HJ, Molloy JC, & Brinsfield CT (2012) 'Reconceptualizing workplace commitment to redress a stretched construct', *Academy of Management Review* 37: 130–151.

Koen J, Klehe UC, Van Vianen AEM, Zikic J, & Nauta A (2010) 'Job-search strategies and reemployment quality', *Journal of Vocational Behavior* 77: 126–139.

Kolb DA (1984) *Experiential Learning*. Prentice-Hall, NJ: Englewood Cliffs.

Kontos M (2013) 'Negotiating the social citizenship rights of migrant domestic workers', *Journal of Ethnic and Migration Studies* 39(3)409–424.

Kontos M, Shinozaki K, Morokvasic M, Catarino C, & Satola A (2009) 'Migrant domestic and care workers', in Kontos M (Ed) *Integration of Female Migrants in Labour Market and Society: A Comparative Analysis*: 44–51. Frankfurt: University of Frankfurt.

Koot W (1996) 'The rhetoric of synergy and the practice of increasing ethnic rivalry in organizations', in Koot W, Sabelis I, & Ybema S (Eds) *Contradictions in Context*: 63–86. Amsterdam: VU University Press.

Kreiner GE, Hollensbe EC, & Sheep ML (2009) 'Balancing borders and bridges', *Academy of Management Journal* 52(4)704–730.

Krizan Z & Suls J (2008) 'Losing sight of oneself in the above-average effect', *Journal of Experimental Social Psychology* 44(4)929–942.

Krueger AB & Mueller A (2011) "Job Search, Emotional Well-Being and Job Finding in a Period of Mass Unemployment: Evidence from High-Frequency Longitudinal Data," *Brookings Papers on Economic Activity*, 42(1)1–81.

Kulik CT, Ryan S, Harper S, & George G (2014) 'From the editors: Aging populations and management', *Academy of Management Journal* 57: 929–935.

Kunda G (1992) *Engineering Culture: Control and Commitment in a High-tech Corporation*. Philadelphia: Temple University Press.

Lamine W, Mian S, & Fayolle A (2014) 'How do social skills enable nascent entrepreneurs to enact perseverance strategies in the face of challenges?', *International Journal of Entrepreneurial Behaviour & Research* 20(6)517–541.

Lapidot Y, Kark R, & Shamir B (2007), 'The impact of situational vulnerability on the development and erosion of follower's trust in their leader', *Leadership Quarterly* 18: 16–34.

LaPointe K (2010) 'Narrating career, positioning identity', *Journal of Vocational Behavior* 77(1)1–9.

Lee MM (2015) 'The History, Status and Future of HRD', in Poell RF, Rocco TS, & Roth GL (Eds), *The Routledge Companion to HRD*: 3–13. London: Routledge.

Lee MM, Letiche H, Crawshaw R, & Thomas M (1996) (Eds) *Management Education in the New Europe*. London: Routledge.

Lewicki RJ & Litterer J (1985) *Negotiation*. Homewood, IL: Irwin.

Li PP (2011) 'The rigour-relevance balance for engaged scholarship', *Journal of Trust Research* 1(1)1–21.

Lincoln Y (2012) 'In and Out of the Black Box', in Lee MM (Ed) *Human Resource Development as We Know It*: 27–37. New York: Routledge.

Litwin H & Shiovitz-Ezra S (2011) 'Social network type and subjective well-being in a national sample of older Americans', *The Gerontologist* 51: 379–388.

Lloyd S & Hartel C (2010) 'Intercultural competencies for culturally diverse work teams', *Journal of Managerial Psychology* 25(8)845–875.

Locke KD (2009) 'Aggression, narcissism, self-esteem, and the attribution of desirable and humanizing traits to self versus others', *Journal of Research in Personality* 43: 99–102.

Lorenzi P (2004) 'Managing for the common good: prosocial leadership', *Organizational Dynamics* 33: 282–291.

Lu C, Schneider MT, Gubbins P, Leach-Kemon K, Jamison D, & Murray CJL (2010) 'Public financing of health in developing countries', *Lancet* 375: 1375–1387.

Maclean M, Harvey C, Gordon J, & Shaw E (in press) 'Identity, storytelling and the philanthropic journey', *Human Relations* 68(10): 1623-1652

Maddi SR, Harvey RH, Khoshaba DM, Fazel M, & Resurreccion N (2009) 'The personality construct of hardiness, IV', *Journal of Humanistic Psychology* 49(4): 292.

Magrath J (2010) 'The injustice of climate change: Voices from Africa', *Local Environment The International Journal of Justice and Sustainability*: 15(9–10): 891–901.

Mason J & Davies K (2009) 'Coming to our senses? A critical approach to sensory methodology', *Qualitative Research* 9(5)587–603.

Mathieu JE & Zajac DM (1990) 'A review and meta-analysis of the antecedents, correlates, and consequences of organizational commitment', *Psychological Bulletin* 108(2)171–194.

McDonald J (2014) 'A fair deal for immigrants? The Truman Administration and Immigration Policy Reform', *Immigrants & Minorities* 32(2)206–233.

McLean G (2004) 'National HRD', *Advances in Developing Human Resources* 6(3)97–110.

Menard J & Brunet L (2011) 'Authenticity and well-being in the workplace: A mediation model', *Journal of Managerial Psychology* 26(4)331–346.

Metz-Gockel S, Morokvasic M, & Munst AS (2008) (Eds) *Gendered Mobilities in an Enlarged Europe*. Opladen: Barbara Budrich.

Meyer JP, Hecht TD, Gill H, & Toplonytsky L (2010) 'Person-organization (culture) fit and employee commitment under conditions of organizational change', *Journal of Vocational Behavior* 76(3)458–473.

Mitra R (2015) 'Proposing a culture-centered approach to career scholarship', *Human Relations* (in press).

Molina-Morales FX, Martinez-Fernandez MT, & Torlo VJ (2011) 'The dark side of trust: The benefits, costs and optimal levels of trust for innovation performance?', *Long Range Planning* 44(2)118–133.

Mollan S & Tennent KD (2015) 'International taxation and corporate strategy: Evidence from British overseas business, circa 1900–1965', *Business History* 57(7)1054–1081.

Morgan G (1986) *Images of Organization*. Beverly Hills: Sage.

Morrill C (1991) 'Conflict management, honor, and organizational change', *American Journal of Sociology* 97: 585–621.

Mudambi R & Swift T (2012) 'Multinational enterprises and the geographical clustering of innovation', *Industry and Innovation* 19: 1–21.

Murithi T (2009) 'Aid Colonisation and the Promise of African Continental Integration', in Abbas H & Niyiragira Y (Eds) *Aid to Africa. Redeemer or Colonizer?*: 1–12. Cape Town: Pam-bazuka Press.

Muzio D, Brock DM, & Suddaby R (2013) 'Professions and institutional change: Towards an institutionalist sociology of the professions', *Journal of Management Studies* 50(5)699–721.

Myers N. (2002) 'Environmental refugees: A growing phenomenon of the 21st Century', *Philosophical transactions of the Royal Society B: Biological Sciences* 357: 609–613.

Nederveen Pieterse A, Van Knippenberg D, & Van Ginkel WP (2011) 'Diversity in goal orientation, team reflexivity, and team performance', *Organizational Behavior and Human Decision Processes* 114(2)153–164.

Ng M, Fleming T, Robinson M et al. (137 authors) (2013) 'Global, regional, and national prevalence of overweight and obesity in children and adults during 1980–2013: A systematic analysis for the Global Burden of Disease Study', *Lancet* 2014(384)766–781.

Ng TWH & Feldman DC (2015) 'The moderating effects of age in the relationships of job autonomy to work outcomes', *Work, Aging and Retirement* 1(1)64–78.

Ouimet G. (2010) 'Dynamics of narcissistic leadership in organizations: Toward an integrated research model', *Journal of Managerial Psychology* 25: 713–726.

Padilla A, Hogan R, & Kaiser RB (2007) 'The toxic triangle: Destructive leaders, susceptible followers, and conducive environments', *The Leadership Quarterly* 18: 176–194.

Pal M & Buzzanell PM (2008) 'The Indian call center experience', *International Journal of Business Communication* 45(1)31–60.

Papastergiadis N (1997) 'Tracing Hybridity in Theory', in Werbner P & Modood T (Eds) *Debating Cultural Hybridity*: 257–281. London & New Jersey: Zed Books.

Parzefall MR & Hakanen J (2010) 'Psychological contract and its motivational and health-enhancing properties', *Journal of Managerial Psychology* 25(1)4–21.

Pascale R (1999) 'Surfing the edge of chaos', *Sloan Management Review* Spring: 83–94.

Payne SC, Horner MT, Boswell WR, Schroeder AN, & Stine-Cheyne KJ (2009) 'Comparison of online and traditional performance appraisal systems', *Journal of Managerial Psychology* 24(6)526–544.

Peacock JL (1981) 'Durkheim and the social anthropology of culture', *Social Forces* 59: 996–1008.

Pearce, F. (2002) 'Mamma Mia', *New Scientist* 20 July: 38–41. London: Reed Business Information.

Peredo AM & Chrisman JJ (2006) 'Toward a theory of community-based enterprise', *Academy of Management Review* 31: 309–328.

Philanthropy Review (2011) *Philanthropy Charter: A Call to Action*. London: Philanthropy Review.

Picketty T (2014) *Capital in the Twenty-first Century*. Cambridge, MA: Belknap Press.

Pittaway L & Cope J (2007) 'Simulating entrepreneurial learning', *Management Learning* 38(2)211–233.

Prasad A (2014) 'You can't go home again: And other psychoanalytic lessons from crossing a neo-colonial border', *Human Relations* 67(2)234–257.

Pun N & Chan J (2012) 'Global capital, the state, and Chinese workers: The Foxconn experience', *Modern China* 38(4)383–410.

Ramirez C (2012) 'How Big Four Audit Firms Control Standard-setting in Accounting and Auditing', in Huault I & Richard C (Eds) *Finance: The Discreet Regulator:* 40–58. London: Palgrave Macmillan.

Resick CJ, Whitman DS, Weingarden SM, & Hiller NJ (2009), 'The bright-side and dark-side of CEO personality', *Journal of Applied Psychology* 94: 1365–1381.

Riach K & Warren S (2015) 'Smell organization: Bodies and corporeal porosity in office work', *Human Relations* 68(5)789–809.

Riad S (2014) 'Leadership in the fluid moral economy of conspicuous consumption', *Journal of Management History* 20(1)5–43.

Ripple WJ, Beschta RL, Fortin JK, & Robbins CT (2014) 'Trophic cascades from wolves to grizzly bears in Yellowstone', *Journal of Animal Ecology* 83(1)223–233.

Rodal B (1994) *The Environment and Changing Concepts of Security (Commentary No. 47).* Ottawa, Ontario, Canada: Canadian Security Intelligence.

Roper J, Ganesh S, & Inkson K (2010) 'Neoliberalism and knowledge interests in boundaryless careers discourse', *Work, Employment & Society* 24: 661–679.

Ruddiman WF, Ellis EC, Kaplan JO, & Fuller OQ (2015) 'Defining the epoch we live in', *Science* 348(6230)38–39.

Ruona WE (2009) 'Programme excellence network of the academy of human resource development', *New Horizons in Adult Education and Human Resource Development* 23(1)41–45.

Ryan RM & Deci EL (2001) 'On happiness and human potentials: A review of research on hedonic and eudaimonic well-being', *Annual Review of Psychology* 51(1)141–166.

Ryan KM, King EB, & Finkelstein LF (2015) Younger worker's metastereotypes and workplace mood, atitudes, and behavior. *Journal of Managerial Psychology,* 30(1)54–70

Salem P (2002) 'Assessment, change, and complexity', *Management Communication Quarterly* 15(3)442–450.

Sankowska A (2013) 'Relationships between organizational trust, knowledge transfer, knowledge creation, and firm's innovativeness', *The Learning Organization* 20(1)85–100.

Sankowska A & Söderlund J (2015) 'Trust, reflexivity and knowledge integration', *Human Relations* 68(6)974–1000.

Schalk R, Timmerman V, & van den Heuvel S (2013) 'How strategic considerations influence decision making on e-HRM applications' *Human Resource Management Review* 23:84–92.

Schieman S, Whitestone YK, & Van Gundy K (2006) 'The nature of work and the stress of higher status', *Journal of Health and Social Behavior* 47(3)242–257.

Schuster P (2015) 'Ebola—challenge and revival of theoretical epidemiology', *Complexity* 20(5)7–12.

Shareef MA, Kumar V, & Kumar U (2014) 'Factors affecting citizen adoption of transactional electronic government', *Journal of Enterprise Information Management* 27(4)385–401.

Sharma A & Grant D (2011) 'Narrative, drama and charismatic leadership: The case of Apple's Steve Jobs', *Leadership* 7(1)3–26.

Sheldon KM & Schuler J (2011) 'Wanting, having, and needing: Integrating motive disposition theory and self-determination theory', *Journal of Personality and Social Psychology* 101(5)1106–1123.

Shenoy-Packer S (2014) *India's Working Women and Career Discourses*. Lanham, MD: Lexington Books.

Shimoni B & Bergmann H (2006) 'Managing in a changing world: From Multiculturalism to Hybridization', *Academy of Management Perspectives* 20(3)76–89.

Sievers B (2003) 'Against all reason: Trusting in trust', *Organizational & Social Dynamics* 3(1)19–39.

Skinner D, Dietz G, & Weibel A (2014) 'The dark side of trust: When trust becomes a "poisoned chalice"', *Organization* 21(2)206–224.

Smith ACT (2004) 'Complexity theory and change management in sport organizations', *E:CO* 6(1–2)70–79.

Spence C, Dambrin C, Carter C, Husillos J, & Archel P (2015) 'Global ends, local means: Cross-national homogeneity in professional service firms', *Human Relations* 68(5)765–788.

Spreitzer GM & Mishra AK (2002) 'To stay or to go: Voluntary survivor turnover following an organizational downsizing', *Journal of Organizational Behavior* 23(6)707–729.

Spreitzer G, Sutcliffe K, Dutton J, Sonenshein S, & Grant AM (2005) 'A socially embedded model of thriving at work', *Organization Science* 16: 537–549.

Stamov-Roßnagel C & Biemann T (2012) 'Ageing and work motivation: A task-level perspective', *Journal of Managerial Psychology* 27(5)459–478.

Stewart J & Beaver G (2003) *Human Resource Development in Small Organisations*. London: Routledge.

Stewart J, Lee MM, & Poel R (2009) 'The university forum for human resource development: Its history, purpose and activities', *New Horizons in Adult Education and Human Resource Development* 23(1)29–33.

Stone DL, Lukaszewski KM, Stone-Romero EF, & Johnson TL (2013) 'Factors affecting the effectiveness and acceptance of electronic selection systems', *Human Resource Management Review* 23: 50–70.

Stone-Romero EF & Stone D (2002) 'Cross-cultural differences in responses to feedback', *Research in Personnel and Human Resources Management* 21: 275–331.

Storey J (1991) 'Do the Japanese make better managers?', *Personnel Management* August: 24–28.

Strohmeier SS & Justus-Liebig RK (2009) 'Organizational adoption of e-HRM in Europe', *Journal of Managerial Psychology* 24(6)482–501.

Sully de Luque M, Washburn NT, Waldman DA, & House RJ (2008) 'Unrequited profit: How stake-holder and economic values relate to subordinates' perceptions of leadership and firm performance', *Administrative Science Quarterly* 53: 626–654.

Tahvanainen M, Welch D, & Worm V (2005) 'Implications of short-term international assignments', *European Management Journal* 23: 663–673.

Tams S & Marshall J (2011) 'Responsible careers: Systemic reflexivity in shifting landscapes', *Human Relations* 64(1)109–131.

Tarrant P (2013) *Reflective Practice and Professional Development*. London: SAGE.

Taylor M (2013) 'Climate change, relational vulnerability and human security', *Climate and Development* 5(4)318–327.

Tomlinson F (2005) 'Idealistic and pragmatic versions of the discourse of partnership', *Organization Studies* 26(8)1169–1188.

Tosti-Kharas J (2012) 'Continued organizational identification following involuntary job loss', *Journal of Managerial Psychology* 27(8)829–847.

Twenge JM & Campbell WK (2009) *The Narcissism Epidemic*. New York, NY: Free Press.

Urban MC (2015) 'Accelerating extinction risk from climate change', *Science* 348(6234)571–573.

Usui C, Colignon RA, & Rosen D (2014) 'The Japanese Approach to Bridge Jobs', in C. Alcover C, Topa G, Parry E, Fraccaroli F, & M Depolo M (Eds) *Bridge employment*: 252–265. London, UK: Routledge.

Valette A & Culié JD (2015) 'Career scripts in clusters: A social position approach', *Human Relations* (in press).

Van der Voet J, Groeneveld SM, & Kuipers BS (2013) 'Talking the talk or walking the walk? The leadership of planned and emergent change in a public organization', *Journal of Change Management* 14(2)171–191.

Victor DG (2015) 'Embed the social sciences in climate policy', *Nature* 520: 27–29.

Villadsen K (2007) 'The emergence of "neo-philanthropy"', *Acta Sociologica* 50: 309–323.

Werbel JD & Henriques PL (2009) 'Different views of trust and relational leadership', *Journal of Managerial Psychology* 24(8)780–796.

Werbner P & Modood T (Eds) (1997) *Debating Cultural Hybridity*. London & New Jersey: Zed Books.

Wodak R & Boukala S (2015) '(Supra)National identity and language', *Annual Review of Applied Linguistics* 35: 253–273.

Ybema S, Vroemisse M, & van Marrewijk A (2012) 'Constructing identity by deconstructing differences', *Scandinavian Journal of Management* 28: 48–59.

Yukl G (2002) *Leadership in Organizations*. Upper Saddle River, NJ: Prentice-Hall.

Zacher H (2015) 'Successful aging at work', *Aging and Retirement* 1(1)4–25.

Zacher H & Bock A (2014) 'Mature age job seekers: The role of proactivity', *Journal of Managerial Psychology* 29: 1082–1097.

Zacher H & Grifn B (2015) 'Older workers' age as a moderator of the relationship between career adaptability and job satisfaction', *Work, Aging and Retirement* 1(2)227–236.

Zerubavel E (1991) *The Fine Line*. New York: Free Press.

Zientara P (2014) 'Flexible transitions from work to retirement: Evidence from Poland', in Alcover C, Topa G, Parry E, Fraccaroli F, & Depolo M (Eds) *Bridge employment*: 90–114. London, UK: Routledge.

Zikic J & Richardson J (2007) 'Unlocking the careers of business professionals following job loss', *Canadian Journal of Administrative Sciences* 24(1)58–73.

17 The Rules We Create

This chapter explores my concerns that codes of ethics do not necessarily promote ethical behaviour, and they do not always provide the individual with appropriate guidance on the 'ethical' thing to do when confronted with a real ethical situation.

Much of the research says that codes of ethics are an important tool in improving ethical performance. Codes are a way for addressing ethical lapses uncovered by research, and they link the ethical climate of organisations to the presence of, and training in, codes of ethics. However, in the former case, the research doesn't actually suggest the code of ethics; it merely offers it as a solution to a problem. In the latter case, the focus on ethics might raise the overall concern for ethical behaviour, but not necessarily the actual adherence to the codes at the moment an ethical dilemma is encountered.

The establishment of a code of ethics can be seen as a mechanism by which a group of individuals delineate some rules by which they come together. I give examples of spontaneous rule creation in Chapters 3 and 15, but here I am talking of the deliberate creation of rules by which we may work together. This is generally taken to be a good thing, and most societies rely upon their rules—and their lawyers! All forward-thinking organisations are assumed to have a code of ethics, and this is an important badge of good practice.

Many writers have questioned the way in which society appears to be progressing. Dalla Costa (1998: 59) says, 'When the government is focused on competitiveness, and society is fixated on budgets, growth assumes greater importance than quality of life', and Korten (1995: 7) argues for the 'creation of life-centred societies in which the economy is but one of the instruments of good living—not the purpose of human existence'. Hatcher (2002) takes this further by arguing persuasively for the need to include ethics and social responsibility within organisations and HRD, not just because this is a 'good' thing, but also because those companies that have codes of ethics outperform those that do not, and because acting ethically is ultimately less expensive than the cost of misbehaviour (also see Chapter 16). Estes (1996) estimated that unethical behaviour associated with organisations and their leaders, ranging from misinformation to deliberate fraud, accounted for losses of almost $3 trillion a year in the United States alone, and, world-wide, the figure may be triple that (Hatcher 2002: 4).

One way to address these issues is through a list of ethical principles to which people in the organisation are expected to adhere: a code of ethics. Many also provide behavioural guidelines and some are punitive, in that people can be punished if they are found to be acting outside the code. Typically, codes of ethics address standards and behaviour at work, work-ing with others, the handling of data, and professional development, with a particular focus on honesty, trust, responsibility, integrity, and confidential-ity. Such a code has tremendous power. It helps establish some norms and socialise newcomers into a profession or an organisation. It delineates and clarifies acceptable and unacceptable behaviours. Most professions have codes of ethics of some sort, though not all have them written down or thought through. Most are in the process of establishing them, such as the Academy for Human Resource Development (1999). This is done in the belief that once we develop a value it becomes a criterion of significance for us (Hultman & Gellerman 2002). Core values (such as peace, equality, freedom, respect, and sustainability) do not change dramatically over time since they represent an end state or outcome (Gilley et al. 2001). Organisa-tions that exhibit core values such as stakeholder service, social responsibil-ity, ethics, and sustainability are able to transcend the conflicts that arise between human fulfilment, environmental protection, and economic suc-cess. The core value, enshrined within a code of ethics, acts with mediating power and as a goalpost. This is particularly true of human rights issues:

> Human rights violations occur through daily HR activities such as employment, recruiting, training, promotion, and laying off of employ-ees. Therefore, by ensuring the security of employees and facilities, identifying and managing environmental issues, and attempting to make a positive contribution to the societies and cultures within which the companies operate, HRD is intimately involved in human rights in many organisations. The capacity of individual HRD professionals to mitigate these and other human rights abuses is in most cases limited. However, collectively, as a profession and as a field of study, we can and should make a significant contribution to upholding human rights (Hatcher 2002: 133).

When we establish that value as an ethical code we are marking what is important for us, both now and as to what we would like to see in the future. Establishing a code of ethics is therefore a way of making a clear signal about how we would like the future to develop, as well as saying something about our current society. The adoption of codes of ethics has a clear impact upon the social, economic, and performance environment of the organisation. They are a collective statement of responsible behaviour.

They form the rules by which organisations can govern themselves in the same way that principles can guide the actions of individuals. In considering and writing down codes of ethics, thereby exposing them to public scrutiny, professions and organisations take a large step towards acting ethically.

Although organisations establish codes of ethics with the best of intentions, one concern is whether or not they really work. For example, it could be argued that recent financial scandals, such as Enron, are a good example of a code of ethics that allowed greed to take precedence over probity. I suggest that codes of ethics are flawed in offering a false sense of authority, in reifying ethical concepts and issues, in avoiding issues of appropriateness to the time and place, in presenting ethical issues through single set of lenses, and in their consideration of the situated role of individuals and emotions.

OFFERING A FALSE SENSE OF AUTHORITY

Codes of ethics form the rules by which organisations can govern themselves in the same way that principles *can* guide the actions of individuals. The establishment of a code of ethics, however, does not mean that those to whom it applies will necessarily act in an ethical manner. Hopfl (1999) makes a distinction between *auctoritas,* or moral authority, and *potestas,* or the rights of office. *Auctoritas* is a capacity to initiate and inspire respect. As an attribute of institutions it has a stabilising effect, whereas as an attribute of an individual it can be linked to initiative and the capacity to set things in motion, and, whilst of value, it does challenge the status quo. It carries the right to be listened to, and elicits respect, but it is *not* a right to command, or compel. In contrast, *potestas* is the right to act derived from an office, and it can be assigned, or withdrawn. The role of the whistleblower is a good example (see Chapter 9). When the whistleblower feels sufficiently compromised to risk their job and colleagues in order to step out of line and call attention to what they see as malpractice, they are asserting their moral authority over that of the power of office. They are saying that their code of ethics is being contradicted by the one that they see in practice around them.

Consider the issue of authorship and authority. I am the author of my world and it is this generic 'I' who interprets whether the situation has ethical connotations and what they might be, and whose individual code of ethics comes to bear. Where they exist, professional or organisational codes might dictate what my ethical behaviours ought to be, but even so, I have the responsibility of deciding if I will comply or suffer the consequences of not complying. Therefore, if we wish to establish a code of ethics, those who are implicated in the process must be able to see it as legitimate.

> Legitimation must establish some plausible connection between what people value already and what is to be legitimated. The strength of the link established between these constitutes the force of the legitimation.

> Plausibility demands at a minimum that what is being legitimated should not be out of proportion to the goods in terms of which it is legitimated: an association that can promise its associates immortality can demand more of them than an association that can merely offer them an attractive package of benefits (Hopfl 1999: 231).

In other words, I am not going to follow a particular code of ethics unless I believe in its benefits.

Let us assume that key people in a profession have deliberated for hours on end, have consulted with their membership, and have designed a code of ethics that (should have) a high level of legitimacy. The question is 'Will I follow it?', and the answer is 'I don't know'! Like many professionals in HR I have a strong desire to work towards a better way of doing things. I dislike hypocrisy and have several times risked a great deal in support of my principles. In other words—like many others—I do reflect upon my actions and thoughts quite regularly with the intention of 'doing my best' for the human condition (which, I hasten to add, includes—at least in my view—doing my best for the environment and non-humans also).

Although I would like to consider myself a principled person, I am not sure I could tell you what my principles are, and as soon as I find I 'have a principle' and start to consider it, I can find a case in which the application of that principle would be counterproductive—or, in my view, unethical. Where do I stand on war? I don't know. How about abortion? I don't know. What of riches? I don't know—and so on. Even hypocrisy can sometimes have its benefits, can it not? This is not because I don't know what ethics are, but because it seems wrong to make an unwavering stand on such emotionally charged issues. When there are many sides to the debate how do we know which is the right one, and what are the dangers in raising that above all others?

REIFYING ETHICAL CONCEPTS AND ISSUES

Reification occurs when we turn an abstract concept into an object. We do this quite often, such as when talking of HRD as if it were an embodied, concrete 'thing'. Once a concept is embodied in this way it is easy to ignore or pay lip service to it, whilst no longer paying attention to what the concept really means, or what is implied by its use. An example of this might be seen as we all sit at the start of a participative training session, and as part of good practice negotiate our 'learning contract'. In doing so we all agree to be open and honest with each other, to maintain confidentiality, and to trust each other. However, do we ever actually do so, and what would be the effects on the session if we really did? In my experience each of these aspects of the learning contract is taken with a pinch of salt. We are open to a certain level but even in sessions designed to bring feelings to the surface, true openness seems hard to achieve, and if it does arise it is often destructive to the people involved and the objectives of the session. Do we not really mean 'open, but in a nice way'?

Similarly, when we agree to confidentiality what do we really mean? That nothing goes outside the room? Can we tell others what happened for us, but not talk of others—and if so, how do we talk about interactions that might have had a lasting effect upon us? When we agree to confidentiality do we not really mean that we won't talk about things that are not important to us? Trust is an even harder one: Do we really mean it when we say that we will trust people that we hardly know—people who (if they are work colleagues) might have a major effect upon our careers in a few years' time? Do we not promise to trust and at the same time reserve the right to only reveal certain aspects of our selves? We successfully manage to survive the training session (as in life) by the application of a certain level of hypocrisy.

In doing so, we fall into the danger of reifying each of these concepts we have agreed upon, such that they take on a life of their own—we know we are honest with each other because we have agreed to this, and thus we do not need to revisit it. Honesty (or whatever) sits like another piece of furniture in the room with us—one that we can ignore now that it is there. We might occasionally refer to it, and take turns to sit on it—but to what extent do we internalise it? We follow the rules *(potestas)* and promise 'honesty', but self-preservation means that we introduce small print that modifies how honest we are in any particular situation—indeed, it might even be more ethical to keep silent on some points *(auctoritas)*. There can be good reasons, at times, to reify the aspects of a code of ethics, but do we really want a code that allows people to pay lip service to it? Does this reduce its legitimacy?

AVOIDING ISSUES OF APPLICABILITY AND TIME-DEPENDENCE

Of course, codes of ethics cannot be set in stone. They need to be able to develop and change as society and the needs of the profession changes. If I may, I would like to share a personal experience that illustrates this point. The medical profession is one that is renowned for its strong code of ethics and its focus upon ethical behaviour—to the extent that malpractice is considered to be extremely serious, and is punished. In the 1970s I was diagnosed as having a hormone imbalance, which at the time was believed to be a direct indication of a brain tumour on the pituitary gland. The particular hormone had only recently been isolated in humans and I was one of the early cases to be identified. I was interested in the field and able to talk to the consultants in a knowledgeable way, and so was not overtly emotional about notions of brain tumours, best methods of operating, and so on. My prolactin levels became extremely high, and in discussing this one of the consultants told me, as a colleague, that my case was being used as a cautionary tale, because a small amount of my blood had been left in the container and contaminated another sample, resulting in a false high reading. The man was wrongly told that he also had a brain tumour. He committed suicide rather than face the tumour. It turned out that my condition was not, in fact, due to an active brain tumour, and although it will remain with me and affect my hormone balance for life, it is manageable. What also remains with me is the awful knowledge that someone committed suicide because of a misdiagnosis based upon my blood.

It seems to me that no ethical principles were broken here. It is easy to say that there should have been no possibility of contamination and the man shouldn't have been misdiagnosed—but at the time medical science was not as advanced as it is now. The consultant was doing the best he could, ethically, in telling as many people as possible of the need to be absolutely scrupulous in avoiding contamination, and this has probably contributed to the much cleaner approach that exists nowadays. It is also easy to say that I should never have been told—but that wasn't the sort of relationship I had or would wish to have. I am sure he would not have told me of this if our relationship had been that of a normal patient and doctor, rather than more like one of colleagues. I want to know as much as I possibly can about my condition so that I am able to make informed decisions, not act as a passive recipient—and that approach carries with it the risk of unwanted knowledge. It is easy to say that it was the doctors who were responsible for the situation, not me—and I acknowledge that, but it does not stop me still feeling responsible, in some way, for another person's death.

Despite working under a strong code of ethics and with the best of intentions, a situation developed under which each of the parties, including the man who committed suicide and myself, could in some way be seen as ethically tainted. The code of medical ethics at the time did not cover this situation, and I can't see how it could be changed to do so, under the circumstances prevailing at the time, without compromising other codes—such as that of my right to information. Having said that, codes of ethics are a reflection of the values of society and of a profession at a particular time in a particular society. To be relevant they need to be changed in accordance with changing societal and professional values. Nowadays we might view the scenario I described above through a different lens.

PRESENTING ETHICAL ISSUES THROUGH A SINGLE SET OF LENSES

The lens through which we view codes of ethics differs, not just with time, but also with the form of society and the nature of the individual. For example, we differ in whether we believe in the need for differentiated ethical codes. Tufts Richardson (1996) suggests that the strength of the perceived need for ethical guidelines is, itself, associated with personality type, and with form of culture—thus for some, and in some less complex societies, ethics were an unnamed part of life, and do not need to be visited or considered as a separate issue or practice. For example:

> 'in the Vedic period in India, harmony and integration were realized through ritual experience. The ritual act brought into being the ethical balance through one's essential participation in the order of the world. Ethics was undifferentiated from affirmation. . . . Native American culture likewise does not differentiate ethics from the upbringing of a traditional culture. The puberty rites include a vision quest, where the young person experiences being apart from the traditional routines long enough to find a personal, separate, vocation or orienting symbol for their life. . . . In societies that are pluralistic, on the other hand, puberty rites need to initiate the young person into commitments into social rules and values that in traditional societies are already internalised and secure. The need for ethics per se therefore tends to evolve in diverse and pluralistic societies, where the individual knows there is more than one truth and multiple ways to live rightly' (Tufts Richardson 1996: 33–34).

From the standpoint of those who do not see society as pluralistic, the collective establishment of codes of ethics, independent from the society's normal mores, is irrelevant—or unnecessary. The development of a code of ethics, therefore, is more relevant to those who are faced with issues of diversity and plurality—as in current complex Western society and in most business and organisational settings. Within Western society, different people follow different spiritual paths, and seek different end points to their spiritual journeys, and these paths are associated with different ethical foci. It follows from this that the code of ethics that I might develop will be different in focus to one developed by another person—though of course, the closer we are in our world view and in our agreement of what is good and evil, right and wrong, and what should be created for the future, the closer our codes might be. A profession, being a fairly homogenous grouping, can suffer from groupthink when developing a code of ethics, and thus risks not addressing individual or cultural differences in ethical aspiration and values. An example is the need for a profession to revisit its code of ethics as it becomes more international and represents multiple cultures. The notion of individual difference in the focus of ethicality raises another concern.

CONSIDERING THE ROLE OF THE INDIVIDUAL AND EMOTION

I have already mentioned problems of reification, through which the very existence of the code can mean that lip service is paid to it such that the import of the code is ignored—in other words, the code can become a 'law' which is followed to the letter, but not in spirit. This is particularly the case in those codes which are punitive, and can thus force people to comply, such as that of the medical profession, and might be seen to occur less in others that are more aspirational. My concern here, however, has a slightly different focus. As we go about our daily business, we encounter situations that feel as if they require some ethical deliberation, yet which require an immediate response or one for which there are no codes to guide us.

I shall illustrate this with another personal experience. I was providing team development and conflict resolution to a senior manager and his close team from a multinational organisation. The team had been having a lot of problems working together, which is why I became involved. The cat's cradle of issues gradually started to untangle and a level of openness started to emerge. As it did so, the atmosphere became tenser and a high level of emotion was clearly just below the surface. In facilitating this, I was making sure everyone had their say and was truly 'listened to' rather than just 'heard'; I was trying to maintain a calm and trustable persona whilst privately being worried about the potentially destructive nature of where we were going. Everyone was on the edge of their seats and fully and deeply engaged, when one member of the team finally made some very personal comments about a senior manager's leadership style.

The room went silent and I knew that I had to intervene within the next second or so, and that the nature of my intervention would be critical. It seemed to me that I could work with the emotional charge to bring the issue to a head, or take a safer route and encourage the manager to rationalise the feedback by asking him what he *thought* about it. I quietly said, 'How do you feel about that?'. He was silent for a second and then started crying. Out tumbled years of tension around caring deeply for his team, and not being able to balance that with the harsh judgements demanded of senior management, and of not wanting to delegate for fear of overloading them. His team were incredibly supportive, both about the problems he faced and of his emotion, pointing out that they much preferred him as a vulnerable 'real person', than the remote 'senior manager' persona he had adopted as a safety blanket. The whole process took several days, and on the night after the turning point I did a lot of soul searching, wondering what the next day would bring.

My thoughts revolved around questioning why I had acted as I did, and what the consequences of that, and acting differently, might be. In encouraging (forcing?) a senior manager in a 'hard' industry to reveal his weaknesses to his team had I in effect destroyed him and his career? What sort of trauma had I put him through? What about his team? Had it completely shattered any chance of them working together? What would be the effects on each of them? What if I had played it safe and asked him what he thought of the comment rather than what he felt—would the same result have been achieved without the emotional breakthrough? I suspect not, in which case we would have ended up with yet more 'talking round the houses', and short-term satisfaction of the team having talked, but no long-term development. Would it have been ethical for me to have 'chickened out', and accepted payment for a half-job knowing that I had not done the best I could? What of the power involved? Was it right that one person should be placed in, or accept, such a position of trust that others could be severely emotionally shaken by their actions? Was I really being trusted to keep people safe whilst being employed and therefore trusted to resolve the conflict? And so on . . .

As it was, people came together the following day in a much more positive mood and with a real impetus to build upon what had happened. Obviously this was not the only issue, but many of the more minor issues resolved themselves as the whole team started to work together in a different way. Feedback I got, both at the time and several years later, suggested that my risk in focusing on feelings in that way had been well worth it for all involved—but what a risk!

The question that remains with me is: 'Where does the responsibility lie for managing people's emotions in a situation like this?' with the correlate, 'Is there any way a that code of ethics that covered responsibility for emotion could have helped?' Given the power that is wielded by the trainer/developer in such situations, it certainly feels as if there is a need for some sort of code of ethics to cover it, but is it possible? Emotions arise quickly and can be focused by a word or a gesture—both the emotion and the trigger are often subconscious, unknown to the actors, until they burst upon the scene. They can't easily be designed or regulated. They require immediate response that doesn't allow for deliberation about the ethics involved. The outcome is unknown, such that we can only guess whether the response might help or harm—and, of course, notions of help and harm are relative to the people and situations involved. We can't develop guidelines from one situation about what might be helpful in another.

Similar examples can be found in online conversations, where it is harder to gauge the other person's reaction to our words without body language to help us. In theory, when online we have more time to contemplate our reply, but in practice, particularly if the topic is emotional, we often reply immediately with whatever words we have available—yet those words when read by another or by ourselves at a later date, become amplified and strengthened, just because they are written down and can be mulled over, such that they have greater power than was intended at the time.

On a daily basis we come across complex situated events in which we have to act—in that even a non-response counts as an act. We might like to think that we are guided by codes of ethics and our own principles, but, in reality, our actions or inactions are down to ourselves as individuals. We might seek to justify them in retrospect by reference to wider generally agreed or upheld ethical considerations, but at the time of decision-making and acting we have to rely on our own patterns of behaviour and interpretation of the situation. Given time, we might turn to an ethics decision-making scheme or process that helps us to make the 'right' decision, but that time does not always exist. Furthermore, in many instances, we cannot make an objective choice, as the consequences of our 'choice' only become apparent once the choice is made, and we have no way of knowing what would have really happened (as opposed to our replayed possible scenarios) if we had acted differently.

In other words, it is the moral authority or *auctoritas* that is brought to bear in any given situation. This might or might not be in accordance with or supported by *potestas* (in this case, the overarching and agreed code of ethics). In acting with moral authority it might be that we come across situations which are, at the least, ambiguous, or even in which we find that we have to break the letter of the law if we wish to preserve its spirit. We cannot assume a close-knit and comfy fit between a code of ethics and the process of acting in an ethical manner. At times we have to assert our personal codes of ethics, and hope that by doing so we contribute to a strengthening, or re-examination, of the collective code of the profession or organisation we are engaged in.

SPIRITUAL JOURNEYS AND FALSE GODS

We need codes of ethics—individually as part of our spiritual journeys, and collectively, to guide our development and help an ethical future emerge— but we also need to be aware of the difficulties and pitfalls: to avoid the false god of reification, and to be aware that the current drive towards the establishment of such codes is, itself, culturally bound and ethically problematic. Furthermore, we need to be aware that the role of *auctoritas* is, at times, to challenge *potestas* and a code of ethics is only as good as the moral authority that underlies it.

This line of thought emphasises that the structures we use are not morally or ethically neutral. Whether implicit, subconscious, or explicit (as in codes of ethics) they are dynamic, situated, co-created, and contested. They are dynamically linked to a wider, holistic, structure, and we, as agents within that holism, create, maintain, question, and destroy them. This short chapter acts as an interlude between the previous chapter that explored the wider picture of where we are, and the following chapter, which explores our becoming.

REFERENCES

Academy for Human Resource Development (1999) *Standards on Ethics and Integrity*. (http://www.ahrd.org/publications/ethics/ethics_standards.PDF). Accessed 14/1/16.

Dalla Costa J (1998) *The Ethical Imperative*. Reading, MA: Perseus Books.

Estes R (1996) *The Tyranny of the Bottom Line*. San Francisco: Berrett-Koehler.

Gilley JW, Quatro SA, Hoekstra E, Whittle DD, & Maycunich A (2001) *The Manager as Change Agent*. Cambridge MA: Perseus Publishing.

Hatcher T (2002) *Ethics and HRD*. Cambridge, MA: Perseus.

Hopfl H (1999) 'Power, authority and legitimacy', *Human Resource Development International* 3(2)217–235.

Hultman K & Gellerman B (2002) *Balancing Individual and Organisational Values*. San Francisco: Jossey-Bass.

Korten DC (1995) *When Corporations Rule the World*. San Francisco: Berrett-Koehler.

Tufts Richardson P (1996) *Four Spiritualities: Expressions Of Self, Expressions Of Spirit*. Palo Alto, CA: Davies-Black Publishing.

18 Becoming

> 'How an entity becomes constitutes what the actual entity is; so the two descriptions of an actual entity are not independent. Its being is constituted by its becoming. This is the principle of process . . . the flux of things is one ultimate generalisation around which we must weave our philosophical system'.
>
> (Whitehead 1929: 28 & 240)

HRD AS ASPIRATION

In this chapter we step into the Heraclitean world of becoming that I discussed in Chapter 2, and question the path we want to walk along in the knowledge that we will never get there. As boundaries become eroded so will HRD find itself facing issues that are about self and other; power and control; identity and ownership; inclusion and exclusion; agency and structure. Throughout this book I have asked questions of our becoming. In our understanding of HRD do we include the child labourer, the sex worker, the illegal alien, the abused and discriminated against? Do we include the self-employed, the unemployed, voluntary workers, not-for-profit organisations, NGOs, or virtual organisations? What form of governance and leadership should the organisation adopt, and how is that supported by the HRD function? How does HRD strike a balance between the thrust for organisational growth (including year-on-year increase in profit) and notions of sustainability and concomitant steady-state economy? At what stage does HRD become the mediator (and facilitator) of individual or global exploitation? Where does HRD stand on issues of cultural imperialism—particularly in relation to migrant workers or satellite organisations? How is information about employees managed—does the written information match that which 'everyone knows' through rumour, innuendo, and off-record discussions? How transparent are the organisational processes? To what extent are ethical codes really followed? What do we aspire to—for ourselves, our organisations, and our societies?

The ideal world of work that started to emerge from Chapter 16 was one in which leaders and managers are visionary and focus on stakeholder values rather than profit, consulting employees in important decisions; are fair, open, and honest; are caring, and display trust. This is a world in which employees work in an organisation with a strong family feel, held together by loyalty and tradition, and are seen as people rather than profit-making resources. Both in the East and in the West, work environments that meet an employee's psychosocial needs for challenge, support, autonomy, and feedback are associated with positive outcomes—such as individual learning, development, satisfaction, and better performance. The sorts of skills that people need are around social intelligence, problem solving, proactivity, cognitive hardiness, and ethicality. People like to be amongst smaller social groupings (of up to about 50 people) in which they are trusted, responsible, and contributing members of the society—a society that they feel they are helping co-create.

This all sounds like it might be rather hard work—however, the problem for those of us who want a quiet and undemanding life is that if (by its very nature) HRD is at the nexus of the human condition, then we cannot avoid our influence on the world. To do nothing is to influence it, though the effects of our existence will be different. Even small steps can be of great influence.

BROADBAND FOR THE RURAL NORTH (B4RN)

I live in an area that used to a broadband black spot—we had telephone, and thus dial-up service, but so much degrading copper wire was required to get to us, that the signal was 0.5 megabit download speeds at the best, with considerably lower upload speeds. There were many isolated farms and hamlets around us who could not get satellite or mobile signal either. The UK government and the incumbent monopolistic telecoms company in the UK were committed to achieving 100% coverage of high-speed broadband (which they defined as over 25 Mbps). That was the rhetoric. In reality they stipulated that 100% would be achieved by reaching 95% of the population, as it would be very costly to deliver to the remaining 5% rural properties. In essence, I and my neighbours felt that the chance of us ever getting well-connected was very slim.

B4RN would not have even started without the collaboration of several key volunteers (each retired and community oriented)—the principal being the current CEO, BF, who has spent his life designing networks and is a close neighbour of mine. Another is CC, a farmer's wife with incredible zest and drive (for herself and others), who, with others, had installed a fibre and wifi network in her local community several years before and was keen to expand the idea. A third was myself, desperate to bring broadband to the area, with experience of organisation, managing projects, and group development. Several years earlier I had tried to bring Wi-Fi to the area and had involved BF in that, but the potential funder dropped out, so when he brought CC and others together with me we looked at the possibility of an optic fibre network. Optic fibre is a long-term solution offering 1000 Mbps upload and download; it doesn't degrade, and, hidden below the ground, it is not sensitive to weather conditions, nor does it impact upon the environment.

We gathered like-minded people, some of whom remain fundamental to the progress of B4RN, and we applied for a grant to set up a fibre to the home (FTTH) network in the area. Whilst we were successful with our bid, the money got absorbed into the county council pot, which then went to the incumbent, who had close commercial ties with the county council. Some of us cried foul! We were so frustrated by this that we decided to take our idea of creating our own network to the wider community and see what the response was, and so B4RN was formed.

We proposed a cooperative community venture, in which any profit had to go back to the community, and in which there was a maximum holding of 20,000 shares, so we could not be taken over or asset-stripped. Landlords would donate the way leaves for the duct to cross their property (a major concession as way leaves can provide landlords with a respectable annual income), and all digging and installation would be done by volunteers from the community. We committed to 100% coverage of our rural areas, however distant or difficult the route. It was a risky prospect to start with, and the incumbent made the whole process much harder through a series of political manoeuvres that I won't go into here, but after our launch in December 2011 we sold sufficient shares to enable us to buy the necessary fibre and ducting, and so started digging in 2012.

The whole process has been much, much more successful than we could have imagined at that time. Three years later BF and I are co-directors of a small telecoms company. CC is still involved, progressing the work day and night, but is particularly interested in the network buildout and did not want the additional responsibility of directorship. We manage a world-class network, built and owned by the community, and all profits going back to the community. We are well beyond our initial planned footprint and are developing rapidly because as we near each small isolated group they become very keen to join us. We encourage one or more champions within each community group, who then work with the local volunteers. There is a hierarchical management system, but it is flexible and emergent. The small, local nature of the groups also helps people become deeply involved and committed to improving their own community. We help them with planning routes and provide the necessary skill and hardware, but essentially they raise the funding and dig to meet us. One community then helps the next community, as they were helped, in a cascading manner. We are now appointing staff and more directors. We have won several prestigious rewards, worldwide news coverage (for example, see Coleman 2014 for an article in *Forbes* about B4RN), and requests for service from as far away as Australia. We refused that one as we thought it might be rather hard to dig that far, but we offer regular information/training days that attendees (from across the world) and nascent groups seem to find very useful.

Part of the success is because this has been about much more than just telecoms. Even after such a short time it is clearly evident that disparate parts of the communities (such as the farmers, going back many generations, and the people from 'off' who have only lived in the area for 20 years or so—see Chapter 11) have talked with each other and worked together, often digging in horrible conditions. The B4RN digging team swung into action during a flood last year, helping others in a concerted and communal way that just would not have happened previously. The excellent connectivity is saving people money, bringing business into the area, employing and training local people, and enabling children to do their homework. There are also broadcasts of community and church events for the housebound, and the ability to trial online medical consultations.

This has grown exponentially from a very small start: A wave of engagement has rippled through communities, changing them as it goes in unplanned and emergent ways. Because of the technical nature of this venture, much of the focus, internally and internationally, has been on the network itself: its design, structure, logistics, and so on. My involvement has deliberately been more back-office, applying for grants, managing the system of community loans, initiating and managing key events, such as a recent visit by HRH Prince Charles, taking responsibility for staffing and HR concerns, and generally being a point of stability in the chaos of interaction. From my point of view, however, it is the changing nature of the B4RN society that fascinates me—and it is that, I think, that is the hardest for other groups to replicate.

Non-Profit Do-It-Yourself Mentality

As I describe in Chapter 11, the farming community has a non-profit barter system approach to life—people are well used to helping each other out and swapping goods and services. They are also well used to making do—if something breaks they find ingenious ways to fix it themselves. Many of the people involved in B4RN are farmers or from the farming community—and that mentality has translated into the B4RN project. As nearby communities have considered whether they want B4RN service there has been a clear split between those who embrace the need to get together to dig towards the nearest point of the existing (and continually spreading) network and so become part of B4RN, and those (mainly businesses and individuals) who expect to pay for B4RN to dig to them and provide them with a service. Though the task we set ourselves (100% coverage of isolated rural areas) was that which the incumbent provider and others had said was unachievable and commercially non-viable, we have had the advantage of an existing community-focused mentality.

The not-for-profit aspect has been particularly important. Aspiring to establish FTTH in isolated rural areas sounds a bit like selling snake oil medicine, and at the beginning people were quite rightly concerned about whether they could trust us—especially as the incumbent and others were vocal about how it could not be done. In about 10 years' time we will be receiving considerable income from service fees, but B4RN is constituted in a way that means that all profit has to go back to the community and it will be up to the shareholders to decide how that is done. They might decide to reduce fees further, although a flat rate of £30 per month for 1000 Mbps symmetrical service is already very cheap. My personal hope is that we will use the money for further projects helping the isolated and socially disadvantaged rural communities. The point to this explanation, however, is that people were willing to buy shares and become engaged in the project because they could see that no one was out to make a personal profit from their efforts. Several other community networks in the UK started by entrepreneurs have not done so well, with people less willing to donate to someone else's pocket.

It has been very important to ensure that no one, CEO, directors or anyone else, has profited from the project. Until recently everyone has been an unpaid volunteer, putting in years of hard labour for the long-term vision. This includes the core of people who have been with the project since the beginning as well as large clusters of geographically based volunteers who have come together to establish the B4RN network in their own particular area. We are now able to pay key staff, but are deliberately keeping levels of remuneration low (the CEO receives less than three times that of the lowest-paid worker) and at interview, in addition to the usual skills fit, we are seeking understanding of, and commitment to, the community-based values of B4RN.

Managing Volunteers

Managing volunteers presents several challenges and opportunities that the main HR literature barely touches upon, yet it raises concerns that are important to the world of paid work, that I have discussed elsewhere in this book. Volunteers identify strongly with the cause and are committed to what they are doing, and the people they are doing it with. They bring themselves, their whole personalities, good and bad. In committing to the job they have their own ideas about how it should be done, and they fully expect to be seen as competent adults working together for a common cause. They do not expect to be ordered around, reprimanded, or treated as if they *have* to work. They are sensitive to potential inequalities between themselves and other volunteers, and being 'taken advantage of'. To manage volunteers is to encourage, enthuse, empathise, and lead by example. These are skills we are told that all managers need:

> By excessive promotion of leadership, we demote everyone else. We create clusters of followers who have to be driven to perform, instead

of leveraging the natural propensity of people to cooperate in communities. In this light, effective managing can be seen as engaging and engaged, connecting and connected, supporting and supported (Mintzberg 2009: 235).

However, managers of paid workers can offer lip service to these things whilst knowing that fundamentally the contract is 'you do what I say and you get the money'. That doesn't work with volunteers!

B4RN seems to attract the eccentric and the retired. These are the people with the time and energy, who are also at a stage of their life when they want to contribute to the community. There are lots of people with strong views and set ways of doing things, who come from all walks of life, and across the full spectrum of difference. Such diversity is to be valued as it helps enhance collective intelligence and the general ability of the group to perform a range of tasks (Woolley et al. 2010), but it can make like difficult! Each volunteer has their own preferences about how, where, when, and on what they want to work, and it is no good telling them to do something they don't want to do. Part of the skill, then, is not about sorting out the jobs first and then seeing who can do them, but about seeing what people want to do and matching everybody up to get the job done. People stop for breaks when they want, they socialise, vent their emotions, and catch up with each other (see Hadley (2014) for the work benefits of catching up over the coffee machine), but the jobs all get done. It can, though, cost a lot in cake. Managing volunteers, therefore, is about co-creating the future, establishing a joint vision, and influencing the activities towards the end goal, but recognising that everyone is going to get there along their own path and in their own sweet time.

The emphasis is slightly different for the directors because we need to ensure that the way forward emerges in a consensual manner. One of the first things we established was a management committee of core volunteers, and one of the first things we had to fight off were volunteers with management-speak who tried to organise people, including the committee, into clear roles and responsibilities. It sounded good and would have looked brilliant on paper, but we were convinced that these things needed to emerge with time so that individuals developed and owned different areas of responsibility (and did not have them allocated). It is only now as we appoint paid employees that we are formalising such things into job descriptions and contracts.

Changing Culture

Apart from a handful of paid staff, everybody in each community that we serve (known collectively as B4RNland) is a volunteer. They have offered their services without payment for the good of the community. Some have dug long distances in foul weather, others have learnt how to install the equipment and have put the connections in all their neighbours' homes ready for the fibre to be blown in. Some have learnt how to blow fibre and go across the country connecting people, whilst others have provided tea and cakes where necessary. B4RN is built upon cooperative volunteer labour and the people in B4RNland are very proud of this. We welcome and support this ethos, whilst appreciating that B4RN-the-business needs to emerge from within and alongside it. Just because we are a community venture does not mean that the community should put up with poor service and ramshackle finances. As B4RN develops it needs to become a sleek telecoms operation whilst maintaining the cooperative community ethos and the willing force of volunteers to continue taking B4RN to outlying districts.

I am in charge of the HR side of the project and have to tread very carefully whilst shifting the culture to accommodate the emergence of a core of a 'proper organisation' within the wider volunteer ethos. We, the employers, and the employees have to get used to management structures, work hours, objectives, and undertaking boring and unwelcome tasks as well as the interesting bits. We are small enough for the family atmosphere to remain, and there is so much varied and rewarding work that the team spirit is strong. At present I have to remind people to take holidays, rather than worry about absenteeism. With reference to the points made in Chapter 16, there are no enormous salaries and people work very hard, but they say that they feel part of the team: trusted, respected, and that their views are taken into account. It helps that B4RN has very high customer satisfaction. This is in part due to the technology, fibre-optic cabling being so much better than copper, but it is also due to the attitude of the staff, who are clearly willing to go out of their way to help people. For example, a recent survey of UK telecoms companies found that B4RN was second fastest in responding to phone calls, with an average pick-up time of under a minute.

Part of the volunteer community ethos comes from the way the organisation is structured, and the way people evolve into groups, but it is also helped by physical structures. For example, we are developing a large open informal area where customers, volunteers, and staff meet and make coffee when they want in the adjoining kitchen. The other day someone came in early and cooked a whole pile of biscuits for everyone—much appreciated!

Social Justice and Equality

The changing culture also brings with it jealousies and feelings of inequality. People who have slaved away without reward suddenly notice that someone else is being paid, and become upset. It is not about the money itself (they were previously doing the job very happily without payment), but it is about what payment signifies. Instead of feeling valued for their contribution they start to perceive that their worth is now judged by others in financial terms—and thus, that they are not valued. One of the key skills during this cultural shift revolves around making people feel that they, their views, and their work, are valued—whether or not they are paid; that they themselves are of importance regardless of their differences, similarities, and eccentric natures. This means that regardless of management status within B4RN, it is important that we maintain the ethos by which everyone is treated as equal, contributing, and responsible adults—even, or especially, during differences of view over how to proceed.

The sense of equality of value to the community is not just about the people involved, but is also about the provision. One of the founding tenets of provision was 100% coverage within each parish. We committed to providing a connection and service to everyone however distant or difficult their property might be. We also committed to one set rate for each household (£30 per month) regardless of how much bandwidth they used. Everyone is treated equally. This actually makes it much easier to manage than ramping up the rate according to usage, or throttling back provision so that marketing bands can be applied, as most telecoms companies do. It also emphasises quite how different we are, and reinforces the sense of social justice and equality of community.

The sense of social justice was very important at the inception of B4RN, and remains in the background. The development of B4RN has often been referred to as a 'David and Goliath' situation. Ironically, it is likely that if the monopolistic incumbent had supported, or even ignored B4RN, then B4RN would have been considerably less successful. However, the incumbent went out of its way to politicise, denigrate, and hamper the development of B4RN in apparent anti-competitive use of their monopolistic power. The ensuing fights have resulted in investigation and censure of their claims about their own provision, and the international recognition of B4RN as offering a visionary way forward. The frustration around what were seen as the continual dirty policies of the incumbent triggered people's innate sense of social justice and fostered a great deal of support for B4RN.

Identity and Ownership

To a large extent the incumbent Othered themselves. In acting as they did the community started to identify much more closely with B4RN and its cooperative not-for-profit principles. Despite spending a great deal of time and effort on applying for grants we never received any government money, largely because the incumbent was able to influence the granting bodies to modify the criteria in a way that excluded B4RN. This was a source of intense frustration but in hindsight was of great help. It is doubtful that the community would have rallied quite so strongly, and owned the project quite so tightly, if they had felt that someone else would be paying for it. Also, all government grants seem to come up with major hoops to leap through, and endless paperwork. Without them we have been able to let the project emerge in a flexible manner that is sympathetic to the needs of the community rather than meet bureaucratically defined stages of development.

The heroic fight against the incumbent and the forces of bureaucracy have led to what Weick (1995: 61) calls 'a good story': a collective identity of valour and community spirit in the face of overwhelming odds, with the added bonus of superb broadband at the end. The collective B4RN identity is not that of a single, stable self but is dynamic, complex, and situated, influenced by the differing identity claims that people bring with them as they interact with B4RN at different times and have developed through different histories.

Long-Term Vision and Hanging Open

It is hard to emphasise how important it has been, on the one hand, to provide and reinforce the long-term vision and maintain the ethos of equal cooperative venture without overtly 'managing' the people and the organisation: being able to hang loose and exercise negative capability (see Chapter 2). Yet, on the other hand and at the same time, it is vital in something as technically and financially detailed as a telecoms organisation, to closely direct, check, and account for the actual network, service, customers, and associated details. This balance needs close attention and has largely been achieved because of the way that different people have focused on different areas within the organisation and so brought to their personal style to bear. Of course, the organisation has had to be sufficiently flexible to accommodate such different styles of working; however, I want to emphasise the individuality within the development.

Around the day-to-day core of technical detail has been the ability to hang loose and be open to emerging opportunities, innovative techniques, requests from new communities, and so on. Over and over again the short-term vision has shifted as different events impacted upon the B4RN community. We would be in a very different place now if we had not been open to such changes. We have been asked by governmental and commercial bodies across the world for our 'model' and we do provide help where we can, with regular training days and workshops. But it seems that we are very hard to emulate, and I put this down to the importance of the individual influences within the much wider picture. These influences are unique, in the same way that every person is unique, and cannot be copied without also copying the wider picture.

Co-Constructing Change

For the purposes of this chapter then, and of discussion of holistic agency within the book, I want to emphasise the unique, situated, emergent nature of change and becoming that can be seen within B4RN. As directors BF and I have helped establish the organisational sense-making, through which we co-constructed a 'definition of the situation' that built a compelling vision and concrete plan for strategic change (Whittle et al. 2015). Everyone involved, however, whether as members, detractors, or people indifferent to the existence of B4RN, has had some effect upon the way in which B4RN developed: B4RN has been co-created by these people and will continue to change for years to come. Some of us have a clear idea of where we would like it to be in 50 years; my preference would be to see it as a community venture providing superb broadband as well as managing other community projects paid for by the service fees generated. Other people's involvement might have finished once they got a good connection for themselves and their neighbours. We don't know how B4RN will develop and how much bigger it will continue to grow, but it is a key part of the community and it melds with all community structures whilst still being open to the influence from one person or one event.

Before I leave this discussion of B4RN I want to emphasise that this is my personal view, but, more than that, I am almost alone in this view. The vast majority of people involved in B4RN would not describe it in the way I do. If asked about B4RN they will talk of the network, broadband, action within the community, and tasks completed and to be done. If they consider the ethos at all, they speak of what a great place it is to work, how much they feel involved, and so on. They don't talk about how it got to be like this, or how else it could have been. This mirrors my concern about HR (that I touch upon later): To all extents and purposes, HR is normally invisible to those it touches, yet it can have a profound effect upon them and their relationships with others.

ALTERNATIVE WAYS?

Throughout this book I have questioned the organisational structures that we, as societies, create and collude with. I have tried to illustrate that as individuals we can and do have some effect upon the structures. I have tried, through the example of B4RN above, to illustrate that it is possible to develop alternative structures within the wider capitalist systems. I have also tried to illustrate in this chapter and throughout the book the sorts of structures that people say they prefer to be within. I have made many of these points through illustration or allusion, but I intend to finish this chapter by looking more directly at the role that HR and the people involved in it play in evolving our futures.

Most of us like the idea of alternative organisations in which we are valued for who we are, and in which finance is not the key driver for all that we do. Most of us hope to enjoy 'work' or at least have it as a meaningful part of our lives—no longer the boring/hectic/stressful hard travail that we escape from when we can. This escape is often equated with escape from the capitalist ethos. Fournier (2002: 189) suggests that 'if one looks at the field of organization studies specifically, one may be forgiven for thinking that there aren't many alternatives to capitalist corporations', though as

Wilson (2013: 720) points out, there is 'the potential for a range of diverse possibilities beyond capitalism'. Like B4RN, alternatives tend to have been built from the bottom up and espouse inclusivity and participative action. They seek to prioritise the well-being of people, communities, and nature above profit maximisation (Langley & Mellor 2002; North 2010). The New Economics Foundation calls for a 'Great Transition' (Ryan-Collins 2009), in order to develop a fundamentally new economy based on sustainability, equality, and stability. This ties in with ideas of social entrepreneurship, which can be seen as the creation of economically sustainable organisations or social enterprises that have as their objective social or community benefits and where the profit is invested in the activities of the venture rather than returned to investors (Chang et al. 2014).

Capitalism and Cooperation

I would like to remind you, however, of the discussion in Chapter 2, in which I described the Parmenidean world as one of integrated structure, and the Heraclitean world as one in which alternative approaches can coexist. My views of holistic agency are predicated upon alternative structures existing and operating within the whole. To talk about alternative structures does not mean that we have to talk about revolution. It is much more complex than that! I use the word 'complex' here deliberately, in order to allude to the 'Matthew Effect' that is found in complex self-organising systems and describes self-reinforcing inequality. This is a general pattern that is empirically identifiable in the study of economic wealth, political power, prestige, knowledge, or in fact any other scarce or valued resource (Rigney 2010). In essence, it is the effect of cumulative advantage—the rich get richer, the powerful get more powerful, and so on.

Fundamentally, capitalism is the extension of the barter system, exchanging goods for money instead of other goods. The difference between the two is the ethos, the way in which money has come to represent more than just goods. To many people money now represents intangible qualities such as security, power, attractiveness, and desirability. The Matthew Effect applies not just to the money itself, but also to what it represents so that the more money one has, the 'better' one is. We can tie this line of thought in with the discussions about narcissism and consumption in Chapters 10, 11, and 16. Within the barter system one can only have so many potatoes or eggs before becoming thoroughly fed up with them, but for those who have taken to heart the capitalist ethos it is impossible to have too much money. The flipside of the rich getting richer is that the poor get poorer, yet this is forgotten in the chase for money. Indeed, people very rapidly become to feel that they are entitled to good luck, winning, or money; their behaviour changes and they become less concerned about others. Although they have achieved this by pure chance they start to believe that they are better than other people and have the right to such good fortune (Piff et al. 2012). It seems to be part of the way in which we 'Other' others that we quickly come to believe that we, the rich, get richer because we deserve it and the poor get poorer because they also deserve it.

B4RN shows, as do many other cooperative ventures, that it is possible for an organisation and its employees to be within the capitalist system but not adopt the core capitalist ethos of entitlement. There are many people who question the capitalist ethos and seek alternative ways of working; however, raising finance offers a particular challenge because 'normal' economic investors remain wary of the desire to pursue social benefits as well as economic gain (Morrissette 2007). Similarly, younger people, particularly those starting families, need to be able to earn sufficient money to live on. As people age they tend to search for meaning in their life beyond the acquisition of wealth and so it is no surprise that the age profile of B4RN and similar organisations is rather older than average. As discussed in Chapter 16, it tends to be the older people who are more focused on giving back to the community and, importantly, have the time to do so. One of the key features of social entrepreneurship is the compassion of the entrepreneur and their desire to create social change and/or to provide social benefits (Choi & Gray 2008). It also tends to be the older people who have the social skills and contacts to be able to bridge diverse stakeholder communities using social connections and relationships to raise resources, both financial and non-financial—in the form of expertise, information, and other provisions—as well as the adaptive skills needed to manage the changing social enterprise environment (Cope et al. 2007).

Sustainability

Appalling levels of inequality, spurious entitlement, and blatant consumption assume a world of infinite resource. As discussed in Chapter 16, our resources are not infinite and our actions are having a dramatic effect upon the planet. Our competition for dwindling resources highlights the distinction I made in Chapter 8 between the world of heroes and villains, in which the good and the mighty win the prize and the villains are vanquished (or otherwise disappear), and the world of symbiosis, in which people work together as equals, finding ways to co-create balance and equality. When addressing this logically most people recognise that we cannot continue plundering finite resources in order for each of us to acquire what we believe we are entitled to without respect for other people's needs. It is however a different matter when we are presented with the need to pay taxes, welcome refugees into the country, or choose a lifestyle that might be good for the soul but not the pocket. We need to bear in mind Wilson & Wilson (2008: 389), who say that

'members of hunter-gatherer groups succeed primarily by teamwork. Selection for teamwork probably began very early in human evolution.

Human infants spontaneously point things out to others, and not merely to get what they want, which chimpanzees do not do at any age. Symbolic thought, language and the social transmission of information are fundamentally communal activities that rely on trustworthy social partners. Exploitation, cheating and free riding do exist in human groups, but what is most remarkable is the degree to which they are suppressed. They loom so large in our thoughts partly because we are primed to suppress them, like a well-adapted immune system'.

See also Wilkinson & Pickett's (2010) discussion of the benefits of more equal societies.

Organisations small and large, and the individuals within them, are likely to benefit if they foster a cooperative, more sustainable approach to life. This does not necessarily mean completely abandoning old systems but it does mean changing the ethos under which we operate. Working within finite resources means that if one person gets richer, then another automatically and necessarily gets poorer. If one person has lots of children, then other people have to have fewer. If one country uses lots of resources, others have to use less. If one society produces lots of pollution, others suffer for it. The boundaries that we create for ourselves and our existence need to include the balancing act of finite resources.

Development

If HRD is at the centre of the way in which societies and organisations develop, then the activities and the ethos enacted by HRD people are at the core of an organisation's becoming. The idea of HRD as aspiration, however, encompasses working together to create a vision in the hope that events will move in that direction. HRD is involved in creating the structures (entrance, monitoring, promotion, and exit) through which people and organisations develop, as well as fostering the development of people within those structures.

From the point of view of a new employee, qualifications aid entry and promotion and give the organisation some idea of what they're getting. Thus systems of qualification are a form of benchmarking and offer a badge of status, but we can question the extent to which they help the individual develop. For the individual, longevity within the organisation depends upon the ability to make valued contributions to the organisation: The qualification itself is of little use, and it is the expertise (or lack of it) that becomes important. As discussed in Chapter 16, an individual's success will depend to a large extent upon their personal qualities (such as cognitive hardiness and proactivity). Also, whether they are within a single organisation, a portfolio worker, or self-employed, they need to be seen to be good at the job and as a repository for resources, to acquire mentors and allies and further development opportunities, and to be able to manage others. Long-term life satisfaction and well-being for the individual and others might well be supported by developing a cooperative community-based ethos.

Notions of employability that now permeate Western society mean that the individual is considered to be responsible for the success or otherwise of their own career path and their own development. As I emphasise throughout the book, however, self-development is not really about neatly planned stages and achievable end points. Chapter 13 shows that we normally act on a subconscious level, and that our consciousness places a retrospective rationale and structure upon our actions or inactions. Self-development is, to a certain extent, a process of beginning to understand and come to terms with how and why we perceive ourselves to be as we are. This requires the difficult and painful skill of being able to think reflexively, learn from the experience, and weave our way through ambiguity.

The individual is likely to be moving from job to job, paid or voluntary, supportive or challenging, in a way that suits their needs at the time. People will develop and co-evolve in their own sweet way regardless of externally planned or organised development, though their path might well be influenced by such structures.

DEVELOPMENT STRUCTURES

Organisations and the people within them are moulded by the systems of reporting, appraisal, and reward: the traditional area of HR. Some of the key boundaries, however, are set by governments, universities, organisations, and professional bodies as they stipulate how they think the populace should develop through the establishment and implementation of systems of education and qualification. I discuss this in Chapters 2 and 16, but want to emphasise here that such systems normally reinforce the status quo, are sensitive to political agendas, and create a short-term vision.

Educational systems are split between a desire to address the development of 'the whole person' and the pervasive need to quantify achievement. As we climb the educational ladder the focus upon qualifications becomes paramount, skewing provision. For example, qualification-based education privileges serial cognitive learning. Those children who are spatially adept, rather than serially able, are less favoured by our educational system, yet it is this ability that is central to the notions of cognitive mapping, creativity, and strategic vision that are important attributes of senior management (Taylor 1994). High-ability females disempower themselves to accommodate the machismic environment of school (Marshall 1984). We are socialised early on into the belief that teachers are dominant because of their expert knowledge, that there are right and wrong ways of doing things, and that mistakes are bad. From an early age talent that does not conform to our educational system is unrecognised and easily discouraged and the very qualities that might be looked for in later life can be seen as difficult to handle and in need of suppression in the early years. This is partially addressed by adult education courses that replicate qualifications that could have been obtained in childhood, but their very existence is an indictment of the system.

Education systems are becoming increasingly achievement oriented— there must be very few educators who have not been questioned about 'value for money', or 'where will this qualification lead?' Similarly, there must be very few employers who do not look, in the first instance, to the academic references of the job candidate. All stakeholders are concerned about the academic reputation and credibility of the institution, the educators, and the qualifying professional body. The need to get a good qualification, heard from infancy upwards, stems from the understanding that it is the quickest and easiest way of getting a good job and hence gaining professional status in a competitive society. We talk of gaining a broad education and developing rounded people, but the need to get the bit of paper at the end, as a passport to eternal happiness, frequently overrides such considerations. Both educational and organisational cultures focus upon the needs of the job, to the detriment of the needs of the person and the health of the organisation.

Organisations are becoming increasingly vocal in their requests for wider provision, and both internal and external providers are attempting to meet these needs. This is particularly noticeable in providers that collaborate more closely with industry. For example, many MBAs now involve elements of personal development, and some computing degrees also provide units on interpersonal relations. A drive towards short-cycle post-experience skills-based courses, and a desire for applicability, criticality, and transferability of learning, means that post-experience students are becoming influential stakeholders in educational provision.

As I describe in Chapter 16, in the early 1990s the UK created a system of wide-based provision that addressed competencies, provided a nationwide system of lifelong learning, and was available to all. In theory integrated competency-based provision might best meet the widely differing needs of the stakeholders (Constable & McCormick 1987). In practice competency-based approaches are driven by assessment of output, and thus, as with other systems of qualification, are skewed away from the less easily measurable aspects of personal development (Smithers 1993). In the UK, reduced government support led to a greater focus upon attracting corporate finance and increasing student fees, which, alongside the need for portable qualifications, has led to individuals becoming more powerful stakeholders. Individuals and organisations are giving providers a wish list of personal development and empowerment that is cheap and immediate. Providers are attempting to meet these needs by changing the rhetoric and the provision.

Long-Term Personal Development

As has been emphasised throughout the book, traditional Western management is seen to be synonymous with an aggressive stance in life. MBA students were taught to demonstrate that they had 'balls' and could compete in an aggressive environment. This view was emphasised by the style of teaching, forms of assessment, and choice of course material (Ashton 1988). The above discussion, however, suggests that it is within the organisation's long-term interests to deliberately incorporate a developmental approach and an appreciation of the issues around empowerment. This can be done by altered appointment criteria and by encouraging the providers to review the long-term usefulness of the courses they offer. The course material is relatively easy to review; changing the attitudes of the tutors and the educational philosophy underlying the provision is much harder. There is a groundswell of applicants for consortial, in-company, and 'ecological' MBAs and other management qualifications that include experiential learning and self-development, as in the MSc in HRD described in Chapter 2. At the start of the programme in that example, the majority of participants reported that the specialist input was of the most value, and they expressed concern and doubt about the more developmental aspects. Towards the end of the programme, however, they emphasised the particular long-term value of the developmental learning obtained—especially during the times that they had previously felt things had gone 'wrong'. This points to one of the difficulties faced by developmental provision. It is often long-term, and requires both the tutors and the funding body to be able to manage initial negative feedback. It takes a special form of organisation to support participants upon this sort of programme and they need to believe in the long-term benefit of facilitating empowerment.

Short-Term Cost Effectiveness

The more a course focuses upon personal development, the more it appears to cost. Personal development is, by its nature, individualistic. A group of students might go through the same experience, but learn different things from it. They might not even be aware of what they have learnt and will need help in thinking reflexively as well as time to assimilate what has gone on. This has immediate implications for staffing and length of the course: namely, a high staff-to-student ratio, and plenty of time to discuss and reflect. This is not to say that all courses that cost a lot are effective; however, it is possible to question the extent to which a one-day course with low staff-student ratio really facilitates long-term development.

Personal development is hard to measure. Is it possible to quantify? How and when do we measure quality? It is here that the split between short- and long-term benefits is crucial. The organisation is likely to want immediate feedback about the effectiveness of a course, and thus there is a continual pressure to demonstrate short-term learning, such that participants can leave courses with vast amounts of literature but little personal development.

Individuals are willing to sponsor themselves through these courses (often at great personal cost) because they believe in the long-term benefits.

Organisations encourage their training departments to adopt such courses for the same reason. However, because of the individual nature of the learning, it is hard to evaluate, and so justify, exactly what each participant has learnt. Personal development is often confusing and painful. Not only does this come as a shock to inexperienced participants but it is also disconcerting for the line manager. Hence the major difficulty of explaining to those who have little understanding of the nature of the learning what the long-term benefits might be (Chapter 15).

In the longer term both the organisation and the course providers can look at how participants have been affected, and the effect that the learning has had on those around them. However, this also presents problems. As Handy et al. (1987) point out, if the course is truly successful and the learning fully integrated, then it is unlikely that it will be fully credited with effecting the change. Participants believe that they have learnt to help themselves.

Managerial life, decision-making, and governance are being driven into the short term by the need to quantify and justify profit and loss. More than that, our systems of development and education are following the same pattern. If the Matthew Effect spawns capitalism, so capitalism spawns short-termism.

I have presented B4RN as an alternative form of organisation, working within the capitalist systems without adopting the capitalist ethos. However, as Gibson-Graham et al. (2013) argue, the very label 'alternative' marginalises non-dominant ways of organising such that their credibility can be questioned. B4RN is just one of many such organisations, and there are many people across the world who question capitalist short-termism and the need to consume and dominate. Short-term approaches to evaluation and education are stunting our ability to develop. We, more than any other creatures in the world, work with symbolism, representation, myth, and vision: It is what we are. We are capable of envisaging futures and acting to make them happen. B4RN started, and continues, because of the long-term vision: people actively working together to create a better future. The generation of a vision for the future, looking to many years ahead, is a core part of influencing one's becoming in a way that one wants to become!

REFERENCES

Ashton DJL (1988) 'Are business schools good learning organisations?', *Personnel Review* 17(4)6–14.

Chang JYC, Benamraoui A, & Rieple A (2014) 'Stimulating learning about social entrepreneurship through income generation projects', *International Journal of Entrepreneurial Behaviour & Research* 20(5)417–437.

Choi DY & Gray ER (2008) 'Socially responsible entrepreneurs: What do they do to create and build their companies?', *Business Horizons* 51(4)341–352.

Coleman A (2014) 'Europe's fastest rural broadband network? British farmers are digging it', *Forbes* 6 February.

Constable J & McCormick R (1987) *The Making of British Managers*. London: British Institute of Management and Federation of British Industry.

Cope J, Jack S, & Rose M (2007) 'Social capital and entrepreneurship', *International Small Business Journal* 3(25)213–219.

Fournier V (2002) 'Utopianism and the Cultivation of Possibilities: Grassroots Movements of Hope', in Parker M (Ed) *Utopia and Organisation*: 189–217. Oxford: Blackwell.

Gibson-Graham JK, Cameron J, & Healy S (2013) *Take Back the Economy: An Ethical Guide for Transforming Our Communities*. USA: University of Minnesota Press.

Hadley CN (2014) 'Emotional roulette? Symmetrical and asymmetrical emotion regulation outcomes from co-worker interactions about positive and negative work events', *Human Relations* 67: 1073–1094.

Handy C, Gow I, Gordon C, Randlesome C, & Moloney M (1987) *The Making of Managers*. London: National Economic Development Office.

Langley P & Mellor M (2002) 'Economy', sustainability and sites of transformative space', *New Political Economy* 7(1)49–65.

Marshall J (1984) *Women Managers: Travellers in a Male World*. Chichester: Wiley.

Mintzberg H (2009) *Managing*. San Francisco: Berrett-Koehler.

Morrissette SG (2007) 'A profile of angel investors', *Journal of Private Equity* 10(3)252–266.

North P (2010) 'Eco-localisation as a progressive response to peak oil and climate change', *Geoforum* 41: 585–594.

Piff PK, Stancato DM, Côté S, Mendoza-Denton R, & Keltner D (2012) 'Higher social class predicts increased unethical behavior', *Proceedings of the National Academy of Sciences* 109(11)4086–4091.

Rigney D (2010) *The Matthew Effect: How Advantage Begets Further Advantage*. New York: Columbia University Press.

Ryan-Collins J (2009) *The Great Transition*. London: New Economics Foundation.

Smithers A (1993) *All Our Futures—Britain's Education Revolution*. University of Manchester: Centre for Education and Employment Research.

Taylor FJW (1994) *Working Party Report: The Way ahead 1994–2001*. Management Development to the Millennium Research, The Institute of Management, Northants.

Weick KE (1995) *Sensemaking in Organizations*. Thousand Oaks, CA: Sage.

Whitehead AN (1929) *Process and Reality*. New York: Free Press.

Whittle A, Housley W, Gilchrist A, Mueller F, & Lenney P (2015) 'Category predication work, discursive leadership and strategic sense-making', *Human Relations* 68(3)377–407.

Wilkinson RG & Pickett KE (2010) *The Spirit Level: Why More Equal Societies Almost Always Do Better*. New York, NY: Bloomsbury Press.

Wilson AD (2013) 'Beyond alternative: Exploring the potential for autonomous food spaces', *Antipode* 45(3)719–737.

Wilson DS & Wilson EO (2008) 'Evolution "for the Good of the Group"', *American Scientist* 96: 380–389.

Woolley AW, Chabris CF, Pentland A, Hashmi N, & Malone TW (2010) 'Evidence for a collective intelligence factor in the performance of human groups', *Sciences* 330: 686–688.

19 Conclusions

In so far as a book about becoming can be said to conclude, then this chapter concludes the book. I hope, however, I have opened more lines of thought than I have closed, and that I have introduced a way of thinking that is constructive rather than limiting. I have referred to 'HRD' throughout the book, because this is one book in a series on HRD, and because that is the field of study that I am addressing, but my model and arguments apply equally to any field of study that involves human development. It is self-referential, in that different fields of study can, themselves, be located within the model. For example, the concerns of psychology could be considered analogous to the self-other construct, and those of sociology to the agency-structure construct. In the same way, more applied areas, such as 'Education', 'Management Learning', 'Behaviour in Organisations', 'Development Studies', and so on, look at the interface between individuals and organisations, and my thesis is relevant to them all.

HOLISTIC VIEW

I am asserting that in exploring the nature of HRD we need to adopt a wide, holistic, view of the world. In this sense, I am using 'holistic' as shorthand for the complex web of social sciences. This includes pulling in information and thoughts from a range of sources, fields of enquiry, and our own experiences. It also means bringing them together to create a coherent story of our existence, in which theory and experience are judged against each other. I have proposed a model of holistic agency that represents the human condition as moulded by two key archetypal constructs derived from evolutionary psychology: namely, self and other, and agency and structure. The model maps our world of *being* onto these constructs, such that it represents our experience of the world, and the many two-by-two matrices that we generate can be patterned on to it. This helicopter perspective, looking down on the patterns of humanity, is intended to accommodate difference. Each area in the model is archetypal: aspirational not definitional, and known by what it is not. Similarly, in order to argue my case I have taken an overarching perspective, drawing from sources that are sometimes contradictory and are spread across the range of human knowledge.

OUR WORLD

I present people as living in worlds of their own construction, individually and collectively. Biological, psychological, and evolutionary evidence shows that our senses, which we believe to be presenting us with immediate information, are actually a form of memory, albeit split-second. These memories have already been processed by our past, present, and future anticipations. Furthermore, we are continually subject to influences of which we are not aware, such as pheromones, our own and others' body language, and even our own gut flora. Our consciousness does not even make us in charge of our own bodies; instead it allows us to imagine and speculate, and to build upon our unique penchants for symbolism, fostering language, myth, culture, and complex society.

Sociological and psychological sources evidence the collective nature of our existence. We create our own understanding of the world and our circumstances, but it is built in relation to other people. We co-create ourselves and our society and we co-evolve our culture. I use the concepts and language of complexity theory and philosophy to explore the complex and at times contradictory ways in which we create and describe our social existence.

These lines of thought build a picture of life through relationships. Everything relates to everything else in some way or another, and it is we who create the boundaries and who say our particular world is this big or that small. HRD (for the want of an alternative title) is about those relationships. It is about how people see themselves and how they relate to others, how they work with others, organise, and manage, and the implicit and explicit rules that they and others form that build societies. HRD, therefore, is at the nexus of a web of *being,* but it is also more than that.

AGENCY

My model of holistic agency is a static, sterile, two-dimensional representation, presenting a balanced, archetypal, and *holistic* view of the human condition, which contains no *agency* other than by implication. Yet, agency is at the core of our existence. Our lives are affected whether we do something or stay still, whether we accept one way of thinking or another. Being alive is about experiencing. It is impossible to use words like evolve, create, and human resource *development* without invoking a sense of direction, of *becoming.*

HRD, by its nature, is personal and directional—about our experiences and how we understand them, about the history and the stories we tell ourselves and others, and about the future. We are agents (by our existence and our nature) and also pawns. We influence the balance, acting within different arenas and across barriers, fostering emergent co-creation within the principle of becoming.

METHOD

My arguments are derived from several bodies of literature, pulled together to present a conceptual overview, but they are also strongly grounded in my experience. I have described my approach as almost-autoethnographic and justified it through reference to the literature, but actually I felt I had little choice. Experiential reflexive methods of enquiry seemed most appropriate for an experiential complex subject area such as this. However, it must not be forgotten that much of what I offer here is based upon hard scientific and experimental data. From climate change to group behaviour, I have relied upon findings from quantitative research—as does HRD. How can we know what is 'normal' without it? Qualitative research looks at those outside the 'norm'. More personal methods such as auto-ethnography emphasise the individual in a way that normative research cannot, and, by their nature, carry with them individual bias. I trust I have made my researcher/participant bias clear where appropriate and that you, the reader, are able to step back and critically evaluate the ideas I am exploring.

CONTENTS

I have concentrated on each of the polar ends of the archetypal constructs in turn, looking first at self and other, then agency, and then structure. This has been a difficult process because each debate, each line of thought, and each experience has aspects of all areas within it. I have chosen to include those chapters that best relate to one area or another, but I can easily accept that if someone else were authoring this book they would make different choices. My intention has been to offer a wide smorgasbord of individual and organisational life, from the painful areas of bullying, discrimination, and stress through to the very positive areas of co-creating the future, and to include wider views of management and organisation than are often presented by the predominantly Westernised and sanitised literature.

Some themes have reverberated throughout the book, such as forms of leadership, micro-cultures, working with difference, and issues of trust. In each case, however, although I have named them here as if they were *topics* they have actually intruded upon the text under different dynamic and situated guises. For example, discussion of cultures and micro-cultures arises explicitly in several places, yet nearly everything I say impacts upon culture in some way. Whether it is just the development of signs and symbols that friends use together as a form of shorthand, or the impact of immigration on national culture, the way in which the relationship shifts with time can be seen as a form of co-evolution of culture.

This book is unusual in the way in which it tries to incorporate ideas of the *whole* person in discussions about work and management. Most theories talk of people as rational decision makers, and forget that we bring with us a world of body odours and assumptions, myths and histories. We might sit around a table and talk politely and intelligently in a meeting, but at the same time we are, without realising it, working on a more animal level. Even the famous Kolb cycle has no space for the subconscious aspects of learning. Take, for example, the use of stories. We actively participate in the creation of culture by listening to stories and telling them—within our organisations we adopt and create symbols and archetypes, legends and myths. Discussions of holistic agency need to include the whole person: embodied and symbolic—warts and all.

Throughout the book I have tried to emphasise the situated nature of HRD, one that goes together with a holistic approach to the situation. Many different things matter at any one moment. Circumstances and people change from day to day, minute to minute, and there can be no reassuringly simple toolkit about what to do under particular circumstances.

HRD can however be about aspiration. As agents within this holistic world we will never 'become' what we aspire to, as we are always becoming—but we might sidestep becoming along a path we want to avoid. We face many global challenges and possibilities, and change is the only certainty! Some ways of working and being appear to suit our desires more than others. We can envisage being part of a community that fosters equality, respect, acceptance of difference, and well-being within a more symbiotic lifestyle. We need to be valued regardless of how lowly our job or how little we earn. We need to feel that there is quality time for family and friends, alongside work that challenges and infuses us. We need to be earning enough money for our needs, but to sculpt our needs so that they do not outstrip the needs of others. We need to feel that we are accepted and valued co-authors of our existence.

From having started by looking at what HRD might be about, I have moved to placing a challenge and a burden onto the shoulders of HRD people. If I am right in my view that development is at the core of individual and organisational life, that to exist is to live in a state of becoming within a holistic world of agency, then my question is simple: So, how shall we become?

20 Antecedents

This chapter is for those who might be interested in the antecedents of the book. As I explained in the introduction, I have been very bad about publishing a nice coherent stream of papers in well-known outlets. This book started as a reprint of some of my work to bring it together a bit more, but I have added, changed, and moved text all over the place. I am not sure where this stands in terms of self-plagiarism (Callahan 2014), but I have obtained all the relevant permissions to reuse my own words.

CHAPTER 2. DEFINING HRD

This was initially presented as a conference paper at the first UFHRD conference held in Kingston University in the UK in 2000, and then slightly revised at the HRD conference (Lee 2001a) when it was judged to be one of the top 10 outstanding papers presented that year, and so also got published in the Cutting Edge series (Lee 2001b). Interestingly, AHRD first rejected it as a conference paper because of dated references. Luckily for me, someone supervising the submissions process reversed that decision, recognising that the references to ancient Greek philosophers still had some small place in the modern world. This paper was then chosen by Jean Woodall for inclusion in a special issue of *HRDI* (Lee 2001c) and won the Monica M. Lee Award given by the AHRD for the best paper published in *HRDI* in 2001. AHRD had honoured me tremendously by naming the award after me but I hasten to add that I had nothing to do with the setting up of the awards or with any of the judging for it. Indeed both the naming of the award and the winning of it with this paper came as a very great surprise to me. At the time of publication this paper challenged a lot of deeply held beliefs and was much discussed. It has reappeared in several compilations since then.

CHAPTER 3. EVOLUTIONARY ROOTS AND HOLISTIC AGENCY

These ideas are rooted in my work as a psychologist and consultant prior to coming to academe. I was struggling then, and still struggle, with how to get all the ideas together in a way that makes sense and links them coherently whilst also being short enough to fit into a modern publication format. I published parts of the model of holistic agency in schematic form (Lee 1991, 1994a) and aspects of development (Lee 1997a), and strategy (Lee 1997b). I continued to try, and failed, to get my model and supporting ideas published in one paper: positive reviews, good feedback, lots of length-based rejections! Normal journals do not like long papers. I had nearly finished writing them as a book when I had my cerebral haemorrhage. Without the circumstances outlined in Chapter 9 my book would have been the first in the Studies in HRD series, and my career would have been very different— though I would have had less varied experiences to draw upon! I presented these ideas (roughly as laid out here) at the initial conference of the newly formed Asian branch of AHRD that was held in Bangalore (Lee 2002a), and, in modified form, at the AHRD conference (Lee 2002b). That paper was also published as a Cutting Edge paper (Lee 2002c). I extended the analysis to concentrate the focus on complexity theory (2003a) and combined these ideas into the OTSC paper (Lee 2005) on which this chapter is based.

CHAPTER 4. FACT, FICTION, AND REPRESENTATION

This chapter is based on a thought piece, sparked by the way I was treated on my early retirement on medical grounds (Lee 2009a).

CHAPTER 5. MEANING AND METHODOLOGICAL CHOICE

This chapter is based on ideas derived from my teaching of quantitative and qualitative methodologies (Lee 2001c).

CHAPTER 6. MEET THE AUTHOR

Darren Short is a past president of the AHRD and he hosted a symposium at the AHRD conference based around several live interviews with 'senior' figures in 2009. This chapter is based upon the interview with me, which has the dubious notoriety of being the first to be published (Short 2010).

CHAPTER 7. THE EMERGENT SELF

This chapter is based on an SCOS conference paper about my experiences at a previous conference (Lee 1995a). Parts of this were also later published as a book chapter (Lee 2002d).

CHAPTER 8. THE FUTURE SELF

The story was first written as a thought piece for students in the early 1990s. I presented it as a conference paper at SCOS (Lee 1996a), and it was picked up by several colleagues, who used it with their own students across Europe, the US, and Scandinavia. It proved to be a great way to bring students in, and to foster discussion and critical evaluation, but its unusual experimental nature meant that it was very hard to publish. I eventually got it published by sandwiching it between explanations at the front and the back of the piece written in proper authoritative academic style. This was ironic, as part of the thrust of the paper was questioning the legitimacy of such style. This version is based on one published as a book chapter (1999).

CHAPTER 9. THE SUBMERGED SELF

This chapter is set in a supposedly enlightened environment, within which some staff are bullied to the edge of endurance. As with the previous chapter, I found it hard to get it published, though for different reasons. This was first presented as conference papers (Lee 2001d, 2002e) that recounted these happenings and many more along the lines presented here. Everything that happened here is thoroughly and completely documented with emails, letters, and internal papers. My paper was initially accepted by one journal after another, but in each case was withdrawn by the journal in the final stages on advice from their lawyers. Each time, they were very apologetic and agreed that I was not saying anything inappropriate, but they did not want to bear the potential cost and time that would ensue if someone took exception to what I was saying. Though they agreed we would win, they did not want the hassle of publishing something that was a bit more realistic than usual. Finally, in order to be acceptable for publication, I had to take myself and my setting out of it by relocating the happenings to a different country in a different sector, by cutting out several of the more horrendous incidents, and by minimising the characters involved into little more than avatars. This felt like intellectual dishonesty, because without the true details how can the reader accurately evaluate the merit of the research that is presented? However, I caved in, and thus it was published. I have since heard several tales of similar stories, of articles about mistreatment in organisational settings that are not published because journals don't want the hassle. This is a sad indictment of our times, and of our field, in which truth telling and whistleblowing remains hidden, and potentially impactful research is sanitised. This is based on a book chapter (Lee 2008).

CHAPTER 10. FREEDOM AND CHOICE

This chapter is based on a paper (Lee 1995b).

CHAPTER 11. DECISION-MAKING AND HIDDEN OTHERS

This line of thought was first presented at a workshop in honour of Burkard Sievers (Lee 2007a). This chapter is based on a subsequent paper (Lee

2009b), which was awarded a 'Highly Commended' at the Literati Network Awards for Excellence in 2010.

CHAPTER 12. DIFFERENCE AND CONFLICT

These ideas were developed when I was working with the cross-cultural role of action learning (Lee 1996a, 1996c). The chapter is based on a paper (Lee 1998) that was republished by Personnel Review Select as one of their best papers (Lee 1999b).

CHAPTER 13. WHO IS THE AGENT?

The core of this chapter acknowledges unpublished work done by Charles Lee in 1974 about the nature of consciousness. His theoretical considerations were ahead of their time, but there is now increasing empirical evidence for the ideas he proposed. This chapter is based on a conference paper (Lee 2004a) in which I matched his proposed imaginary-time mechanism to my own experiences. It is now updated, incorporating more recent research findings.

CHAPTER 14. AGENCY AND IMPOTENCE

This chapter is based on a paper outlining some of my experiences as a school governor (Lee 1999c).

CHAPTER 15. THE ISOLATION OF AGENCY

The thoughts presented here sprang from my experiences with management and consultancy and my concern that, at the time, very little of the literature addressed what it was really like. I wrote several other papers, each of which concentrated on one part or another of the ideas given here (Lee 1992, 1994b, 1996b). This chapter is based on a conference paper that pulled some of these ideas together (Lee 1994a).

CHAPTER 16. BOUNDARIES AND CHANGE

I have explored these ideas in several different arenas. I presented my earlier thoughts as a keynote speech to the Asian HRD conference in Korea (Lee 2004b), and then revised the findings in line with updated climate change predictions for a keynote speech to the UFHRD conference in Oxford (Lee 2007b). I updated these further around the diffusion of boundaries in my reply to a keynote speech at the UFHRD conference in Pécs, Hungary (Lee 2010a). This chapter is based upon a paper (Lee 2010b); however, here, I have again revised the findings to capture more recent research.

CHAPTER 17. THE RULES WE CREATE

This chapter is based on a paper (Lee 2003b).

CHAPTER 18. BECOMING

This chapter is very loosely based on a paper that was awarded a 'Highly Commended Paper' by the Emerald Publishing Group (Lee 1995c). It has been changed considerably, however, to accommodate the discussion of B4RN and the needs of the book.

REFERENCES

Callahan JL (2014) 'Creation of a moral panic? Self-plagiarism and the academy', *Human Resource Development Review* 13: 3–10.

Lee MM (1991) 'Organisational culture and change: Theoretical correlates of organisational archetypes', *Proceedings of European International Business Association Conference*, Copenhagen.

Lee MM (1992) 'Interpersonal skills and the manager as a process consultant', *Proceedings of Learning Company Conference*, Warwick.

Lee MM (1994a) 'The Isolated Manager: Walking the Boundaries of the Microculture', in Westall O (Ed) *Proceedings of British Academy of Management conference:* 111–128. Lancaster: British Academy of Management.

Lee MM (1994b) 'Locating Empowerment: The Role of Management Education in Meeting Individual and Organisational Needs', in Hopfl H (Ed) *Challenging Learning: The Experience of Management:* 132–147. Bolton: Bolton Business School.

Lee MM (1995a) 'The Opposing Self: The Truth Is That There Is No Truth', in Gustafsson C (Ed) *Proceedings of 13th Standing Conference on Organisational Symbolism, Self and Identity in Organisations,* Turku.

Lee MM (1995b) 'Working with freedom of choice in Central Europe', *Management Learning* 26(2)215–230.

Lee MM (1995c) 'Learning for work: Short-term gain or long-term benefit?', *Personnel Review* 24(6)29–43.

Lee MM (1996a) 'Text, Gender and Future Realities', in Goodman R (Ed) *Proceedings of Standing Conference on Organisational Symbolism, Exploring the Post-industrial Sub-culture:* 109–125. Los Angeles: Jossey Bass.

Lee MM (1996b) 'Action Learning as a Cross-Cultural Tool', in Stewart J & McGoldrick J (Eds) *Human Resource Development: Perspectives, Strategies and Practice:* 240–260. London: Pitman.

Lee MM (1996c) 'Holistic Learning in the 'New' Central Europe', in Lee MM, Letiche H, Crawshaw R & Thomas M (Eds) *Management Education in the New Europe: Boundaries and Complexity:* 249–267. London: Integrated Transport Planning.

Lee MM (1997a) 'The Developmental Approach: A Critical Reconsideration', in Burgoyne J & Reynolds M (Eds) *Management Learning:* 199–214. London: Sage.

Lee MM (1997b) 'Strategic Human Resource Development: A Conceptual Exploration', in Torraco R (Ed) *Proceedings, AHRD Conference:* 92–99. Atlanta, Georgia.

Lee MM (1998) 'Understandings of conflict: A cross-cultural investigation', *Personnel Review* 27(3)227–242.

Lee MM (1999a) 'Text, Gender and Future Realities', in Goodman R (Ed) *Modern Organisations and Emerging Conundrums: Exploring the Post-Industrial Sub-Culture of the Third Millennium:* 109–125. Lanham, Maryland: Lexington Books.

Lee MM (1999b) 'Understandings of Conflict: A cross-cultural investigation', *Personnel Review Select* 2(3)138–146.

Lee MM (1999c) 'The Lie of Power: Empowerment as Impotence', *Human Relations* 52(2)225–262.

Lee MM (2001a) 'A Refusal to Define HRD', in Aliaga O (Ed) *Proceedings, Academy of HRD:* 1072–1079.

Lee MM (2001b) 'A Refusal to Define HRD', in Poell R (Ed) *Defining the Cutting Edge 2001:* 3–12. AHRD: AHRD.

Lee MM (2001c) 'On Seizing the Moment as the Research Question Emerges', in Stewart J, McGoldrick J, & Watson S (Eds) *Understanding Research into HRD:* 18–40. London: Routledge.

Lee MM (2001d) 'Come, enter, the Department of Management Violence', *Proceedings of 2001 SCOS Conference,* Dublin.

Lee MM (2002a) 'The Evolution of HRD?', in Pareek U, Osman Gani AM, Ramnarayan S, & Rao TV (Eds) *Proceedings of Human Resource Development in Asia:* 695–702. New Delhi: Oxford & IBH Publishing Co.

Lee MM (2002b) 'The Complex Roots of HRD', in Egan T & Lynham S (Eds) *Proceedings of the AHRD Conference,* Hawaii. AHRD.

Lee MM (2002c) 'The Complex Roots of HRD', in Rocco T (Ed) *Defining the Cutting Edge 2002:* 3–12. AHRD: AHRD.

Lee MM (2002d) 'Who Am I? An Introduction to Self Development in Organisations', in Pearn M (Ed) *Individual Differences and Development in Organisations:* 17–34. Chichester: Wiley.

Lee MM (2002e) 'The Power of Stories: A Story of Power', in S. Watson (Ed) *'HRD Research and Practice across Europe'* proceedings of the 3rd European HRD Conference, Edinburgh.

Lee MM (2003a) *HRD in a Complex World.* London: Routledge.

Lee MM (2003b) 'On codes of ethics: The individual and performance', *Performance Improvement Quarterly* 16(2)72–89.

Lee MM (2004a) 'Blind sight and consciousness, culture and organisations', *Proceedings of 'Organisational Wellness' SCOS Conference,* Cambridge.

Lee MM (2004b) 'HRD: Looking to the Future', *Keynote Speech, 3rd Asian Conference, KAHRD,* Seoul, Korea, November (www.kahrd.org).

Lee MM (2005) 'Complex archetypal structures that underlie the 'human condition', *Organisational Transformation and Social Change* 2(2)49–70.

Lee MM (2007a) 'Sticks and Stones: Decision Making by Rumour', in *Proceedings of 'The (un)conscious of organising: thoughts of and about Burkard Sievers' thinking and writing',* Leusden, Netherlands.

Lee MM (2007b) 'Locating HRD from a holistic perspective', *Keynote Speech, The 8th International Conference on Human Resource Development Research & Practice across Europe,* 27–29 June. Oxford.

Lee MM (2008) 'Goddess: A story of myth and power', in Kostera M (Ed) *Book II. Organizational Epics and Sagas: Tales of Organizations*: 40–54. Basingstoke: Palgrave Macmillan.

Lee MM (2009a) 'On the loss of a room: An autoethnographic assay of fact', *Human Resource Development International* 12(3)343–349.

Lee MM (2009b) 'Sticks and Stones: Decision making by rumour', *Society & Business Review* 4(2)123–132.

Lee MM (2010a) 'Some thoughts on the diffusion of boundaries and borders', Academic response to Keynote 'HRD Strategies in a European Borderless Postal Market: A Hungarian Perspective', Ildikó Szűts, CEO, Magyar Posta Zrt', *11th International Conference on HRD Research and Practice across Europe,* June 2010, University of Pécs.

Lee MM (2010b) 'Shifting boundaries: The role of HRD in a changing world', *Advances in Developing Human Resources* 12(5)524–535.

Short D (2010) 'Better know a HRD scholar: A conversation with Monica Lee', *Human Resource Development International* 13(3)361–374.

Index